Culture, Ethnicity, and Identity

CURRENT ISSUES IN RESEARCH

Culture, Ethnicity, and Identity
CURRENT ISSUES IN RESEARCH

Edited by

WILLIAM C. McCREADY
Center for the Study of American Pluralism
University of Chicago
Chicago, Illinois

1983

ACADEMIC PRESS

A Subsidiary of Harcourt Brace Jovanovich, Publishers

New York   London

Paris   San Diego   San Francisco   São Paulo   Sydney   Tokyo   Toronto

ACADEMIC PRESS, INC.
111 Fifth Avenue, New York, New York 10003

United Kingdom Edition published by
ACADEMIC PRESS, INC. (LONDON) LTD.
24/28 Oval Road, London NW1 7DX

Library of Congress Cataloging in Publication Data

McCready, William C.,   Date
    Culture, ethnicity, and identity.

    1. Ethnic relations--Addresses, essays, lectures.
2. Ethnicity--Addresses, essays, lectures.
3. Pluralism (Social science)--Addresses, essays, lectures.   I. Title.
GN496.M38 1982   305.8   82-22651
ISBN 0-12-482920-1

PRINTED IN THE UNITED STATES OF AMERICA

83 84 85 86   9 8 7 6 5 4 3 2 1

Contents

23   THE ETHNIC NUMBERS GAME IN INDIA: HINDU–MUSLIM CONFLICTS OVER CONVERSION, FAMILY PLANNING, MIGRATION, AND THE CENSUS

Theodore P. Wright, Jr.

Contributors

Numbers in parentheses indicate the pages on which the authors' contributions begin.

Irving Lewis Allen (1), Department of Sociology, The College of Liberal Arts and Sciences, University of Connecticut, Storrs, Connecticut 06268

Abdo I. Baaklini (17), State University of New York at Albany, Albany, New York 12222

Richard Basham (57), Department of Anthropology, The University of Sydney, N.S.W. 2006, Australia

Betty L. Chang (79), School of Nursing, University of California, Los Angeles, California 90024

Lee E. Dutter (301), Department of Political Science, College of Liberal Arts and Sciences, University of Illinois at Chicago Circle, Chicago, Illinois 60680

Peter K. Eisinger (95), Department of Political Science, University of Wisconsin-Madison, Madison, Wisconsin 53706

Donald V. Fandetti (111), School of Social Work and Community Planning, University of Maryland at Baltimore, Baltimore, Maryland 21201

Joshua A. Fishman (127), Ferkauf Graduate School of Professional Psychology, Yeshiva University, New York, New York 10461

Stephen S. Fugita (223), Department of Psychology, The University of Akron, Akron, Ohio 44325

Donald E. Gelfand (111), School of Social Work and Community Planning, University of Maryland at Baltimore, Baltimore, Maryland 21201

Albert I. Goldberg (139), Faculty of Industrial Engineering and Management, Technion, Haifa, Israel 32 000

J. Barry Gurdin[1] (149), Sociology and Anthropology Department, St. Xavier College, Chicago, Illinois 60655

Gedaliahu H. Harel (139), Faculty of Industrial Engineering and Management, Technion, Haifa, Israel 32 000

Charles Hirschman (381), Department of Sociology, Cornell University, Ithaca, New York

Phylis Cancilla Martinelli (181), Department of Sociology, Arizona State University, Tempe, Arizona 85281

Peter Y. Medding (195), Department of Political Science, The Faculty of Social Sciences, The Hebrew University of Jerusalem, Jerusalem, Israel 91 905

Jacqueline S. Mithun[2] (209), Culture Learning Institute, East-West Center, University of Hawaii, Honolulu, Hawaii 96848

David J. O'Brien (223), Department of Sociology, University of Akron, Akron, Ohio 44325

Jonathan Y. Okamura (241), Department of Anthropology, University College London, London WC1 6BT, England; and Culture Learning Institute, East-West Center, University of Hawaii, Honolulu, Hawaii 96848

Stephen O. Olugbemi (265), Department of Political Science, Faculty of Social Sciences, University of Lagos, Lagos, Nigeria

Peter G. Ossorio (283), Department of Psychology, University of Colorado, Boulder, Colorado 80309

Albert Ramirez (283), Department of Psychology, University of Colorado, Boulder, Colorado 80309

Paul Ritterband (291), Department of Sociology, City College and Graduate Center, City University of New York, New York, New York 10036

Ofira Seliktar (301), University of Haifa, Haifa, Israel

Rita J. Simon (327), College of Communications, Institute of Communications Research, University of Illinois at Urbana-Champaign, Champaign, Illinois 61820

Bryan Thompson (341), Department of Geography, College of Liberal Arts, Wayne State University, Detroit, Michigan 48202

Morton Weinfeld (361), Department of Sociology, McGill University, Montreal, Quebec H2A 2T7 Canada

[1]Present address: To Love and to Work: An Agency for Change, Chicago, Illinois 60637.

[2]Present address: Minnesota Association of Professional Anthropologists, Minneapolis, Minnesota 55419.

Morrison G. Wong (381), Department of Sociology, Texas Christian University, Fort Worth, Texas 76129

Theodore P. Wright, Jr. (405), Department of Political Science, Graduate School of Public Affairs, State University of New York at Albany, Albany, New York 12222

Preface

This volume is essentially concerned with the subject of diversity. It is especially concerned with the phenomenon of diversity among human groups and individuals within those groups. It is noteworthy that whereas we admire differentiation in the lower forms of life, and in fact find it both stimulating and beautiful, our own diversity is frequently perceived as threatening and primitive, a facet of life that needs to be improved. The general reason for this is that we tend to link many qualitative differences to those signs of our own cultural and social differentiation. While it is certainly true that many of our past and present conflicts have centered around our diverse identities, it is also true that the diversity does not manufacture the conflicts.

What do we mean when we say that differentiation is a good in its own right and does not necessarily have to be linked with conflict? Quite simply we mean that diversity is a facet of human existence. People have always tended to divide themselves into groups of various kinds for various reasons. Some of those reasons have been for defense or aggression, but some have been for definition as well. One of the themes that has run through many recent studies of ethnicity is the role that differentiation plays in formulating our individual identities, not because individuals are weak and require a group identity to support them, but rather because there is a commonality in the group experience that is valued and deemed worthy of preservation. It is a sign of our own maturity that we can examine our differences without feeling as though they must be eliminated, but rather that they contain valuable and uncommon insights as to what makes us most human.

Among the recent writings of self-psychologists can be found new insights into old concepts, such as narcissism, that had been previously defined as exclusively negative. Along with these insights have come new modes of help for persons with emotional and psychological difficulties and limitations. Yet the insights have been developed because scholars were unafraid of taking a traditional abstraction and turning it on its head. The study of groups is at about the same stage, although it is relatively primitive at this time. Because human conflicts have frequently focused on national, religious, racial, linguistic, or other cultural differences, many thought the differentiation was the essential source of the conflict. In fact there is another aspect of differentiation: the way in which it functions as a part of the process of social and individual identity. Humans tend to use a variety of ways to express and symbolize their individuation, and they attach various degrees of importance to those ways.

If we equate ethnicity with heritage, then everyone is an ethnic. Almost all of us have families that started out in other countries, perhaps a long time ago, but nevertheless somewhere else. The United States is not like older countries, which have long national histories and long periods of cultural development. Rather it is a stopping-off place to which people came from somewhere else. This is an essential element of our self-definition as a nation and is increasingly an important element of the way we define ethnicity. In other words, we are using a subjective identification of ethnic heritage rather than a compositional definition. I have been involved in research in which it was expected that people who said that ethnicity was an important factor in their lives would be different from those who said it was not. In fact just the opposite was found. Ethnicity, to the extent that it is a factor in people's lives, is a factor independent of people's consciousness of it. Sociologists call this a latent, or hidden, effect. Ethnicity is a characteristic that resides a bit below the surface of the personality. We may not acknowledge it very often and we may not think of it very often, but it does influence many of our thoughts, attitudes, and behaviors, and for this reason is called a social fact.

An important part of one's ethnic identity, or heritage in a larger sense, is one's religious identification. Ethnicity and religion have to be viewed in tandem as social facts for either one of them to make sense. It may surprise some people to know, for example, that those in the United States who identify themselves as "Irish" may also identify themselves as "Protestant." And these people are very different in many ways from those who identify themselves as both "Irish" and "Catholic." Our heritage, a combination of religious and ethnic identity, is an important social variable because it can both influence and reflect the way we think about reality; and every so often it is worthwhile for us to reflect upon our heritage and the meaning that it has for us.

There are two issues here. The first is the meaning that the heritage has for the rest of the people in society, and the second is the meaning that it has for those people who share a common heritage. The meaning that ethnic heritage has in the mass society is frequently that of a stereotype and can be found in derisive jokes and stories about different ethnic groups. For the purpose of correcting some of the stereotypes, observe the following facts. Most of the European immigrant groups have made remarkable economic and educational strides since coming to the United States. The Irish Catholics in the country are second only to the Jewish population in terms of average years of education. Italian and Polish Catholics, as well as Irish Catholics, are rapidly moving up the income ladder and can hardly be considered lower class anymore. The Catholic ethnic groups are also considered politically conservative, especially on issues of race and social welfare. The data do not support this contention, and in fact it can be shown that the Catholic ethnic groups are disproportionately *liberal* on most of these issues. It is also generally considered that these groups are no longer the target of discrimination, but if we look at the occupational prestige rankings and their proportion of representation in the opinion-shaping segments of society, we can see there is still a fair amount of discrimination against certain Catholic groups, particularly those from Middle and Eastern Europe. These stereotypes persist in part because it is useful for the larger society to have them, but they also persist in part because it is useful for Catholic ethnics not to fight them. For years Catholic ethnics somehow considered it un-American to cry out against the discrimination they knew existed. It was as though they had to prove how loyal they were by not complaining about what they knew was happening. This is no longer the case, and various people are pointing out the continuing ethnic and religious discrimination in our society; however, much more needs to be done along this line.

While the general society has had one view of ethnicity, people who share the same ethnic heritage have had another view. In our contemporary society, what is the advantage of reflecting upon one's own ethnic heritage? What can we learn by looking at the community of people from which we have come? I think there are two major points that we can learn by reflecting upon our heritage. The first is the necessity of belonging to a people in this pluralistic society, and the second is the strength that comes from celebrating the differences within society rather than trying to make them all disappear. One of the reasons that ethnic groups have persisted within our society is that people need a sense of belonging somewhere. It is not just a matter of being on a different team or picking sides in a conflict (although that has certainly happened in the past and will probably happen in the future). What is more important is the sense of belonging somewhere and having a group of people who you consider your own. This gives the individual a great deal of strength to sustain him- or herself against the various pressures that occur in everyday life. If we are secure in the knowledge of where we have come from, then we are able to deal with the difficult relationships that we are going to have with people who are different from us.

The fact that there are in our society differences as well as people of different backgrounds, races, and cultures bothers some social thinkers. They wish the differences would go away. Differences are not only messy; they also can produce conflict, and for that reason some social thinkers would prefer that we work to obliterate all differences. A more reasonable position is to celebrate the differences and use them as sources of strength rather than focusing on them as points of weakness. In this regard it becomes very functional for individuals to reflect upon their ethnicity and heritage as sources of knowledge and strength rather than to hide, be ashamed of, and be told to forget them.

There is also the question of fairness. It is not fair to tell people that they can celebrate their heritage, that because they have been discriminated against in the past the society will make up their losses, and that they may now exhibit their background with pride and demand their true rights; while at the same time they need not respect people of other heritages. And yet in a strange way that is what has been happening in our society with the rather selective definition of minority status according to racial and ethnic categories, rather than according to need. To celebrate the diverse heritages that exist in our society actually means to respect all of the heritages, and that is about all that any people want. We want to feel as though the larger society respects the place from which we have come.

These two factors, belonging to a people and being aware of a heritage that we respect, have a lot of significance for our society today. Social policies and various programs meant to help people will be much more effective if they are built on an awareness of these two social facts rather than conscious ignorance of them. Through research, we are finding more and more instances in which heritage and identity play an important role in people's behaviors and attitudes and the way they pass these along to their children. Unless we reflect upon our heritage from time to time, we will lose touch with it and, therefore, with a source of strength not only for ourselves as individuals but for our communities and for our society as well. People in leadership and opinion-molding positions, particularly those who are involved in organizational roles such as parish and diocesan committees, ought to be especially aware of this.

Ethnicity and the importance of our heritage are not external social issues that we can discuss dispassionately; rather they touch and involve each and every one of us individually. These are deep, personal, almost primordial social factors and as such need to be taken very seriously. Heritage is not something that deals exclusively with our past; rather it is an integral part of who we are right now. And the more we can learn about our heritage and learn to appreciate the differences between our heritage and other heritages, the more powerful our reasons for cooperating with each other and for respecting each other. Ethnicity, then, is not a nostalgic social issue, an impersonal source of discussion material, or something that exists only in the older big-city neighborhoods; it is rather a basic social characteristic that we need to reflect upon and use profitably lest we waste it. Ethnicity is not this year's crusade to be dropped in favor of whatever fad comes along next year; rather it is an important characteristic of ourselves and our groups, one that ought to be appreciated more deeply as our society matures.

Work needs to be done on the many new questions that some of the contributors to this volume raise, but perhaps most of all we need to begin to construct new models for the ways in which ethnicity and culture change over time within a pluralistic population. In many ways, neither assimilation nor acculturation is a sufficient paradigm. Perhaps the notion of a mutation, taken from the biological sciences, would be more descriptive. Ethnic and cultural identity mutates over generations, losing some of its elements and refocusing on others, while still others lie dormant for a time only to spring up again when we least expect them. Whatever the future of ethnic and cultural research holds, we can hope that it continues to be as sprightly, scholarly, and stimulating as the articles that have been compiled in this book and their many predecessors in the journal, *Ethnicity*. The contributors should certainly be thanked for their finè work, as should all who have contributed to *Ethnicity*'s pages over the years. Most particularly I express sincere appreciation to the editorial board and my colleagues at the Center for the Study of American Pluralism at the National Opinion Research Center who have been so supportive during this endeavor. Special gratitude is due to Pastora Cafferty, Leon W. Chestang, Robert Coles, Walker Connor, Charles Ferguson, Nathan Glazer, Philip Gleason, Andrew M. Greeley, J. David Greenstone, Herbert Gutman, Ruth F. Hale, Matthew Holden, Jr., Donald L. Horowitz, Chun-tu Hsueh, Harold Isaacs, John A. Jackson, Lyman Kellstedt, Dorothy Kocks, Mary Kotecki, Alice Kassis Kuroda, Frederick A. Lazin, Seymour Martin Lipset, Helena Z. Lopata, Arthur Mann, Martin E. Marty, Lawrence J. McCaffrey, Daniel Patrick Moynihan, Tae Y. Nam, Orlando Patterson, William Petersen, Richard Pipes, Richard Rose, Peter H. Rossi, Julian Samora, Timothy L. Smith, Rudolph Vecoli, and Sidney Verba.

Culture, Ethnicity, and Identity

CURRENT ISSUES IN RESEARCH

1

Variable White Ethnic Resistance to School Desegregation: Italian-American Parents in Three Connecticut Cities, 1966*

Irving Lewis Allen

INTRODUCTION

Why do certain white ethnic groups, such as the Irish in South Boston, protest so much against school desegregation and busing, whereas other white groups living in the same neighborhoods and facing the same prospect seem less concerned with defending the neighborhood against external threats? I propose that the simple fact of majority status of an ethnic group in a plural community explains variations among white ethnic groups. Any group that has been the largest group and has had the greatest cultural influence in a plural community will most actively try to conserve the status quo and to retain its control over aspects of community life, such as the neighborhood schools.

This is a familiar description of the "conservative" behavior of majority groups. In some metropolitan areas white Protestants are a majority, but they and the middle class of other groups have long since moved to the suburbs and are not required to deal with the issue of school desegregation. The suburban majorities, as every effort at metropolitan school consolidation indicates, resist desegregation as vigorously as central city groups.

This study compares seven white, central city groups of ethnic parents in Bridgeport, Hartford, and New Haven by their attitudes toward

*The University of Connecticut Research Foundation supported this study. I thank Harold J. Abramson for commenting on an early version.

1

CULTURE, ETHNICITY,
AND IDENTITY

the prospect of neighborhood school desegregation. The study focuses on Italian-Americans, which is the largest group of parents of school-age children, in order to show why different white ethnic groups are associated with protest against desegregation in different cities and in different parts of the same cities. Which group is most likely to protest, and to protest hardest and longest, is not simply a matter of who is being required to conform with school desegregation.

Neighborhoods in mature, central cities, so often designated for de-segregation by busing, are sometimes white ethnic enclaves. These neigh-borhoods are often Catholic and working class and have high rates of home ownership. Journalists and other observers of desegregation and busing protests in the North and Midwest sometimes focus on the par-ticipation of certain white ethnic groups, usually working-class segments of a Catholic group (e.g., Schumacher, 1979; and many others). The case of the Irish in South Boston is a recent and widely publicized example. Some observers anticipate that Slavic groups in cities such as Chicago and Detroit and the Italians in New England will react similarly when they are confronted with this issue. These diverse ethnic groups have a common characteristic. The group associated with protest is usually the largest white "minority" group in a city or the largest group in a section of a large city, such as the Irish in South Boston. We do not know whether the largest group evokes media attention because its members are the most visible and numerous participants or whether they actually behave differently.

In seeking an answer to this question, I do not claim to inform either the present school-desegregation and busing controversy or the question of "white flight." The national climate of opinion, the schools, the cohorts of parents, and the demographic characteristics of cities have changed too greatly since 1966 to make any inference to the present situation. Similarly, this study tells us nothing of public attitudes today in Bridge-port, Hartford, and New Haven. This is, rather, a "historical" study that seeks to answer the general question of why some white ethnic groups become greatly involved in desegregation protest whereas other groups in the same situation seem to remain more aloof.

THE PRINCIPLE OF THE LARGEST GROUP

There are theoretical reasons to believe that the largest group in a plural community behaves differently in controversies over social change be-cause it is both large and largest. Large group size stimulates the emergence of secondary subculture along ethnic lines. Part of this subculture may be to rationalize and justify the status quo of ethnic stratification in the community. Fischer (1975) argues that large size of ethnic and other groups may constitute a "critical mass" that induces and galvanizes subcultures. Mayhew and Levinger (1976) use the variable of size as explanation for a variety of interactive phenomena. Blau (1977:19–44) develops several structural theorems about intergroup relations, which derive from group size and number in a dichotomous (plural) society. Yancy, Ericksen, and Juliani (1976) organized a mass of literature and theorized that a complex of ecological and economic characteristics of American cities structured and maintained ethnic subcultures.

The political factor in secondary ethnic formations, moreover, is a venerable idea that receives less attention than it deserves. Max Weber (1922/1968:385–398) thought that, in industrial societies, group beliefs in common ethnicity and the formation of ethnic groups had "artificial" origins in memories of immigration, rational association, and political experience. Cohen (1974:95–98) similarly argues that much of what we call "ethnicity" in complex society is less primordial culture than political consolidations that correspond with ethnic lineages and that result from intensive competition with other groups.

Bergesen (1977), in a comment upon Yancey et al. (1976), argues that "emergent ethnicity" is mainly a defensive political protest. Bergesen asserts that the Irish of South Boston express ethnic solidarity not because they share common occupational experience, status, institutions, and residential areas but because of defensive reaction to an external threat to their privilege of controlling schools. This is similar to white "backlash" hypotheses (e.g., Glazer, 1976:168–195; Greeley, 1974:186–241; Rubin, 1972:39–73, 1976), which are the prevailing explanations of white ethnic resistance. "Backlash" hypotheses, however, do not explain why some ethnic groups organize and vociferously resist whereas other groups do not, though they may be similarly situated and exposed to the same "threat." The questions remain of whether "backlash" varies with ethnicity and, if so, why.

Stack (1979) makes a historically informed explanation why the Irish of Boston reacted as they did in the recent desegregation controversy. "Irish opposition to busing was overwhelmingly oriented around such interests as stability of neighborhoods, property values, jobs, and the safety of school children rather than simply irrational fears and prejudices [p. 24]." He points to the seeming paradox that studies of public opinion show that Irish- and Italian-Americans are no more opposed to desegregation than other white groups. Stack goes on to make essentially a "backlash" hypothesis that the busing crisis "resurrected long sub-merged ethnic antipathies" that expressed a long history of intergroup relations in Boston and the frustrations of rising expectations and relative deprivations.

Useem (1980) studied three Boston neighborhoods, including South Boston, that were greatly affected by busing orders. His sample of white respondents was collected in 1977–1978 and was confined to persons in the 25 to 53 age category in order to include many parents of school-age children. His tests of the "solidarity" and "breakdown" hypotheses of recruitment into social movements showed that two characteristics con-tributed to support of and participation in the antibusing movement: strong ties to and involvement in the local community and, indepen-dently, relative deprivation.

Buell (1980) found the roots of resistance to busing in South Boston during 1974–1977 in the "defended neighborhood," an idea developed by Suttles (1972) and others. The defended neighborhood is character-ized, among other traits, by strong community ties and involvement, such as Useem (1980) found related to recruitment into the antibusing movement in South Boston. Buell found that South Boston met every criterion of the defended neighborhood, including a history and tradi-tions of solidarity, extensive networks of primary group relations, and great community involvement and satisfaction. South Boston, Buell ar-gues, is also geographically isolated, which contributed to the emergence of the defended neighborhood.

Buell found that the numbers and the cultural influence of the Irish were important but did not wholly account for the emergence of a defended neighborhood in South Boston. The working-class Irish, he shows, were especially involved in social networks and had a strong tradition of mutual aid. By 1970, the Irish were only 36% of the foreign stock population in South Boston, a decline from 62% in 1905, though South Boston still had the largest concentration of Irish in the city. If Buell had taken third- and later-generation Irish into account, the Irish may still be largest in numbers as well as in cultural influence.

But the question remains of why "backlash," community solidarity, and the defended neighborhood do not seem to involve equally all ethnic groups in the plural community. We might reasonably expect an anti-busing coalition of ethnic groups to develop in the symbolic community of South Boston, such that all groups would protest equally. What is special about the Irish in South Boston or the Italians in Boston's North End? I propose that group size and the related factor of cultural dom-inance account for variable white ethnic resistance to busing and school desegregation.

A COMPARATIVE STUDY

The hypothesis can be assessed partially and indirectly by comparing different white ethnic groups living in similar community situations but varying with respect to the independent variables of relative group size and absolute number.[1] The setting is the three largest central cities in Connecticut—Bridgeport, Hartford, and New Haven, as they were in 1966. The study compares seven groups of parents of school-age children and focuses upon the largest group of parents—native-born Italian-Americans. Many were third and fourth generation, and the vast majority were working class.

The Italian communities (parents and nonparents of school-age children) in 1966 were the largest European ethnic group in these cities, comprising 20% of the white population. Prominent enclaves were in each of the cities, and New Haven, in particular, had large enclaves of urban character in the inner suburbs. For most of this century the Italians in these cities have been a white working-class majority, though many have entered the middle classes. Among Catholic groups, the Italians were the largest (38%) group in these cities. Among blue-collar residents, the Italians were again the largest (39%). In addition to having been and remaining the largest white ethnic group, the largest Catholic group, and (aside from the blacks) the largest blue-collar group, the Italians were the most visible of the European groups because of residential enclaves. Italian immigrants were more inclined than groups arriving earlier to settle and remain longer in enclaves, which perhaps only re-flects their arrival on an already changed urban industrial setting. Other white groups were smaller and residentially more dispersed; some, such as the Poles and French Canadians, were perhaps more dispersed be-cause they were smaller.

White ethnic resistance to housing and school desegregation is often explained as a simple geographic circumstance of ethnic enclaves being sited in older areas of central cities (e.g., Conforti, 1974). Italians in many cities, it is said, are just more often in the path of black social and spatial

[1] A complete test of the hypothesis would entail not only a comparison of different groups within similar community settings but also a comparison of different cities in different parts of the country, such that the largest (and most cohesive) group also varies by ethnicity. The secondary analytic nature of this study, moreover, constrains the oper-ational definition of the dependent variable to a single hypothetical question about self-predicted behavior in response to a school desegregation that had not, in fact, yet been proposed by community authorities. A full test of the hypothesis, in addition to a com-parative study of variant plural settings, would need to develop a conceptually complete index of community defense and reaction to a real situation.

mobility. Italian community patterns in Connecticut cities are probably similar to those elsewhere in the nation and, particularly, to those in the cities and suburbs of the Northeast and Midwest where Italians are concentrated. Greeley (1977:120) reports 1970–1976 National Opinion Research Center (NORC) data from the metropolitan North that shows the Italians, compared to other Catholics, are less supportive of integrated education, and this might be attributed to their urban circumstance.

A *New York Times*–CBS Poll (Reinhold, 1976) showed that Italian-Americans nationally were more "conservative" than other ethnic groups on a variety of social issues. Yet, Taylor, Sheatsley, and Greeley (1978) showed that in the 1970 to 1976 period, especially in the 1970 to 1972 interval, national attitudes, toward racial integration in particular, generally became more liberal for all white groups. The Italians, who were among the least liberal groups in 1970, rose markedly, such that by 1976 they resembled most other white groups on integration issues. This trend is undoubtedly true as well for Italians in these Connecticut cities.

Italians, like other groups, identify with the "social turf" of neighborhood (e.g., Greeley, 1971:95–102). Attachment to place is a frequent explanation of defensive reactions. Conforti (1974), for example, argues that the ecological patterns peculiar to the cities of the Northeast, where Italian communities are juxtaposed with mobile black communities, makes the Italians first to respond defensively and thus to bear the calumny of bigotry. When confronted, says Conforti, Italians resist suburbanization because of a tenacious attachment to neighborhoods. The attachments, however, may be more to social networks than to particular houses and streets. Firey (1947:178–192ff.), for example, wrote that Boston Italians of the North End had few sentimental attachments to neighborhoods *as place*. Place was mainly a mechanism to maintain contact and community organization. Resistance to desegregation requires more explanation than a group's simply being in the path of change and having sentimental attachments to place.

Political consolidation among the Italians in these three cities vis-à-vis the blacks, nonetheless, may grow in some part from their ecological situation. The Italians and the blacks, each representing 16% of the total city population, were highly visible to the other because of color and residence in enclaves. Suttles (1968:102–103, 120–121) describes a tension between the Italian and black communities in the Addams area of Chicago that stemmed in part from their juxtaposition, both ecological and historical. Suttles (1968:120–121, 1972:146) suggests that relatively large, working-class Italian cultural communities evolve a "zero sum" game strategy when pitted in competition with other ethnic communities, particularly blacks at this point in American urban history. This entails an "oppressive belief that benefits of social life make up a fixed quantity and [are] already being used to the maximum [1968:103]." Gains of blacks, in this case access to white schools, are seen as a threat to white control of the schools, and are resisted. Working-class segments of other Catholic groups, which are smaller and without a history of numerical and cultural dominance, therefore, more easily accommodate and are less likely to see their own and their children's fortunes and mobility impaired by black gains in access to community facilities. For the Italians, beliefs about the exhaustibility of the public weal and resentments of black encroachment are perceptions consensually defined through interaction in ethnic social networks. Consolidation, thus engendered, reinforces resistance to the prospect of school desegregation and the community change it symbolizes.

The purpose of the study is not to explain the behavior of Italians per se but to explain why defensive reactions to the prospect of community change are characteristic of some ethnic groups but not others in otherwise similar community situations. In other cities and in other ecological and plural settings the explanation would apply to other ethnic groups. I hope to elucidate why different ethnic groups become engaged in desegregation controversies in different cities without primary reference to original culture, to simple geographic circumstance, or to working-class "backlash."

SURVEY METHODS

The Samples

Sample survey interviews were conducted in late 1966 with 1783 adult residents in the central cities of Bridgeport, Hartford, and New Haven, which are the three largest cities in Connecticut. This is a secondary analysis of a subsample of 286 white ethnic parents of school-age children. Several national surveys, such as NORC's General Social Survey, collect data on ethnic background and attitudes toward school desegregation but sample sizes do not permit manifold comparative studies in community contexts. Each of the three city samples is a strict two-stage area probability sample of households.[2] The subsample includes

[2] The second stage of the area sampling was conducted by a procedure that minimizes cluster error. Each resident over 20 years of age in each selected household was listed, and one such person was randomly selected to be interviewed. No substitution of households or respondents was permitted. These strict sampling procedures, ipso facto, apply to the subsample of 286 parents.

all white, non-Puerto Rican parents who had one or more children of ages 5 through 17 enrolled in the public schools. Puerto Rican parents are omitted because the study focuses on comparing the reactions of different groups of European background to the prospect of school de-segregation. The subsample includes 60 Italian-American parents, smaller numbers of six other white ethnic groups of parents, and "others."

The city sample sizes are proportionate to the relative size of each city and are combined and treated here as a single sample, as are the subsamples of parents from each city. The samples reflect similar com-munity contexts in a single and integrated urban region (see Meyer, 1976). Interview completion rates were about 85% in each city. All respondents were coded into one of seven categories of religio-ethnicity or into an eighth "other" category containing the many ethnic groups too small to analyze and the ethnically nondescript.[3]

The Temporal and Political Context

These 1966 data, which are now in the nature of recent urban history, were collected in the temporal and political context of the first public discussions and media attention to prospects and means to school de-segregation in these cities. The public school enrollments in 1966 were approximately one-third black, whereas the proportion is much greater today. Bridgeport, Hartford, and New Haven are typical of many middle-sized and larger cities in that they have been steadily losing their white population to the suburbs for several decades, while the black and Puerto Rican populations have been steadily increasing because of in-migration. Census data show that between 1960 and 1970 these cities together lost to the suburbs over 16% of their white, non-Puerto Rican population. Fourth count U.S. Bureau of the Census (1970) data indicate that the white ethnic composition of the suburbs was closely similar to that of the central cities, and there were a number of ethnic, especially Italian, enclaves in these suburbs. Many whites still in the cities were not living

[3] For the Religio-Ethnicity Index, data were collected on respondents' race, ethnic self-concept and nativity, ethnicity and nativity of both parents, respondents' religion, and religion of both parents. If the respondent's ethnic self-concept and present religious "preference" corresponded to one of the seven categories, he or she was coded directly, as was the case for most. Respondents who identified as "American" only or as having no religion presently or as having converted to another as adults were placed into one of the categories by the nativity or ethnic origins of their fathers (presuming an importance of surname for ethnic identification) or by parental religion. This procedure allocated 85% of the cases into seven categories that shall be called ethnic "groups," although they vary widely in ethnic network involvement.

in ethnic communities of place but in extra-local networks of ethnic identity and kinship, which are also important for ethnic behavior and cohesion (see, e.g., Parenti, 1967).

The surveys, moreover, were conducted in the late phase of the civil rights movement, just before the first outbreaks of racial violence in these cities in the summer of 1967, the assassination of Martin Luther King, Jr., in 1968, and the subsequent phase of black militancy. Some speculate that the "resurgence" of white ethnic identity was in some part a response to black militancy and racially changing neighborhoods and schools in the late 1960s and early 1970s. These surveys are a historical picture of ethnic attitudes before any galvanizing of ethnic identities as a conse-quence of those events and provide a glance at ethnic politics on a now topical issue before the issue was greatly topical or, in fact, real.

THE FINDINGS

The 286 parents of school-age children were asked: "Do you think you would consider moving to another neighborhood if many Negro [the conventional term of 1966] children began attending your child's school?" Table 1 shows that 27% of all parents said they would consider such a move. The French Canadian, Irish, and Jewish parents were least apt to give this response, and the Italian parents (42%) were most apt. Other cross-tabulations (not presented here) show that the finding for the Italians is pronounced in each of the three cities.

Though resistance is expressed as a willingness to move, the expe-rience of South Boston and elsewhere make it clear that community defensiveness is acted out either by staying and fighting or, for some of those who can afford it, by moving to the suburbs, which achieves com-munity defense finally and absolutely. The question asked of the re-spondents, which gets at the defensiveness potential only indirectly, invited the response of "would consider such a move," and it is not surprising that that response was forthcoming. Thus, all the question really measures is a certain contrariness toward the prospect of school desegregation. But my interest is in the group differences in expressing a negative reaction to school desegregation.

Table 1 shows that, in the aggregate, blue-collar parents were slightly more apt to say they would consider such a move (29%) than were white-collar parents (23%). Eight in ten of the Italian parents were blue-collar, and a majority of the other Catholic groups were blue-collar as well. The disproportionate number of blue-collar parents in these central city

Table 1

Ethnicity of Parents Who Say They Would Consider Moving if Child's School Desegregated, by Occupational Status and Home Tenure Status

Ethnicity[a]	All parents		White-collar		Blue-collar		Owns home		Rents home	
	%	N	%	N	%	N	%	N	%	N
Catholics										
French Canadian	15.8	19	—	4	13.3	15	—	3	12.5	16
Irish	10.8	37	20.0	15	4.5	22	11.8	17	10.0	20
Italian	41.7	60	25.0	12	45.8	48	41.9	31	41.4	29
Polish	25.0	20	—	7	30.8	13	—	9	36.4	11
Protestants										
British Isles	30.3	33	33.3	15	27.8	18	—	8	36.0	25
German	27.3	22	—	8	28.6	14	—	4	22.2	18
Jews, all national origins	13.8	29	16.0	25	—	4	15.8	19	10.0	10
Others	30.8	65	28.0	25	32.5	40	29.0	31	32.4	34
Total	27.0	285	23.4	111	29.3	174	26.2	122	27.6	163

[a]Percentage not shown when cell base N is less than 10.

samples, which are not subsamples of general populations, and the small
N of white-collar parents in some groups virtually preclude an analysis
by class. Nonetheless, I shall later adjust in a regression procedure for
occupational status differences among the (predominantly blue-collar)
parents. Neighborhood tenacity is often associated with home ownership. Table 1, which arranges responses according to home tenure status,
also shows that (in the aggregate and for each group whose cell frequencies reasonably permit percentaging) home-owning parents did not
respond differently from their home-renting counterparts; this is also
true of the Italian parents.

A dummy-variable regression procedure (8 minus 1 ethnic groups)
is used to make a stronger test of the proposition that Italian parents
are incipiently most resistant.[4] All variables in the equation, including
all the control variables or covariates, are rendered to dummy or dichotomous form. Unstandardized partial regression coefficients (Table 2) are
used to rank each ethnic group by its additional probability to give the
defensive response. The partial regression coefficients are adjusted for
11 controls in dummy form as 29 factors. Most of the controls are in the
nature of variables, other than desegregating schools per se, that could
influence a decision to move or stay and that could vary among ethnic
groups.

Control variables were selected that reasonably could be related to
ethnicity, on one hand, and independently to the dependent variable,
on the other. These were reduced to 11 by a preliminary stepwise regression procedure. The control variables are

1. Duncan's (Reiss, 1961:109–161) SEI for households (10 minus 1
   categories as dummy factors)
2. Annual family income (6 − 1 categories)
3. Gender or sex of parent (2 − 1)

---

[4] There are arguments for and against using ordinary least-squares regression instead
of a "log-linear" technique for such a problem, especially with a dichotomous dependent
variable (e.g., Gillespie, 1977; Knoke, 1975). The simple aims of adjusting partial coefficients
for a large number of covariates, without attention to interactions, and ranking independent
variables make regression a practical choice. Regression also reduces the problem of few
cases for subpopulations and uses information that would be lost in dichotomizing manifold variables for log-linear procedures. Multiple Classification Analysis (MCA) is another
procedure that lends itself well to problems generally of this type. But the decision to use
12 control variables obviated MCA for practical reasons. In settling on the present procedure
because of its practicality and prima facie interpretability, several alternative procedures
were explored within their own constraints. The results are the same in any case. The
object of this procedure, moreover, is to test an hypothesis rather than to maximize prediction; all the independent factors explain (R^2) only about 14% of the variance of the
dependent variable.

4. Perceived direction of recent "neighborhood" racial change $(2-1)$
5. Respondents' estimates of the number of blacks living in the "neighborhood" already $(5-1)$
6. Proportion of households on the block that were occupied by blacks $(2-1)$
7. Proportion of housing physically deteriorating on respondent's block $(3-1)$ (U.S. Bureau of the Census, 1960)
8. Home-owner or renter $(2-1)$
9. City of residence $(3-1)$
10. Whether respondent currently had experience of child in a racially balanced school $(2-1)$
11. Whether first, second, or third-and-later generation $(3-1)$

These were introduced as 29 control factors.

Because the seven independent variables, all 29 cofactors, and the dependent variable (a dichotomous yes or no response) are all in dichotomous form, the unstandardized partial regression coefficients can be interpreted directly as adjusted percentage deviations from the reference group of "others" and as adjusted percentage differences between groups. Table 2 shows that the Italian parents had the highest coefficient of .171, representing a substantial deviation from other groups.[5] Although this does not seem a high coefficient, it represents a departure of 13% to 41% from the other groups. The French Canadians and Irish were least inclined to consider moving, whereas the two Protestant groups, the Poles, and the Jewish parents were so similar to "others" that their coefficients are near 0.[6]

---

[5] It would be theoretically pertinent, in addition, to test the hypothesis more directly by making the independent variable the percentage of the sample that is the number of respondents in each ethnic group. This would, in effect, order ethnic groups by the theoretical principle of size. In this sample (and community context), however, the sizes of ethnic groups (except the Italians), especially the working-class segments of Catholic groups, are roughly the same (except for the many yet smaller groups in the "other" category), and each is about a third or less than the size of the Italian subcommunity. A scale by the relative size of each group (not including the many small groups among "others") would result in an effective dichotomy. Therefore, the dummy independent variable regression procedure loses little or nothing in this regard.

[6] F scores and tests of significance for regression coefficients with dummy dependent variables are not applicable because of problems of heteroscedasticity. However, the coefficients are unbiased and their relative sizes can be interpreted directly. If one wishes to ignore the problem, he or she should note that the coefficients for the Italians as well as for several other of the groups have corresponding F scores that indicate significance at conventionally high levels.

Table 2

Regression Coefficients for the Influence of
Ethnicity on Whether Parents Would Consider
Moving if Child's School Desegregated

	B
Catholics	
French Canadian	− .240
Irish	− .194
Italian	.171
Polish	− .045
Protestants	
British Isles	− .014
German	.045
Jews, all national	
origins	− .037

CONCLUSIONS

Assuming that these procedures have factored out or adjusted for most background and situational factors specific to each group, there remains a distinct ethnic effect for the Italian parents. They were more apt to express a reactive intention toward neighborhood change than parents of any other group. In contrast, the other Catholic groups—the French Canadians, the Irish, and the Poles (all of whom were also predominantly blue-collar but much smaller groups)—were markedly less apt to say they would move in response to the hypothetical situation of desegregating schools. The two Protestant groups and the Jewish parents had responses close to the population average. The direct association between the implicit independent variables of group size and cultural dominance and the dependent variable of defensive reaction is "circumstantial," though it is unlikely that it is coincidental or spurious.

The least likely interpretation is that these differences reflect primordial or original cultural differences—that Italians are somehow more "conservative." Most of these parents of school-age children were younger persons of the second and third-and-later generations. There is no evidence here for an interpretation of this behavioral particular in terms of a survival of an original culture, or even as a residue after assimilation. But that does not preclude the possibility of subcultural differences that are relatively "new" or that have emerged as a consequence of living in large ethnic communities in plural cities.

Working-class, white ethnic groups are most often in the path of desegregation in central cities, and their children are more subject to the imposed requirements of racial balancing. One might expect all groups to respond roughly the same, but they do not. Explanations that rely upon general "backlash" or upon simple geographic situation need to be qualified. That these 1966 data were collected before the social changes and events of the late 1960s and early 1970s, which supposedly galvanized the "new" ethnic resurgence, suggests an already existing base of subculture inclined toward resistance. This seems further to qualify "backlash" hypotheses. Explanations that deemphasize ethnicity and attribute all to the commonality of class condition similarly need to be qualified as to why the "ethnic factor" still emerges as a variable.

Variations in community solidarity and the emergence of "defended neighborhoods" best explain why certain neighborhoods resist more than others. Ethnic groups in such neighborhoods probably will vary accordingly in resistance. But community solidarity of plural neighborhoods, like South Boston or these Connecticut cities, does not explain ethnic variations within defended neighborhoods.

In conclusion, the largest white group in a plural community is more likely than smaller white groups to resist desegregation. When white "minorities" are in a position of majority in a local community, they tend to behave like "majorities." Any group could be the largest group, but it is the Irish, Italians, and Slavic groups that are now experiencing desegregation in many big city neighborhoods. Members of the largest group are most "conservative" because they have the most control, status, and privilege to conserve. Moreover, the largest group, by reason of numbers, often has the "critical mass" that gives rise to a consensus of resistance and its public display. Smaller groups, otherwise similarly situated, have less to lose and may accommodate to externally imposed change with less vociferous resistance. On the other hand, members of smaller groups may join a protest movement, but they are not seen as among the vanguard and, thus, do not catch the attention of the media. Resistance to desegregation of schools and probably also of housing has little to do with ethnicity in itself.

REFERENCES

Bergesen, A. J.
    1977   Neo-ethnicity as defensive political protest. *American Sociological Review* **42**:823–
           825.

Blau, P. M.
  1977   *Inequality and Heterogeneity*. New York: The Free Press.
Buell, E. H., Jr.
  1980   Busing and the defended neighborhood: South Boston, 1974–1977. *Urban Affairs Quarterly* **16**:161–188.

Cohen, A.
  1974   *Two-Dimensional Man*. London: Routledge & Kegan Paul.
Conforti, J. M.
  1974   WASP in the woodpile: inequalities and injustices of ethnic ecology. Paper presented at the annual meeting of the American Sociological Association, Montreal, Quebec, Canada.

Firey, W.
  1947   *Land Use in Central Boston*. Cambridge, Mass.: Harvard University Press.
Fischer, C. S.
  1975   Toward a subcultural theory of urbanism. *American Journal of Sociology* **80**:1319–1341.

Gillespie, M. W.
  1977   Log-linear techniques and the regression analysis of dummy-dependent variables: further bases for comparison. Paper presented at the annual meeting of the American Sociological Association, Chicago, Illinois.
Glazer, N.
  1976   *Affirmative Discrimination*. New York: Basic Books.
Greeley, A. M.
  1971   *Why Can't They Be Like Us?* New York: E. P. Dutton.
  1974   *Ethnicity in the United States*. New York: John Wiley & Sons.
  1977   *The American Catholic*. New York: Basic Books, Inc.

Knoke, D.
  1975   A comparison of log-linear techniques and regression models for systems of dichotomous variables. *Sociological Methods and Research* **3**:416–434.
Mayhew, B. H., and Levinger, R. L.
  1976   Size and density of interaction in human aggregates. *American Journal of Sociology* **82**:86–110.
Meyer, D. R.
  1976   *From Farm to Factory to Urban Pastorialism: Urban Change in Central Connecticut*. Cambridge, Mass.: Ballinger.

Parenti, M.
  1967   Ethnic politics and the persistence of ethnic identification. *American Political Science Review* **61**:717–726.

Reinhold, R.
  1976   Many Connecticut Italians disenchanted with Carter. *New York Times* **October 23**:23.
Reiss, A. J., Jr.
  1961   *Occupations and Social Status*. New York: The Free Press.
Rubin, L. B.
  1972   *Busing and Backlash*. Berkeley, Ca.: University of California Press.
  1976   White against white: school desegregation and the revolt of middle America, in *School Desegregation* (F. H. Levinsohn and B. D. Wright, Eds.), pp. 67–93. Chicago: University of Chicago Press.

Schumacher, E.
   1979   School violence in Boston reflects a deep-seated racial animosity. *New York Times*
          October 22:A-16.
Stack, J. F., Jr.
   1979   Ethnicity, racism, and busing in Boston: the Boston Irish and school desegre-
          gation. *Ethnicity* **6**:21–28.
Suttles, G. D.
   1968   *The Social Order of the Slum*. Chicago: University of Chicago Press.
   1972   *The Social Construction of Communities*. Chicago: University of Chicago Press.
Taylor, D. G., Sheatsley, P. B. and Greeley, A. M.
   1978   Attitudes toward racial integration. *Scientific American* **238**:42–49.
U.S. Bureau of the Census
   1960   *U.S. Census of Housing: City Blocks*. Washington, D.C.: U.S. Bureau of the Census.
   1970   U.S. census of the population, fourth count summary tape, Connecticut. Wash-
          ington, D.C.: U.S. Bureau of the Census.
Useem, B.
   1980   Solidarity model, breakdown model, and the Boston anti-busing movement.
          American Sociological Review **45**:357–369.
Weber, M.
   1968   *Economy and Society*. Vol. 1. (G. Roth and C. Wittich, Eds.) New York: Bedminster
          Press. (Originally published, 1922)
Yancey, W. L., Eriksen, E. P., and Juliani, R. N.
   1976   Emergent ethnicity: a review and reformulation. *American Sociological Review*
          41:391–403.

2

Ethnicity and Politics in Contemporary Lebanon

Abdo I. Baaklini

INTRODUCTION

Ethnic conflict has taken many shapes and forms (see, e.g., Enloe, 1973; Connor, 1972). In his paper in this volume Wright identifies 11 ways in which one group may try to shift to maintain the numerical—and thereby power—balance in its favor. This paper will discuss how ethnicity manifests itself in contemporary Lebanon. It will analyze the extent to which the civil war in Lebanon between 1975 and 1982 is a manifestation of ethnic political conflict. In the process of doing so, the various approaches that have been advanced to explain this civil war will also be reviewed and evaluated.

Three main propositions underlie this study. The first is that ethnic conflict is started and exacerbated by competition *within* the various groups of the same ethnicity as much as by competition *between* different groups. Thus, according to this viewpoint, the conflict in Lebanon was as much a product of competition within the Christian and Moslem groups themselves as it was between Moslems and Christians. The main actors were competing to increase their political power not only vis-à-vis the actors of the other ethnic group but also vis-à-vis competitors of their own ethnicity.

The second proposition is that political groups adhering to universalistic ideologies and political visions are more likely to initiate ethnic conflict by refusing to play by the rules of the game than are those

17

adhering to parochial pragmatic views. Groups adhering to universalistic ideologies tend to transcend ethnic boundaries by appealing to members of other groups as a means to increase their power base. I shall call this method of extraethnic appeal on the basis of a universalistic political ideology *power accumulation*, or increasing a group's size through political conversion, a modern counterpart of traditional religious conversion.

The third proposition is that in many cases ethnic conflict cannot be resolved through integrative institutions long-advocated by political scientists and political actors concerned with development. Examples of these institutions are a strong army, a mobilizing political party, or a strong executive. Ethnic conflict usually can be contained through mediating and compromising institutions such as legislatures. Political groups that seek national integration and assimilation as a means to resolve ethnic conflict may end up exacerbating the conflict rather than resolving it.

A caveat is in order at the outset. The analysis of the Lebanese conflict contained in this paper highlights the internal dimension of the conflict. This is not intended to belittle or ignore the international dimension of the 1975-1982 war in Lebanon. The approach one follows reflects the variables that one intends to emphasize. In this paper I am interested in exploring the internal dimension of the war by examining the inter-ethnic variable and its contribution to this conflict. A full understanding of the Lebanese war, however, requires a thorough examination of the role played by the various non-Lebanese actors, whether they are Arab, Israeli, or non-Middle Eastern actors.

This paper will therefore conceive of the conflict as a synthesis between internal and international forces, with the emphasis on the internal dimension. Making Lebanese actors the unit of analysis is not intended to exclude international actors. In this case the international actors (Arab and non-Arab) are regarded as resources, similar to funds, military power, ideology, and information, which the various local forces mobilize to increase their power base. Because they are non-Lebanese citizens, the Palestinians pose a special problem for our analysis. At one time during the early stages of the conflict they were regarded and mobilized as an external force. As the conflict developed, however, they became closely associated with one side of the conflict. The Palestinians in Lebanon are now estimated at close to 500,000. Their interaction with Lebanese society enabled them to penetrate and be penetrated by the various Lebanese political forces. Nevertheless, they are considered by most analysts as an external force with considerable impact on the balance of power among the various groups constituting Lebanese society, and we shall treat them as such.

ETHNIC CONFLICT IN THE LEBANESE POLITICAL SYSTEM

Democracy in recently independent nations of the Third World brought with it some advantages and a host of problems that those nations had not previously faced. One of these problems is the question of distribution of power among the various groups in society. In pluralistic, multiethnic societies such as Lebanon, this issue assumes a paramount importance because the viability of the system depends on its ability to ensure that power is satisfactorily distributed among the main groups in the country.[1]

Under colonial rule, power distribution was handled by the arbitrary authority wielded by the colonial state and by various mechanisms the state developed to ensure that the main groups were either kept satisfied or were adequately controlled—by the forces of colonial armies, if necessary. In traditional societies direct election of power holders was not the practice. Distribution of power was achieved in accordance with custom, tradition, convenience, and, ultimately, by the domination of one group over another regardless of their relative size.

With the advent of representative democracy and universal suffrage, power distribution was to take place through balloting, giving one person one vote. The size of an ethnic group became very significant. Dominant groups in society had to ensure that they remained in power by ensuring that they retained the numerical majority, by converting others to their ranks, by eliminating others, by holding key positions in the nonelected jobs, or by structuring the political game and electoral process in such a way that their preeminence might last irrespective of their size. Lebanon's dominant Christian elite has tried several of these strategies throughout modern history.

1. *Religious conversion.* Beginning with the early nineteenth century, when Lebanon was still part of the Ottoman Empire but ruled by its feudal families, the Maronite Christians were successful in converting some of the most prominent Moslem feudal families to Maronite Chris-

---

[1] Sectarianism in Lebanon is treated in this study as a form of ethnicity, yet this mode of analysis is rejected by many scholars and political actors in Lebanon, especially those with nationalistic or leftist orientations.

tianity. This was possible because of the decline of the authority of the Ottoman Empire and the aggressive wave of Christian European colonialism. The conversion of such families as the Abi Lama', the Shihabs, and the Harfoush added political power and prestige to the emerging Maronite Church and enabled it to play a leading role in working for an independent Lebanon tailored to Christians' needs in the late nineteenth century and early twentieth century. However, after the middle of the nineteenth century and the emergence of Arab nationalism, conversion on any significant scale stopped. Islam became a national culture; even Christian Arabs extolled its virtue and used it against both Ottoman hegemony and, later, French and British colonialism

2. *Territorial division.* Another method utilized after the disintegration of the feudal system in 1842 by the Maronites was to divide Mount Lebanon into two autonomous districts, one dominated by the Christians, the other dominated by the Druze. This is also a step that some Christian parties, the Phalange, and the National Liberals allegedly now advocate as a solution to the present Lebanese crisis (see, e.g., Salibi, 1965; Tarbein, 1968). For reasons discussed elsewhere, this solution was doomed to failure. It led to civil war in 1860 and had to be replaced by another formula. The same reasons that led to its failure then are believed to be relevant now, suggesting that any territorial division may not be in the best interest of the Christian population of that country.[2]

3. *Sectarian allocation of political powers.* With the active participation of European powers, the new system that emerged in 1864 after the 1858-1860 civil war called for the establishment of one locally autonomous region under the Ottomans. Within this autonomous region (which included most of Mount Lebanon), power in the form of offices was to be shared proportionately by the various religious sects. A non-Lebanese Christian was to be the governor, assisted by an indirectly elected central administrative council representing the various sects constituting Mount Lebanon at the time. The following table shows the distribution of the members of the council by sect and by region.

---

[2] This experiment at partition failed because of the resistance of the feudal aristocracies of both Christians and Druzes. The Maronite peasants resisted it because they saw in it a regressive measure against their newly won gains. The two areas contained mixed population which were ruled by different laws. Finally, the Church opposed it. In the present conflict, many of the Christian populations live in mixed areas outside the so-called Maronite enclave in the mountains east and north of Beirut. Furthermore, many Christians subscribe to liberal nationalistic ideologies in diametric opposition to the Phalange party. Finally the Maronite Church and leading members of the Christian business community view any such partition as detrimental to their interest. For details, see Baaklini (1976a:41–49).

		Sect					
Region	Maronite	Greek Orthodox	Greek Catholic	Sunni	Shia	Druze	Total
Kisrawan	1						1
Batroun	1						1
Jazzin	1			1		1	3
Matn	1	1			1	1	4
Shuf						1	1
Koura		1					1
Zahle			1				1
Total	4	2	1	1	1	3	12

Source: Baaklini, 1976a:49. Copyright © by Duke University Press, Durham, N.C.

The sectarian formula was continued after Lebanon was enlarged in 1920 by France as the mandatory power under Maronite pressure to include regions in the North, South, and East that were previously part of Syria and were predominantly inhabited by Moslem Sunni or Shia but retained an overall Christian majority. The French Mandate, under which Lebanon was ruled between 1920 to 1943, crystallized and institutionalized the sectarian sharing of power. By the time of independence in 1943 the pattern was already established whereby the president of the republic was to be a Maronite Christian, the prime minister a Sunni Moslem, and the president of the Parliament a Moslem Shia. Membership in the Parliament was distributed according to the ratio of six Christians to five Moslems. This arrangement was contained in an informal understanding between the spokesmen of the Maronite and Sunni known as the National Pact. The various electorate laws of independent Lebanon specified the ways in which the National Pact was implemented (al-Khouri, 1947; al-Haj, 1961)

After independence the question of the numerical strength of each of the religious sects became important. The formula devised by the French and adopted by the leaders of independent Lebanon was based on the 1932 official census, which the French undertook. It showed the Christian population as representing 54% of the population, whereas the Moslems represented 46%.[3] If the Christians were to maintain their political prominence, they had to maintain the reality or the myth that they were numerically superior to the Moslems, or they had to neutralize whatever numerical edge that the Moslems might develop. Otherwise, the principle one man—one vote would subvert the existing sectarian formula of power sharing.

[3] The late 1932 census has been contested since the time it was undertaken. For a vivid illustration of how the French falsified the census, see al-Riachi (1953).

The Numbers Game after Independence

In 1943, the newly independent state under the influence of the Christians resorted to a number of strategies to keep the numbers game in their favor. The Moslems reluctantly accepted these strategies as temporary measures that were soon to be eliminated with the coming of independence and the expected modernization of the country. These strategies will be discussed under three headings: "Manipulation of the Census," "Engineering of Electoral Laws," and "Domination of Law and Order Institutions."

Manipulation of the Census

The last official census in Lebanon was taken in 1932 during the French mandate. According to this census and against the objection of many Moslems, the Christians were found to have the numerical edge. The 1943 formula for distributing power between the sects, known as the National Pact, was based on it. Since then, in spite of frequent protests by sects believed to be underrepresented (like the Shia), Lebanon has steadfastly refused to undertake an official census. Several problems have been raised as obstacles that need to be settled before it could be undertaken. The Christians have maintained that it is important first to settle who is a Lebanese and who is not. Would the census count only those living in Lebanon, or would it also include the millions of Lebanese living overseas either on a temporary or permanent basis? If only those Lebanese residing in Lebanon were counted, there is no doubt that the Moslem segment of the population would be in the majority, perhaps constituting 60% to the Christian 40%. Apparently the birthrate among Lebanese Moslems is higher than among Lebanese Christians. The Christians maintained, therefore, that any census would have to include the overseas Lebanese. If this were done, the Christian element would undoubtedly dominate because most emigrants are Christian. To give substance to their claim, the Ministry of Foreign Affairs was named Ministry of Foreign Affairs and Emigrants. Since Shamun's presidency in the late fifites, an organized campaign was launched to mobilize the Lebanese overseas and encourage them to return to Lebanon and declare their citizenship. Chapters of the Lebanese League sprang up in Africa, Latin America, and North America to instill the overseas Lebanese with a new commitment to the motherland. Each year a world congress of the overseas Lebanese was held in Lebanon with the encouragement of the government. Although the official expectation of this mobilizing campaign was to reawaken a Lebanese nationalistic feeling among the overseas Lebanese, which might benefit the country both economically and politically, the Christians entertained another expectation. By keeping the overseas Lebanese in close touch with the motherland, they hoped to keep them interested in being counted as Lebanese in case a census were to be undertaken. Lebanon is one of the few states where dual citizenship is officially recognized.

Another means by which the Christians manipulated the census to their advantage was in controlling the ways noncitizens may acquire citizenship. If a noncitizen can establish that he or she is of Lebanese ancestry, he or she is guaranteed a citizenship. By establishing their Lebanese ancestry, many of the Egyptian–Lebanese Christians who fled Egypt in the fifties and sixties and many of the Palestinian Christians were able to acquire citizenship overnight. Many Armenians from Syria and other Arab countries were also granted citizenship by establishing a relationship to Lebanese Armenians. On the other hand, thousands of the Moslem Kurds living in Lebanon for over 25 years were denied citizenship. Similarly, thousands of Arab Moslem tribesmen living in the north of the country (Arab Wadi Khaled) were denied citizenship allegedly because of their Syrian origin.

Finally, many rich Christians were able to buy their citizenship through bribery and influence. Few Moslems succeeded in this game, either because they lacked financial resources or influential government contact or because they assumed that Lebanese citizenship will soon give way to Arab nationalism.

The resolution of the citizenship question was deadlocked, and for over 30 years the Lebanese political leadership failed to agree on a formula to regulate the acquisition of citizenship by aliens living in Lebanon. Undoubtedly, the need for a new census and a new law regulating citizenship will be at the top of the agenda of the regime that deals with the post-civil war problems of Lebanon. Palestinians living in Lebanon, however, were considered temporary aliens while they struggled to regain their land and establish their own state and citizenship. With the exception of Jordan, none of the Arab countries offered them citizenship. Their leaders resisted any attempt to eliminate the Palestinian identity through the acquisition of another citizenship.

Engineering of Electoral Laws

The sophistication of the Lebanese system rests on the way the electoral laws were designed to maintain two principles in balance. First, if Lebanon was to qualify as a working democracy, it had to accept the principle of one man–one vote. Yet if Lebanon was to survive as a political entity, it had to ensure the stability of the formula defining the distribution of power among the various sects. The electoral laws were designed to ensure that both the one man–one vote principle as well as the stability of the power distribution formula were upheld.

The common characteristics of the various electoral laws that Lebanon has witnessed since independence are the list system and the sectarian distribution of the seats in Parliament.[4]

A permanent feature of the electoral laws of Lebanon since independence is what has come to be known as the list system. Each district in Lebanon has had more than one seat to be filled. The 1960 electoral law (which is presently still in effect), for example, divided Lebanon into 26 electoral districts. Only one of those districts (the city of Saida) was made into a single-member district. The remaining 25 districts are multiple-member districts, ranging in size from two seats in Batroun and Bshari to eight in the first district of Beirut and Shuf. The multiple-member districts vary not only in size but also in terms of sectarian and ethnic composition as indicated in Table 1.

In multiple-member districts, where the voters are asked to choose among contestants who belong to the same sect, the competition is intersectarian. The issues are normally local and center around local leaders. Alliances are in terms of what strength each candidate brings to the list. Normally, a list includes a representative of a very strong and influential family or a candidate who can secure a certain geographical area within the district. Thus a list in Zgharta will invariably have a representative of the Franjieh, the Dweihi, or the Muawad family. In Koura district a successful list will need a representative of the Ghusn or the Boulus family. In Matn, in addition to sectarian and political considerations, a successful list needs to have a representative of the coastal towns, the middle ridge, and the upper highlands. Thus, geographical, sectarian, family, and political considerations enter into the formulations of lists. In no cases are these alliances permanent or ideological. In many cases they crystallize at the last moment before the election only to break as soon as the election is over. The main uniting force for an alliance is the utilitarian consideration of winning the election. In mixed areas where candidates from more than one sect compete, competing lists are composed of candidates from the sects who are entitled to seats in that area. Thus the competing alliances in Baa'bda will be between two or more lists, each composed of three Maronites, one Druze, and one Shia.

Candidates who are unable to join a list or to formulate a list of their own may compete for a particular seat independently. Regardless of their

[4] This section is based on material contained in Baaklini (1976a:145–152). Copyright © by Duke University Press, Durham, N.C.

Table I

Districts and Sectarian Distribution Since 1960[a]

Sect	District	Sectarian distribution of seats[b]	Total no. of seats
Purely Maronite	Kisrawan	4M	4
	Zgharta	3M	3
	Bshari	2M	2
	Batroun	2M	2
Purely Shia	Bint Jbeil	2Sh	2
	Sour	3Sh	3
	Nabatiya	3Sh	3
Purely Sunni	Saida	1S	1
	Villages of Tripoli	2S	2
Pure Greek Orthodox	Koura	2GO	2
Mixed Christians	Matn	3M, 1GO, 1AO	5
	Jezzin	2M, 1GO	3
	Beirut First	1M, 1GO, 1GC, 1P, 1AC, 3AO	8
Mixed Christians-Moslems	Saida–Zahrani	1Sh, 1GC	2
	Marjeoun	2Sh, 1GO, 1S	4
	Shuf	3M, 2S, 2D, 1GC	8
	Aley	2M, 2D, 1GO	5
	Baa'bda	3M, 1D, 1Sh	5
	Jbeil	2M, 1Sh	3
	Zahle	1M, 1S, 1Sh, 1GO, 1GC	5
	Rachaya–West Beka	1S, 1Sh, 1GO	3
	Baalbeck–Hermel	1S, 4Sh, 1M, 1GC	7
	Beirut Second	4S, 1GO	5
	Beirut Third	1S, 1Sh, 1Mi	3
	Tripoli	4S, 1GO	4
	Akkar	2S, 1M, 1GO	4

[a]Source: Baaklini, 1976a:146. Copyright © by Duke University Press, Durham, N.C.

[b]M, Maronite; GO, Greek Orthodox; GC, Creek Catholic; S, Sunni; Sh, Shia; D, Druze; AO, Armenian Orthodox; AC, Armenian Catholic; Mi, Minority; P, Protestant.

sects, voters have the right to elect a whole list or to choose their candidates from more than one list or from independents. In other words they are not bound to choose any one single list. They can choose as many candidates as the number of seats in that district, provided they observe the sectarian distribution. Thus a voter in the Baa'bda district referred to earlier, regardless of sect, may choose any five candidates running in the district provided the five he or she chooses include three Maronites, one Druze, and one Shia. The voter cannot choose more than five candidates nor can he or she alter the sectarian distribution by voting, for example, for two Druzes instead of one. A voter is, however, entitled to choose one candidate for a particular seat and leave the other seats vacant. This means that although the sectarian distribution of seats in a particular district is specified by the electoral law, the voter is left with the freedom of formulating a list in accordance with his or her preference and with no restriction stemming from political parties or formal alliances among candidates. Any formal alliance among candidates is not binding unless it meets with the voter's preference. This places the voter in a strong position vis-à-vis the party or the list maker. For an alliance to be successful the preferences of the voters have to be respected or else they do not vote for the whole list.

Although running a list is no guarantee that a candidate will win, running independently is almost a sure way to lose, as the following figures show.

	1960	1964	1968	1972
No. of individual candidates	123	66	78	137
No. of those who succeeded	4	—	2	2

Source: Baaklini, 1976a:148. Copyright © by Duke University Press, Durham, N.C.

Of the 99 Chamber members, less than 2% have been elected independently. The remaining 98% have been candidates who have run on one list or another. The following figures indicate the number of lists in four parliamentary elections that have managed to win an election by having all their members elected.

	1960	1964	1968	1972
No. of lists	15	20	13	17
No. of deputies	48	65	44	56

Source Baaklini, 1976a:149. Copyright © by Duke University Press, Durham, N.C.

With the exception of the 1964 election when the Shihab regime played an active part in eliminating the opposition and the forging alliances, approximately 50% of the deputies have been elected as members of completely successful lists. The remaining deputies have managed to be elected from various competing lists and as independents. This is a very clear indication of the independence of the voter in asserting himself or herself by going beyond the confines of one single list. It is not uncommon to find that in a district of five seats, two may have been elected from one list and the other three elected from another list.

This independence, enjoyed and exercised by the voter, poses certain problems for political parties and independent political leaders. Political parties cannot ensure that their members can be relied upon to vote for the whole list regardless of the nature of the alliance they enter into. Ideological political parties like the Ba'ath party and the Syrian Social Nationalist Party are even more hampered. If their candidates are to have any chance of winning an election, they have to join a list. But to join a list involves cooperation and many compromises with local leaders and forces that are considered by these parties to be "traditional," "feudal," or "reactionary." If they do cooperate, they face the prospect of insubordination and possible defection among their party regulars. If they do not, they are certain to lose the election and possibly leave their followers frustrated with both the system and the party. This is why the only political parties that have been able to send representatives to Parliament are the nondoctrinaire, compromising political parties that manage to accept political divisions in society as natural and healthy (see Table 2).

Although doctrinaire political parties have suffered under the list system by being unable to play by the rules of the game and yet maintain their ranks intact, compromising political parties and local political leaders have flourished. To be successful under the list system, one has to keep open all the options for alliances. In order to do this, political parties and political leaders normally maintain close relationships with their political base, not through ideological extremist platforms, but through ambiguous general programs and, most importantly, through personal relationships and constituency services. This ensures that supporters will follow the candidate regardless of which list he or she chooses. Because they have not been galvanized around a particular issue but around allegiance to their candidate, they are willing to trade votes with the supporters of other candidates on the list to ensure that the list stands a chance of winning. Double-crossing by supporters is usually avoided for fear that the supporters of the candidate on the list being double-crossed will retaliate by doing the same.

Because electoral success depends on compromise, the ability to join a list, and, most importantly, the ability to maneuver politically without losing one's political base, candidates in mixed districts who belong to different sects find that the best strategy is to avoid capitalizing on sectarian issues. Intersectarian competition may exclude one from finding a listmate from another sect. Furthermore, one's real competitor is not

Abdo I. Baaklini

Table 2

Parliamentary Membership of Parties in Lebanon 1951–1972 [a,b]

Party	1951	1953	1957	1960	1964	1968	1972
Syrian Social Nationalist Party	—	—	1	—	—	—	—
Ba'ath (Arab Renaissance Socialist Party)	—	—	—	—	—	—	1[c]
Arab Nasserite Coalition	—	—					1[c]
Dashnak (Armenian Party)	2	2	3	4	4	3	2
Najjads	—	—		1		1	
Progressive Socialist Party	3	2–4	3	6	6	5	4
National Action Movement	—	—	—	—	1	1	1
National Appeal	(Membership flexible and indeterminate)						
National Organization	—	—	—	1	—	—	—
Kataeb (Phalange)	3	1	1	6	4	9	7
Constitutional Union	Flexible and indeterminate			5–8	5	4	—
National Bloc	2	3	4	6	2	5	3
National Liberals	Party nonexistent			4–5	6	8	7
Democratic Socialist Party	—	—	—	—	—	—	3[c]
Democratic Party	—	—	—	—	—	—	1[c]
Total	10	8–10	12	32–37	28	36	30
Total members in chamber	77	44	66	99	99	99	99
Percentage of members in political parties	13	24	18	35	28	36	30

[a]Source: Baaklini, 1976a:181. Copyright © by Duke University Press, Durham, N.C. See Crow, 1970:284; Suleiman, 1967:265.

[b]The following parties were unable to elect any members to the parliament: Lebanese Communist Party; Moslem Brethren; Ibad-ar-Rahman (The Worshipper of God); Moslem Group; Tahreer; Hunchak (Armenian Party); Ramgavar Azadagow (Armenian Party).

[c]The election of 1972 brought to the parliament representatives of three parties that were never represented before, and the creation of a new party, the Democratic Socialist Party, headed by Mr. Kamel al-Assa'd.

the candidate from another sect but his or her coreligionist. Hence the main rational behind the Lebanese sectarian list system, according to its advocates, is that it contains, rather than encourages, sectarian conflict.

In addition to the advantages of the list system and sectarian distribution characteristics of the electoral laws of Lebanon, the Christians reaped some further advantages. By dividing the country into districts

Table 3

Over- and Underrepresented Districts[a]

District	Number of seats in excess of population	District	Number of seats in short of population
Beirut First	1	Baa'bda	1
Shuf	2	Matn	2
Aley	1	Akkar	2
Baalbeck–Hermel	1	Kura	1
Nabatiyah	1	Batroun	1
Jezzin	1		
Total	7	Total	7

[a]Source: Harik, 1972:134.

of unequal sizes, the power of the sectarian voter was diffused. Furthermore, voters who participate in the selection of eight candidates, like the Shuf and Beirut First Districts, exercise more power than voters who select one or two candidates. Finally, some districts such as Shuf, which had two powerful leaders (Shamun and Jumblat), received more seats than the number of its population justifies, whereas other districts receive less seats than their population justifies. Column 1 of Table 3 shows the districts that have been more parliamentary seats than their population justifies; column 2 shows the districts that are represented by fewer seats than their size justifies.

On the whole, with the exception of the Druze sect, the imbalance in representation worked in favor of the Christian population. In view of the centrality of the electoral laws to the way the ethnic numbers game is played in Lebanon, it is no wonder that demands for political reforms have centered around those laws. Ideological and doctrinaire political parties have spearheaded the attack against the list system and its sectarian distribution. Those parties have maintained that true democracy can be achieved only after the sectarian system is abolished and the list system is replaced by a more equitable system based on one man–one vote, such as the proportional representation system, on the basis of party affiliation. Moslem political parties, on the other hand, have advocated the readjustment of the sectarian distribution to reflect their real number in society. They have also protested the gerrymandering that the present districts manifest, charging that it was intended to dilute their vote and in some cases ensure that they are not represented altogether.

Domination of Law and Order Institutions

Another way the ethnic numbers game is played in Lebanon is through distribution of higher civil and military posts among the various sects. Although this process is not highly formalized as was the case in the electoral laws, it manifests similar characteristics. One major difference, however, is that this process is dynamic and flexible. This explains its ability to accommodate certain socioeconomic changes that the formal electoral process was not intended to accommodate.

At the time of independence most of the higher civil and military jobs of the newly created republic were dominated by Lebanese Christians. Moslem Lebanese, who by and large refused to cooperate with the French colonialists or because they lacked certain formal educational qualifications, found themselves at a disadvantage. The new Lebanese state was called upon to balance two contradictory forces. On the one hand, Lebanon's survival as a political entity depended on the extent its Moslem populations were willing to accept and participate in its political institutions, which meant opening the civil and military service to them. On the other hand, if the stability of the country was to be maintained as defined by the country's Christian elites, it was important that certain sensitive positions dominating law and order institutions be kept with the Christians. Moslems were not given equal access to those institutions for fear that they would not protect the status quo as zealously as their Christian counterparts.

The Civil Service

Within the realm of civil service positions Lebanon pioneered what is presently labeled in the United States the affirmative action approach to recruitment.[5] Although its personnel laws called for recruitment through the competitive merit system, the application of those laws followed what may be termed a qualifying system with some general consideration for quota distribution. All of those who passed a certain civil service examination were listed by sect in accordance with the score they attained. After 1958, the established quota in the civil service followed the ratio of six Christians to six Moslems as opposed to the six to five ratio then prevalent. Those who ranked top in each sect were, therefore, selected to whatever positions were available in accordance with the sectarian distribution. Top political appointments to the civil service continued to be handled by the political leadership, in this case

---

[5] Regarding the Lebanese civil service system, see Baaklini (1963), Bashir (1965), and Iskandar (1964).

the president, prime minister and his cabinet and quite frequently in consultation with religious and parliamentary leaders. Over the years the civil service was able to absorb many of the mobilized and educated Moslems into its ranks. The continued expansion of the civil service and the addition of new functions and departments enabled this process to take place without really displacing the Christians who are already in or who are likely to join.

Another favorable development is the rapid expansion of the private sector, under a laisse-faire economic policy, in which many of the emergent Christian talents found their opportunities. Yet the Moslems, who found this way to the top of the civil service, were not totally satisified. From where they stood, they could feel the discrimination more than before, especially since the real power in Lebanon was never concentrated in the public sector but remained in the private sector and big business. Second, many of the classically prestigious posts in the Ministries of Foreign Affairs, Transportation, Defense, and Interior and the presidential staff remained in Christian hands. Moslems were put in charge of recently established ministries and departments that, although economically and socially important (such as labor, social welfare, community services, youth and sport, and so on), were not as influential as the posts dominated by Christians. In no other place was the discrimination as apparent as in the military and police services.

The Military Service

More than any other Lebanese institution, the top military service (both the armed forces and the internal security forces) was and remained the exclusive domain of the Christian elites. In 1975, at the beginning of the civil war, close to 70% of the leadership positions in the armed forces were in Christian hands.[6] This disproportion was a product of both historical circumstances and conscious design.

Beginning in the late nineteenth century, displaced Christian aristocracy found a refuge in the special internal security forces of Mount Lebanon, which were established by the 1864 Protocol under European pressure even when the Ottomans were still in control. The drift of the Lebanese Christian aristocracy toward the military was done for economic, social, and nationalistic reasons. Economically, it provided them

---

[6] There are no official data on the composition of the top military leadership in Lebanon by sect. However, as late as 1976, the commander-in-chief admitted that although the Moslems have 52% of the privates in the army to the Christians 48%, at the top of the command the percentage is 70% Christians and 30% Moslems. See Khoweiry (1977:4–9). See also Baaklini (1976b) and Khalidi (1976:67).

with an income to replace the loss they incurred as a result of losing their feudal rights. Socially, it provided them with a new source of power and status, and nationalistically it guaranteed them that their internal affairs were under their control, thus ensuring them a measure of local autonomy under the Ottomans.

Under the French Mandate this trend continued with added impetus. To maintain law and order and to ensure the preservation of an eventually independent Lebanon, the French recruited mainly from among the Christians. Young Moslems, who had the qualifications and felt the urge to join the military, preferred to join the Arab forces in Syria, Iraq, and Palestine and eventually remained in the Syrian armed forces. This was the case because many Moslems opposed the creation of an independent Lebanese state. Such a state was considered a colonial creation to be abolished and replaced by a Syrian or Arab state as soon as independence was achieved and colonialism defeated.

After independence the military institutions continued to resist opening up their higher ranks to the hitherto unrepresented part of the Moslem population. The leadership of both the armed forces and the internal security forces remained predominantly in Christian hands.

To maintain their leadership, the Christians deployed a number of strategies. In spite of the deteriorating general security conditions in the region, Lebanon refused to employ full and general conscription. Instead it maintained a small, select, all-volunteer, professional army. Lebanon consistently refused to be entangled with the regional armed conflict between Israel and the Arab states surrounding it. Furthermore, it trained, equipped, and defined the mission of the army in terms of internal security needs. For its external security needs, Lebanon depended on the goodwill of the big Western powers—first, France and Britain and, later, the United States. Finally, to ensure that the leadership of the army remained in Christian hands, Lebanon restricted entry by defining the admission qualifications to include certain education and language requirements favoring the Christians and those graduating from Christian-dominated schools. Under popular pressure, especially after the Six Day War of 1967, the army relaxed its admission to the rank and file and the junior officer class. It was not, therefore, surprising that during the recent Lebanese civil war, one of the main demands of the Moslem and nationalistic forces was the reorganization of the leadership of the military institutions of the country. The discrimination of the military institutions in favor of the Christians and the emergence of the armed Palestinian resistance movement in Lebanon in alliance with Arab nationalistic and leftist forces in Lebanon were major factors contributing to the Lebanese civil war. Had the leadership of the military been well integrated and representative of the major sects in the country, its ability to intervene and stop the bloodshed would have been greatly enhanced. Being a Christian-dominated institution, the military was mistrusted by Moslem and other Arab nationalistic forces. Even traditional Moslem leadership who would have favored the deployment of the army to separate the combatants found it politically very costly to do so, because they feared that the army might favor the Christian side.[7] Under pressure from their political base Moslem leaders in the government and in the Parliament refused to approve a state of emergency in which the army could be deployed. The Lebanese civil war is unique in the sense that for seven years of intense and brutal fighting the state was unable even to declare a state of emergency.

When the Lebanese army split in 1975, it was not surprising that many of the rank and file that joined the nationalist pro-Palestinian front were Moslems led by a junior Moslem officer named Ahmad al-Khatib. On the other hand, most of the senior Christian officers and their units either continued to support the legitimately elected government or openly aided or joined the Christian forces under the leadership of the Kataib party. In the south, near the Israeli border, a whole contingent was created and armed by Israel under a renegade army officer, Major Saad Haddad, a Christian.

As of this writing a major stumbling block for political reconciliation among the Lebanese warring factions is the composition and role of the armed forces. The front of Lebanese forces insists that the Syrian and Palestinian forces should be withdrawn from Lebanese territories to be replaced by the newly reconstituted and strengthened Lebanese army as a necessary condition for any political reconciliation. It views the role of the Lebanese army to preserve law and order within Lebanon and to separate and disarm the various Lebanese warring parties. The nationalist front, on the other hand, opposes such a role for the Lebanese army. They are critical of its composition and structures, which, they argue, favor the Christians. They also object to its role as a law and order institution for internal security matters, proposing instead that its mission should be to support the Syrian, Palestinian, and Lebanese nationalist forces in a common front against the common enemy, Israel.[8]

---

[7] To deploy the army internally, the president must declare a state of national emergency. The Christian president can declare a state of emergency for only one week, if he has the approval of his Moslem prime minister. After one week the approval of the Parliament is necessary. In the recent Lebanese civil war no Moslem prime minister was willing to authorize the deployment of the army because they feared that its predominant Christian leadership would use the army to suppress their supporters and their allies. For details on this important constitutional point, see Baaklini (1976b:266–267, 273–277).

[8] On June 6, 1982, while this paper was being written, Israel invaded and occupied all of Lebanon south of Beirut. The war lasted for nearly five months, and at this writing, its implications are yet to unfold.

Ethnic Conflict and the Lebanese Civil War

From the preceding discussion, it is very tempting to conclude, as many did (see, e.g. Hudson, 1976 and Dekmergian, 1978), that the Lebanese civil war was an inevitable by-product of the structure and processes of the political system and its sectarian characteristics, which it preserved if not encouraged. In the view of this author such a hasty conclusion would be unwarranted and misleading. Lebanon's ethnic-sectarian character-istics preceded the establishment of the state and were not a product of it. Granted, the system was not intended to eliminate these conflicts, but it did not try to encourage such conflicts either. It was designed to contain and manage these conflicts while preserving the cultural and religious identities of the groups involved. To explain the Lebanese civil war, we need a less simplistic approach. The ethnic-sectarian mode of explanation will not suffice.

As I mentioned earlier, the stress in this chapter is on the internal dimension of the Lebanese conflict with specific emphasis on the sec-tarian ethnic variable. Yet the international dimension of the conflict cannot be overemphasized. Therefore, before I proceed to discuss the internal actors and the dynamics of their actions, I shall briefly identify the international actors and the ways in which they exacerbated the tension within the delicately and perhaps precariously synchronized Lebanese political system. There are five groups of international actors: the Israelis, the Palestinians, the Syrians, other Arab states, and the big powers.

The Israelis

Israeli actions in Lebanon are perhaps more responsible for the de-stabilization of the Lebanese system than any of the other international or domestic actors. It is the cause of the presence of other international actors, especially the Palestinians and later the Syrians. After the 1967 war all of Palestine was occupied by Israel, and all Palestinians either became refugees or lived under Israeli occupation. Until 1971, the Pal-estinians used Jordan as a base for their military operations against Israel. Between 1970 and 1971, the Palestinian military presence in Jordan was eliminated after a series of bloody confrontations with the Jordanian army. Lebanon then became their base for political mobilization and military operations. Consequently all of Israeli military might was di-rected against Lebanon, first to force the Lebanese government to curb

the Palestinian presence, and, since 1975, to directly liquidate the Palestinian movement as a political and military factor.

The direct Israeli military operation in Lebanon has had the unin-
tended consequences of weakening and deligitimizing the Lebanese government, strengthening the Palestinian political and military presence,
exacerbating the conflict between the Christian Lebanese and the Moslem-Nationalistic Palestinian supporters, and finally necessitating the
1976 Syrian military intervention to halt the raging civil war. To counter
the Palestinian's increasing strength, the Israelis sided with the Christians, training and arming them, thus rendering reconciliation among
the Lebanese parties more unlikely. In 1978 and most recently in 1982,
the Israelis invaded Lebanon. At this writing they control all of Lebanon
south of Beirut.

The Palestinians

Although the Palestinian presence was initially not a crucial factor,
the escalation and prolongation of the conflict has made it a decisive
one. At present any formula for resolving the Lebanese conflict must
deal with the status and role of the Palestinians in Lebanon. For our
purpose here, it is important to point out that the Palestinian armed
presence in Lebanon and their need and strategy to forge an alliance
with Lebanese sympathizers led them to support the Moslem-nationalistic front. It is inconceivable to imagine that the Moslem-nationalistic
front would have entered in an armed conflict against the Christians.
More importantly, the Moslem-nationalistic front would not have been
able to carry and prolong the fight once it was initiated. The Christians,
assisted by the central government and Israel, would have prevailed or
would have been willing to concede some of the legitimate demands of
the aggrieved Moslem segments of the population. Figure 1 identifies the
various groups that constitute the Palestinian armed presence in Lebanon, which is currently estimated at 30,000 fighters.

The Syrians

Of all Arab governments, the Syrians, because of history, geography,
and national security interests, have always played a leading, if not decisive, role in internal Lebanese affairs. In 1976, at the apex of the Lebanese civil war, the Syrians, sensing a nationalist-Palestinian victory and
an imminent Israeli and/or Western intervention (U.S. and France), entered Lebanon to protect the Christians, to preserve Lebanese territorial

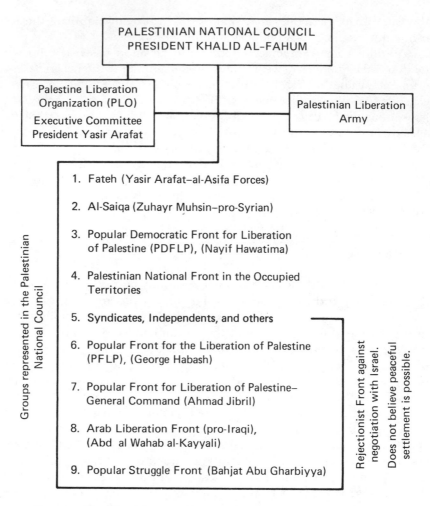

Figure 1   The Palestinian resistance movement. Source: Baaklini, 1980:355.

integrity, and to safeguard their national security interests. As the conflict continued and in the face of increased Israeli military operations in Lebanon against the Palestinians (especially after the occupation of South Lebanon in 1978 and the increased and open support Israel began giving to the front of Lebanese forces) the Syrian role in Lebanon changed from supporters of the Christians to defenders of the Palestinians and their Lebanese allies. The increased cooperation between the Israelis and their Christian Lebanese cohorts brought the Syrians in direct conflict with the Christians on many occasions, especially in 1979 and 1981.

Other Arab States

Being the only pluralistic democratic country in the area, Lebanon always served as an outlet for inter-Arab conflict. Its free press and the multiplicity of its political parties were excellent forums to air Arab views that were normally suppressed in their own countries due to the nature of the political regimes and the censorship they imposed on the press and the freedom of political associations. As long as inter-Arab conflict took the form of dissemination of information through the Lebanese press and the financial support of various political groupings, Lebanon thrived and indeed, benefited from inter-Arab infighting. However, after the 1967 war and the collapse of the regular Arab army and the rise of the Palestinian resistance movement in Lebanon, inter-Arab fighting in Lebanon took a violent form. The death of President Nasser in 1971 robbed the Arab world of the only leader who had a national stature that enabled him to mediate and peacefully resolve inter-Arab conflict. A vacuum was created and various Arab leaders rushed unsuccessfully to fill it. The scrambling to fill this vacuum translated itself on the Lebanese scene into funds and arms to various Lebanese competing factions. The Palestinian problem became a cause célèbre for ambitious Arab leaders.

After the 1973 October war and the movement of Sadat's Egypt toward a peaceful accommodation with Israel, the Arabs were divided into two camps: the moderates pushed for some sort of peaceful resolution of the conflict, and the confrontationists or rejectionists adhered to the legitimate and just Palestinian rights and nationhood. The battle line was drawn and each group vied for Palestinian support or else Palestinian containment and suppression. Lebanon again became the battleground for these various forces. The principal actors on the side of the Palestinians, in addition to the Syrians, were the Libyans, Iraqis, and Algerians. The Egyptians, Saudis, and Jordanians championed the so-called forces of moderation. Each of these countries had their armed supporters on the Lebanese scene.

The Big Powers

Traditionally the Middle East has and continues to be a fertile ground for big-power confrontation and cold war strategies. Its geopolitical location straddling three continents (thus vital for the NATO defense) and its natural resources (energy) have pitted the Western world against the Soviet Union.

After 1973 and the oil embargo that ensued, it became very clear to the United States that the preservation of the Western world's access to Middle Eastern oil required a resolution of the Arab-Israeli conflict. Again the Palestinians were considered the stumbling block, and their elimination or taming in Lebanon was considered a necessary step before a "strategic alliance" against the Soviet Union could be possible. The success of the first and second Sinai disengagements and recently the Camp David agreement necessitated a docile and acquiescent Palestinian movement in Lebanon. From a Soviet perspective, especially after having been dismissed from Egypt in 1972, their presence and influence depended on the degree they were identified with the Palestinian movement and other resistance movements and regimes in the area. In addition to political campaigns and cold war rhetoric, each side embarked on arming its client states and supporters in the region. The internal Lebanese warring factions did not escape this big power rivalry and ended up receiving arms and support directly, or in most cases indirectly through the client regimes in the region.

Within this international climate the internal Lebanese actors found themselves being manipulated rather than the manipulators.

Nonetheless the dynamics of the internal conflict in Lebanon has its own logic as well as its own course and objectives.

THE INTERNAL ACTORS IN THE LEBANESE CONFLICT

The internal actors in the Lebanese conflict appeared under many different names; at present, however, they can be divided into two main groups: the Front of Lebanese Forces, under the leadership of the Kataib party, representing the Christians; and the National Front, under the leadership of the late Kamal Jumblat and presently his son Waleed, representing the Moslems, nationalists, and leftist forces in Lebanon. Tables 4 and 5 present details on the various groups. Of the estimated 20,000 Christian fighters, more than 15,000 belong to the Kataib; 3,000 of the 4,000 belonging to the national movement are Druz supporters of Kamal Jumblat.[9] From these figures it can be seen that the fight has been between the Kataib–Israeli front and the Palestinian–National Movement

[9] These figures were cited by Harik (1981:3). However, as the war has proceeded, the number and distribution of the nationalist movement has changed. No official estimate is available, but it is now believed that Amal Movement representing the Shia has increased its forces significantly (2000–3000), so has the Syrian Social National Party (SSNP). After the death of Kamal Jumblat his forces declined significantly and became less of a factor in the Lebanese conflict.

Table 4

Front of Lebanese Forces[a]

Name of party or group and leader	Religion of leadership	Religion of membership	Political ideology	Geographical distribution of membership	Position after entry of Syria, June 1976[b]
The Phalange Party (Pierre al-Jumayil)	Maronite Christian	Mostly Maronite Christian with some other Christians	Lebanese reformists but internationally conservative	Wherever Christians are found	Support Syrians
National Liberal Party (Camille Shamun)	Mixed, but dominated by Christians	Mostly Maronite Christian with some other Christians	Conservative both internally and internationally	Wherever Christians are found	Support Syrians
Zogharta Liberation Army (Toni Franjieh)	Maronite Christian	Maronite Christian	Conservative	In Zogharta and its surroundings	Support Syrians
The Guards of the Cedars (Etian Sakr)[c]	Christian	Christians	Conservative	In Christian areas	Support Syrians
Maronite Monastic Order (Sharbel Kassis)	Maronite Christian	Maronite Christian	Conservative	In Kisrwan	Support Syrians
Lebanese Cooperation Front (Saed Akl)	Maronite and Catholic Christian	Maronite and Catholic Christians	Conservative	In Zahle's and its surroundings	Support Syrians

[a]Source: Baaklini, 1980:353–354.
[b]The support of the Syrians has changed. With the exception of the Zogharta Liberation Army, all the groups are now against the Syrian intervention in Lebanon.
[c]A secret group that emerged in 1975.

Table 5

The National Front [a]

Name of party or group and leader	Religion of leadership	Religion of membership	Political ideology	Geographical distribution	Position after entry of Syrian troops in June 1976
Progressive Socialist Party (Kamal Jumblat, now his son, Walid)[b]	Druze	Mixed, but mostly Druze and Muslim	Moderate socialist	In most Lebanese regions	Against Syrians
Baa'th Socialist Party (Syria: Asim Quansuh)	Mixed, but mostly Muslim	Mixed, but mostly urban Muslim	Arab nationalist and socialist	In urban areas and Beka	With Syrians
Baa'th Socialist Party (Iraq: Abd al-Majid, al-Rafii and Niqula al-Firzili)	Mixed	Mixed but mostly Muslim	National and radical socialist	In Muslim and urban areas	Against Syrians
Lebanese Communist Party (George Hawi)	Mixed	Mixed	Moderate communist	Over most Lebanese regions	Against Syrians
Communist Action Organization (Muhsin Ibrahim)	Mixed	Mixed	Radical Marxism and Arab Nationalism	Few urban centers	Against Syrians
October 24 Movement (Farouq al-Mugaddam)	Sunni Muslim	Sunni Muslim	Arab nationalist	In Tripoli	With Syrians

40

Organization					
Syrian Social Nationalist Party (Inam Ra'd, PPS)	Mixed	Mixed	Radical Syrian nationalist	In most of Lebanon	Ambiguous, yet continued with the National Movement
Movement of the Deprived (Musa al-Sadr)[c]	Shia Muslim	Shia Muslim	Reformist	In south Lebanon and Beka	Accommodation with the Syrians
Independent Nasserite Movement (Ibrahim Qulaylat)	Sunni Muslim	Sunni Muslim	Arab nationalist	In western Beirut	Against Syrians
Popular Nasserite Organization (Mustafa Sa'd)	Sunni Muslim	Sunni Muslim	Arab nationalist	In Sidon	Against Syrians
Nasserite Organization—Union of Popular Labor Forces (Kamal Shatila & Najah Wakim)	Mixed	Sunni Muslim and some Christians	Arab nationalist	In western Beirut	With Syrians
Nasserite Organizations. Corrective Movement (Isam Arab)	Sunni Muslim	Sunni Muslim	Arab nationalist	In western Beirut	Against Syrians
Arab Socialist Union (Kamal Yunis)	Sunni Muslim	Sunni Muslim	Arab nationalist	In western Beirut and a few urban centers	Against Syrians

[a]Source: Baaklini, 1980:350–352.
[b]Kamal Jumblat was the overall spokesman.
[c]Amal, withdrew in 1978, but remained pro-Syrian and Palestinian.

Front; beginning in 1978, the Syrians supported the Palestinians against the Israelis and on occasions against the Kataib.

This is not the place to review the various strategies used by each group and the changing alliance they formed. One of the apparent puzzles of the Lebanese conflict was the fact that violence was not restricted to intergroup fighting but extended to intragroup fighting. Between 1977 and 1980, the Kataib was able to consolidate its grip on part of the Christian mountain areas, first by eliminating the Zogharta Liberation Army leadership (causing this group to withdraw from the Lebanese front and ally with the Syrians) and, second, by eliminating the military presence of the Shamun, National Liberal Party. This was achieved at a high cost in lives. Among the National Movement, the intragroup fight has not yet abated. It is a daily occurrence that pits one group against another, especially Amal forces against leftist forces, traditional Sunni Moslem forces against pro-Syrian forces, and recently pro-Iranian forces against pro-Iraqi forces. The bloodbath among the nationalist forces has yet to end.

Approaches to the Lebanese Civil War

Social scientists and political observers of the Lebanese scene have been busy trying to untangle the international and internal webs that may explain the conflict in Lebanon. Various theories and approaches have been proposed.[10]

Five distinct approaches can be identified. The conflict has been viewed as (1) Christians versus Moslems, (2) rich versus poor, (3) Left versus Right, (4) Lebanese versus Palestinians, and (5) a consequence of the Lebanese political system. Each approach has its own proponents and opponents.

Christians versus Moslems

At the risk of oversimplification, proponents of this approach conceive of the conflict as essentially a fight between the Christians and the Moslems over the division of political power and resources in the country. They argue that the 1943 National Pact, which regulated the division of political positions among the various groups in Lebanon, as well as the form of the government and directions of its economic and foreign policy,

---

[10] Some portions of this analysis appeared in Baaklini (1980).

favored the numerically declining Christian elements of the population to the detriment of the Moslems. Some suggest that although the National Pact may have been appropriate to the national and international realities of 1943, it became irrelevant to the realities of the 1970s of both Lebanon and the Middle East. Between 1943 and 1975, Lebanon's Moslem population has increased at a higher rate than the Christians and is thought to constitute now about 60% of the population. The persistent government refusals to undertake the necessary adjustment to reflect this change in the structure of power, through legalistic maneuvers of defining who is Lebanese, and through the granting of citizenship to Christian aliens while denying it to Moslems, led to the recent explosions seeking to redress the injustices of the system. Another variant of this approach argues that the Moslems accepted the 1943 pact reluctantly and only as a stage to ensure the withdrawal of the French colonialists from Lebanon. All along, the Moslems of Lebanon have not accepted the Lebanese state nor its national identity. Their goal was always a Syrian or Arab national identification.

Opponents of this approach point out the merits of the National Pact and proceed to argue that the existing conflict in Lebanon goes beyond religious identification. Many Christian groups are fighting on the side of the Moslems, and many Moslems have benefited from the National Pact and, therefore, are among its ardent supporters. In all cases, opponents of this approach propose one of the other approaches as a better explanation of civil war in Lebanon. Most of the advocates of the Christian versus Moslem approach are to be found among the foreign press and social scientists.

Although none of the Lebanese combatants have or are likely to endorse this approach, many of their actions and reform proposals seem to lend credence to the supposition that the religious factor plays a role at least as far as some of the participants in the conflict are concerned.[11]

Rich versus Poor

Advocates of this approach argue that the nature of the Lebanese economic system encouraged the worst type of exploitation. By adhering to a laissez-faire economic system, the Lebanese state became the guardian of a vicious and irresponsible capitalism. Lebanon's economic system adhered to the principles of social Darwinism, where the weak are devoured by the strong. The system of taxation, education, public works,

[11] For an illustration of this mode of analysis, see Barakat (1975; 1977), Deeb (1971), al-Jisr (1971), Lebanese Socialists (1969), Meo (1965), Qubursi (1954), and Tabbarah (1966).

banking, public health, and custom regulations were all worked out with the interest of the rich in mind. In the absence of a strong government role to ensure equal redistribution of resources through progressive taxation and appropriate provisions of social services needed by the poor, Lebanon's poor became poorer and its rich richer. With the recent inflation that swept the world and the increased oil revenues of many Arab states, Lebanon's imports as well as its limited domestic resources rose beyond the purchasing ability of the majority of the Lebanese. Thus, the civil war was a necessary consequence of this economic reality.

Opponents of this approach contest the economic rationality as well as the facts and figures of this analysis. They argue that Lebanon's prosperity, as compared to its neighbors who are endowed with favorable natural resources that Lebanon lacks, was directly related to its enlightened economic system. By adopting a laissez-faire economic system, Lebanon became the banker and the market for all the Middle East. Lebanon, they argue, has no natural resources to protect or to depend on. Therefore, its economic system, which stressed the service sector, was a reflection of its economic realities and its geographical location. Since Lebanon's wealth was accumulated by the Lebanese either through operations they conduct outside Lebanon or through the willingness of foreigners (Arabs and non-Arabs) to invest and spend in Lebanon because of its economic climate, any strong government intervention would scare off both sources of income. They also suggest that even the government intended to play such a strong interventionist role, it could not because the resources under question are elusive and can easily be withdrawn from the country.

Although not completely dismissing the existence of poverty in Lebanon, this group argues that Lebanon's poor are better off than many of the middle class or even the rich of many of the surrounding countries. Through government social and developmental programs (albeit limited), through the open economic system, and through the individual efforts and remittances of overseas Lebanese, each citizen has access to a better educational and health system, better roads, more consumer goods, and a superb and rich social and cultural life. Thus, the poverty in Lebanon turns out to be relative richness if compared with the bleakness and poverty existing in other countries in the region.

Undoubtedly, both views contain some merits. For our purpose in this analysis, an approach is considered relevant or irrelevant to the extent that there are political actors who believe or do not believe in it. In this case, at least some of the participants in the conflict, especially the leftist and some national and socialist parties, subscribe to the notion that the conflict is not between Christians and Moslems but between the rich and the poor (Palestine Liberation Organization, 1977). However, most members of the Front of Lebanese Forces do not perceive the conflict as that between rich and the poor. They point out that many of their members are the real poor in Lebanon, whereas many of the leaders and followers of the leftist-nationalist alliances are among the richest in the country (Phalange Party, 1974–1976; Chamoun, 1977).

Left versus Right

This approach conceives of the conflict in Lebanon as a struggle between the Left and the Right. The intellectual roots of this approach go as far back as the cold war era. At that time political forces in developing countries were conceived of as being either with the West or with the Soviet Union. Any local conflict was normally viewed as a manifestation of this basic conflict between communism and capitalism.

There is no doubt that several political actors in Lebanon and in the Arab world view the conflict as a struggle between the Left and the Right. The Kataib party, one of the principal actors in the current fighting, has repeatedly declared that it is fighting the international Left supported by the "undisciplined" elements of the Palestinian Liberation Organization (Phalange Party, 1974–1976). The purported support that the Lebanese forces have been receiving from conservative regimes such as Jordan, Saudi Arabia, and possibly Egypt cannot be viewed except as a support against the extreme Left. Even Syria's intervention on the side of the Lebanese forces in 1976 is thought to be against an "uncontrollable" Left, which if successful in Lebanon, could pose a threat to the moderate regime of President Hafiz al-Assad of Syria.

The conception of the conflict as a Left versus Right conflict is not limited to the political actors among the Lebanese and conservative forces. At least some actors among the National Movement forces conceive of it in similar terms. However, a large group in this front is caught in the middle and is less interested in the ideological orientations of the conflict. Many of the Moslem and nationalist groups, including their late leader, Kemal Jumblat, are as much opposed to leftist outlooks as they are to a rightist orientation. The bulk of the forces of the Palestinian Liberation Organizations, as represented in Al-Fateh, are not ideological save for their all-embracing Palestinian Nationalism, which is open to all Palestinians regardless of their political persuasion. In other words, the leftist–rightist approach overlooks one of the most significant elements in the current Lebanese conflict—namely, nationalism—whether it takes the shape of Lebanese, Syrian, Palestinian, or Arab nationalism. Although each of these nationalist orientations may have a position regarding the Communist–Western conflict, such a position is either transient or cannot be regarded as a determining characteristic of those nationalisms. The histories of Syrian and Arab nationalism are cases in point; their orientation toward the Communist–Western conflict was determined by their national interest at the time. The Left–Right approach suffers from the fallacy of assuming that what is relevant to the analyst is or should be relevant to the actors. It assumes a political and ideological vacuum in many developing countries that can only be filled either by communism or capitalism. It is, therefore, a popular and appealing approach for many journalists and social scientists who are the product of the climate of the cold war, as well as those who grew up on a liberal ideology reacting against the cold war ethos.

Lebanese versus Palestinians

To the Front of Lebanese Forces (FLF), the conflict is essentially between Lebanese and Palestinians, who are aided by the international Left. It is significant to note that the Left was not called the Lebanese Left but the international Left. This was done deliberately to avoid the conception of the war as Lebanese against Lebanese. All through the conflict the FLF, especially its core the Kataib party, has insisted that the conflict was not among the Lebanese and, therefore, could not be regarded as a civil war. Rather it was a conflict between the Lebanese, on one side, and the forces of the Palestinian and international Left, on the other side. After 1977, the Syrians were added to the list of "foreigners" who are responsible for the conflict in Lebanon. Consequently, the conflict was always viewed by the Kataib party as a foreign invasion of Lebanon and as a threat to Lebanese autonomy and sovereignty. The FLF has always favored the internationalization of the Lebanese conflict as a means of resolving it.[12]

It should be mentioned that the logic of the FLF did not exclude several issues over which many Lebanese were either already in disagreement or were likely to disagree upon. They contended that Lebanon has always been a country of minorities and political pluralism. Therefore, disgreement over a whole range of issues among Lebanon's constituent elements was and is not a novelty. In fact, the whole structure and logic of the Lebanese political system was predicated on the as-

[12] The entry of Syrian troops and the recent attempts by the Phalange party and the National Liberals to internationalize the conflict to drive the Syrians out of Lebanon are illustrations of this approach.

sumption that conflict was endemic to the system and, therefore, needed to be contained and managed rather than eliminated. Elimination of conflict in Lebanon could be achieved only through enormous human sacrifices that might bring down the whole system and could be achieved only through a form of genocide. The FLF conceded that certain elements of the Lebanese population might have legitimate political, social, and economic demands. These demands, however, could only be dealt with within the context of the Lebanese system and within the sovereignty of the state.

The National Movement forces and its Palestinian allies view the conflict in different terms. Although conceding that the conflict may have started between the PLO and some Lebanese elements, they do not see it as a Lebanese versus Palestinian conflict. In the first place, they argue, the FLF spearheaded by the Kataib party cannot possibly claim to represent Lebanon or the full spectrum of the Lebanese population. These forces are represented in both the Parliament and in the government, and at no time did the Lebanese government or the Parliament ever resolve to wage a war of extermination against the Palestinians. In the second place, the opposition of the FLF to the Palestinians is based on the support that the Palestinians have been giving to the legitimate claims of the nationalist and leftist forces in Lebanon. In other words, the Palestinians are not opposed because they are Palestinians but because they tend to support the claims of those who work against the existing power structure in Lebanon. Finally, the Lebanese political system is such that any hope to achieve desired reforms through peaceful means is unrealistic. The system had had ample time to address the grievances brought to its attention but failed to do so. Therefore, revolutionary action supported by the Palestinians was the only way remaining.

There is an element of truth in both conceptions. Under normal circumstances (i.e., in the absence of a strong Palestinian military presence), the Lebanese system has successfully contained and managed many of its endemic conflicts. It is unrealistic to expect the Lebanese system, or for that matter any political system, to resolve all its conflict, especially in a pluralistic, multiethnic, multireligious country like Lebanon. Although the various grievances were not new to the system, it cannot be maintained that the system was oblivious and indifferent to these demands. Throughout the political development of the country since independence in 1943, the system has made adjustments and shown responsiveness to the majority of the Lebanese needs. It is, therefore, reasonable to assume that in the absence of a strong Palestinian military presence in Lebanon the National Movement would have resorted to the normal channels that the system provides for bringing about change. These channels include a free press, freedom of political association and action, and the comparative presence of regular and free elections.

On the other hand, it is reasonable to assume that part of the hostility of the FLF toward the Palestinians is based on the role that the Palestinians started playing in support of the National Movement. This supportive role was partly due to ideological commitments of some Palestinian organizations, and partly the result of political necessities for the survival of the Palestinian National Movement after it had been singled out and liquidated in Jordan in 1970 and 1971. Thus, by allying themselves with the National Movement, the Palestinians hoped to protect themselves from being disarmed by the Lebanese power structure and its international supporters, similar to what happened to them in Jordan.

The Lebanese Political System

This approach assumes that all the abuses mentioned in the previous four approaches are the product of the Lebanese political system. It asserts that the sectarian nature of the Lebanese political system protected and strengthened the religious differences in the country but failed to devise strategies intended to weaken or eliminate sectarianism and promote adherence to a single nationalism. The sectarian system worked to perpetuate the advantage of the Christian minority over the Moslem majority because it favored the rich of both the Christians and the Moslems against the poor of both religions. In the words of one commentator (Deeb, 1971), it divided the country vertically (along religious lines) so as to prevent its division horizontally (along economic classes). Finally, the sectarian political system is blamed for the country's inability to provide political mobility for elements belonging to the national and leftist forces. It perpetuated the power of the political establishment, some of whose members entered the Lebanese Parliament in the mid-1920s and most of the others in the 1940s. They have since continued to monopolize the poltical and economic life of the country. Most of the parties in the National Movement, as well as many political scientists, subscribe to this approach (Crow, 1962; Hottinger, 1966; Hudson, 1968; Khalaf, 1968).

Although admitting many flaws in the Lebanese system, the FLF nonetheless argues that it is essentially the system that best fits Lebanon. The problem, it contends, is not in the system but in the diverse nature of its population as well as its external adversaries with their Lebanese supporters. It contends that the problem with the Lebanese system is that it is the only democratic system in an Arab area ruled mostly by military dictators. Lebanon's problems are those faced by any democracy in its confrontation with dictatorships. Its hospitable ground, its free press, its guarantee of individual liberty and political associations enabled many Arab and non-Arab forces to abuse these liberties by spreading division and animosity among the Lebanese and by fighting out their differences in Lebanon rather than in their own countries. Lebanon's "crime," this group contends, is that it opened its doors to all the political refugees and all the persecuted in the Arab countries. These guests, including the Palestinian movement, which grew and developed within the permissive liberal climate of Lebanon, misused and violated the Lebanese hospitality. Although Lebanon tolerated such diverse ideological confrontation as long as it was fought in the Lebanese press, it could not accept it threatening the existence of the country. The recent military conflict is the transformation of the verbal warfare among the various non-Lebanese participants into military warfare. In a way, it is the merit of the political system rather than its shortcomings that led to the conflict.

As to the sectarian nature of the political system, this group maintains that Lebanon is the only country in the Arab Middle East that is genuinely "secular." Whereas all other countries insist on Islam as being the religion of the state and as the main source of legislation and law, Lebanon separated the state from the church by guaranteeing to each its proper jurisdiction. The state refrained from interfering in matters such as family and personal laws that have traditionally been the domain of the church and that had preceded the establishment of the state. The state, however, enforces decisions reached by religious courts. Distribution of political power among the various religious groups was intended to contain, rather than encourage, intersectarian conflict. The various electoral laws worked in the same direction by substituting intrasectarian competition for an intersectarian one. As for the economic rationality of the system, it was discussed earlier under the second approach.

This is not the place to settle the controversy about the merits of deficiences of the Lebanese political system. Suffice it to say that within the context of an independent Lebanon, characterized by the various pluralisms discussed previously, the Lebanese system was a reasonable answer to an unpleasant or unwieldy situation (Cheha, 1966; Harik, 1971; Lijphart, 1968; Salem, 1973; Ziadeh, 1960). Independent Lebanon was not afforded the luxury of achieving political integration around one nationalism or one political or religious ideology. Its population subscribed to different nationalisms (Lebanese, Syrian, Arab, or even pan-Islamism).

It included all religous persuasions as well as the full spectrum of political ideologies. Therefore, unless one was to conceive of Lebanon as part of a Syrian or an Arab entity, the various criticisms levied against the system lack serious validity. This is not to suggest that the Lebanese system was in no need for reform and change; it merely suggests that those reforms and those changes, if construed within an independent Lebanese system, do not undermine the essential and basic rationality, soundness and appropriateness of the system.

Summary

Regardless of what the "objective" social, economic, and political reality is (if such an "objective" reality does exist), these are the dynamics and the visions within which the conflict in Lebanon is taking place. Although no single group of political actors or analysts advocates one approach to the exclusion of others, in their political logic one approach is invariably stressed over the others. In fact, the various approaches lend themselves to two essential configurations. The one configuration puts the Moslem, poor, Left, Palestinian, and anti-Lebanese system on one side and the Christian, rich, Right, anti-Palestinian, and pro-Lebanese system on the other side. However, such a division is merely a simplification that should not be conceived of as a comprehensive expression of the ideology or vision of any single group in the conflict.

THE POLITICAL APPROACH

The "political" approach does not directly refute any of the preceding approaches. Instead it attempts to integrate the various approaches into a coherent and comprehesive one. Essentially, the political approach views the main groups in the Lebanese conflict as political actors, each engaged in a game seeking to expand their political base and numbers, and, consequently, their share of power. As players in a political game they develop various strategies, and in the process mobilize their ideological, religious, economic, military, and information resources. The appropriate mixture of these resources depends upon the particular strategy being played as well as the anticipated and the actual action of the other players in the game. Thus, it is conceivable for the same groups to use different resources while playing this political game.

The Kataib party, for example, when trying to mobilize its Christian supporters, may stress the religious factor; when trying to mobilize the

Lebanese and Arab Moslem conservatives, it may stress the presumed threat of the international Left; when dealing with the Palestinians, it may stress a mixture of Lebanese territorial integrity, sovereignty, and military power. In its bid to win the support of the Lebanese army, it upheld the army's integrity against its critics. Similar analysis could be made of the strategies employed by the other political actors.

This is not intended to suggest that politics in Lebanon is immoral or that Lebanese politicians have no values to realize beyond their power struggle. On the contrary, history has taught us that quite often the fiercest and perhaps the most brutal power struggle takes place among morally motivated participants. In fact, the conflict in Lebanon was pre-cipitated not by the so-called compromisers or traditional leaders but by the modernist, ideological, and secular leadership that was morally commited; the achievement of power was simply a means to the real-ization of its goals and values.

A unique feature of the political approach just described is that it does not assume that the conflict is limited to that between the Christians and the Moslems, the Left and the Right, or the Lebanese and the Pal-estinians. Rather, it conceives of the political conflict as going on as much within each group as between groups. For example, to understand what is happening in Lebanon, one should not conceive of the conflict as being one of Christians against Moslems. The Lebanese war is as much a product of the conflict within the Christian political groups and within the Moslem groups as it is between the Christians and the Moslems.[13]

Finally, the political approach does not subscribe to the deterministic undertones characteristic of the other approaches. The other ap-proaches convey the impression that what has happened was inevitable because of the rift between the Christians and the Moslems, the rich and the poor, the Left and the Right, or the Lebanese and the Palestinian or because of the nature of the poltcial system. The poltcial approach suggested in this analysis assumes that what happened was not inevi-table and the strategies that could have been developed and put to use are varied and numerous. What happened was a result of deliberate actions by some parties to the conflict that have either miscalculated their resources, misjudged the strategies and resources of their adver-

---

[13] In 1978, for example, former President Franjiah withdrew from the Front of Lebanese Forces, denounced its leaders for their criminal acts and treason, and threw his support behind the Syrian-Arab deterrence force in Lebanon, which was engaging in a cruel fight with the Kataib and National Liberal parties. In 1980, the Kataib liquidated the military presence of the National Liberals. At this writing the 1982 conflict between the National Movement and the traditional Moslem leadership over the establishment of local com-mittees is still raging.

saries, or failed to predict the consequences. In some cases, the cata-strophic consequences of the Lebanese war to the country as a whole actually may have brought benefits to some groups engaged in the con-flict. Lebanon's loss cannot be assumed to be the loss of each group in the conflict unless one adheres to the view that society is an organismic whole with perfect integration. Such an assumption cannot be sustained in regard to Lebanon or any other country.

According to the political approach, two main developments led to crippling of the Lebanese system and prevented it from handling the normal ethnic-sectarian conflict that it is specifically intended to handle. The first is the emergence of the armed Palestinian resistance movement on Lebanese soil, and the second is the growing power and ambitions of the Kataib party. It is beyond the scope of this paper to detail the contribution of these two factors to the Lebanese civil war. Yet an outline summary is in order.

The emergence of the armed Palestinian resistance movement brought with it a challenge to the system that it was not equipped to solve. It is a military challenge of a revolution versus a state. In addition to the armed forces of the Palestinians themselves, the Palestinian resistance was able to mobilize around it all of those elements and political parties that have failed to make inroads to the system through the electoral process. When discussing the electoral law and the list system, I men-tioned that ideological and doctrinaire political parties found it difficult to compete for elected offices because they lacked the flexibility and pragmatism needed to enter into alliance to win an election. These elements and other underprivileged elements in the population found in the Palestinian movement a convenient cause around which they could rally to push not only the goals and aims of the Palestinian move-ment but their own. Through its inter-Arab dimension the Palestinian movement succeeded also in Arabicizing the Lebanese conflict, making Lebanon an arena for the inter-Arab cold war. Finally, through its resis-tance to Israeli occupation, the Palestinian movement succeeded in in-ternationalizing the Lebanese conflict; this brought with it a massive Israeli retaliation against Lebanese villages and targets, which under-mined the political legitimacy of the Lebanese state as well as the eco-nomic and social foundations of the system.

All of those developments might have been tolerated and perhaps contained by the Lebanese system had it not been for the growing power and ambitions of the Kataib party. This party, sensing the seriousness of the threat posed by the Palestinian movement and its nationalist-leftist alliance to the Lebanese system and to the ambitions of the party, seized the opportunity to emerge as the champion of the Christian cause, if

not the whole Lebanese cause. By picturing the conflict as an international leftist attempt against the Lebanese system, it tried to appeal to
the Moslem population in Lebanon, to the conservative Arab regimes
and to Western interests in the area. With these ingredients the Lebanese
system was now called upon to deal not merely with an ethnic-sectarian
conflict, but also with an international armed struggle involving Lebanese, Arab, and Israeli forces, funds, weapons, and ideologies. Given
such a combination of factors, no wonder the Lebanese system failed to
contain and manage the conflict. Yet one also wonders whether any
other system, given the combination of those factors, would have done
better. Perhaps, it is to the credit of the system that in spite of seven
years of conflict, the same leaders and the same institutions continued
and are being revived to lead the process of reconstruction. Whatever
reforms or changes may be introduced, they are not likely to change the
ethnic-sectarian nature of the system. The system would have been able
to generate and accommodate peacefully and gradually these reforms
and changes, and they do not, therefore, justify seven years of savagery
and destructiveness.

CONCLUSIONS

As in other multiethnic societies, Lebanon's dominant groups played
and perfected the ethnic numbers game. In fact, this game was being
played even before the emergence of an independent Lebanese entity.
After independence some of the institutions already in existence were
formalized. Three methods in particular dominated this game in Lebanon: manipulation of the population census, engineering of electoral
laws, and domination of positions dealing with law and order.

The ethnic-sectarian nature of the Lebanese system and the way it
operated undoubtedly contributed to a certain degree of conflict and
tension, thus giving the system a certain degree of dynamism and fluidity.
Yet the sytem was equipped to deal with these conflicts and tensions.
This is what normal politics is all about in Lebanon or for that matter
in any democratic, pluralistic society—to mediate and arbitrate among
the various groups constituting the system. What Lebanon was not prepared to face and solve was an international armed conflict fought on
Lebanese soil and involving in the process Lebanese elements. The threat
it faced was not a mere peaceful sectarian competition over scarce resources but an international armed and secular conflict over which
neither Lebanon nor any one state or combinations of Arab states in the
region have any ultimate control. If anything, the conflict in Lebanon
was a secular conflict pitting a revolution against a state.

This study supports three propositions with regard to the dynamics of ethnic conflict. First, intraethnic conflicts are sometimes as important as interethnic conflict in explaining tensions in pluralistic societies. Second, secular, nationalistic forces appealing across ethnic boundaries are likely to exacerbate and accentuate ethnic conflict in pluralistic societies. In the Lebanese case the Palestinian movement and its Lebanese national and leftist allies were threatening not only the Christian leadership but the Moslem as well.[14] The threat they posed was not an ethnic-sectarian threat but a secular-nationalistic one. To a limited extent a similar threat was posed by the Kataib party, which tried to outbid and overshadow other Christian leadership in as much as it tried to undermine the authority of the newly emerging Moslem leadership. Finally, the inability of seven years of war to produce a substitute to the Lebanese institutions and the present attempt to revive these very same institutions that were supposed to be at the base of the civil war are other proofs that multiethnic societies can better manage and contain their conflicts through mediating and compromising representative institutions such as legislatures.

REFERENCES

Baaklini, A.
    1963   The civil service board in Lebanon. Unpublished M.A. thesis, Department of Political Science and Public Administration, American University of Beirut.
    1976a   *Legislative and Political Development: Lebanon 1842–1972*. Durham, N.C.: Duke University Press
    1976b   Civilian control of the military in Lebanon: a legislative perspective, in *Civilian Control of the Military* (Claude Welch, Ed.), pp. 225–282. Albany, N.Y.: State University of New York Press.
    1980   Political ethnicity in Lebanon: A historical perspective, in *Mobilization of Collective Identity: Comparative Perspectives* (J. A. Ross, A. B. Cottrell, R. St. Cyr, and P. Rawkins, Eds.) pp. 325–358. Lanham, Md.: University Press of America.
Barakat, H.
    1975   Al Nizam al Assiyasi Bayna al Kiam al hadariyah al taqleediyah walhadeetha [The political system between the traditional and the modern civilized values], in *an-Nizam assiyasi al-afdal lil-i'nma'* [*The Preferred Political System for Development*] (The Lebanese Development Studies Association, Ed.), Beirut: Oweidat Publishing House.
    1977   *Lebanon in Strife*. Austin: University of Texas Press.
Bashir, I.
    1965   *Planned Administrative Change in Lebanon*. Beirut: American University of Beirut.
Chamoun, Camille
    1977   *Crise au Liban*. Beirut: Author.

[14] This explains the increasing hostility of the Moslem Sunni and Shia traditional leadership to the Syrians, Palestinians, and their Lebanese allies.

Cheha, M.
    1966   Lebanon today. *Les Conferences du Cenacle* 20th year, nos. 9–10 (December).
            Beirut.
Connor, W.
    1972   Nation-building or nation-destroying?" *World Politics* **V** (xxiv April):319–355.
Crow, R. E.
    1962   Religious sectarianism in the Lebanese political system. *Journal of Politics*,
            24(August):489–520.
    1970   Religious Sectarianism in the Lebanese Political System, in *Legislatures in De-
            velopmental Perspectives* (A. Kornberg and L. Musolf, Eds.), pp. 273–302. Dur-
            ham, N.C.: Duke University Press.
Deeb, G.
    1971   al Nizam assiyasi wa al mowatin fi Lubnan [The political system and the citizen
            in Lebanon] in *an-Nizam assiyasi al-afdal lil-i'nma'* [*The Preferred Political Sys-
            tem for Development*] (The Lebanese Development Studies Association, Ed.),
            Beirut: Oweidat Publishing House.
Dekmerjian
    1978   Consociational Democracy in Crisis—Case of Lebanon. *Comparataive Politics*
            10:251–265.
Enloe, C.
    1973   *Ethnic Conflict and Political Development.* Boston: Little, Brown.
al-Haj, K.
    1961   *Falsafat al Mithag al-Watanl.* Beirut: al Rahbaniyya al Lubnaniyya.
Harik, I. F.
    1971   The ethnic revolution and political integration in the Middle East. *International
            Journal of Middle East Studies* **Spring**.
    1972   *Man Yahkom Lubnan* [Who Rules Lebanon?]. Beirut: Dar an. Nahar.
    1981   *Lebanon: Anatomy of Conflict. American Universities Field Staff Reports*, No. **49,**
            Asia. Hanover, N.H.: American Universities Field Staff Reports.
Hottinger, A.
    1966   Zua'ma in historical perspective, in *Politics in Lebanon* (Leonard Binder, Ed.)
            pp. 85–105. New York: John Wiley & Sons.
Hudson, M. E.
    1968   *The Precarious Republic: Political Modernization in Lebanon.* New York: Random
            House.
    1976   Lebanese Crisis—Limits of Consociational Democracy. *Journal of Palestine Stud-
            ies* **5**:104–122.
Iskandar, A.
    1964   *Bureaucracy in Lebanon.* Beirut: American University of Beirut.
al-Jisr, B.
    1971   An nizam assiyasi fi Lubnan bein al-mithaq al-watani wa al-talahom al-watani
            [The Political system in Lebanon between the National Pact and the National
            Solidarity], in *an-Nizam assiyasi al-afdal lil-i'nma'* [*The Preferred Political System
            for Development*] (The Lebanese Development Studies Association, Ed.). Beirut:
            Oweidat Publishing House.
Khalaf, S.
    1968   Primordial ties and politics in Lebanon. *Middle East Studies* **4**(April):243–269.
Khalidi, W.
    1976   *Conflict and Violence in Lebanon: Confrontation in the Middle East.* Cambridge,
            Mass.: Harvard Center for International Affairs.

al-Khouri, B.
   1947   *Khutab al-rais al-Shaykh Bishara al-Khouri.* Beirut: no publisher.
Khoweiry, A.
   1977   al-Harb fi Lubnan [*The War in Lebanon: 1976*]. Vol. II. Beirut: Abjadiah Press.
Lebanese Socialists
   1969   *al-Amal al-ishtiraki watanaqudat al wade' al Lubnani* [*The Socialist Work and the
           Contradictions of the Lebanese Situation*]. Beirut: Dar al-Talia.
Lijphart, A.
   1968   Typologies of democratic systems. *Comparative Political Studies* 1(1 April):3–
           44.
Meo, L.
   1965   *Lebanon: Improbable Nation.* Bloomington, Ind.: Indiana University Press.
Palestine Liberation Organization
   1977   Maza Karat al-harb al Lubnamiah [*Diaries of the Lebanese War*], Vol. I and II.
           Beirut: PLO Press.
The Phalange Party
   1974–1976   Fi al-Kadiah al-Lubnamiah [*The Lebanese Question*]. Beirut: al-Amal Press.
Qubursi, A.
   1954   *Nahn wa Lubnan* [*We and Lebanon*]. Beirut: Lebanon Press.
al-Riachi, J.
   1953   *Qabl wa-ba'd.* Beirut: Maktabat al-Arfan.
Salem, E.
   1973   *Modernization without Revolution: Lebanon's Experience.* Bloomington, Ind.:
           Indiana University Press.
Salibi, K.
   1965   *The Modern History of Lebanon.* New York: Praeger.
Suleiman, M.
   1967   *Political Parties in Lebanon.* Ithaca, N.Y.: Cornell University Press.
Tabbarah, B.
   1966   Al-muassasat assiyasiyat [The political institutions]. *Les Conferences du Cenacle*
           20th year no. 7–8 March. Beirut.
Tarbein, A. L.
   1968   *Lubnan Munzu ahd al-muta-sarrifiyya ila bidayat al-intidab, 1861–1920.* Cairo:
           Nahdat Misr Press.
Ziadeh, N. A.
   1960   The Lebanese election, 1960. *Middle East Journal* 14(Autumn):367–381.

3

National Racial Policies and University Education in Malaysia

Richard Basham

INTRODUCTION

Ethnic diversity produced by the arbitrary carving of national boundaries or importation of foreign merchant and labor communities during colonial times is one of the most serious issues confronting nations of the Third World (Basham, 1978:205–297). Nowhere has the task of building a unified nation-state been more difficult than in Malaysia,[1] which was faced with the dilemma of forging a nation from four major groups— Malays, Chinese, Indians, and various indigenous peoples—with the departure of the British in 1957. The fact that none of the groups has a majority of the population has added to the difficulty of the task: In 1970, Malays constituted 46.8% of the population, Chinese 34.1%, Indians 9.0%, and the various indigenous peoples of Northern Borneo and the Malay

---

[1] Research for this paper was conducted in 1973–1974 at the Universiti Sains Malaysia in Penang, Malaysia, during which time I was employed as a lecturer in anthropology and was teaching courses in race relations and urban studies. Although at times this paper is critical of government policy, I am aware of the difficult problems faced by the Malaysian government and that most officials within this highly competent service do not seek to exacerbate ethnic tensions, although their actions often have this unfortunate effect. See Loh (1975) for an historical discussion of the ethnic aspect of Malaysian education and van den Berghe (1975) for discussion of the impact of a plural society upon university education at a Nigerian university. I have adopted the Malaysian usage of *race* in this paper to capture the flavor of Malaysian discourse, although *ethnic group* is the more appropriate term.

57

CULTURE, ETHNICITY,
AND IDENTITY

Peninsula 8.7% (Government Press, 1970:Table 1). Also, the problem has been seriously exacerbated by marked group disparities in income and an extreme ethnoprofessionalism in which Malays tend to be found in farming or the civil service, Chinese in business, and Indians in rubber-tapping and certain liberal professions (Gardner, 1975; Government Press, 1971:38).

For a time after independence in 1957 it seemed that Chinese, Malay, and Indian Malaysians had found a modus vivendi in the governing Alliance political party formed principally from the three major race-based parties: the United Malay National Organization (UMNO), the Malayan Chinese Association (MCA), and the Malayan Indian Congress (MIC). During elections the Alliance sponsored one member of UMNO, MCA, or the MIC in each electoral district to maximize its electoral chances and minimize competitive voting along racial lines; ministerial positions were also allocated among the parties, although the posts of prime minister and deputy prime minister remained with UMNO, the senior member of the coalition.

Although the Malay-dominated coalition made efforts to wield its political power in the economic and cultural spheres through favoring Malays in employment and development schemes and promoting the spread of the Malay language and religion (Islam), it appeared that Chinese and Indians would be permitted to flourish in economic and professional activities. This era of relative domestic tranquillity ended, however, with the bloody race riots of May 13, 1969, which were directly precipitated by rejection of the Alliance by non-Malay voters in favor of what Malays felt were extremist parties that actively sought to undermine the special preferences given to Malays and Malay culture. The success of the non-Alliance Democratic Action Party (DAP) and Gerakan in both the state and federal elections held on May 10, 1969, provoked outrage among Malays who felt they were being manipulated by Chinese duplicity in the Alliance (through the MCA) into making political, economic, and cultural concessions to non-Malays only to see the non-Malays desert the Alliance in support of even more radical demands (see Goh, 1971; Means, 1976:393–400).

During the state of emergency that followed the riots, the government sought to allay Malay grievances through promulgation of policies that emphasized the special position of the Malays and other indigenous peoples (together referred to as *bumiputra*, "sons of the soil"), the Malay language, Islam, and the Malay king and sultans, as well as the need for an equitable distribution of wealth among the races and the right to citizenship for those non-Malays who were able to qualify for it. These various policies were elevated to the level of national ideology, and measures were taken to prevent dissent by declaring them to be officially "sensitive issues," criticism of which was considered seditious even on the floor of Parliament. Implementation of the new policies focused on the crucial issues of special Malay preferences in allocation of educational and economic opportunities and in promotion of the Malay language as the national language of work and education.

Given the tremendous importance of education in Malaysia and the rest of the developing world (indeed one can almost speak of an ideology of education and development, which gives educational issues an even greater emotional salience than they have in most developed countries), it is not surprising that much of the government's effort to enact its post-1969 policies has concentrated on this crucial arena. And it is in the area of education, especially higher education, in which the other races have felt their opportunities dwindle in favor of the Malays, that the government has faced the greatest challenges to its racial policies. The ultimate effects of policies of "positive discrimination" in favor of one group over others are, of course, difficult to predict. They are doubly so in a nation such as Malaysia where independent research on the "sensitive issues" is officially discouraged by the government (Opportunities for Research, 1976:7). However, as an anthropologist who taught courses in race and ethnic relations at a Malaysian university, I was able to observe the effects of such policies on the strategically important university community. In this paper I attempt to assess the impact of Malaysia's racial policies by focusing on an ethnographic perspective of their effects on students of one university. Although I have necessarily restricted my discussion to a single university, I am convinced my observations are more widely applicable, both to Malaysian society and to other nations that confront similar problems.

NATIONAL RACIAL POLICY AND EDUCATIONAL ASPIRATIONS

In 1973, the Ministry of Education of Malaysia published results of a study designed to uncover attitudes toward education among primary and lower secondary school pupils. The study had been undertaken in order to develop strategies to encourage students to continue their schooling. The most surprising result of this *Drop-out Study* was the discovery that Malay secondary students, rather than Chinese or Indians, were most highly motivated to continue studies to the university level

(Ministry of Education, 1973).[2] The study contradicted most conventional assumptions, which rate Chinese as placing more emphasis on education than Malays. It also contradicted our knowledge of the relative importance of greater wealth and higher levels of urban residence on educational aspirations, factors which should enhance Chinese educational aspirations.[3]

Malay educational goals, however, seem not to be associated with high levels of academic achievement. University lecturers in Malaysia usually acknowledge Chinese to be the best students, followed by Indians and then Malays. As such information is considered sensitive by the government, quantitative substantiation of this point is difficult to obtain (see Lim, 1978:266–271, for substantiation at the primary level). However, during my tenure as a university lecturer, I was able to gather complete data on grades and degree levels of 128 graduates in the social sciences for the 1973–1974 academic year (see Table 1).

These results confirm impressions that Chinese students tend to perform better academically than their Malay counterparts. Upper-second class honors were awarded to 31.9% of the Chinese graduates; in effect, this was the highest degree because only one individual, in this case an Indian, was awarded first-class honors. Most Malays (75.4% as opposed to 61.7% of the Chinese) received lower-second degrees. The lowest degree, the general or pass degree, was received by 18% of Malay students and only 6.4% of Chinese students.

A breakdown of degrees by sex reveals the marked academic achievement of the Chinese females. Fully 47.6% of all Chinese females graduated with upper-second class honors, a percentage figure four-and-one-half times that of all other groups considered together (including Chinese males). Ranking a poor second to Chinese females were Chinese males who received 19.2% upper-seconds. Next in order of performance were the Indian males (first-class and upper-second combined), followed by Indian females. Ranking below both Chinese and Indian sexes in overall quality of degrees awarded were the Malay males with 10.8% receiving upper-second honors. Finally, at the lowest level of achievement were Malay females, who received no degrees above lower-second class honors.

---

[2] Thirty percent of urban Malays, 9% of urban Chinese, and 17% of urban Indians attending Form III (age 15 +) scored high on the educational motivation scale. Rural Malays, Chinese, and Indians evidenced high motivation in 25%, 10%, and 12%, respectively, of their total responses (Ministry of Education, 1973:22–23).

[3] Of the Chinese population, 46.3% live in urban areas and 53.7% in rural areas in contrast to the Malay population, which is 15% urban and 85% rural (Government Press, 1970:Table III).

Table 1

Level of Degree Awarded to 1974 Social Science Graduates of
Universiti Sains Malaysia by Sex and Ethnicity

Ethnicity	Level of degree	% of males awarded degree	% of females awarded degree	% of total group awarded degree
Chinese	Upper-second	19.2	47.6	31.9
(N = 47)	honors	(N = 5)	(N = 10)	
	Lower-second	69.2	52.4	61.7
	honors	(N = 18)	(N = 11)	
	General (pass)	11.5	—	6.4
		(N = 3)		
Malay	Upper-second	10.8	—	6.6
(N = 61)	honors	(N = 4)		
	Lower-second	75.7	75	75.4
	honors	(N = 28)	(N = 18)	
	General (pass)	13.5	25	18.0
		(N = 5)	(N = 6)	
Indian	First-class	8.3	—	5.0
(N = 20)	honors	(N = 1)		
	Upper-second	8.3	12.5	10.0
	honors	(N = 1)	(N = 1)	
	Lower-second	58.3	62.5	60.0
	honors	(N = 7)	(N = 5)	
	General (pass)	25.0	25.0	25.0
		(N = 3)	(N = 2)	

Additionally, a review of the students' grade records showed that strict association between level of degree and the usual grade average required for that degree would have increased the gap between Malay and Chinese degrees and increased the Indian students' relative standing.[4] Thus, 47.5% of the Malays, 28.3% of the Chinese, and 15% of the Indians were awarded degrees above the level of their academic performance. By virtue of this aid a very large number of Malay individuals who would have received "pass" or "general" degrees were graduated with honors.

Given the great emphasis placed on education in traditional Chinese culture, the greater wealth and urbanization of the Chinese community, and the greater academic success of Chinese university students, what factors underlie higher Malay educational aspirations?

[4] Award of an upper-second degree requires a grade average of "B," a lower-second requires a "C," and a general degree requires a "D"; "C" is the usual grade and "A" is fairly rare.

Malaysia's employment system places great emphasis on the level of degree received. In a sense, an academic caste is created at conferment and persists through life. An individual receiving first-class honors is certain to gain excellent employment or financial support for further education. Upper-second class degree holders have the option of graduate study or fulfilling careers, whereas lower-second honors students not only begin careers that offer a greater chance for advancement than those awarded general degrees but also gain significantly greater remuneration. In 1974, honors graduates entering government service could anticipate monthy starting salaries of $M750, or almost 10 times the national per capita income, whereas general degree holders could expect to earn initially only about $M525. Since a majority of Malay students anticipate entry into government service after graduation, the distinction betwen general and lower-second honors is crucial; failure to gain upper-second honors, however, is unlikely to influence their career greatly.

The significance of degree distribution does not rest in cultural factors that may underlie it but in articulation with Malaysian national racial policies. As a nation Malaysia has both thrived because of, and agonized over, its ethnic composition. Ethnic occupational distribution symbolized by Malay dominance in agricultural and governmental realms, Chinese control of the commercial sector, and Indian concentration in rubber estates has helped provide some of the tremendous economic strength of Malaysia. On the other hand, its plural society has fostered some of its most troubling problems: the Emergency of the 1940s and 1950s in which largely Chinese communist guerillas engaged in a protracted civil war with both the colonial and Malaysian governments; the expulsion of the predominantly Chinese city-state of Singapore; the great economic differential between urban and rural areas with its clear ethnic overtones; the linguistic and cultural gulfs between its populations; and the race riots of Bukit Mertajam, Penang, and Kuala Lumpur, which set the stage for the disastrous May 13, 1969, "incident" (see Fletcher, 1969; Freedman, 1960; Goh, 1971; Mahathir, 1970; Purcell, 1948; Ratnam, 1964).

Years of communal segregation had produced a nation in which Malays perceived Chinese as holding a stranglehold over the economy, and Chinese and Indians saw Malays as wielding effective political control and exercising it in a self-serving manner. In the wake of the May 13th riots the Malay-dominated government decided to press toward rapid "restructuring" of Malaysian society and development of "national unity" through promulgation of the "Second Malaysia Plan." The first goal, the

restructuring of Malaysian society was designed to correct economic imbalance, so as to reduce and eventually eliminate the identification of race with economic function. This process involves the modernization of rural life, a rapid and balanced growth of urban activities and the creation of a Malay commercial and industrial community in all categories and at all levels of operation, so that Malays and other indigenous people will become full partners in all aspects of the economic life of the nation [Government Press, 1971:1].[5]

Uplift of the Malay population was to take place "in the context of an expanding economy" (1971:1) so as not to deprive the Chinese and Indian communities of their respective levels of prosperity. To achieve the ambitious goal of elevating the Malays without seriously undermining the absolute economic position of the non-Malays, the government urgently needed overseas funds and expertise; consequently, multinational corporations were encouraged to locate in Malaysia, although not without opposition from local political radicals (Basham, 1979).

The crucial, yet more subtle, problem of national unity was to be approached through

the formulation of education policies designed to encourage common values and loyalties among all communities and in all regions; the cultivation of a sense of dedication to the nation through services of all kinds; the careful development of a national language and literature, of art and music, the emergence of truly national symbols and institutions based on the cultures and traditions of the society [Government Press, 1971:3].

In the aftermath of the 1969 riots, Malaysian universities were more directly incorporated as arms of national policy. In addition to the University of Malaya at Kuala Lumpur, new universities, the Malaysian University of Science at Penang and the Universiti Kebangsaan, were opened

[5] Constant government pressure is placed upon companies, especially foreign companies, to hire Malays in executive positions. Consequently, many companies have felt compelled to hire token Malays without substantial duties at relatively high salaries. One senior bank consultant informed me that a major task in recent times is the hiring of conspicuous Malays and their placement in areas where lack of experience and qualifications would not harm the company. Because the government's goal is the development of a real Malay managerial elite, to its credit it has rejected such a response as being in neither the country's nor the Malays' interest. The government has demanded instead that companies train Malay recruits to permit them to assume positions of serious responsibility. One Malay master's candidate, already receiving substantial support, left the university to assume a post in the private sector at a salary comparable to what he would have earned with a Ph.D. One phenomenon resulting from government pressure to hire Malays in the commercial sector is "Malay raiding," in which a company lures qualified Malays from others through strong salary inducements, often before the employee has been in his post long enough to master it. Tengku Razaleigh Hamzah, chairman of a government bank and responsible for development of "bumiputra" executives, cited an instance of a man earning M$1400 (US$575) monthly who left his position for a sequence of several short-term posts, each involving a salary increase, until he reached the monthly level of M$2500 (US$1025). Then, within six months of his departure from his original job, he reapplied to the same company for an executive post at M$3000 (Mohamed Taib (Tengku), 25 March 1974:20).

to promote, respectively, development of science and higher education in the Malay language. University control over educational policy and enrollment was restricted so Malays and other indigenous peoples would be guaranteed greater representation in the university and in the particular fields (e.g., the sciences) in which they were underrepresented (Mohamed Suffian 1973:72).

The policy of Malay preference has today resulted in an overrepresentation of Malay students in universities. In 1977, 5953 students were accepted for admission to Malaysian universities from a total of 25,998 applicants; 4457 of the successful applicants were Malay, 1187 Chinese, 226 Indians, and 43 "others." Because all or nearly all Malays who applied for university admission were accepted for matriculation, it is estimated some 20,000 non-Malay students were denied places (Fernandez, 1978:53; Lim, 1978:263). Additionally, the government has refused permission to leaders of the Chinese community to establish a private university to accommodate students denied admission to state universities—an action that has reaffirmed the feeling of non-Malays that their relative exclusion from higher education results not from economic necessity but from unexpressed government policy (Das, 1978:28). Indeed, as the Merdeka University (the proposed name for the new university) group emphasized in a submission to the federal court in Kuala Lumpur, the actual cost of higher education to Malaysian society would be reduced by the new university as fewer Malaysian Chinese would have to incur the tremendous costs of overseas education (Natarajan, 1982). Additionally, fewer Chinese would feel compelled to migrate to Singapore and overseas to protect their children's futures.

This firm extension of national policies into higher education is the essential cause of high educational aspirations of Malays and much of the disappointment and resentment of the non-Malays. Far from being abstract and remote concepts, the intended restructuring of Malaysian society and promotion of national unity are having profound effects on Malaysian universities and, in turn, weigh heavily in assessments made by non-Malays of their future in Malaysian society.

RESTRUCTURING OF SOCIETY THROUGH EDUCATIONAL POLICY

Malay preference in scholarship awards and government employment directly affects the structure of universities. By provision of the national constitution, those who have been awarded federal or state scholarships, loans, or other public financial assistance—a group that is overwhelmingly Malay—shall not be denied admission to a university except with the agreement of the Minister of Education. In effect, this provision means many students who would not otherwise gain admission to a university are granted admission on the basis of "race," that is, they are Malay. In 1973, the operation of the preferential scholarship system reserved approximately one-third of the positions at Universiti Sains Malaysia to Malay scholarship holders, and another one-third of admissions were set aside for "special" cases; only about one-third of the admissions were based solely on merit.

Government justification for Malay scholarship preference is based on expressed need to elevate rural Malays "from isolated areas where teaching facilities are inadequate and where it is difficult to induce good teachers to devote long service [Hamzah Sendut, 1973:3]." In reality, however, the preference given is ethnically, rather than rurally, based, and a significant portion of urban middle-class Malays are brought in through the scholarship system along with their rural counterparts.

Despite the government's rationale, scholarship preference is a very sensitive issue to non-Malays and an issue that frequently engenders bitterness, as the following student quotations illustrate:

My father works hard and we are not rich. I graduated at the top of my class and didn't receive a state scholarship. A middle-class Malay girl who graduated below me did. It isn't fair. [Why didn't you receive a scholarship?] Race! [At this point the student broke into tears.] [Chinese female, daughter of a farmer, final year].

Most Indians agree rural Malays should have help but there are too many wealthy Malays who are profiting. Most Indians are poor and rural, too, and we get nothing [Indian male, final year].

Increasingly, university teaching positions are being filled by young Malays returned from government-supported educational sojourns abroad. This development is ominous to many Chinese students, especially those whose upper-second diplomas in the past would have directed them toward graduate work and a future post as a university lecturer or administrator. Malays are conspicuously present in the higher posts of university administration, although often deputied by Chinese, Indian, European, and Eurasian assistants who may possess a great deal more experience than their Malay superiors. Not surprisingly, this has led to charges of "Ali Babaism,"[6] in which the non-Malay is purported to "do the work" while the Malay is his or her "sleeping partner."

Today, young educated Malays often return from schooling abroad and assume their posts only to find the past situation in which Malays

[6] A commonly used term for the formation of a Malay (Ali)–Chinese (Baba) partnership to gain special government preference.

were thought of as oppressed has shifted to one in which Malays are seen as oppressors. Thus, one Malay lecturer found himself faced with "a real barrier between myself and the Chinese students. It really makes me feel strange. I never felt anything like it before. I don't know how to get their trust." The "barrier" is illustrated by an incident in which a Chinese student met him in front of his office with a broad smile of greeting and subtle "Thanks for giving me a 'D'—lah."[7] Infuriated, the lecturer could barely restrain himself from attacking the student: "He was accusing me of giving him a 'D' because he was Chinese! He *deserved* that 'D'!"

Malay preference on campus naturally enough extends to allocation of food concessions. Although the population of Penang is predominantly Chinese, the two Chinese food services for university students and staff were replaced by Malay ownership to the extreme irritation of non-Malay students and staff who felt service and quality of food had been sacrificed to government policy. Patronage dropped markedly, although it eventually returned at one facility since prices and location were strongly in its favor. However, non-Malay grumbling continued as students complained that "The Malays are afraid a Chinese manager will put some pork in the food [Chinese male]." "When we get slow service at the canteen, the non-Malays tolerate it saying, 'What do you expect? This is a Malay business' [Indian female]."

It might be argued that Chinese objections to change of concessionaires represented unwillingness to permit Malays access to the commercial sphere of the society rather than a justified rejection of inferior services. But this is probably an unfair critique. For example, one new Malay concession holder was an individual who had failed to gain credentials as an accountant during studies abroad. His casual, playboy persona on campus, his lack of attentiveness to business, his Jaguar, and his European wife suggested once again that ethnicity, not poverty, was the government's real concern.

Malay university students are also favored in post-university employment. Non-Malays frequently point to existence of a 4:1 Malay to non-Malay government hiring quota in the nontechnical service as evidence that Malays "just have to get a degree, any kind of degree" to guarantee employment, whereas Chinese and Indians are forced to scour the nongovernment sector for employment. At the same time the government is pressing so forcefully for preferential Malay hiring in private business that the vice-chancellor of the university complained:

---

[7] Lah is added for emphasis and often appears as a suffix to both Malay and English words.

Low wage levels make it difficult for the university to achieve an ethnic balance in the composition of the administrative, academic, professional, technical, clerical and other supporting staff. This is because every time a Malay staff member is recruited for service, he is attracted by higher salaries elsewhere. Even the training programmes attract few Malay scholars because of greater remuneration offered by other institutions [Hamzah Sendut, 1973:12].

Not surprisingly, non-Malays who feel discriminated against in university admissions and financial aid bitterly resent preferential treatment granted Malays in government—and increasingly in private—employment.

Contending that they are faced with discrimination at all levels without recompense, non-Malays assert that

When we complain about Malay preference we are told that it is a myth that the Malays are first-class citizens who have all the privileges, even if it is only for the "time being." But it is not a myth that the Chinese are well-established in the economy so we must balance the society [Chinese male, third year].

Malays have "rights," others "duties" . . . it is the *duty* of the Chinese to employ a labour force "reflecting the racial composition" of the country even disregarding realities when there are 10 Malays suitable for the particular type of job in contrast to 200 Chinese [Chinese female, third year].

Malays always talk about the need to have more Malay scholarships, more Malay control of the economy. We wouldn't object if they would give us some political control. What about their 4:1 government hiring ratio and their two-thirds control of Parliament? Why do you think Tun Tan wanted to resign [reference to the highest-ranking Chinese politician and former finance minister who had been passed over for appointment to Deputy Prime Minister in favor of a Malay]? Do you think they would ever let a Chinese become Prime Minister? Friends of mine have given up and left for Canada and Australia. I'll probably leave, too, but not until I've fought [Chinese male, third year].

Resentment of Malay preference peaks during the third and final year of university studies as students search for employment. Non-Malay students who are not unsympathetic to Malay desires frequently awake to a feeling that the Malays have gone too far. One especially gifted Chinese female who had studiously avoided criticism of government "racial" policy began to express strong resentment as she sought employment and "was told that I had what they were looking for but unfortunately [I] am handicapped by my sex and *race* [emphasis hers]."

Other Chinese and Indian students who graduated at the highest levels also entered the search for work only to find that their "race" weakened their opportunities. In contrast to most Malay graduates who arranged employment well in advance of graduation, one Chinese female sought government employment for almost a year in a state in which the Chinese greatly outnumber Malays—although the highest ranking officials are Malays—only to be thwarted at every turn. She finally found a job, but only after she had been passed over for a number of posts and had refused to be denied an interview for one for which she was exceptionally well-qualified. "I was the only Chinese interviewed. I expect some others were not called because of Bahasa Malaysia [see discussion in following section]. I think I got it because there were three vacancies for the post. Otherwise I wouldn't have had a chance."

The curious problem of strong Malay motivation toward higher education is resolved in the light of preference given to Malays in university admissions, financial aid, and postgraduate employment. Indeed the fact that Malays are virtually assured of high salaries and rapid advancement if they receive any honors degree may explain why Malay university graduates displayed such a strong clustering at the lower-second honors level. It may also explain why the faculty, under the strong direction of the dean of the school, recommended that many Malay graduates be awarded degrees above their actual academic level—an action that primarily served to elevate students from general to lower-second honors degrees.

Given the realities of Malay society in which males predominate in the economic life of the family, it is not surprising that Malay men gain higher degrees than Malay women; women are increasingly taking jobs outside the home in the light of recent governmental policies, but they still generally assume a family-centered role, only providing supplemental income. Sexual allocation of opportunity also operates in Chinese society. Chinese men generally enter the commercial sector, and the level of their degree is not especially significant. In contrast, Chinese females have no readily available employment path. To succeed in employment they must often enter teaching or another area of government service, and because entry into graduate school virtually requires an upper-second degree, high performance is a necessity for one who hopes to teach at advanced levels. Opportunity for government employment requires superior qualifications for one "handicapped by sex and race."

Not surprisingly, Malay students generally express satisfaction with government policies of preference toward them. Their objections do not follow those made by non-Malays against the system itself but rather express the idea that the government is not doing enough for Malays. Malay "radicals" commonly complain that "the government is not really helping poor Malays enough but just trying to create a few rich Malays" and "the government has not yet implemented the 'quota'."[8] Many Malays

---

[8] This "quota" is the 4:1 goal in government hiring, which the government has not yet been able to achieve, especially in technical fields. Full-scale implementation would virtually end government hiring of non-Malays.

also object to non-Malay criticism of Malay preference as exaggerating the reality of its implementation. Despite the fact that "race," not residence or income, is the criterion for discrimination, they argue that the goal of government policy is to aid the poor, especially the rural poor who are largely Malay. As worthy as this goal is—and I encountered no significant non-Malay objection to it—it appears to many non-Malays a mere smoke screen of rationalization. The salience of "race," not poverty, is illustrated by the recollection of an urban, middle-class Malay female university student that her reluctance to accept a government scholarship abroad was acerbically countered by the government officer tendering the offer: "What kind of Malay are you? Do you want the Chinese to strangle us?"

THE UNIVERSITY AND PRODUCTION OF A NATIONAL CULTURE

Malaysia's 11 million inhabitants display a tremendous degree of cultural and linguistic diversity. Ethnicity, especially Malay and Chinese ethnicity, is a factor of tremendous salience. Student research papers, too, reflect the society's preoccupation with race. One student of Chinese origin adopted by a Malay family told of aloof treatment by Malay strangers, which ceased when he established he was Malay; initial acceptance by Chinese strangers changed to hostility when he replied in Malay to questions posed in Chinese. A Chinese student who one day wore a "baju kurung," a traditional Malay dress, "just for something different," found her casual tampering with an emblem of ethnicity gained friendly comments and stares from Malays but evoked open sarcasm from Chinese, who asked one another, "Is she Chinese or is she Malay?" Another student's detailed survey of several high schools discovered that, except for Indian students, friendships were strongly intraethnic and were not significantly altered by enrollment in integrated schools over segregated ones.

Given the nation's lack of unity, the government is attempting to develop a national culture and to promote acceptance of a common language, culture, religion, and royalty. Royalty, in the persons of the sultans and the king, is intended to serve as a symbol of unity for all Malaysians. But its success in meeting this goal is hindered by the fact that few Chinese and Indians grant the country's royalty any status beyond "very important Malays," and many young Malays consider the royal houses irrelevant to modern Malaysia.

Islam is potentially a more potent unifying force since, unlike allegiance to royalty, it requires a clear and expressed commitment. But although the government encourages conversion and rewards it with concessional preferences, most Chinese regard the conversion of one of their number to Islam as a traitorous act. Although newspaper articles frequently report conversion of Chinese to the national religion, little real progress toward national unity on this point can be expected. Most non-Muslims merely tolerate such symbols of Islam as the religious holiday of Hari Raya Puasa, the assembly of pilgrims journeying to Mecca, the presence of the crescent moon on the flag and currency, the abhorrence of pork and dogs, and the National Koran Reading Contest, and turn deaf ears to lectures on the importance of Islam as an instrument of national unity.

Islamic influence in the university is strong among Malays; for non-Malays it is limited primarily to a de facto prohibition of pork and dogs on campus (although cats are permitted to roam campus cafeterias in search of table scraps), the partially shared observation of Muslim holidays with their Malay fellow students, and periodic divisions among students concerning support for the state of Israel.[9]

The idea of a national culture, by which is meant a culture "based on the Malay culture but [which] includes suitable elements of the culture of the other races" (Datuk Ali quoted in Lim et al., 1974:4), is rejected by most non-Malays as Malay culture in thin disguise. This assertion that "national culture is Malay culture" has not been effectively countered by the Malaysian government. On the contrary, the assumption gained added credence when Culture, Youth and Sports Minister Datuk Ali Haji Ahmed announced in Parliament that the lion dance—the most frequently offered example of a possible Chinese contribution to national culture—could not be absorbed into Malaysian culture as "it is a Chinese dance and reflects the characteristics of a culture which grew outside this region [Straits Times, 7 February 1974:5]."

Unlike other pillars of Malaysian unity, the use of a common national language can be encouraged by rewarding its command. Culture, religion, and royalty as instruments of unity can easily be ignored, but language is not so easily dismissed. Although officially "sensitive" and closed to real debate, it is at the core of an indirectly expressed, yet intense, division within the society: Should Malaysia have a national

---

[9] Many Chinese students, perhaps in response to their own sense of engulfment in a Muslim world, support Israel in its dispute with its Arab neighbors. Despite student union sanction, demonstrations in support of the Arabs draw remarkably few Chinese.

language whose command is mandatory for occupational success and, if so, should that language be Malay (Bahasa Malaysia) or English?

Many university courses in Malaysia at present continue to be offered in English despite the Government's emphasis on development of Bahasa Malaysia as the national language. Persistence of English is attributable to numerous factors, chief of which is that it is the language of maximum competence of most university lecturers and the language in which most students until quite recently received primary and secondary education. Gradual implementation of the Malay language as the national language has begun with establishment of national medium primary and secondary schools throughout the country, a vigorous effort to recruit Malay-speaking lecturers, and efforts to develop the technical vocabulary of Malay. By 1983, all first-year university courses are to be conducted in Bahasa Malaysia (Universiti Sains Malaysia, 1973:21). Current Universiti Sains efforts to promote Malay center on the requirement that all university graduates must successfully complete a three-year course in Bahasa Malaysia and that a percentage of all course examination scripts be completed in Bahasa Malaysia, despite the fact that most lectures are in English.[10]

Effects of the government's implementation of Bahasa Malaysia, more than the goal of linguistic unity per se, have incurred resentment among non-Malays. Although few students question the desirability of the eventual establishment of a common national language, many non-Malay university students would opt for English as the national language were it not for the government's nonnegotiable decision that Malay should become the language of Malaysia's citizens. "What good is Malay when there are almost no textbooks in it and all scientific and technical words are borrowed from English" and "The Malays only want to force us to learn Malay so they can pass us in [their command of] English" are sentiments expressed by Chinese students and commonly held among non-Malays.

Non-Malay objections to implementation of Malay as a national language center on its use as an instrument of discrimination. A survey ($N = 597$) in 1973 of Universiti Sains Malaysia students indicated 63.3% of respondents had received primary education in English, 22.4% in

---

[10] Due to the shortage of individuals capable of marking Malay scripts, the U.S.M. School of Comparative Social Sciences was only able to require that 40% of the 1974 final examinations of first-year students be answered in Malay (although all could be written in Malay if the student desired to do so). For the second and third years, 20% (maximum 60%) and 0% (maximum 20%), respectively, of the final papers had to be in Malay.

Chinese, less than 1% in Tamil, and 12.5% in Malay-medium schools.[11] The preponderance of English as the medium of instruction in secondary schools was even more marked: 92.5% of students had studied in English-medium schools, whereas only 4.1% had studied in Malay schools and 2.6% in Chinese schools. Thus, although many of the 34.4% of the respondents who were Malay had attended primary school in the Malay language and spoke Malay at home (29.3% of the respondents came from homes in which Malay was the dominant language), few Chinese had benefit of either Malay education or of early linguistic familiarity with Malay.

One of the curiosities of the pervasive factionalism characterizing Malaysian society is the assumption made by many Malays that Chinese favor English because it is their language. Despite the fact that only 7.9% of students spoke "mostly English" at home (a figure that undoubtedly includes Indian respondents) and that over 35% of the students reported a Chinese dialect (or Mandarin) was the primary means of communication at home, English is often seen as a Chinese language.[12] Thus, the comment of one Malay male "When I failed English I didn't complain. Why should the Chinese always complain when they do poorly in Malay?" was seconded by most of his fellow Malay students.

Given acute linguistic strain among many Chinese and an inadequate knowledge of Malay, it is not surprising that Chinese students report required "Bahasa" examination answers "are treated as throwaways by

[11] In this survey 36.4% of respondents were Malay, 52.2% Chinese, 8.6% Indian, 0.2% Eurasian, and 2.5% "others." In general, use of questionnaire surveys in Malaysia to tap attitudes toward race should be viewed with a great deal of skepticism, especially when the instrument is designed to measure social distance. When called on to respond to such questionnaires, Malaysian students, especially, are probably inclined to provide relatively "liberal" answers that may not reflect true feelings. It is, of course, quite an easy matter for a Malay to check a questionnaire indicting willingness to marry a Chinese. It is altogether another issue to actually follow through with such an expressed "attitude." Rabushka's research, especially, seems to suffer from a mistaken notion of the value of such survey research in Malaysia, although he admits he was warned in advance by Professor K. J. Ratnam, one of the leading experts on Malaysia's plural society. Thus, when analyzing the returns from a mailed questionnaire to University of Malaya students, he concluded, "The relatively higher rate of willingness to marry compared with the low rate of actual intermarriage further reinforces the distinction between behavior and attitudes [1969:61]." As one who has conducted ethnographic research on the same topic, I feel it reflects a weakness in survey methods, not a "distinction between behavior and attitudes." (See also Rabushka, 1971, 1973).

[12] About 25% of Chinese students indicated both English and Chinese were spoken at home. The usual pattern is conversation in Chinese with parents and young siblings and in English with older siblings who have attended English-medium schools.

the Chinese" because it is assumed "Malays will obviously do better." In the mind of another Chinese student the requirement is

designed to discriminate against the Chinese as most of us already have to speak our dialect, a little Mandarin, English and Bazaar Malay. They are forcing us to spend all of our time learning languages but if this thing [the national language policy] continues then Malays are going to be surprised to discover that the Chinese will be the best Bahasa Malaysia students.

Writing portions of examination papers in Malay has also created dissension among faculty, many of whom agree with non-Malay accusations that the requirement imposes a major discriminatory burden on non-Malay students. A school board meeting held to evaluate the faculty's ability to grade examinations in Malay produced a virtual consensus of opposition to the policy based upon shared feeling that requiring Malay responses to courses presented in English could only gratuitously aid Malays in examinations and hurt non-Malays. The lecturers' continued objection to the policy was terminated only when a local lecturer reminded the meeting in an irony laden voice, "Our discussion is becoming subversive."

Attempts to foster national unity through education are also thwarted by communal attitudes that inhibit relaxed interaction on campus. Responses to the 1973 race relations survey produced ethnic stereotypes paralleling those of the community at large, which clearly influence interaction with members of other groups.[13] Malays, for example, are ranked highest in the following attributes (in descending order): religious, pleasure-loving, cooperative, sensitive, traditional, idealistic, aggressive, clean, trustworthy, and stupid. Chinese predominate in such attributed characteristics as (in descending order): hardworking, materialistic, ambitious, individualistic, and intelligent. Thus, during the course of a discussion explaining why they preferred to avoid sharing rooms with Malays, one of several Chinese females criticized her former Malay roommate as having "spent all of her time playing her radio . . . [and] she and her friends didn't show any respect for my possessions or privacy," whereas a Malay girl said she would prefer a Malay roommate because "They're [Chinese] unfriendly and too serious." Most obvious of the barriers between groups is the Muslim prohibition on eating pork, which is generally assumed by Chinese students to prohibit eating of pork on campus (it is not served in any campus facility). Although Chinese are encouraged

[13] Attributes are tallied from all student responses, undifferentiated by ethnicity, so they contain both "esoteric" and "exoteric" stereotypes in one summation. However, agreement on stereotypes across groups tends to minimize the effect of lumping.

to attend to Malay dietary sensibilities concerning public display and ingestion of pork on campus and in the society as a whole, appetite for pork among Chinese students appears, if anything, to have been heightened by the prohibition. "I don't like the Malay food in the canteen," one Chinese student told me, "so my sister brings me some food, usually a ham sandwich, from home every day."

Muslim proscriptions on eating pork and keeping dogs may seem rather insignificant to non-Malaysians. But in reality they are central emblems of ethnic division. Malays regard both as deeply polluting, whereas Chinese either ignore Malay attitudes or respond even more assertively by clinging to these ethnic symbols. The pervasiveness and absurdity of this division is illustrated by a response given by one Chinese female to my suggestion that she pet a cat sitting beside her in a cafeteria: "*I* don't like cats; *Malays* like cats."

Chinese–Indian friendships appear to develop more readily than do Malay–Chinese or Malay–Indian friendships. However, intermarriage and interracial dating are still strongly disapproved of, especially by the Chinese community. A Chinese female who dated an Indian student and planned marriage admitted her behavior was deviant and anticipated paying a price few Chinese students would risk: severance of family contacts.

I haven't even told my parents I'm dating him. They would cut me off if they knew. [What will happen when you get married?] They'll disown me. I will probably never see them again. [Don't you think that's unfair of them?] How can I? They won't have any choice. They grew up in a different world. They don't understand race like I do. They think Indians are dirty because of their color.

Finally, presence on campus of foreign lecturers has both divisive and unifying effects. Frequently, staff encourage students to question national policies, often focusing on those related to preferential Malay treatment. Chinese and Indian students are thus given support in their objections to government policy, and the wedge between Malays and non-Malays is unfortunately strengthened. As frequently as they are divisive forces, however, expatriate lecturers serve as foils against which students can unify. Many students and administrators resent foreign lecturers as a neocolonial elite exemplifying the unspoken assertion that locals are not yet ready to manage their own affairs. Lecturers who are too opinionated or insufficiently aware of their marginality are occasionally shocked to discover themselves objects of the emotionally devastating charge of harboring racist attitudes toward "Asians." During the fall of 1974 an incident resulted in major demonstrations and boycotting of classes at Universiti Sains. An Australian lecturer's failing of ten students in a midterm review was countered by demonstrations accusing him of being a racist and suggesting he return to his "kangaroo soil." In 1973, the university's vice chancellor circulated a memorandum to all lecturers after a "meet-the-students-session" noting that students had registered frequent complaints that most lectures lacked "relevance to the Malaysian setting" and "questioned me on the attitude of the university towards recalcitrant lecturers, lecturers who obviously reveal a cultural gap and others who show a lack of understanding of the sensitivities prevailing in the Malaysian society."

CONCLUSIONS

The government of Malaysia has promoted its national racial policies in the university system as elsewhere as efforts designed to promote "national unity," "nation building," and to "eradicate poverty." It has made criticism of them a very serious business by elevating even dispassionate inquiry to the level of sedition. If non-Malays could be persuaded to accept the government's goals as in the nation's best interests and not just avoid public criticism out of fear of Malay retaliation, Malaysia would achieve a major step toward national unity and restructuring of its society. Unfortunately, communalism throughout the society is often heightened by government actions that seem designed principally to convert Malay political dominance into economic power.

In higher education in particular, special treatment of Malays incurs tremendous resentment among strongly motivated, hard-working non-Malay students, who have had their aspirations dashed at the same time those of the Malays have been heightened. Under these circumstances non-Malays have learned to accommodate to the realities of firmly wielded political power. But most have also developed resentment and cynicism, which will make true national unity even more difficult to achieve. Even implementation of a common national language has probably proven more divisive than unifying, at least when viewed from a short-term perspective.

Many Malay, Chinese, and Indian students feel a genuine need to attack the problems of the society together, without regard to ethnicity, and to aid the poor of all races. Unless non-Malay resistance can be broken and the country made into a Malay nation, government policy may continue to discourage unity because it precludes development of intergroup alliance around the one issue that offers the potential to improve the life of the nation's citizens without further alienating the various racial groups from each other: an attack on poverty, whether found in urban or rural areas or among Chinese, Malays, or Indians.

REFERENCES

Basham, R.
   1978   *Urban Anthropology: The Cross-Cultural Study of Complex Societies*. Palo Alto: Mayfield.
   1979   Malaysia and the "Committee against Repression in the Pacific and Asia." *Australian Anthropological Society Newsletter* **2**:5–7.
Das, K.
   1978   Malaysia: a test of strength on education. *Far Eastern Economic Review* **102**(4):28–29.
Fernandez, J.
   1978   A sulphurous documentary. *Asiaweek* **August 2**:53.
Fletcher, N. M.
   1969   *The Separation of Singapore from Malaysia*. Ithaca, N.Y.: Cornell Southeast Asia Program, Data Paper no. 73.
Freedman, M.
   1960   The growth of a plural society in Malaya. *Pacific Affairs* **33**:158–168.
Gardner, S. W.
   1975   *Ethnicity and work: occupational distribution in an urban multi-ethnic setting—George Town, Penang, West Malaysia*. Unpublished Ph.D. thesis, Department of Sociology, University of California, Berkeley.
Goh, C. T.
   1971   *The May Thirteenth Incident and Democracy in Malaysia*. Kuala Lumpur: Oxford University Press.
Government Press
   1970   *Population and Housing Census: Community Groups*. Kuala Lumpur: Government Press of Malaysia.
   1971   *Second Malaysia Plan*. Kuala Lumpur: Government Press of Malaysia.
Hamzah Sendut (Tan Sri Professor)
   1973   *A New University in the Making*. Penang: Universiti Sains Malaysia.
Lim, K. S.
   1978   *Time Bombs in Malaysia*. Petaling Jaya, Malaysia: Democratic Action Party.
Lim, T. B., Cheong, M. S., and Dorall, C.
   1974   Restructuring the nation's wealth. *Straits Times* **February 1**:4.
Loh, F. S.
   1975   *Seeds of Separatism: Educational Policy in Malaya 1874–1940*. Kuala Lumpur: Oxford University Press.
Mahathir bin Mohamad
   1970   *The Malay Dilemma*. Singapore: Asia Pacific Press.
Means, G. P.
   1976   *Malaysian Politics* (second ed.). London: Hodder and Stoughton.
Mohamed Suffian bin Hashim
   1973   Problems and issues of higher education in Malaysia, in *Development of Higher Education in Southeast Asia* (Y. H. Yip, Ed.), pp. 57–78. Singapore: Regional Institute of Higher Education and Development.

Ministry of Education
    1973   *Kajian Keciciran* [Drop-out Study]. Kuala Lumpur: Ministry of Education of Ma-
           laysia.
Mohamed Taib (Tengku)
    1974   Room at the top, but where's the talent? *Straits Times* **March 25**:10, 20.
Natarajan, L.
    1982   Wrong to say varsity is not viable: QC. *New Straits Times*, **Feburary 19**:3.
Opportunities for Research
    1976   Opportunities for research: Malaysia. *Far Horizons* **9**:1.
Purcell, V.
    1948   *The Chinese in Malaya*. London: Oxford University Press.
Rabushka, A.
    1969   Integration in a multi-racial institution: ethnic attitudes among Chinese and
           Malay students at the University of Malaya. *Race* **11**:53–63.
    1971   Integration in urban Malaya: ethnic attitudes among Malays and Chinese. *Jour-
           nal of Asian and African Studies* **6**:91–107.
    1973   *Race and Politics in Urban Malaya*. Stanford: Hoover Institution Press.
Ratnam, K. J.
    1964   *Communalism and the Political Process in Malaysia*. Kuala Lumpur: University
           of Malaya Press.
Straits Times
    1974   Lion dance reflects outside culture. *Straits Times* **February 7**:5.
Universiti Sains Malaysia
    1973   *Maklumat Am*. Penang: Universiti Sains Malaysia.
van den Berghe, P.
    1975   *Power and Privilege at an African University*. Cambridge, Mass.: Schenkman.

4

Care and Support of Elderly Family Members: Views of Ethnic Chinese Young People

Betty L. Chang

INTRODUCTION

The Changing Role of the Elderly

In the later years of life various needs arise due to decreased physical abilities and potential social and economic dependency. The family is often seen as the major source of support for the elderly. With an increase in life expectancy increasingly large numbers of families are being confronted with the responsibility for the care of elderly family members. Although literature exists on supportive systems and filial piety in the majority society (e.g., Rosow, 1970; Shanas, 1968, 1979; Sussman and Burchinal, 1968), little empirical data exist on the attitude of minority families toward the care of the elderly. This study specifically examines the views of young men and women of Chinese descent living in the United States (ethnic Chinese) regarding the responsibility for the care of the elderly.[1]

Early literature in family sociology has maintained that the modern family has become more nuclear and isolated from their extended kin

[1] The term "ethnic Chinese" is used in preference to the more popular term "Chinese-American" because the former term refers to a person of Chinese descent who may or may not be an American citizen; whereas, "Chinese-American" technically refers to a person of Chinese descent who has obtained American citizenship either by birth or naturalization.

79

(e.g., Parsons, 1943; Wirth, 1938) and that there has been a decline in the protective aspects of the family toward the elderly. However, more recent literature indicates that the nuclear family exists within kinship systems, which are capable of providing assistance to its members (Gelfand and Fandetti, 1980; Shanas, 1968, 1978, 1979; Sussman and Burchinal, 1968). Theorists suggest that modified extended families exist in the United States. Moreover, they fulfill the functions necessary for the care of the elderly and remain the preferred source of support. These include physical care, shelter, transportation, affective support, and assistance with household tasks.

Although elderly family members may live apart from their children, mutual services and interrelationships can be maintained by living near younger family members. Shanas (1979) notes that the proportion of older Americans in 1950 with children who lived *with* at least one child is constant with today's proportion of older Americans with children who live with *or near* at least one child. Shanas attributes this shift to increased financial flexibility, which allows each generation to have separate households and maintain the type of supportive relationships previously found in extended households.

Further, there have been attempts to broaden sources of support of the elderly to include friends and/or neighbors. These sources have been important in domains of assistance not supplied by family members (Arling, 1978; Rosow, 1970). For example, whereas elderly persons may call upon family members for financial assistance, they may be more willing to call on a neighbor or friend for assistance in transportation or shopping.

Attitudes toward the Elderly

In a rapidly changing technological society, elderly people tend to be undervalued because their knowledge is often considered outdated and unusable for everyday living. Although their knowledge of history and ancestral roots may be interesting to young people, the elderly's ideas about behavior are not valued by the young in matters of behavior (Cowgill, 1972). This negative attitude toward the opinions and knowledge of the aged leads to demeaning stereotypes, and presumably affects feelings and behavior regarding the care of elderly people.

Studies on attitudes toward the aged have been inconclusive. A large number of studies have revealed that a negative attitude toward the aged exists in the United States (Bennett and Eckman, 1972; McTavish, 1971; Tuckman and Lorge, 1953). This has been found to exist in all age groups:

children (e.g., Hickey and Kalish, 1968a), high school and college students (Ivester and King, 1977; Kogan, 1961; Tuckman and Lorge, 1953), and adults (Harris and Associates, Inc., 1975).

Other studies reveal a more neutral or positive attitude. Hickey and Kalish (1968a) showed third-grade children described old people as kind and friendly three times as often as mean or unfriendly. Kogan (1961) and Ivester and King (1977) found college and high school students tend to view the aged more favorably than unfavorably. Lutsky (1981) reported that an analysis of work on attitudes over the past 8 years has failed to reveal a consistent negative attitude. He contends that although attitudes toward the aged were shown to be somewhat negative in relation to other age groups, those attitudes were still neutral or positive in character. Only minimum investigation has been undertaken of the minorities' attitudes toward the elderly. Two reasons may be suggested for this: (1) until recent years, the study of minorities has received little attention in gerontology, and (2) when minorities were included in studies, they constituted so few that the analysis was undifferentiated. This is particularly true with Oriental or Asian subjects in predominantly white and occasionally white and black samples (e.g., Ivester and King, 1977).

Cultural Influences in Ethnic Chinese

The type of family structure usually associated with Chinese families in the United States is that of the extended family found in rural China. This has not been supported by available literature on Chinese Americans. Several studies (Chang, 1981; Kalish and Yuen, 1971; Sung, 1971; Wu, 1975) indicate that Chinese young people in the United States tend to maintain nuclear family structures. Exceptions are found to exist in the crowded areas of Chinatown and in families where financial and/or other concerns have caused the elderly and younger generations to share households.

Regardless of family living arrangements, Chinese tradition dictates that elderly family members receive respect, care, and support from the younger generations. This belief has been attributed to the principles of filial piety or *Hsaio Ching*, which explicates the responsibility a son or daughter has for the aged parents: to give respect, honor, and devotion, and provide for the happiness and financial needs of the aged person. It teaches that the elderly are entitled to harvest all they have given to their offspring.

The concept of *Hsiao Ching* was derived from the teachings of Confucius. His teachings include basic principles pertaining to a person's relationships with his or her parents and describe behavior expected of all human beings. The responsibility to care for one's parents is seen not only as an obligation but as an opportunity and a source of joy. To be deprived of such an opportunity causes shame and sorrow.

In a study of elderly Chinese in Los Angeles, Wu (1975) suggests that the Chinese families are so Americanized that filial piety has lost its place. However, it is unknown to what extent young men and women of Chinese descent continue to view the elderly with a sense of responsibility for their care. Anecdotal and impressionistic accounts of families (Chang, 1981; Kalish and Yuen, 1971; Sung, 1971) indicate a decrease in support of the elderly; however, it is unclear whether the decrease is widespread. In this paper I explore the opinions of young men and women of Chinese descent in relation to one aspect of the concept of *Hsaio Ching:* the care of the elderly.

Past experiences and degree of acculturation to Western industrialized society may influence the views of Chinese-Americans toward the elderly. It is reasonable to expect that, within the Chinese group, subgroups with different historical and immigration experiences may hold different views. Chinese young people may be roughly divided into three major subgroups based on their immigration patterns to the United States: (1) Chinese who were born in the United States, (2) those who came here from Taiwan, (3) Chinese from Hong Kong.

In order to examine the differences, if any, among the three subgroups, the study addressed the following specific research questions: (a) Who should care for the elderly with long-term illnesses? (b) Who is responsible for the nutritional and social needs of elderly? and (c) Do offspring want to live with the elderly if given a choice?

In addition, exploratory questions were asked to investigate (a) what broadened sources of support were actually used by the elderly to maintain physical, social, and emotional health; (b) what young people viewed as ideal environments for living conditions; and (c) what sources of support they felt were necessary for the care of the elderly.

METHOD

Sample

Subjects were 80 ethnic Chinese in Los Angeles[2] who had contact with at least one grandparent (those who lived close by or in the same home when they were old enough to remember the experience). Twenty-

[2] For the purpose of the present study, only subjects both of whose parents were Chinese were included.

Table 1

Percentage of Subgroups in Various Living Arrangements

Subgroup	N	Alone or with friends	With parents and siblings	With parents and grandparents	With spouse and children	Other
			Percentage of total sample			
American-born	24	3.8	17.7	1.3	7.6	0.0
Taiwan-born	28	11.4	11.4	1.3	8.9	2.5
Hong Kong-born	27	17.7	7.6	1.3	5.1	2.5
Total	79	32.9	36.7	3.8	21.5	5.1

four (30%) were American-born Chinese, 28 were from Taiwan, and 27 from Hong Kong. The subjects ranged in age from 18 to 32, the majority being in the 18- to 28-year-old group. The majority of subjects were students ($N = 59$ or 73.8%). Because the respondents were students, they were asked to estimate the approximate annual family income of their parents in U.S. dollars. Although the figures might not have been precise, it was felt this was a more accurate estimate of their financial status than their earnings as a student. It was also recognized that the purchasing power of the U.S. dollar in Taiwan and Hong Kong varies from that in Los Angeles. The majority of subjects reported lower-middle and middle incomes of $5001 to $15,000 (30–37.5%) and $15,001 to $25,000 (16–20.0%).

The majority of subjects from Taiwan (60%) and Hong Kong (62%) have been here less than 5 years. Table 1 shows the subjects' present living arrangements. Very few in each of the subgroups lived in extended households (1.3%). The American-born Chinese who may have been expected to live with grandparents were more frequently found in nuclear households living with parents and siblings (17.7%).

Operational Definitions

The opinions of the interviewees concerning the expectation that young people should care for the needs of the elderly in illness and health were first measured by two single Likert-type items. These addressed the first two specific research questions mentioned earlier. The scores ranged from 1 (strongly disagree) to 6 (strongly agree). The questions, posed here as statements to which the respondent agreed or disagreed, were phrased as follows: (1) "Chinese young people should care for their elderly parents and grandparents in long-term illness," and (2) "Chinese young people should provide for the nutritional and social needs of their parents and grandparents."

These items were direct questions based on face validity constructed for this study. To obtain concurrent validity, the score of each item was correlated with the subject's score from Kogan's (1961) Old People Scale, assuming that attitudes toward old people in general may tap a similar dimension as views toward the care of the elderly in long-term illnesses. Correlations of item 1 with odd pairs of the Old People Scale were .69 and of item 2, .74.

To address the third specific research question, the study posed the following open-ended question: "Would you like to live in the same household with your grandparents if you had a choice?" Additional questions included those pertaining to sources of support actually used by the elderly to maintain health: "What kind of health care have your grandparents actually received?" "Whom do your grandparents call in times of trouble?"

Finally, to explore what young people felt were ideal environments and to explore whom they felt should be responsible for the support of the elderly, the following open-ended questions were asked: "What do you feel would be an ideal environment for the elderly? Whom do you feel should be responsible for the support of the elderly?" These two questions were asked because they were not addressed in the Likert-type items.

Procedure

A nonrandom sample was obtained by contacting Chinese student organizations, churches, and Chinese community centers in the greater Los Angeles area for permission to explain the purpose of the study during a regularly scheduled meeting of the organization. In some cases permission was obtained to approach members where they congregated in order to explain the purpose of the study. They were informed that this was a study to examine the views of the younger generation toward the elderly. Their answers to the questions were to be anonymous and confidential, and they maintained the freedom to participate or withdraw from participation at any time. Those who consented were interviewed at a setting mutually convenient for the interviewer and respondent. The majority of the interviews were conducted at the organization's meeting site; a few were scheduled at the interviewee's place of residence (dormitory), and a few were conducted on campus. The refusal rate was low. Only one person did not show for an appointment and subsequently refused to participate.

Answers to the questions were recorded in writing by the interviewer at the time of the interview. Answers to the Likert-type questions were

Table 2

Subgroup Means and Standard Deviations of Scores
on Variables Related to Expectation That
Offspring Will Care for the Elderly[a]

Variables	American-born		Taiwan-born		Hong Kong-born		All groups	
	Mean	S.D.	Mean	S.D.	Mean	S.D.	Mean	S.D.
1. Chinese old people expect their children to care for the elderly in long-term illnessess.	4.792	.779	5.037	1.126	5.296	.953	5.051	.979
2. Chinese young people should provide for the nutritional, social, and health needs of the elderly.	4.458	1.059	5.000	1.054	4.963	.979	4.823	1.059

[a]Scores are based on answers of (1) strongly disagree, (2) moderately disagree, (3) mildly disagree, (4) mildly agree, (5) moderately agree, (6) strongly agree.

processed as descriptive data (frequencies, chi-squares, and one-way analysis of variance). Responses to the open-ended questions were tabulated for frequency wherever possible. Content rich in verbal description was analyzed for major themes.

RESULTS

Responses to Specific Research Questions (a) and (b)

As indicated in "Method," two single Likert-type items were used to assess respondents' views regarding the expectation that young people should care for the old in illness and health. The range for the responses was from strongly disagree to strongly agree. However, as shown in Table 2, the *means* of all groups were from "mildly agree" to "moderately agree." The American-born subgroup generally answered "mildly agree" to both items, whereas the groups from Taiwan showed slightly higher scores.

Table 3

Chi Square of Desire to Live with Elderly by Subgroup[a]

	Subgroup						
	American-born		Taiwan-born		Hong Kong-born		
	Yes	No	Yes	No	Yes	No	Significance
Would like to	6	17	16	12	14	13	.65
live with elderly	(7.7)	(21.8)	(20.5)	(15.4)	(17.9)	(16.7)	

[a]df = 2. Percentages are shown in parentheses.

The differences, however, were not statistically significant in an analysis of variance test. Similarly, a comparision of mean scores of males and females for the items showed no statistical significance between sexes.

Responses to Research Question (c)

An open-ended question was asked to ascertain whether respondents would like to live with the elderly if they had the choice. Their answers (see Table 3) indicated that the majority of the American-born subgroup preferred not to live with the elderly; the yes and no responses were fairly evenly divided in the other two subgroups. A chi-square to test the relationship between the desire to live with the elderly and the subgroups failed to reach significance. Many respondents provided the reasons for answering as they did. Some indicated they would prefer not to live with elderly grandparents because elderly people had "outdated" ideas and interfered in their (young people's) private lives. They also cited that different food preferences (e.g., bland foods for the elderly) caused problems because of shared cooking in the home. Those who wished to live with the elderly gave reasons supporting their choice: grandmother helped to babysit, clean house, and cook; grandfathers were valued for telling historical stories and teaching young people karate.

Exploratory Question (a)

Table 4 shows the kind of health care that respondents indicated their grandparents actually received during times of illness. The majority of the total group, as well as each subgroup, sought care from physicians. However, a greater proportion of subjects from Taiwan (15 out of 28) than

Table 4

Chi Squares of Type of Health Care by Various Immigration Subgroups[a]

| Type of health care | Subgroup | | | | | | Significance |
| | American-born $n = 22$ | | Taiwan-born $n = 28$ | | Hong Kong-born $n = 25$ | | |
	Yes	No	Yes	No	Yes	No	
Physician (M.D.)	18	4	22	6	19	6	.886
Herbalist	4	18	15	13	9	16	.036[b]
Acupuncturist	1	21	0	28	0	25	.295
Clinic, public health	0	22	1	27	2	23	.373
Hospital	6	16	6	22	9	16	.497
Care by nurses	0	22	0	28	0	25	
Neighbor	1	21	0	25	0	25	.295
Relatives	2	20	3	25	0	25	.255

[a]df = 2.
[b]Cramer's V = .30.

from the other two subgroups reported that they sought care from herbalists. A chi-square test indicated the differences in proportion were significant at the .04 level. Since chi square is influenced by sample and table size, a Cramer's V was calculated to adjust for the sample and cell sizes to estimate the strength of the relationship. For care by herbalists the strength of the association with subgroups was .30 (where the range is 0–1).

The person contacted when the grandparent was in need was seen as an indication of whom the elderly may perceive as close and responsible for aspects of their care. Table 5 shows that the majority of all groups contacted their own sons and daughters. Very few contacted grandchildren, neighbors, or friends.

Exploratory Question (b)

This open-ended question pertained to what young people thought would be an ideal environment for the elderly. The responses were similar for all respondents. The major themes were (1) the ideal environment for the elderly should be a quiet, peaceful place; (2) the ideal environment could be in the countryside, or urban area, depending on the elderly person's preference; (3) the ideal environment should not have grandparents living with young people unless the house was very large and could provide each person with privacy and separate cooking facilities; and finally, (4) there should be easy access to health care, shopping, recreation, museums, Chinese opera, mahjong games, and the homes of offspring.

Exploratory Question (c)

This question pertained to the source of support and responsibility for creating the ideal environment for the elderly people. All respondents included the offspring as a source of support; however, a majority in the American-born and Hong Kong subgroups felt the government, community, and voluntary agencies should also provide support, particularly in meeting health care and transportation needs. The need for Chinese-speaking personnel in the hospitals and in the information and referral services was clearly mentioned. Most respondents stated that the offspring should be asked to support the elderly first, and, if unable to do so, old people should seek alternative sources. This was followed by expressions of a sense of guilt and failure on the part of young people and a reluctance to receive any kind of charity. It was notable that 10 respondents (out of 28) from Taiwan felt that a good son should provide for all his parents' needs.

DISCUSSION

The present study explored the views of young men and women of Chinese descent toward their responsibility for care of the elderly. Although it is recognized that the generalizability of the findings may be limited in this exploratory study due to the composition of the sample, the small sample size, and the descriptive nature of the study, several observations can be made in relation to other groups similar to the one in the present study.

Results indicate that the young people generally "slightly agreed" with the statement that the offspring are expected to take care of the elderly who are chronically ill and that they should also provide for the nutritional and social needs of the elderly. It is important to note that great variations existed in the range of responses. The stereotype that Chinese like to live in the extended family as in rural China was not supported. This is not to say that this differs from people of other racial groups, but perhaps it points out that they, like other groups in the American society,

Table 5

Distribution of Persons Contacted by Elderly When in Need[a]

| Person contacted when in need | Elderly | | | All groups (total) |
	American-born n = 23	Taiwan-born n = 28	Hong Kong-born n = 25	n = 26
Own sons and daughters	22	22	22	66
Grandchildren	0	2	2	4
Others (neighbors, friends)	1	4	1	6

[a]Only respondents who answered this item and belonged to one of the subgroups were in the analysis.

do not feel the extended family is ideal. In Gelfand and Fandetti's study (1980) of suburban and urban white ethnics, the subjects were asked to indicate the living arrangements they preferred for elderly subjects whose spouses were deceased. Over one half of the Italian men favored the elderly living outside their homes regardless of the older person's physical condition. The majority of the Chinese-born Americans preferred not to live with the elderly if they had the choice. Reasons cited for not living with the elderly included their tendency to pry into the young people's affairs, their "outdated" ideas, the need to cater to special needs incongruent with the rest of the family, and their dominance in running the household. When the elderly people were in good health, they could contribute to the household by cooking, cleaning, and babysitting, and other special skills that supported the notion of reciprocity in goods and services (Sussman and Burchnal, 1968). It may be that because America is future oriented, past deeds and services that the elderly have rendered (in rearing the offspring) may not be valued to the extent that the teachings of Confucius have recommended.

The majority of respondents' grandparents sought care from physicians when they were ill. This was consistent with the results of a larger study of Mexican Americans, blacks, and whites in Los Angeles (Ragan, Grigsby, and Torres-Gil, 1976) in which physicians were consulted most frequently. Acupuncture was not as widely used as may have been assumed. The group from Taiwan made greater use of herbalists than respondents from the other two groups. This may have been related to the nature of medical practice in Taiwan, where both Eastern and Western medicine are widely practiced. It is interesting to note that the grandparents made little use of clinics or public health centers. This may be partially explained by their association of clinics with poverty and low income, and those reluctant to seek help from a clinic consulted private physicians. Another possibility is that the elderly may have had a language barrier and preferred to seek help from a private physician who may have spoken their dialect of Chinese.

The sons and daughters of the elderly were seen as a major source of support and the ones to be contacted in case of need. The family remains the strongest bulwark of support in the ethnic Chinese groups, which supports findings on white subjects reported by Brody (1966), Gelfand and Fandetti (1980), and others. That is, elderly people tend to become dependent on their family for their needs. In addition, the off-spring are seen as a source of emotional and spiritual support. This point was further emphasized in the open-ended statements about ideal environments. Respondents indicated that although grandparents should live under a separate roof, the elderly should be able to visit their offspring often. A majority of respondents felt that the government, community, and voluntary agencies should assume a greater responsibility for the health, social, and recreational needs of the elderly, but they recognize the importance of emotional ties to one's offspring. Seelbach (1977), Arling (1978), and Shanas and Sussman (1977) stress the role of family members in the emotional well-being of the elderly in a society whose bureaucratic structures have taken over many of the family functions.

The subgroup from Taiwan held most strongly to the idea that the offspring should be responsible for the care of the elderly. This may have been related to the fact that subjects from Taiwan were more traditional in their thinking, reflecting a closer adherence to the teachings of Con-fucius. The traditional belief that the sons are responsible may have been based in part on the patriarchal system in China in which only the males were heir to the family's wealth. Another possible explanation for the responses of the subjects from Taiwan may be the relative economic status of the subjects' families from Taiwan. The Taiwan subgroup may have been more financially able than the other two groups. This was established by the lack of significant differences in income among the subgroups, when calculated in U.S. dollars. When compared with the lower cost of living in Taiwan, this subgroup indeed may have had a higher economic status in Taiwan than the other two subgroups, who had the same income, but were in a country where the cost of living was considerably higher. A study of Mexican Americans, blacks, and whites in the Los Angeles area showed that differences in attribution of responsibility for the care of the elderly disappeared when socioeco-nomic status was controlled (Ragan and Grigsby, 1976).

In contrast to the subgroup from Taiwan, the American-born and Hong Kong subgroups felt the government, community, and voluntary agencies should play a larger role. Respondents particularly cited the need for health care, transportation, and Chinese-speaking personnel in services and information and referral.

Summary

The present study was based on interviews with 80 young people of Chinese descent (ethnic Chinese) regarding their views on the care of the elderly. They were categorized according to their pattern of immigration to the U.S.: American-born, Taiwan, and Hong Kong subgroups. Findings indicated that they generally agreed in principle with the idea that the offspring should care for the elderly, but that the majority also agreed that they would prefer not to have the elderly live with them. If they had to share the same household, they suggested that the home should be sufficiently large to provide privacy and separate cooking facilities for each generation.

The group from Taiwan advocated the idea that the offspring should be responsible for the care of the elderly. The American-born and Hong Kong subgroups felt the government and community should play a larger role. The present methods of government assistance (charity) and clinics were not acceptable because they connote a loss of self-esteem. A major problem that requires creative problem-solving is overcoming the language barrier. Training bilingual service employees, hiring interpreters, or employing bilingual elderly people who are in good health may help to bridge the communication gap.

Further research is recommended to examine the perceptions of the elderly toward their own health care, and their perception of the role of the family in providing support in old age. Future research may also identify areas of stress that occur from a conflict in values between the older and younger generations. The helping professions should also become more in touch with the community in order to communicate their concern for health care and the alternative programs that are available in a way acceptable to health care recipients. Only with that additional knowledge on background beliefs and present family situations can the helping professions promote good health and counsel the ethnic Chinese families realistically in the care of the elderly.

REFERENCES

Arling, G.
  1978   Social reciprocity, and natural supports. Paper presented at the Annual Meeting
          of the Gerontological Society, Dallas, Texas.
Bennett, R., and Eckman, J.
  1973   Attitudes toward aging: A critical examination of recent literature and impli-
          cations for future research, in *The Psychology of Adult Development and Aging*
          (C. Eisendorfer and M. P. Lawton, Eds.), pp. 575–597. Washington, D.C.: American
          Psychological Association, Washington, D.C.
Brody, E. M.
  1966   The aging family. *The Gerontologist* **6**:201–206.
Chang, B. L.
  1981   Nursing care of Asian-American patients, in *Transcultural Health Care* (G. Hen-
          derson and M. Primeau, Eds.), pp. 255–278. Menlo Park, Calif.: Addison-Wesley.
Cowgill, D. O.
  1972   Aging in American society, in *Aging and Modernization* (D.O. Cowgill and L. D.
          Holmes), Chap 16. New York: Appleton-Century-Crofts.
Gelfand, D. E., and Fandetti, D. V.
  1980   Suburban and urban white ethics: attitudes towards care of the aged. *The
          Gerontologist*, **20**(5):588–594.
Harris, L. & Associates, Inc.
  1975   *The Myth and Reality of Aging in America*. Washington, D.C.: National Council
          on Aging.
Hickey, T., Hickey, L. A., and Kalish, R.
  1968a   Children's perceptions of the elderly. *Journal of Genetic Psychology* **112**:227–
          235.
Hickey, T., and Kalish, R.
  1968b   Young people's perception of adults. *Journal of Gerontology* **23**:215–219.
Ivester, C., and King, K.
  1977   Attitudes of adolescents toward the aged. *The Gerontologist* **17**(1):85–89.
Kalish, R. A., and Yuen, S.
  1971   Americans of East Asian ancestry: aging and the aged. *The Gerontologist* **2**(1):36–
          47.
Kogan, N.
  1961   Attitudes toward old people. *Journal of Abnormal and Social Psychology* **62**(1):44–
          54.
Lutsky, N. S.
  1981   Trends in research on attitudes toward elderly persons. Paper presented at the
          XII International Congress of Gerontology, Hamburg, Germany.
McTavish, D. G.
  1971   Perceptions of old people: a review of research methodologies and findings.
          The Gerontologist **11**:90–101.
Parsons, T.
  1943   The kinship system of the contemporary United States. *American Anthropologist*
          45:22–38.

Ragan, P. K., Grigsby, J. E, and Torres-Gil, F.
   1976   *Responsibility for Meeting the Needs of the Elderly for Health Care, Housing, and Transportation: Opinions Reported in a Survey of Blacks, Mexican Americans and Whites*. Los Angeles, Calif.: Minority Aging and Social Policy Project, Andrus Gerontology Center, University of Southern California.
Rosow, I.
   1970   Old people: their friends and neighbors. *American Behavioral Scientist* **14**:59–69.
Seelbach, W. C.
   1977   Gender differences in expectations for filial responsibility. *The Gerontologist* **17**(5):421–425.
Shanas, E.
   1968   Family helping patterns and social class in three countries, in *Middle Age and Aging* (B. L. Neugarten, Ed.), pp. 296–305. Chicago: The University of Chicago Press.
   1978   The family as a social support system in old age. *The Gerontologist* **19**(2):169–174.
   1979   Social myth as hypothesis: the case of the family relations of old people. *The Gerontologist* **19**(1):3–9.
   1977   *Family, Bureaucracy, and the Elderly*. Durham, N. C.: Duke University Press.
Sung, B. L.
   1971   *The Story of the Chinese in America*. New York: Collier Books.
Sussman, M. B., and Burchinal, L.
   1968   Kin family network: unheralded structure in current conceptualizations of family functioning, in *Middle Age and Aging* (B. L. Neugarten, Ed.), pp. 247–254. Chicago: The University of Chicago Press.
Tuckman, J., and Lorge, I.
   1953   Attitudes toward old people. *Journal of Social Psychology* **37**:249–260.
Wirth, L.
   1938   Urbanism as a way of life. *American Journal of Sociology* **44**:1–24.
Wu, F. Y. T.
   1975   Mandarin-speaking aged Chinese in the Los Angeles area. *The Gerontologist* **15**(3):271–275.

5

Black Mayors and the Politics of Racial Economic Advancement*

Peter K. Eisinger

INTRODUCTION

Except for a few isolated survivors, the traditional urban machine, that marvel of disciplined organization in pursuit of bread-and-butter goals, may safely be pronounced a thing of the past, a colorful exhibit in the gallery of political Americana.[1] Even if the current tone of city politics has lost little of the intensity it had during the heyday of the machine, its practice nevertheless now represents the triumph of an occasionally overrationalized public administration. The widely accepted reasons for the demise of the machine are legion: for example, the supplanting of the machine reward system of selective patronage and side-payments by bureaucratized social welfare programs, the economic assimilation of the ethnic groups that once ran the machines, the spread of municipal civil service coverage and the concomitant decline of patronage oppor-

* This research was supported by funds granted to the Institute for Research on Poverty by the Department of Health and Human Services pursuant to the provisions of the Economic Opportunity Act of 1964. The conclusions expressed are those of the author. This paper was originally presented at the Western Political Science Association meetings, San Francisco, March 26–29, 1980.

[1] A few machines still apparently exist. Johnston (1979), for example, reminds us of the continuing vitality of machine politics in New Haven, Connecticut. But, on the whole, the machine is an anachronism.

95

tunities, and the rationalization of municipal contracting and purchasing.[2]

What these changes mean is that most people now find that they can produce economic benefits for themselves similar to or better than those the machines once offered without making the sorts of commitments of political energy and loyalty that the urban machine organizations required and without regard to whether "their" side has won or lost in a local political contest. The production of income occurs for the most part outside the domain of municipal politics. Even for members of the winning side, income gained through the preferential acquisition of jobs and contracts is no longer a very important goal to be sought through local political action. Certainly this is the case in most places, where issues of equity and efficiency in service delivery, local economic development, the quality of the urban environment, and the effort to reduce the size and cost of the public sector dominate political debate rather than the possibilities for particularistic income redistribution or augmentation. Those individuals and groups who do seek to affect income levels through the manipulation of political institutions generally focus instead on the government in Washington, the source since the Depression of public welfare benefits and the presumptive master of macroeconomic tools to regulate wages and prices.

There is, however, an important emergent development in cities with black mayors, counter to the common drift of municipal politics, which involves the effort of the newly victorious group in city hall to use its control over city government to affect the distribution of income among local residents. If such uses of city government recall traditional machine politics, the techniques in pursuit of these income goals are products of the new public administration. The purpose of this paper is to analyze what is essentially a new-style post-machine patronage politics involving the adaptation of these rationalistic, reform techniques to the traditional aims of ethnic income advancement.

At the outset it must be made clear that the quest for jobs and contracts no longer seems so motivated by the need to reward and control electoral supporters, nor are these efforts the concern exclusively of black mayors; but like much of the machine politics of old, current efforts to use the local polity to augment income reflect, in the hands of black mayors particularly, a politics of ethnic (or racial) advancement. The income goals sought by black politicians specifically for their black constituents occupy a high place in the mayors' agendas and influence their basic strategies of governance.

[2] Greenstein's article (1964) is the classic summary of these reasons.

The major techniques black mayors use in quest of income opportunities for their black constituents involve, first, a variety of affirmative
action rules that bear on public and private sector employment and on
the distribution of city contracts. In addition, since increased black participation in the local labor market and the contracting system require
a healthy local economy, black mayors have pursued a vigorous politics
of economic development, producing a style of governance dominated
by the need to establish close relations with the white business community in their respective cities. The consequences of these efforts, as
we shall see in the data that follow, have been to expand black participation in a variety of public sector income-producing activities in a very
short period of time.

Data pertaining to several aspects of black participation in public
sector employment and in municipal contracting were gathered for six
large cities that had black mayors in office in 1978 (Atlanta, Georgia;
Detroit, Michigan; Gary, Indiana; Washington, D.C.; Los Angeles, California; and Newark, New Jersey). Because no public central depository of
such material exists and because cities are compelled neither to reveal
nor even to save data on these matters, there tend to be gaps and a lack
of comparability in the presentation. Nevertheless, a combination of site
visits and telephone interviews produced sufficient information to suggest an important preoccupation in these cities with using control over
the institutions of local government to enlarge black access to public
money and private payrolls.

ADAPTING THE SYSTEM TO BLACK INCOME GOALS

In contrast to practices in existence in the machine era, nearly all municipal hiring and purchasing today are governed by bureaucratized,
competitive rules. Civil service regulations require hiring largely on the
basis of merit qualifications; city contracts on everything from multi-
million dollar airport expansion to paper clip supplies are let on the
basis of secret, competitive bidding. How, then, have the black mayors
adapted this rationalized system to serve the goal of racial economic
advancement through participation in the receipt of public expenditures? Three principal techniques bear on public sector operations: the
aggressive pursuit of affirmative action strategies, the use of racial criteria
in exercising appointment powers in city government, and the imposition of city residency requirements for municipal civil servants.

Affirmative Action Strategies

Nearly all cities now have local affirmative action laws bearing on municipal employment, and all cities are bound by the 1972 Equal Employment Opportunity Act to hire in a nondiscriminatory way and to report periodically to the federal government on their affirmative action performance. Nevertheless, the existence of such pressures does not necessarily mean that city administrations will pursue affirmative action policies vigorously or even place the hiring of minorities high on the agenda of priorties. For example, although a post of affirmative action officer was created in Atlanta by the white mayor who preceded Maynard Jackson, it was not filled until the black mayor came into office nearly a year and a half later. A study of 16 southern cities averaging more than one-third black in population, none of which had black mayors, found not only that blacks were severely underrepresented in local government service, particularly at the managerial level, but that only 2 of the 16 cities had even developed affirmative action plans in 1975 (King, 10 July 1978:A20).

In cities with black mayors, affirmative action has been used to take the offensive. In contrast to the passivity of personnel officials in cities like Oakland, California, in the early 1970s (Thompson, 1975), personnel departments in contemporary black-mayor cities have not waited for black applicants to appear on their doorsteps but have initiated active recruitment searches. Detroit's personnel office, for example, began a program whereby it identified promising black students in college and offered them internships during their senior year in the hopes of attracting them to city government service after graduation. Atlanta's search for minority city employees took recruiters into surrounding black colleges and even high schools. In both cities the black mayors ordered the reevaluation of selection procedures, which led to a deemphasis on written examinations. In at least five of the six black-mayor cities the head of the personnel office was black. (The race of the sixth was not ascertainable.)

In the five black-mayor cities for which some data are available, it is clear that black public sector employment has been a focus of affirmative action efforts (see Table 1). In the three cases for which data over time are provided, black employment sharply increased. Indeed, this was the case in Atlanta and Detroit, even though total municipal employment in those two cities was decreasing. Black public employment in Los Angeles and Atlanta increased faster than the local black population over the course of the decade. Indeed, black representation in the Los Angeles and Gary city work forces slightly exceeded the proportion of blacks in

Table 1

Black Gains in City Employment, 1973–1980[a]

City[b]	% black population, 1980	% blacks hired[c]	
		1973	1980
Los Angeles (1973)			
Total	17.0	22.0	24.0
Administrators		1.3	6.7
Professionals		5.0	8.8
Newark (1970)			
Total	58.2	—	49.6
Administrators		—	19.5
Professionals		—	51.6
Atlanta (1973)			
Total	66.5	41.5	60.7
Administrators		13.5	35.0
Professionals		19.0	47.2
Detroit (1973)			
Total	63.0	45.1	55.2
Administrators		12.1	41.2
Professionals		22.8	39.2
Gary (1967)			
Total	70.3	—	77.3
Administrators		—	72.3
Professionals		—	70.8

[a]Source: Personnel departments of each city. Washington, D.C., data were not made available.
[b]Date in parentheses is date of the first election of a black mayor.
[c]A dash indicates that data were not available.

those cities. Perhaps most important of all are the sizable advances made by blacks at the top of the civil service employment hierarchy, namely at the administrative and professional levels. In Los Angeles, Detroit, and Atlanta the rate of increase in these categories was substantially more rapid than the rate of increase in total black municipal employment.

The importance of the black mayor in implementing affirmative action polices is suggested by a study of black public employment patterns in 43 large U.S. cities (Eisinger, 1982). Although variations in the percentage of blacks in the municipal work force were largely a function of the proportion of blacks in the population, the presence of a black mayor still explained an additional increment of the variance when black population was controlled in a multiple regression model.

As figures in Table 2 show, black increases in police employment in particular are also dramatic. In the space of 10 years, black representation in the Detroit police force increased sixfold and in Newark and Atlanta

Table 2

Blacks on Police Forces[a]

City	% black in selected years[b]	
Los Angeles	5 (1971)	6 (1978)
Newark	9 (1970)	25 (1977)
Atlanta	9 (1967)	33 (1978)
Detroit	5 (1967)	30 (1978)
Washington, D.C.[c]	22 (1968)	44 (1978)
Gary	22 (1968)	47 (1977)

[a]Source: Police departments of each city.

[b]Record keeping varies markedly from city to city. Some places have data that predate the election of the black mayors; others do not. Dates in parentheses in the first column are the closest to the date of the first election of a black mayor; dates in the second column are the latest for which data were available.

[c]Washington, D.C.'s black mayor was appointed in 1967; the first popular election of a mayor took place in 1974.

threefold. Starting with a higher base, the percentage of blacks on the forces in Gary and Washington, D.C., still doubled. The only exception to this growth occurs in Los Angeles, significantly the only city on the list without a black majority and one of the two cities (the other is Washington, D.C.; Preston, 1976:125) that did not have a black police chief during the mid-1970s.

Besides seeking to expand black employment opportunities in the public sector, black mayors have also attempted to expand the participation of minority-owned firms in city contracting and purchasing. The figures offered in Table 3 are not strictly comparable from city to city because the basis on which statistics are kept varies widely. Nevertheless, the data for Newark, Detroit, and Atlanta show plainly that black participation in public purchasing contracts has swelled from virtually nothing at the beginning of the 1970s to a substantial share by 1980.[3] Such increases cannot be explained by the imposition of federal minority "set-aside" requirements, some of which—regarding public works, for example—date as far back as the Lyndon Johnson administration, because these apply only to federal grants. Rather, initiatives taken by the black-mayor administrations to influence the spending of local revenues appear to be the decisive factors.

[3] Early lack of black participation was not necessarily a function of lack of black enterprises. The number of black-owned businesses with employees in 1972 in Atlanta was 442; in Detroit, 1104; in Gary, 199; and in Washington, D.C., 773 (Howard, 1978:7).

Table 3

City Contracting and Purchasing Awarded to
Minority- Owned Enterprises[a]

City	% of purchase dollars awarded to minorities		In millions of dollars
	1973	1980	1980
Atlanta[b]	2	14	18.2
Washington[b]	—	10[c]	2.5[c]
Detroit[d e]	6	15	22.5
Los Angeles[d f]	—	3	1.9
Newark[f]	1	5	.5
Gary[f]	—	40	6.4

[a]Sources: Individual purchasing, engineering, and redevelopment departments. A dash indicates that data were not available.

[b]Data on total city spending, including equipment, professional and maintenance services, public works, supplies, real estate.

[c]Percentages for first 6 months of 1978 only; dollar amount for 1978. Later figures not available.

[d]Data only on spending handled through a central purchasing department.

[e]Includes nearly all major expenditures and contracts except for professional services and repairs and maintenance.

[f]These figures do not include public works construction spending. Newark spent 18% of its public works funds with minority firms, while 64% of Gary's public works money went to minority firms.

The participation of minority firms in city business has been increased in part by advertising efforts of city purchasing departments that are designed to let black entrepreneurs know the range of products and services the city buys. In Detroit, Los Angeles, and Newark, minority businesspeople are invited to visit the city purchasing department to discuss city needs; Atlanta sends copies of all bid requests to minority business organizations. Los Angeles routinely advertises its needs in the minority print media. In addition, some black-mayor cities have developed more elaborate devices to make possible greater minority business involvement.

In Atlanta, joint venturing enables many small minority firms that could not have submitted bids on their own to participate in city business. All firms in that city that submit a bid on a municipal purchase or project must meet minority hiring goals established by the city's contract compliance officer; a firm not in compliance may have its bid turned back, even if it is the lowest. However, a white-owned firm not in compliance may be allowed to undertake a city contract if it develops a good-faith hiring plan and if it agrees to a joint venture—an arrangement in which the white-owned firm is joined by a black-owned firm in order to merge resources, perform the contractual obligation jointly, and share in the profits on the basis of a negotiated formula. Joint ventures in Atlanta's massive airport expansion project accounted for an estimated $36 million worth of contracts for minority firms in 1977.

Detroit has established a preference system for local firms when its city purchasing department reviews bids. Although not all local firms are minority owned, of course, the preamble to the city ordinance establishing preferential treatment expressly states the intent of the law "to aid those small business concerns which . . . are owned by socially or economically disadvantaged persons [City of Detroit, 1975]." In comparing bids, the ordinance provides that the bid of a local firm is treated as the better bid even if it is as much as 2% higher than that of a firm based outside of Detroit.

It should be noted that in all cities 10% of federal public works funds are set aside by federal law for minority contractors. Newark, however, attempts on its own initiative to set aside a minimum of 25% of these expenditures for minority entrepreneurs, and Gary's redevelopment department maintains a 40% quota. In addition, local ordinances in all six cities require that private firms interested in bidding on city contracts or firms that take advantage of publicly financed tax abatement or economic development plans must meet affirmative action hiring criteria. Although there are few reliable data bearing on the impact of such rules on the racial makeup of the private sector labor force, city officials nevertheless believe that they possess a modest tool to enlarge minority job opportunities in private firms. As the contract compliance officer in Atlanta commented in an interview (May 19, 1978):

We have generated untold numbers of jobs for minority persons in Atlanta, and it's because firms are dependent on city business. Some firms have gone from zero to 20 percent minority workforce. . . . Any overall figures would be soft, but we do know that the policy has changed the composition of the laboring force.

An official in Detroit's economic development agency noted (May 22, 1978) that, "When we lend money to a private firm at a favorable rate or guarantee a loan, we can put plenty of pressure on them to employ people from the neighborhood—like in the East Jefferson auto plant deal that's in the works."

City Government Appointments

A second technique black mayors have used to expand black income opportunities through public sector employment is the appointment of a high proportion of black supervisors to head city agencies. Appoint-

Table 4

Mayoral Appointments of Blacks to
City Government, 1977–1978[a]

City	Department and agency heads %	Boards and commissions %
Atlanta	55.5	46
Gary	66.7	—
Detroit	51.3	44
Los Angeles	—	35
Newark	—	51.4
Washington, D.C.	—	—

[a]A dash indicates that data were not available.

ment powers vary from city to city, but the black mayors of Detroit, Atlanta, and Gary—all strong mayor cities—have appointed blacks to more than half the department head positions (see Table 4). Because department heads ultimately evaluate and promote employees under them, getting blacks into these key "gatekeeper" positions is seen as critical to black employment and advancement opportunities (personal interviews, May 18, 1978; May 23, 1978). Even in Newark, where the mayor's appointive powers are relatively limited, the mayor has been able to appoint blacks in majority numbers to the Affirmative Action Review Council, the Newark Human Rights Commission, and the Committee on the Status of Women, all of which exert influence on agency personnel practices.

City Residency Requirements

A third device that black mayors have used to increase black employment opportunities is the imposition of city residence requirements on municipal workers (see Table 5). Requiring city employees to live within the city limits has recently become an issue laden with racial overtones. Playing particularly on the image of white police forces whose members commute to their jobs from the suburbs as occupying armies in the ghettos, black politicians have been prominent in the call for residency laws. With the city no longer obligated under such laws to draw from the predominantly white metropolitan labor force, black job aspirants in the increasingly black central city face a more favorable structure of competition. Residency requirements are not, of course, designed solely to aid central city minority groups; in regard to police employment, for example, three quarters of all cities over 250,000 have

Table 5

City Residency Requirements for Municipal Employees

City	Action taken under black mayor
Atlanta	Executive order requiring city residence for all appointees (1974). City residency requirement for new police and fire department employees (1976).
Washington, D.C.	City residency requirement for all city employees (1980).
Newark	City residency requirement for all city employees except police, fire, and school personnel, who are exempted by state law (1975).
Gary	City residency requirement for all city employees (1978).
Los Angeles	None. The California state constitution forbids residency laws.
Detroit	None. A general residency requirement was passed in 1968.

such rules (ICMA, 1974:222). It is striking, however, that residency laws were passed in four of the six cities under discussion during black-mayor regimes. In Detroit, Mayor Coleman Young has been a vigorous defender of the residency law when it has come under periodic attack by the Detroit Police Officers Association.

BLACK POLITICAL ALLIANCE WITH WHITE ECONOMIC POWER

Expanding black income opportunities is viewed by urban black mayors as a central issue facing their cities (Hatcher, 1971:123, 128). The quest for jobs and the rhetoric about saving their cities through economic development have at their core a concern with black poverty and unemployment. Reflecting on his Cleveland mayoralty, Carl Stokes (Williams, 1974) once remarked:

Serving all the people is nothing more than campaign rhetoric. No matter what a black candidate for mayor says in his campaign, on taking office he should profess his real responsibility: to help those who are most dependent on government and what it can do for them. That is the blacks. All the ethnic mayors—the LaGuardias, the Fitzsimmonses—have done just that. They have gotten into office and tried to lift the dispossessed, the economically powerless—their people—up the ladder [p. 11].

To produce income opportunities, most black mayors have pursued a strategy designed to establish a partnership with the dominant white business and industrial interests in their city. As Detroit Mayor Coleman Young (Stuart, 1979) puts it, "What is good for the black people of this city is good for the white people of this city [p. 110]." The black mayors operate on the basis of a simple equation: private economic development in the city produces jobs in the private sector and tax money that may be used for jobs and purchases in the public sector. Through the various affirmative action devices discussed earlier, a certain proportion of these jobs and purchases may be channeled to the black community.

Mayor Carl Stokes established the basic pattern when he set out to mobilize a fragmented business community that had shown little interest in the rebuilding of Cleveland (Rogers, 1971:120). The revival of downtown Detroit and the erection of new insurance industry skyscrapers in Newark are to a large extent the fruits of the coalition strategies of Mayors Coleman Young and Kenneth Gibson (on Newark; see Maurer, 10 July 1978:6; *New York Times*, 3 May 1978:A24). Airport expansion and the construction of a mass transit system serving the downtown are the product of Maynard Jackson's occasionally tentative alliance with Atlanta business interests. In Los Angeles, Mayor Tom Bradley was so assiduous in his pursuit of downtown redevelopment in league with the city's business interests that he jeopardized his support in the 1977 election campaign in some segments of the black community, which claimed that he had forgotten them (Nordheimer, 4 April 1977:A18; Hollie, 11 April 1980:A10).

The decision to follow a strategy of coalition with white business means that a number of other possible governing strategies must be foregone. Black autonomous development or separatism is seen not only as too radical in a biracial city but as economically doomed to failure. Coalition with poor whites—that is, the pursuit of a politics of class— is seen as a threat that could drive white business from the city. Coalition with the white middle class, a possible third strategy, is viewed as the least productive alternative of all, because it is among the dwindling central city middle class that opposition to school integration and the sharing of public sector jobs with blacks (on the police force, for example) is lodged. Thus, the black mayors have come to the ironic conclusion that to use the local political system to create income opportunities for blacks, they must forge a coalition with local private money. In a period in which federal grants are insufficient to offset the inflation that local governments face, it is assumed that private investment finally determines whether local tax revenues will reach sufficiently high levels to permit the hiring of new policemen or enable the city to meet the matching requirements of job- and contract-producing federal public works grants.

Thus, in most black-mayor cities, the governing coalition represents an alliance of white economic power and the black political power. Although it is not yet entirely clear how much these alliances are affecting black income levels on an aggregate basis, there are in the meantime certain negative costs to bear. Black mayors are occasionally accused by black groups of having sold out to the white corporate rulers, and therefore must spend a good deal of time performing rituals of reassurance before ghetto audiences. There is also a problem in such coalitions of finding a meaningful role for the white middle class to play in the affairs of the city. Certain of their political resources—their votes and their money—are virtually superfluous. Yet they constitute the clientele for many of the institutions and activities that give a city its character—its cultural amenities, shops, restaurants, libraries, universities, and so on— as well as a significant proportion of the city's taxpayers. The consequences of their possible loss of interest in a city in which they play no great role in the governing process are grave.

THE POLITICS OF ECONOMIC ADVANCEMENT

Machine politics in American cities began to disappear, according to accepted doctrine, in large part because the federal government began to take over, universalize, and bureaucratize the machine's income functions. The character of urban government, whatever it became, was no longer defined by its income-producing activities. To win control of city hall these days is no longer considered an achievement of great substantive value. Power is said to reside elsewhere: in metropolitan bodies, in Washington, D.C.; in the state capital; in public employee union halls. Cities are too dependent economically on sources of revenues that they do not control, and their powers are constrained by restrictive charters. It has taken the emergence of black urban mayors, however, to rediscover the possibilities for expanding income opportunities for ordinary people through a new style politics of post-machine patronage.

A complete assessment of the impact of affirmative action policies on black employment patterns would, of course, have to take into account the gains made by black workers in private sector jobs as well as public employment. To an unknown degree, new jobs in the private sector for blacks are created in part by affirmative action pressures on those contractors who work with the city and on firms that take advantage of public economic development subsidies. Other jobs are undoubtedly created as a result of the expansion or formation of black-owned firms in response to the new business opportunities in city contracting.

It is clear from the figures on public employment alone, however, that public sector affirmative action does not offer a strategy for full employment. The impact of public sector jobs is, at least in terms of numbers, a relatively limited one. Assuming for the sake of argument that each worker supports a family of four people, black public servants would support a total of no more than 6–8% of the total black population of the cities under examination. But this is not to say that the public sector labor corps is unimportant to the black community. If nothing else, employment in the municipal civil service helps to create a sizable, secure middle-class group in the black community. Bound by residency laws to the city, this group may be expected to use its considerable civic and financial resources, not in the surrounding bedroom suburbs, but in the place they work. The economic security of black civil servants cannot be minimized: despite fiscal pressures on cities, civil service employment provides steadier work than the private sector; it is generally better paid for similar work; and it provides more generous fringe benefits (Perloff, 1971). In addition, the public sector offers many blacks a chance to learn managerial skills that may possibly provide lateral access to the private sector at a high level. In theory, such an economically stable group should provide a certain measure of leadership for the larger black community.

But there are other gains for the black community at large in the entry of large numbers of blacks into public service. The presence of blacks in policy-making and policy-implementing positions in the municipal bureaucracy may be expected to do much to remedy some of the tensions and dissatisfactions bred by the social asymmetry between civil servants and those they serve (Yates, 1977:132–133). Finally, the members of this group provide a stable platform in the social mobility ladder for their children.

Establishing historical comparisons with other ethnic groups to put these figures and this analysis into perspective is a difficult task. However, the Irish experience provides the most obvious analogy. Irish political power in American cities developed in the decades around the turn of the century. A major consequence of their local political success was the capture of a disproportionate share of public sector jobs at all levels and of government contracts. Although the general pattern is well known and innumerable case studies exist of Irish patronage and municipal employment strategies, there are few hard data to make direct, aggregate comparisons with the current black experience.

Stephen Erie's (1978) work on San Francisco, however, permits a limited comparison by allowing us to estimate the extent to which local municipal employment supported the Irish population in that city in 1900 (a year in which the Irish dominated the city's politics and municipal work force). Irish city employees in San Francisco, constituting slightly more than one-third of the entire public service work force, probably supported no more than 10% of the Irish population.[4]

Set against the extraordinary level of Irish socioeconomic achievement by the 1970s, such a figure does not seem insignificant. Public service jobs seem to have established for the Irish an economically secure lower middle and middle class, which, if initially small, nevertheless provided the resources to support and encourage the advancement of succeeding generations. By 1970, the Irish ranked as the most successful gentile group in the United States on most measures of socioeconomic achievement (Greeley, 1976:45–56).

Since the days of Irish dominance in city jobs, the public sector has grown significantly, opening up more substantial employment opportunities for blacks than the Irish had. Furthermore, black politicians have a battery of affirmative action tools, unknown to the Irish, to bring pressure to bear on private employers. Black business and black labor may also be expected to grow as local government spending increases and with the additional opening of the municipal purchasing and contracting process to black entrepreneurs. All of these gains, upon which a certain segment of the urban black population may be expected to build a substantial level of economic security for succeeding generations, have come in large part as a consequence of manipulating the local political system. Winning influence in or control of city hall, then, is no mere symbolic achievement for blacks: mastering local government can have significant economic consequences for blacks.

[4] My calculations were made as follows. The first- and second-generation Irish population in San Francisco in 1900 amounted to approximately 80,500. Irish workers held a combined total of 2551 public service jobs in federal, state, and local government. Generously assuming that 2000 of these jobs might have been municipal in character and multiplying by a factor of 4, we arrive at a figure of slightly less than 10% of the Irish population supported by the city payroll. (For the figures on which my calculations were based, see Erie [1978:281].)

REFERENCES

City of Detroit
    1975   Ordinance 52-H. Detroit: City of Detroit.
Eisinger, P.
    1982   Black employment in municipal jobs: the impact of black political power. *American Political Science Review* **76**(June): 380–392.
Erie, S.
    1978   Politics, the public sector and Irish social mobility: San Francisco, 1870–1900. *Western Political Quarterly* **31**(June):274–289.

Greeley, A.

    1976   *Ethnicity, Denomination, and Inequality.* Beverly Hills, Calif.: Sage.

Greenstein, F.

    1964   The changing pattern of urban party politics. *Annals* **353**(May):1–13.

Hatcher, R.

    1971   The black man in United States politics, in *The Black Politician* (M. Dymally, Ed.), pp. 120–134. Belmont, Calif.: Duxbury.

Hollie, P.

    1980   Downtown Los Angeles getting new focus. *New York Times* **April 11**:A10.

Howard, J.

    1978   A framework for the analysis of urban black politics. *Annals* **439**(September):1–15.

International City Management Association (ICMA)

    1974   Police and fire personnel policies in cities over 50,000. *Municipal Yearbook.* Washington, D.C.: International City Management Association.

Johnston, M.

    1979   Patrons and clients, jobs and machines: a case study of the uses of patronage. *American Political Science Review* **73**(June): 385–398.

King, W.

    1978   Southern blacks, women, found in low city jobs. *New York Times* **May 25**:A20.

Maurer, A.

    1978   "Going the route" with Newark and Gibson. *New York Times* **July 10**:6.

New York Times

    1978   Editorial. *New York Times* **May 3**:A24.

Nordheimer, J.

    1977   Los Angeles, despite problems, regards vote for mayor passively. *New York Times* **April 4**:A18.

Perloff, S.

    1971   Comparing municipal salaries with industry and federal pay. *Monthly Labor Review* **94** (October):46–50.

Preston, M.

    1976   The limitations of black urban power: the case of black mayors, in *The New Urban Politics* (L. Masotti and R. Lineberry, Eds.), 111–132. Cambridge, Mass.: Ballinger.

Rogers, D.

    1971   *The Management of Big Cities.* Beverly Hills, Calif.: Sage.

Stuart, R.

    1979   The new black power of Coleman Young. *New York Times Magazine* **December 16**:102–114.

Thompson, F. J.

    1975   *Personnel Policy in the City.* Berkeley: University of California Press.

Williams, R.

    1974   America's black mayors: are they saving the cities? *Saturday Review* **1**(May 4):10–13.

Yates, D.

    1977   *The Ungovernable City.* Cambridge, Mass.: MIT Press.

6

Middle-Class White Ethnics in Suburbia: A Study of Italian-Americans*

Donald V. Fandetti
Donald E. Gelfand

Introduction

In his comprehensive overview of European ethnicity in the United States, Greeley (1974) developed an extended discussion around the question, Does ethnicity matter? Despite extensive writing on the topic, the issue of ethnicity's importance has yet to be resolved. In order to move toward a greater agreement concerning the importance of ethnicity, there first needs to be continued clarification of the importance of ethnic identity and ethnic culture in a variety of behaviors and attitudes. Second, more widespread agreement on what would constitute valid evidence is required. Third, the discussion and examination of ethnicity need to be extended to a wider variety of populations. In this sense we are talking not only about studying additional ethnic groups, but also about refraining from generalizing from population groups that remain based in inner-city areas when large segments of the metropolitan population have shifted to the suburbs. In this paper we report on an initial, but certainly not final, effort to examine the role of ethnicity among a primarily third-generation, suburban, Italian-American population.

* This research was supported in part by a grant from the Graduate School of the University of Maryland at Baltimore. We are grateful for the cooperation of Melvin Kohn throughout the course of this research. The comments of Anthony Conto and Charles Harris on earlier drafts of this paper were also greatly appreciated.

ETHNIC IDENTIFICATION AND CHANGE

In recent years social scientists such as Parenti (1967), Issacs (1972), and Greeley (1974) have attributed increased importance to ethnic identification as a developing social phenomenon. There has also been renewed interest in the persistence of ethnic cultural differences as the acceptance of melting pot theories of assimilation continues to decline. The persistence of ethnic cultural traits, is, of course, not necessarily dependent on a continuing sense of awareness and identification with ethnic background and culture.

The importance of this distinction should not be underestimated. Individuals who have negated any conscious identification with their ethnic heritage may still internalize its value system and implicitly transmit these values to their children. Greeley's (1972) emphasis on child socialization thus seems particularly pertinent:

> I am convinced that certain ethnic traits can be passed on through the early childhood socialization process, whereby a child learns role expectations in relation to parents, siblings, cousins, aunts and uncles, close friends. . . . I think this may be the most important aspect of ethnic heritage, and it is not less important because it can occur without conscious concern for such transmission on the part of parents or children [p. 8].

Our interest was to explore (1) the degree to which Italian-Americans who are not living in ethnically cohesive communities in the inner city maintain a strong sense of identification with their Italian heritage; (2) the degree to which ethnic culture is influential in their values and social orientations.

The focus upon Italian-Americans allowed us to examine a frequently studied group whose cultural traditions have been viewed as markedly distinct from those of the majority American society.

In order to place the study sample and the findings in an appropriate framework, we must briefly review the contemporary social science portrayal of Italian-American culture.

ITALIANS AND ITALIAN-AMERICANS

Contemporary literature on Italian-Americans has focused on the first-generation immigrant family and their second-generation offspring in the industrial cities of the Northeast and Mid-Atlantic. Unfortunately, ethnic culture among third- and fourth-generation Italian-Americans remains a relatively unexplored area of empirical research. Summarizing the prevailing literature provides a picture of the history of Italian-Americans and their presumed common characteristics.

History of Immigrants

Italian immigrants to the United States during the early part of the twentieth century came largely from provinces to the east and south of Rome, a region known as the *Mezzogiorno*. The migrants from this region were illiterate peasant farmers and propertyless agricultural day workers. The social structure of their region was characterized by grinding poverty, a closed class system, and exploitative economic and political institutions (Iorizzo and Mondello, 1971). The attitudes and behavioral patterns spurned by this socioeconomic environment in southern Italy have been the focus of numerous investigations.

Southern Italian Attitudes and Behavior

According to sociologists and anthropologists, the degradation and harshness of the southern Italian social structure fostered among Italian peasants a tradition of resignation characterized by the belief that the individual had little control over his or her life situation. The emphasis was on the role of *destino*, or fate (Rosen, 1959). The southern Italian male learned to be a man of "patience." In this case patience implied inner control, reserve, waiting, and planning rather than reacting impetuously or in an ill-controlled fashion (Gambino, 1975). This orientation, however, cannot be viewed as uniquely Italian; southern Italian orientations to change are comparable to the pattern of other peasant societies. In the face of misfortune and the forces of nature, fatalistic attitudes among peasants reflected a belief that individual or collective efforts did not make a difference (Papajohn and Spiegel, 1975).

Southern Italian Family and Society

Studies suggest that in southern Italy a sharp bifurcation existed between the immediate family and the rest of the society. Living in a social structure where the major institutions were only marginally effective and where the country was frequently dominated by a foreign power, the Italian family was viewed as the only reliable institution. Little trust was extended to outsiders beyond the family circle (Gans, 1962). For the southern Italian peasant the village was the true *patria*, or country. The world, in this view, extended only as far as the sound of the village church bell. Individuals from other towns were strangers to be viewed with suspicion (Covello, 1967; Vecoli, 1974), and extrafamilial institutions were viewed with contempt. Laws were obeyed only because of the fear of punishment. In his well-known study, Banfield (1958) concluded that moral values among southern Italians applied primarily to family members. The southern Italian peasant thus acted to maximize the material short-run advantage of the family and assumed that all others did the same (Gans, 1962). More recently, Lopreato (1970) challenged the tendency to portray the ethnic content of Italian folkways in a negative light.

In the *Mezzogiorno* the individual was not perceived as independent of the family unit. Members of the family tended to be tied to expected and predictable roles by a general conformity that ensured the continuity of the family's normative system (Tomasi, 1972). The basic value orientation in this social structure was collateral rather than individual, stressing the primacy of family goals and welfare over individual aspirations. The young southern Italian existed in a closed familistic system in which obedience, dedication, and respect were centered on parental figures (Tomasi, 1972).

Italian-American Culture

A review of *Mezzogiorno* culture is important, since Italian-American culture is usually depicted as a compound of southern Italian and urban working-class folkways (Vecoli, 1974). In the environment of the new world, the second-generation offspring of immigrant parents were confronted with a struggle to reconcile the old ways of their immigrant parents with urban American social values and institutions. Under the dual socialization of southern Italian and American culture, second-generation Italian-Americans experienced personal conflict affecting their social identity and their adaptation to American institutions. Some writers continue to find evidence of conflict. Gambino (1975), for example, has argued that young third-generation Italian-Americans in contemporary American society continue to experience identity conflict. Their problem, he asserts, centers on a "pervasive identity crisis" that undermines the Italian-American's capacity for initiative, self-confidence, and assertiveness.

SAMPLE AND METHODS

The sample studied in this research is distinctly different in socioeconomic attributes from the national composition of Italian-Americans cited by Roof (1979). The Italian men included in the present study were residents of Columbia, Maryland, a "new town" strategically located midway between Washington, D.C., and Baltimore. Since its opening in 1967,

Columbia has been one of the most successful new town developments undertaken during the past 20 years.

During its initial stage, the community attracted individuals committed to its promise of planned residential, recreational, and business facilities. Columbia now appears to be attracting a mix of individuals, including many families who are less interested in the new town concept than the good schools available in Columbia and the relatively reasonable housing prices. A recent study by the Columbia Association (1978) indicates that Columbia's growth is now based not only on individuals moving from other regions of the country but on families moving from expensive yet less desirable suburbs in the Baltimore–Washington area. We thus believe that the demographic, socioeconomic, and attitudinal characteristics of the Columbia sample are representative of many upwardly mobile middle-class individuals in suburban communities.

To provide some understanding of the role of ethnicity among suburbanized Italian-Americans, a sample of 200 males with Italian surnames was drawn at random from the 1979 Columbia phone directory. Based on a recent needs-assessment of the elderly in a similar Maryland county (Burkhardt, Annan, and Dietz, 1977), we assumed that this directory included 97% of all Columbia residents. Because of the problem of name changes resulting from marriage, only males were included in the sample.

The questionnaire mailed to the sample focused on three major parameters: (1) the identification of the respondents with their Italian backgrounds measured by Sandberg's "ethnic group cohesion scale" (1974) originally utilized in a study of Poles in Los Angeles, (2) a 13-item index on parental values for children, and (3) a 45-item value index containing measures of social orientation and self-conception. These two latter indices were used by Kohn (1977) in his study of occupational values and class and reanalyzed by Greeley (1972, 1974, 1977) for ethnic differences. In order to limit the time commitment required from respondents, the mail questionnaire utilized only the items that had high loading in Kohn's factor analysis. The reduction in the items does not allow for replication of the factor analysis originally undertaken, but an analysis of the importance of individual items has been carried out through extensive cross-tabulations and correlational analyses. Two mailings and follow-up phone calling resulted in 113 usable responses, a total response rate of 56%.

The demographic and socioeconomic characteristics of the Columbia men responding to the questionnaire are comparable to the sample of the overall Columbia population studied by the Columbia Association in 1978. Eighty-three percent of the respondents had either a college or graduate school degree and were overwhelmingly employed in professional and managerial positions. Over half of the men had family incomes over $30,000, and an additional one-third had family incomes over $20,000. The median age was 36.

Columbia was not the area of second settlement for these men, only 4% of them having moved to the community directly from an ethnic neighborhood. The vast majority, however, had lived in the mid-Atlantic region before coming to live in Columbia. Thirty-six percent of the men had been raised in an ethnic neighborhood. Because there were few first-generation immigrants in the sample, the major division was between second- and third-generation Italian-Americans. Among the third-generation respondents 70% had been raised outside an ethnic community, and three-fourths of the entire sample was married to non-Italians.

Moving to Columbia meant moving away from the ethnic community and also living at a distance from relatives. Unlike a Baltimore working-class sample recently studied (Fandetti and Gelfand, 1976, 1978), almost 60% of the respondents did not live in close proximity to either parents or siblings; these relatives lived more than 200 miles away. Although the men in the study asserted that they spent their holidays with relatives, their network of social relationships was by necessity built around friends in the immediate vicinity. Because of the heterogeneity of the community and the respondents' attitude toward ethnicity discussed later, the majority of these friends were non-Italians. Interaction with family members was maintained through phone contact. Two-thirds of the respondents contacted their parents at least once every other week.

Although the move to Columbia must attentuate the daily direct contact with relatives that is stressed in the literature on Italians, it does not necessarily imply a substitute "joining" mentality that was associated with suburbia by writers in the 1950s. The list of formal organizations that the sample belongs to was not impressive. Only 25% belonged to a community association; 12% were members of a local school organization. Eleven percent belonged to church groups, and only 7% belonged to an ethnic organization such as the Sons of Italy. In sum, the sample forming the focus of this study is comparable to the Class I and II (Hollinghead index) individuals in the sample reported by Kohn (1977).

FINDINGS

Ethnic Identification

As is true of other global terms, "ethnic identification" is not a monolithic concept. Few researchers have been able to come to grips with the complex set of elements that must be included in any ethnic identification scale. As Manual (1978) notes, validation of the utility of the Sandberg scale for studying minority groups has yet to be undertaken, but few alternative scales of ethnic identification are yet available.

Sandberg's scale utilizes an ethnic identity model based on a composite of four major factors: (1) Cultural; (2) National: (3) Religious Associational; (4) Religious Communal. In toto, the Sandberg scale includes 30 items, 10 assessing the cultural subconstruct, 10 national, and 10 that combine religious associational and communal.[1]

On a Likert scale ranging from 1 (strongly agree) to 6 (strongly disagree) the mean subscale scores of the Columbia sample were Cultural, 3.36; National, 3.94; and Religious Communal, 4.27. The strongest reaction was the negative response to the associational aspects of the church, 4.6.

Although the mean scores on the subscales do not indicate strongly negative or positive feelings about ethnic identification, analysis of individual items provides a clearer picture of the feelings of this middle-class population than can be seen from the combined means. The most discriminating items are shown in Table 1, which includes all items at least one standard deviation from the mean of all scale items.

The scores in Table 1 indicate important attitudinal stances among these Italian men. First, Columbians objected to the suggestions that other Italians could not be relied upon, or that they would feel more comfortable with fellow Italians. Second, they objected strongly to any assertion that they could be influenced by the fact that a political candidate was of Italian background.

The belief that an Italian church is preferable because it allows the individual to be with his or her own kind was rejected, as was any emphasis on the use of Italian in church services. Third, what was viewed as most important was the transmission of Italian culture and history and the maintenance of organizations that could serve as transmitters of this heritage. Despite this stress on Italian heritage, the belief in endogamous marriages among the sample was not strong.

As in previous research on white ethnics (Fandetti and Gelfand, 1976, 1978), the importance of generation in attitude formation and maintenance cannot be overlooked. In the present study there were significant differences by generation of immigration in total ethnic scores, $(p < .05)$;

---

[1] The Cultural subscale measures responses to key indicators of cultural life apart from religion and nationality. Religious Associational deals with feelings regarding participation in ethnic church services and the importance of the church to the individual. The Religious Communal subscale focuses on the value of the church for others in the kin and ethnic group and feelings of personal responsibility for reaching out to them. The National subscale measures the importance of ethnic solidarity, feeling of peoplehood with others of similar background, and sensitivity to ethnic background.

Table 1

Discriminating Items on Ethnic Cohesiveness Scale:
Scale Items 1 Standard Deviation from Mean

Item	Score[a]
Cultural	
Organizations which carry on Italian culture are important.	2.2
Our children should learn to speak Italian.	3.0
Maryland does not need an Italian newspaper.	3.1
We don't need to know the history of the Italian people.	4.6
National	
An Italian neighborhood is a friendlier place to live.	3.1
It is better to marry someone of your own nationality.	4.6
I would vote for an Italian political candidate rather than any other nationality regardless of political party.	5.1
If you're in trouble you cannot count on Italian people to help you.	5.4
Religious	
I feel more comfortable in an Italian church.	4.5
Our people should get their families to the Italian church on Sundays.	4.5
It is important for me to contribute my time, talent, and finances to the Italian church.	4.8
I prefer a church where services are in the Italian language.	5.0
You should belong to the Italian church even if it is far from your home.	5.2

[a]Scale items range from 1, "strongly agree" to 6, "strongly disagree." Mean for all 30 scale items = 3.87; S.D. = .7.

third-generation men expressed significantly less identification with their Italian background than their second-generation counterparts. Ethnic identification was also weaker among individuals who were raised outside of an ethnic neighborhood ($p < .02$) and lower among individuals who socialize primarily with friends rather than with relatives ($p < .02$).

Italian Suburbanites and Parenting

The values probed by Sandberg's scale provide a sense of ethnic group cohesiveness among Columbians, but they fail to probe other important attitudes. Kohn's (1977) national study has provided researchers with a valuable resource for examining parental values related to the child socialization process and in assessing important general value orientations among class, religious, and ethnic groupings.

The Kohn index of parental values consists of a list of 13 commonly valued characteristics. Columbia respondents were asked to choose the 3 most desirable characteristics and the 1 most desirable of all. They also chose the 3 least important and the 1 least important of all.[2] These choices were only made for boys.

The index measures characteristics that the respondents consider to be important but problematic in realizing. Four characteristics (good manners, being neat and clean, obedience to parents, and acting like a boy) reflect a traditional value orientation stressing conformity to imposed external standards. The other characteristics, except "tries hard to succeed" and "gets along well with children," reflect an orientation toward self-direction. The self-direction orientation stresses internal dynamics such as thinking for oneself, flexibility, and empathetic regard for other persons. This description of the index does not fully coincide with Kohn's. The major difference lies in Kohn's assumption that a valuation of honesty reflects conformity. His belief is that honesty connotes self-directed behavior among middle-class individuals but not among lower-class populations. Because of the high socioeconomic status of our sample, we have chosen to consider honesty as an indicator of the individuals' self-direction.

Table 2 shows that the differences between Kohn's findings and our data are slight. The traditional characteristics (good manners, being neat and clean, acting like a boy, and obedience to parents) tend to be even less valued in Columbia than in the national sample. In sum, the mean scores of the Columbia men and Kohn's Class I and Class II individuals are comparable. All three of these groups reject the values associated with conformity. Interestingly, the item that provoked the strongest feeling among Columbia men was the issue of whether a boy should "act like a boy." The suburban men obviously reject any implications that they have implicit sex-based role orientations. Wright and Wright's (1976) analysis of the parental values index scores of a 1973 national sample indicated a response pattern consistent with our data. The major differentiation among the Columbian sample was the stronger emphasis they placed on "good judgment."

In contrast to the findings on ethnic identification, generation of immigration, being raised in an Italian-American neighborhood, or socializing with friends rather than relatives does not provide any differentiation among individuals on the parental values. There is also limited relationship between total ethnicity scores of respondents and these parental values. As in the Kohn national sample, the Columbia data show

---

[2] Respondents' valuations of each characteristic were scored on a five point scale: 5, the most valued of all; 4, one of the three most valued, but not the most valued; 3, neither one of the three most nor one of the three least valued; 2, one of the three last valued, but not the least valued; 1, the least valued of all.

that the degree of ethnic identity among respondents in Columbia does not appreciably change the picture regarding their parental values.

Social Orientations

Conceptions of the external world among Columbia men were examined by several questions taken from Kohn's indices of social orientation and self-conception. Responses to these questions indicated the extent to which the Columbia sample deviated from the norms associated with southern Italian culture. Using Kohn's approach, we investigated four aspects of social orientation: Authoritarianism, Criteria for Morality, Trustfulness, and Stance toward Change (Kohn, 1977).

> 1. *Authoritarian Conservatism*. Definition of what is socially acceptable. At one extreme rigid conformance to the dictate of authority; at the other, openmindedness. The average percentage of agreement among Columbians with authoritarian assertions was 14%.[3]
>
> 2. *Criteria for Morality*. A continuum of moral positions, from opportunistic to highly responsible. The average percentage of agreement on opportunistic assertions was 15%.[4]
>
> 3. *Trustfulness*. The degree to which men believe that their fellow men can be trusted. The average percentage of agreement on assertions of trustfulness was 65%.[5]
>
> 4. *Stance toward Change*. Men's receptiveness or resistance to innovation and change. Twelve percent of the Columbian respondents thought it best to keep on doing things as before. Seventy-two percent said they work toward definite goals. Twenty-five percent stated that they were the first to try something out, 10% would wait and see, and 66% felt that their actions depended on the action or object that was in question.[6]

[3] Indexed by agreement with such assertions as: Young people should not be allowed to read books that are likely to confuse them. In this complicated world, the only way to know what to do is to rely on leaders and experts. People who question the old and accepted ways of doing things usually just end up causing trouble. There are two kinds of people in the world: the weak and strong.

[4] Indexed by agreement or disagreement with the statements: If something works, it doesn't matter whether it's right or wrong. It's all right to get around the law as long as you don't actually break it. It's all right to do anything you want as long as you stay out of trouble. It's all right to do whatever the law allows.

[5] Indexed by agreement to the statements: Human nature is really cooperative. If you don't watch out, people will take advantage of you. Most people can be trusted.

[6] Indexed by responses to the following: It generally works out best to keep on doing things the way they have been done before. Are you generally one of the first people to try out something, or do you wait until you see how it's worked out for other people? Are you the sort of person who takes life as it comes, or are you working toward some definite goals?

Table 2

Parental Values for Columbia and National Sample Classes I and II

	Mean Score[a]		
Characteristic	Columbia $N = 113$	Kohn's Class I $N = 74$	Kohn's Class II $N = 192$
Honest	3.89	3.59	3.55
Good sense and sound judgment	3.84	3.18	3.10
Considerate of others	3.47	3.41	3.36
Responsible	3.47	3.09	3.05
Gets along with other children	3.39	3.06	3.32
Tries to succeed	3.26	2.91	2.72
Interested in how and why things happen	3.13	3.09	2.99
Obeys his parents	3.07	3.42	3.61
Self-control	2.91	2.95	2.90
Good student	2.91	2.55	2.48
Good manners	2.64	2.84	2.94
Neat and clean	2.37	2.26	2.40
Acts as a boy should	1.80	2.79	2.77

[a]High valuation is indicated by a score of 5, low by a score of 1.

Based on their scores on these four indices, Columbia respondents can be characterized as open-minded, responsible, trustful, and willing to work toward new goals rather than remaining rooted in previous behavior patterns.

Conceptions of Self

Self-conceptions of the Columbia sample were investigated along four dimensions also utilized by Kohn (1977): Self-confidence, Self-depreciation, Attribution of Responsibility, and Idea-Conformity. Responses to questions related to these four aspects of self-conception provided an indication of whether Columbia men viewed themselves as competent, effective, and in control of the forces that shaped their life.

1. *Self-confidence*. The positive component of self-esteem: the degree to which men are confident in their own capacities. The average percentage of agreement with assertions of self-confidence was 94%.[7]

---

[7] Indexed by agreement with such assertions as: I generally have confidence that when I make plans I will be able to carry them out. I take a positive attitude toward myself. I feel that I'm a person of worth at least on an equal plane with others. I am able to do things as well as other people can.

2. *Self-depreciation.* The self-critical half of self-esteem: the degree to which men disparage themselves. The average percentage of agreement with assertions of self-depreciations was 21%.[8]

3. *Attribution of Responsibility.* Men's sense of being controlled by outside forces or of having some control over their own fate. Seventy-seven percent of the Columbia Italians viewed themselves as partly or mostly to blame for problems. Only 5% felt that what happened to them was the result of events over which they had no control. Eighty-eight percent attributed some responsibility to themselves when "things go wrong."[9]

4. *Idea-Conformity.* The degree to which men believe their ideas mirror those of the social entities to which they belong. The average percentage of respondents indicating that their ideas differed from relatives, friends, persons of the same religion, and most other people was 94%.[10]

These four conceptions of self highlight a group of Italian-American men who are confident about themselves and willing to take responsibility for their actions and blame for their failures. They also assert a confidence about adopting ideas that may not exactly conform to those of the groups to which they belong.

A correlational matrix of social orientation and conception of self indicators did not illuminate any theoretical relationships. As was expected, however, there were significant correlations between indicators of self-conception and generation of immigration, being raised in an ethnic neighborhood, and socializing with friends rather than relatives. The correlations (.2 to .3) had a consistent directionality with generation, place of rearing, and socializing patterns correlating with attitudinal stances contrary to traditional Italian values. Thus, being third generation, raised outside an ethnic neighborhood, and socializing primarily with nonrelatives correlates positively with self-direction and self-confidence.

[8] Indexed by agreement with such assertions as: I feel useless at times. I wish I could be as happy as others seem to be. I wish I could have more respect for myself. At times I think I am no good at all. There are very few things about which I am absolutely certain.

[9] Indexed by the following: To what extent would you say you are to blame for the problems you have? Do you feel that most of the things that happen to you are the result of your own decisions or of things over which you have no control? When things go wrong for you, how often would you say it is your own fault?

[10] Indexed by the following: According to your general impressions, how often do your ideas and opinions about important matters differ from those of your relatives, friends, people of your religious background, most people in the country?

The responses of the Italian men in Columbia are consistent with Kohn's (1977) conclusion that the "higher the social class position, the more men value self-direction and the more confident they are that self-direction is both possible and efficacious [p. 86]." As was true in the case of parental values, the social orientations and self-conceptions of the Columbians thus closely resemble the upper-class individuals in Kohn's sample.

The Continued Importance of Ethnicity

The overall neutral responses on Sandberg's ethnic cohesiveness subscales are reminiscent of the "apathetic reaction" described by Child (1943) in his early study of second-generation Italian-Americans. Child found that most second-generation Italians failed to react strongly as they adapted to American culture. The majority were apathetic in the sense that their dual socialization experience elicited no strong personal reactions about their ethnic background. Most members of the second generation accommodated to both the old ways of the immigrant parents and the larger culture of the United States. Typically, they gradually attempted to gain full membership in American society. A smaller number of second-generation Italians rebelled against their Italian background or remained closely tied to southern Italian folkways of their immigrant parents.

Importantly, Columbia Italians tend to reject ethnic religious organizations and any localized orientations that these organizations suggest. They do not favor voting for fellow ethnic political candidates and reject any suggestion that it would be more appropriate for them to live in ethnically cohesive neighborhoods. We can assume that their common feeling was that their income, education, and occupational status now provides them with the options to determine each of these decisions on an individual rather than a group basis.

However, the responses of Columbia Italians on items related to cultural heritage and history on the cultural subscale (Table 1) are consistent with the Hansen (1938) thesis that successful third-generation descendants of immigrants would seek to reestablish a sense of continuity with their cultural roots. The Columbia data tend to lend support to Greeley's (1975) prediction that successful Italian-Americans continue to legitimate ethnic cultural pluralism. Our data suggest that Italian-Americans with high socioeconomic status seek to keep their ethnic groups' historical experience alive in the United States.

Parental Values and Social Orientations

The Columbia data on social values do not appear to support the point of view that the cultural heritage of southern Italy persists among second- and third-generation Italian-Americans. The open-minded, self-confident men in the sample do not match the response pattern that would be predicted on the basis of knowledge of southern Italian cultural orientations.

Born during the "baby boom" period, this sample appears to have internalized many of the values that become common during the 1950s. Their parental beliefs are consistent with the trend toward self-direction noted by Wright and Wright (1976). Their emphasis on good judgment is not suprising among such an upwardly mobile group. Kohn found Italians to be one of the most "conforming" of all of the nationality groups included in his study; however, as opposed to the Columbian sample, 46% of Kohn's Italians were in Class IV and 33% in Class III. The self-conceptions and the values of the Columbian Italians fit the common description of an upper middle-class group.

As Greeley (1977) has argued, it is very likely that the fatalism of first-generation Italian-Americans has been overstated. In contrast to the apathetic second-generation Italians whom Child studied, upwardly mobile third-generation individuals may have merely regained the earlier determination of their grandparents to improve their position in the New World.

ETHNIC CHANGE IN COLUMBIA AND THE UNITED STATES

The Columbia respondents represent a group that has been able to achieve considerable economic and social success in the business and professional worlds of the United States (Greeley, 1977). Their value orientations, ethnic identifications, and living patterns seem considerably altered from those traditionally viewed as part of Italian-American culture. Their high rate of intermarriage and their low rate of visitation with relatives would also appear to be contrary to patterns among Italian-Americans.

It is thus possible that the Columbia respondents represent a self-selected group of individuals who have moved to the suburban community because it meets their cultural needs rather than a group that is representative of change in the larger Italian-American community. Behavioral indicators of change from other studies, however, indicate that the pattern among the Columbia sample may be consistent with that of Italians nationwide. Alba and Kessler (1979) noted that intermarriage rates among Italians are high and increasing with each succeeding age cohort. Greeley's (1977) data also indicate that increased occupational status among Italians is associated with a lessening of interaction with relatives.

CONCLUSION

Examined together, the Columbia, Kohn, and Wright and Wright analyses indicate a general convergence among middle-class Italian Americans to the parental and social values of the dominant society. It would thus appear that social mobility and acculturation will diminish many of the distinctive values that have typified white ethnic groups in the United States. As Italian-Americans become a significant segment of the suburban middle class and raise their children in heterogeneous suburbs, we may find the fourth-generation descendants of the "new" immigration of the late 1800s sounding more like their middle-class Anglo-Saxon neighbors. Farber's (1979) analysis of Jews in Kansas City would lead us to predict a shift in some ethnic values among many groups. White ethnics will maintain a strong desire to transmit their proud ethnic heritage to their children but not to transmit the values they regard as parochial or inhibiting of "success."

REFERENCES

Alba, R., and Kessler, R.
    1979   Patterns of interethnic marriage among American Catholics. *Social Forces* **57**:1124–
           1140.
Banfield, E., and Bainfield, L.
    1958   *The Moral Basis of a Backward Society*. New York: The Free Press.
Burkhardt, J., Annan, S., and Dietz, S.
    1977   *The Status and Needs of Montgomery County's Senior Citizens*. Rockville, Md.:
           Westat.
Child, I. L.
    1943   *Italian or American: The Second Generation in Conflict*. New Haven: Yale Uni-
           versity Press.
Columbia Association
    1978   *Columbia Survey: Preliminary Results*. Columbia, Md.: Columbia Association.
Covello, L.
    1967   *The Social Background of the Italo-American School Child*. Leiden, Netherlands:
           E. J. Brill.
Fandetti, D., and Gelfand, D.
    1976   Care of the aged: attitudes of white ethnic families. *Gerontologist* **16**:544–549.
    1978   Attitudes towards symptoms and services in the ethnic family and neighbor-
           hoods. *American Journal of Orthopsychiatry* **48**:477-485.

Farber, B.
    1979   Kinship mapping among Jews in a midwestern city. *Social Forces* **57**:1107–1123.
Gambino, R.
    1975   *Blood of My Blood*. New York: Anchor Books.
Gans, H.
    1962   *The Urban Villagers*. New York: The Free Press.
Greeley, A.
    1972   *That Most Distressful Nation*. Chicago: Quadrangle Books.
    1974   *Ethnicity: A Preliminary Reconaissance*. New York. John Wiley & Sons.
    1975   An Irish-Italian? *Italian-Americana* **1**:239–245.
    1977   *The American Catholic*. New York: Basic Books.
Hansen, M.
    1958   The third generation: search for continuity, in *Social Perspectives on Behavior*
            (H. Stein, and R. Cloward, Eds.), pp. 139–144. New York: The Free Press.
Iorizzo, L., and Mondello, S.
    1971   *The Italian-Americans*. New York: Twayne Publishers.
Issacs, H.
    1972   The new pluralists. *Commentary* **53**:75–79.
Kohn, M.
    1977   *Class and Conformity*. Chicago: University of Chicago Press.
Lenski, G.
    1963   *The Religious Factor*. New York: Anchor Books.
Lopreato, J.
    1970   *Italian-Americans*. New York: Random House.
Manuel, R.
    1978   Social research among the minority aged: providing a perspective for a select
            number of issues, in *Research and Training in Minority Aging* (G. Sherman, Ed.),
            pp. 16–30. Washington, D.C.: National Center on the Black Aged.
Papajohn, J., and Spiegel, J.
    1975   *Transactions in Families*. San Francisco: Jossey-Bass.
Parenti, M.
    1967   Ethnic politics and the persistence of ethnic identification. *American Political
            Science Review* **61**:717–727.
Roof, W.
    1979   Socioeconomic differentials among white socioreligious groups in the United
            States. *Social Forces* **58**:280–289.
Rosen, B.
    1959   Race, ethnicity and the achievement syndrome. *American Sociological Review*
            24:47–60.
Sandberg, N.
    1974   *Ethnic Identity and Assimilation: The Polish-American Community*. New York:
            Praeger.
Tomasi, L.
    1972   *The Italian American Family*. New York: Center for Migration Studies.
Vecoli, R.
    1974   The Italian Americans. *The Center Magazine* **7**:32–43.
Wright, J., and Wright, S.
    1976   Social class and parental values for children: a partical replication and extension
            of the Kohn thesis. *American Sociological Review* **41**:527–537.

7

Language and Ethnicity in Bilingual Education

Joshua A. Fishman

AN ASSUMED BUT UNDEFINED LINK

Both bilingual education and ethnicity have old and deep roots in American history. In *Language Loyalty in the United States* (Fishman, 1966) I have tried to show how they have both constituted ingredients of the American experience from earliest colonial times to the present. However, they have both been "reborn" during the past decade, in the sense of arriving at more general recognition, and the simultaneity of their appearance (to many who had not realized that they were both there before) has led to the uncritical conclusion that they are inherently, causally and conflictually interrelated. As a result we now encounter those who are in favor of and those who are opposed to bilingual education on the basis of its assumed link to ethnicity. Unfortunately, most of those in the argument have no precise knowledge of either bilingual education or of ethnicity. In fact, there is a great deal to be known about both of them that would serve to enrich and sensitize our understanding of their American context in general and of their most recent "rebirth" in particular.

In bilingual education we are dealing with a worldwide phenomenon that has a history of some 3500 years in the Euro-Mediterranean world, which is to say that the records of it go back as far as do our records of formal (and admittedly elitist) educational history (Lewis, 1976). With respect to ethnicity and its link to language there is, similarly, a continuing dialogue of equally distinguished vintage between social theorists (be they prophets, philosophers, or social scientists) of the entire Euro-Mediterranean world (Fishman, 1977). It behooves us to be familiar with the entire panorama traced by both of these phenomena, rather than merely with their most recent outcroppings, if we are to understand our own American situation with respect to them both and the extent to which it is typical or unique.

THE ETHNICITY EXPERIENCE

Bilingual education can be succinctly (though superficially) defined as education that utilizes two media of instruction in connection with subjects other than and beyond language learning per se. No similarly adequate brief definition is available for ethnicity, perhaps because its variability—that is, its developmental and phenomenological change as society itself changes—is more crucial than its elements of constancy. These elements can be listed easily enough. Ethnicity is a bond (self-perceived and/or ascribed by others, with or without objective justification) to a historically continuous authenticity collectivity. Thus, ethnicity assists individuals in coping with the existential question of "Who am I?" and "What is special about me?" by contextualizing these questions in terms of putative ancestoral origins and characteristics. These questions are therefore illuminated in terms of "Who are my own kind of people?" and "What is special about us?" and come to be answered at the level of peopleness *being* (biological continuity and, therefore, physical triumph over death), peopleness *doing* (behavioral fealty even in the course of behavioral change) and peopleness *knowing* (i.e., ethnicity includes not only native philosophy but historiosophy and cosmology: a *Weltanschauung* or world view). Language is a central component in all three of the above experiential components.

However, as with all social behaviors, ethnicity is not only experienced from the inside but reacted to from the outside. The nature, quality, and saliency of the ethnicity of "others" are of concern to beholders, indeed of as much concern as their own ethnicity and often even far beyond claims for or interest in their own ethnicity. The Western world in general has a long history of being concerned with the ethnicity of "others" and with downgrading, criticizing, suspecting, and, not infrequently, counteracting the ethnicity of "others." Many Americans in particular are heirs to a peculiar intellectual-emotional history vis à vis ethnicity: it is seen as "out there" (not in us), peripheral to the mainstream, divisive rather than integrative, and backward looking rather than modernizing. In short, ethnicity has a ready-made "bad press" as a result of a social and intellectual tradition that is many centuries and even millennia old (Fishman, in press), a tradition in which the ethnicity of "others" has been more frowned upon than smiled upon.

SOME ROADBLOCKS TO A FULLER UNDERSTANDING

Why is it that the original fifteenth, sixteenth, and seventeenth century English meanings of *ethnic* and *ethnicity* (and of such now obsolete forms as *ethnish* and *ethnicize*) pertain to pagans and paganism; heathens and heathenism; materialism and uncouthness; wildness; and lack of cultivation, refinement, and gentility? Even now, after a decade of the rebirth and semantic rehabilitation of ethnicity, ethnic hairdos, ethnic music, and ethnic dress imply the offbeat or the exotic, rather than the refined. Why should that be, particularly since the Greek etymology, *ethnos*, seemingly pertains to nationality, peopleness, and their attributes?

To answer this question, we must push back to "pre-Greek" social theory with respect to peopleness, to a theory of the early Hebrews. This theory viewed peopleness as a "mixed bag," including both good and bad potentialities. At its best, peopleness was sanctified, rule-governed, and regulated by lofty and spiritual considerations and superhuman precepts and commandments that led peoples to seek justice and to love mercy in distinctive ways. A peopleness collectivity of this elevated sort, whether they were the Hebrews themselves or another people, was referred to as an *'am*. However, the Hebrews sorrowfully recognized another kind of peopleness, one marked by greed, lawlessness, materialism, inequity, and iniquity. The Hebrew prophets thundered against this sort of peopleness *among their own*, as well as among peoples that attacked, corrupted, devastated, or misled the Hebrews. This sort of peopleness, the negative pole, so to speak, of a continuum that had its distinctly positive pole as well, was referred to as *goy*, whether Hebrews or non-Hebrews were involved. Our current term *ethnic*, or *ethnicity*, stems from the Greek (Septuagint, third century CE) translation of the *Pentateuch* (and perhaps of the entire Old Testament) and from the need to cope with the *'am-goy* distinction in an Indo-European language in which the distinction had not arisen. The negative semantic field of *goy* necessarily contributes an original negative semantic field to *ethnic* or *ethnicity* ("pagan" or "heathen") in English and other languages and is still there today, both in common parlance and in professional thought, notwithstanding the semantic rehabilitative events of very recent years. However, this disparagement of the total ethnicity concept has also been rejected, of course; thus, the association of bilingual education with ethnicity has immediately involved it in a controversy, in a tug of war, and in a conflict of loyalties not of its own making.

CLASSICAL HEBREO-GREEK SOCIAL THEORY: THE MAINTENANCE IDEAL

The Greeks did not need classical Hebraic ambivalence with respect to peopleness in order to arrive at an ambivalence all their own in this connection. Among the eternal dilemmas argued by Plato and Aristotle is also the dilemma of whether the energizing and internally altruizing affective bonds of ethnicity fully counterbalanced the injustice, favoritism and self-centeredness that these bonds fostered. In Plato's scheme for good government via a special class of Gaurdians he explicitly provides for their "deethnization" so that government can be dispassionate, even-handed, and open to new ideas from whatever quarter they might emerge. Aristotle, on the other hand, refused to throw out the baby with the bath water and warned that any governing body that is not bound by ties of immediate affection and relatedness to the governed is more to be feared than desired. Aristotle implied that although ethnicity exacts a price, it should not be (and could not be) extirpated, being part and parcel of some of the very best traits in the human condition: love, altruism, self-sacrifice, resilience, ingenuity, and the willingness to struggle against overwhelming odds.

The classical Greeks and Hebrews both saw themselves as central to mankind, as essentially different from each other, and as even more different from *all the others*. However, they also long held fundamentally similar views of language and ethnicity. Both peoples traveled the length and breadth of the known world, settled everywhere, learned (and used) all languages with which they came into contact, and yet considered transethnification of their own kind to be unnatural, a grievous tragedy of cataclysmic or catastrophic proportions. Other languages had important and well-established (often diglossic[1]) functions for them, but not at or near the inner core of their own sense of peopleness: their own

[1] Diglossic, the adjectival form of "diglossia," pertains to stable and widespread societal multilingualism such that two (or more) languages are culturally accepted as legitimated in their respective functions.

holiness, genius, uniqueness, and specialness in the larger order of things. They and the eternal civilizations that they both founded remain very much alive as a continuing (Eastern Mediterranean) tradition in Western thought. The autocephalic churches of Eastern Christianity and their (as well as the early Islamic) assumptions, that God sends prophets to speak to each people in its own language (for how else could He give to each of them its mission?) and that the Tower of Babel (aiming as it did to unify mankind in disrespect of God's authority) was destroyed so that the many-splendored nature of God could be appreciated by a world made up of different peoples, undergird a recurringly powerful senti-ment among others as well.

The classical Hebreo-Greek tradition, particularly as it developed in far-flung diaspora colonies from Gibraltar to the Euphrates, frequently engaged in bilingual education involving languages other than those of their own respective peopleness. Over the centuries these "other" lan-guages were successively replaced. At times some of them displaced the "own" languages as vernaculars. More frequently they merely supple-mented or replaced the "own" languages in connection with ethnically less encumbered pursuits in commerce, industry, government, and gen-eral scholarship, even though they constantly influenced the "own" lan-guages lexically, morphosyntactically, and even phonologically. However, the concept of "own," classical authenticity, and elevated and language-embedded uniqueness was never lost, no matter how much it was com-promised. It remained a beacon even to ordinary folk of "one's own kind" and certainly a rallying symbol for elites and proto-elites attempting to mobilize the masses. Classic traditions differ from others, not in being petrified (for they too change, grow, and are reinterpreted), but in being unforgettable. Such unforgettability—sanctified to be sure—is a tremen-dous force on behalf of ethnic and linguistic maintenance, at least in certain protected rounds within the entire role repertoire. It has been such not only for Jews, Greeks, Moslems, and Eastern Orthodox Chris-tians, but also for various relatively modern, secular, Western movements of self-determination and preservation that have been influenced by them (Jakobson, 1945, 1968; Deutsch, 1942, 1968).

Ethnocentric though this ideal has been at times, it has rarely been racist in the sense of considering "own" peopleness defined entirely on biological grounds. (Neither *doing* nor *knowing* is essentially biological.) Nor has it posited hierarchies of mankind on biological grounds, sepa-rating the superhuman (and exquisite) from the subhuman (and ex-pendable). The Eastern Mediterranean vision has commonly been a vision of a world of different peoples, each addressed to the mission that is its lot. It is a celebration of diversity—with good and bad existing in each camp—and a reflection of a world view that sees such diversity, simultaneously ethnic and linguistic, as a necessary creative and self-renewing aspect of social life. Who needs all those little peoples and languages out there? The Eastern Mediterranean vision answers, "They need themselves, and that is enough!" A type of bilingual education has arisen to serve this vision, and it is known as language-maintenance bilingual education.

THE WESTERN VISION: ETHNICITY AS TRANSITIONAL, EXPANDING, AND OPPORTUNITY RELATED

The classical Eastern Mediterranean vision is a by-product of a particular, early, small-scale, socioeconomic political reality. Is it any wonder then that other realities have given birth to other visions of language and ethnicity (and of education to correspond to them)? Even the Eastern Mediterranean itself, in later centuries, nurtured other visions that corresponded to changed, more transethnically integrative circumstances there, but the prototype theories of this latter kind carry the imprimaturs of the Western church and the Western empire. From Cicero and various apostles to early church councils and medieval moral philosophers, the view is presented that ethnicity at any particular time is no more than a building block for a yet more inclusive integration to come. For the integrative power (the church or the empire) smaller scale ethnicity nevertheless represents a parsimonious opportunity for dealing with and regulating sizable populations through the leaders that they already recognize and with whom they have an established affective bond. If these leaders can be successfully transethnified, by offering them greater rewards, privileges, and opportunities, they then become the mechanisms for transethnifying their kinsmen. In general, it is believed, there is a constant "cosmic" flow of mankind to higher and more inclusive levels of integration. This is viewed as a natural flow, following the lines of constantly growing understanding, interaction, shared experience, shared technical capacity, and shared benefits. Man's affections begin as a small circle, close to hearth and home, and naturally expand to the widest, most inclusive, and rewarding limits available. Only the vicious and the inept retain a more provincial bond in preference to a more universal one that is made available to them.

This Roman dream of universalization has left very deep roots in all of us, particularly in us as Western intellectuals and in us as Americans. It is there not only in our ecumenical religious thought but in the American experience of transethnification and in the French Revolution's Jacobin promise of a clear slate and full equality and fraternity thereafter. It is there in *capitalist assumptions* that political stability creates its counterpart in historically arbitrary but morally legitimate ethnic identity; *in Marxist assumptions* that ethnicity is a mere by-product of selfish and doomed cleavages in the control of means of production and that these cleavages will give way to the greater proletarian brotherhood; and in purportedly neutralist *sociological assumptions* that *Gemeinschaft* (intimate community) will vanish and *Gesellschaft* (impersonal society) alone will reign supreme in a world dominated by the truly unifying experience of modern times: the invincible processes of the rational marketplace.

The fundamental view that any ethnicity is merely the accident of a temporary level of integration, that it is merely a way station along the road to a higher and ever higher level of reethnification, and that the masses easily leave lower levels behind and flow in the directions in which their own reethnified leaders and greater rewards beckon has its counterpart in nineteenth- and twentieth-century philosophies of American public education. The recent chapter of American bilingual education is also almost completely under the penumbra of this view. It views education in general and bilingual education in particular as part of the great transethnification opportunity of American life—an opportunity that only the warped and the malignant would seek to deny. Bilingual education is, therefore, viewed as justified to the extent that it admits unfortunates into the greater opportunity system of Anglified, urban, industrial life. It is hoped that bilingual education, if properly managed, will make English-speaking Americans out of the last benighted holdouts. If it does not do that, then, many of its supporters believe, there is not only no justification for it but it is downright objectionable. Unless it transethnifies toward a higher Anglo-status, it may rigidify identities that could and should go away; it may dignify lower levels of integration and as such reinforce divisiveness rather than a better future for the erstwhile ethnics.

Whereas both capitalist and communist social theory with respect to language and ethnicity see them both as temporary, changeable, and dependent variables responding to more basic and fundamentally political-economic factors, at least one major sociologist has begged to differ. Although Comte, Saint-Simon, Emile Durkheim, Alexis de Tocqueville, Ferdinand Tönnies, and Talcott Parsons have all sounded an unrelieved dirge for ethnicity in modern life, Max Weber alone has cast doubt upon this line of reasoning. In several justly famous volumes he argued that the economic forces of ancient Israel, classical China–India, and Reformation Protestantdom were all governed by their particular ethnocultural traditions. Thus, rather than ethnicity being merely a passive by-product of more basic political–economic patterns, Weber argued that it helps shape those patterns and makes them assume particular directions, tempos, and styles. Weber has yet to be fully examined for his implications as to the relationship between bilingual education, ethnicity, and the process of integration into Anglo society. One implication may well be that cultural mechanisms become functionally independent. Once they are put into place, they simply refuse to fold their tents and silently fade away. They become a factor in their own right in the creation of future economic and political developments. Modern market-dominated life may very well limit the scope of ethnocultural differences, but it is itself heavily influenced by ethnocultural establishments. Marx might say today that bilingual education is a trivial and delaying intermediate step. Participation in economic benefits and economic control can and should be achieved directly, and if seized or made available, they will have their inevitable transethnifying consequences. Weber, on the other hand, would say that bilingual education itself shapes a separate economic base for its participants and does so at least partially in accord with their own traditions. Any transition that occurs via bilingual education will thus be slower, Weber might say, although it might well be experienced as more indigenous, less conflicted or imposed, and more humane. Who needs all those funny little peoples out there? No one really needs them, Weber might answer, as would Lord Acton, John Stuart Mill, Friedrich Engles, Karl Marx, and the founding fathers of modern sociology, and indeed, their *own* need for their various differences is constantly decreasing. But, he might add, if they find their way into the mainstream of modern *Gesellschaft*, they can do so only via a route that is, in part, distinctly their own, partly on their own terms, with an establishment that is, in part, their own. Perhaps that is exactly what bilingual education helps them to do.

HERDER AND WHORF: THE VISION OF ENRICHMENT

The promised universalist paradise either has not come, or it has not brought the blessings originally promised. Those funny little people out there, called ethnics by their betters, have not gone away nearly as much nor as fast as predicted. Indeed, since the middle of the nineteenth century, Europe itself, and even Western Europe, the heartland of long entrenched "higher order" political and economic establishments, has been shaken by the protests of ethnic collectivities that have refused to die, integrate, or transethnify. Actually, the latter have turned on their heads the capitalist and Marxist claims that they were nothing but by-products. No, they have said, it is we who are original causes. It is not the political and the economic realities that create languages and eth-nicities, but, on the contrary, it is language and ethnicity collectivities that deserve to have and create their very own political and economic structures. Such counterclaims were particularly dangerous for the mul-tiethnic Austro-Hungarian and Czarist empires and for the fledgling Communist movement, but they were certainly embarrassing as well for the great Atlantic seaboard polities that had benefited first and most from the mercantile, industrial, and colonial revolutions. Predictions and dictums have maintained that the Irish, Scots, and Welsh were dead or dying; that the Bretons, Occitans, and Alsatians were gone or going fast; that the Catalans, Basques, and Gallegos were no more than relics of a bygone age; and that the Frisians were a figment of necromancers. And when these dead nationalities, these so-called peoples without histories (Fishman, 1972)—for if they had bona fide histories they might deserve recognition—and the untold many more in Central and Eastern Europe, insisted that the rumors of their deaths were highly exaggerated, the intellectual and ideological heads of Western civilization replied, as they often do today: "But who needs all those little people and funny languages out there? They simply impede the wheels of progress; they are anach-ronisms; they are divisive of the greater good that we (and only we) can bring to mankind without them!"

A major voice that arose in opposition to the self-serving and self-congratulatory integrative visions of those who claimed that they rep-resented—nay that they *were*—the wave of the future was that of the German philosopher, poet, and literary scholar Johann Herder (1744–1803). He went beyond his initially anti-French stance (occasioned by French control of German political, cultural, intellectual, and economic life) to a general social theory of language and ethnicity. He also went beyond the earlier Hebreo-Greek view (of which he was well aware) by claiming that no people could retain its creativity, spirit, individuality, and genius unless it maintained its linguistic and ethnic authenticity, and by developing the view that the future of mankind itself, of civilization as a whole, depended on the diversity of values, ideas, ingenuity, and insight that only the diversity of language and ethnicity collectivities could provide. As a Romanticist, Herder despised the rational and me-chanistic market-dominated society that the Enlightenment sketched. Where is spontaneity? he asked. Where is creativity? Where is affection? Where is hope? Where is the fortitude to triumph over the problems not yet fully visible but already on the horizon? Herder was convinced that only the little peoples out there—the ones that were still untrammeled by *Gesellschaft*, still uncorrupted by the West, still unspoilt, and still faithful to their ancestral ways and tongues—could save the world, for only they had preserved the authenticity necessary to do so. Thus, Herder not only inspired (and inspires today) countless nationality movements of submerged collectivities, but he is the modern fountainhead of cultural pluralism as a good, a resource, and a treasure for all of mankind. Therefore, he advocated learning not only one's own authentic and ancestral language but as many others as possible. For him, languages were not only keys to great sensitivity, wisdom, and originality but also great dynamos. They each had within them a spirit of their own that could make people think differently, see differently, understand differently, and behave differently. Its own language made a people wiser. Many languages made an individual wiser, greater, and better.

A century and a half later the American anthropological linguist Benjamin Lee Whorf formalized much of Herder's thinking and restated its underlying principle of relative linguistic determinism in more directly testable (although still ambiguous and somewhat tautological) terms. However, for Whorf too there was a more fundmental goal, a more basic motive underlying his view of language systems as the causal mainsprings of ethnocognitive differences. Like Herder before him, he feared that the West was intellectually and spiritually depleted and not up to solving the problems that were increasingly engulfing it. He too concluded that only a more diversified pool of talent, solutions, and perspectives could save mankind from the deadening grip of Western routinization. Thus, like Herder, he answered the question, "Who needs all those funny little people and languages out there?" with a resounding "We all do!" He believed that the very future of human life on this planet depends on their cultivation for the sake of the enrichment that all can gain from them. Not only will the social sciences and the humanities be different if enriched from diverse linguistic sources but the natural sciences themselves have something to gain from being reformulated in Navaho, Hopi, and in other supposedly exotic non-Western languages. The spirit of Herder and Whorf is not far away today whenever enrichment bilingual education is being advocated. By claiming most for the language and ethnicity link, they seem also to have raised it to a universal, with as much potential for human good as the Roman ideal of transethnification (Fishman, 1982).

IS BILINGUAL EDUCATION INHERENTLY CONFLICTED?

The roseate panacea of bilingual education to cure the world's ills that derives from Herdian and Whorfian thinking contrasts starkly with the opposition to bilingual education as a spoke in the wheels of eternal-progress-via-higher-order-transethnification. In truth it must be admitted that bilingual education is often beset by conflict. It is so beset in the USSR (to the degree that I was not permitted to enter the country on one occasion because I had made known my hopes of observing it) because that country has inherited both Marx's antilanguage-and-ethnicity stance and Herder's messianic glorification of diversity exactly on that basis. It is conflicted in the United States, where Roman`integrationism and Jeffersonian cultural democracy are both deeply ingrained, colegitimate components of our ethos and of our ethics. It is conflicted in Canada because the Herdian *Volksgeist* (national élan or spirit) of the Quebecois is feeling its oats as it comes out from under the suffocating embrace of Anglophone certainty that all the world would become English speaking and, thereby, English learning, *as a first priority*, if only enabled to do so. However, it is *societies*, rather than bilingual education as such, that are conflicted. If societies can come to accept (value?) and make an option of (permit?) ethnolinguistic diversity, so that some can treasure it for maintenance purposes, others for enrichment, and others for transitional purposes, bilingual education will quickly become what it should be: an internally diversified alternative kind of education for those who want it.

REFERENCES

Deutsch, K. W.
    1968   The trend of European nationalism: the language aspect in *Readings in the Sociology of Language* (J. A. Fishman, Ed.), pp. 598–606. The Hague: Mouton. (Originally published, 1942 in *American Political Science Review* **36**:533–541.)
Fishman, J. A.
    1972   *Language and Nationalism*. Rowley, Mass.: Newbury House.
    1977   Language, ethnicity and racism. *Georgetown University Roundtable on Language and Linguistics* **1977**:297–309.
    1982   Whorfianism of the third kind: ethnolinguistic diversity as an international good. *Language in Society* **11**:1–12.
    n.d.   *'Am* and *Goy* in The Old Testament: Explorations in the Continuing Perjorative Connotations of the Term "Ethnicity" in *Language and Ethnicity: American and International Perspectives*. The Hague: Mouton. In press.
Jakobson, R.
    1968   The beginnings of national self-determination in Europe, in *Readings in the Sociology of Language* (J. A. Fishman, Ed.), pp. 585–597. The Hague: Mouton. (Originally published, 1945 in *The Review of Politics* **7**:29–42.)
Lewis, G. E.
    1976   Bilingualism and bilingual education: the ancient world to the Renaissance, in *Bilingual Education: An International Sociological Perspective* (J. A. Fishman, Ed.), pp. 150–200. Rowley, Mass.: Newbury House.

8

Sensitivity to Ethnic Discrimination: The Case of Israeli Production Foremen

Albert I. Goldberg
Gedaliahu H. Harel

INTRODUCTION

Achievement, not background, is considered the primary basis for personnel selection and reward in the industrial work system of any developed society.[1] Nevertheless, managers are more likely to be members of higher ranking ethnic groups, even in those plants where the majority of production workers are from lower ranking ethnic groups.[2] An explanation of this common finding, which still conforms to the view of an achievement basis to the industrial system, attributes this inconsistency to factors from outside the work place; for example, higher ranked ethnic groups are more likely to obtain the college education demanded for many managerial positions (Jencks and Riesman, 1977:61–154). The existence of an achievement system in industry might therefore be measured better by examining the criteria used in selecting foremen because this position does not usually require a college education and is more dependent on factors intrinsic to the work place.

---

[1] A discussion of the shift in industrial societies from universalistic–ascriptive to universalistic–achievement patterns can be found in Parsons (1951:533). Disagreeing with this evaluation, Hechter (1976) suggests that industrialization, through its maintenance of a division of labor, perpetuates ethnic differences in the work force.

[2] For a comparative community discussion on discrimination in the work place, see *Industrial Relations* (1970:277–355).

CULTURE, ETHNICITY, AND IDENTITY

The work of a foreman combines a need for technical competence with a need for skill in supervising other workers.[3] It would seem natural in the competitive world of industry to select foremen on the basis of achievement measures. The foremen, however, also play an important role in the linkage between higher management and workers: they often are the individuals who implement general corporate policy through their direct supervision over the line production workers. In this case, management might prefer hiring someone for the position with the same ethnicity as higher management under the assumption that such an individual would hold similar work norms and values and therefore be more compliant to their wishes.

In this study the extent to which lower ranked ethnics obtain foreman positions is considered an indicator of the use of achievement criteria in industry. In addition, reports from the ethnics themselves on the existence of ethnic discrimination are utilized as a measure of the perceived reality of the work place. This sensitivity to ethnic discrimination will be found to vary with other background characteristics of the foremen, and the direction of this changing pattern of backgrounds will allow us to predict the extent to which such discrimination may be experienced in the future.

SAMPLE AND METHOD

This study of ethnic discrimination was done within the electronics and metals industries of Israel.[4] These two branches of industry have seen tremendous growth in Israel over the last 30 years as they have changed from basically craft work to the utilization of technologically and organizationally modern plants. This relatively short period of development should make visible the natural tendencies of such industrial systems to adapt achievement criteria. The relatively small size of the total system also provides an opportunity for studying the complete system in these branches.

The Jewish ethnic division of Israel is primarily between two groups, Sephardim and Ashkenazim, each of which represents approximately half the Jewish population of Israel (Peres, 171:1021–1047). The Sephardim are Jews who originated primarily from countries in North Africa and

---

[3] Discussions on the role of foremen can be found in Dunkerley (1975:28–33, 76–79) and Roethlisberger (1965:22–37).

[4] An early paper on the Israeli industrial scene that gives some idea of its rapid development is Derber (1963:39–59).

the Middle East, whereas Ashkenazim are Jews originating primarily from countries in Europe and America. Even though all Jews share a common culture, irrespective of origin, customs and beliefs have developed that differentiate the two communities. In Israel, Sephardim are presently a group with a lower average income (Remba, 1973:199–214), are more likely to hold low-ranking occupations (Porath, 1973:215–235), and face possible discriminatory practices in employment (Toledano, 1973:333–347).

The data were collected in the winter of 1973–1974 as part of a study (sponsored by the Israel Ministry of Labor with the cooperation of the Israel Institute for Productivity) on the training needs of these foremen (Goldberg, 1976). Questions were included in the instruments to probe the added dimension of ethnic discrimination. In total, 360 production foremen were interviewed in 53 different enterprises; of these 110 were Sephardim and 250 were Ashkenazim. All foremen were interviewed in the smaller plants, and 20 foremen were randomly selected in the larger plants.

Sensitivity to discrimination was measured by a battery of 22 questions asking the foremen to indicate what they considered important for success as a foreman in their plants. The foremen showed high agreement that such factors as a good technical education and good relations with workers were important for success. Being of the same ethnic group as management was 21st on this list. Still, 32% of all foremen gave this factor some importance, with Sephardi foremen having a greater likelihood of giving this response. Because higher management is almost universally Ashkenazi in these plants, it is assumed that when a Sephardi foreman indicates success is dependent on being of the same ethnicity as managers in his plant, he is expressing a specific sense of discrimination related to his own position in the plant.

THE OBJECTIVE POSITION OF ISRAELI SEPHARDIM

The Sephardim of Israel are underrepresented in the higher status positions of the society (see Figure 1). Sephardim are proportionately 47% of the total Jewish population and 41% of the total Jewish labor force (Israel Central Bureau of Statistics, 1975). However, they have been found to be only 16% of first-degree university students (Israel Central Bureau of Statistics, 1975:627) and 15% of the members of the Israeli parliament (Smooha and Peres, 1975:63–79). In the industrial scene, they are 6% of the line managers in this study. The 29% of foremen found to be Se-

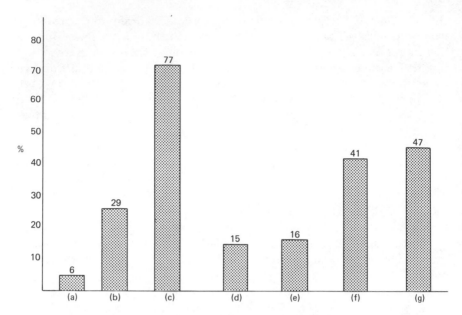

Figure 1   Proportion of Sephardim (based on father's birthplace) found in various Israeli population groups. (a), line managers (N = 99; Israeli metals and electronics industries data, 1974); (b), foremen (N = 363; Israeli metals and electronics industries data, 1974); (c), production workers (N = 139; Israeli metals and electronics industries data, 1974; based on four of the companies sampled in de Haan [1975]); (d) members of Israeli parliament, 1970 (N = 113; Smooha and Peres, 1975:72); (e) first-degree university students, 1972–1973 (N = 32,542; Israel Central Bureau of Statistics, 1975:Table xxii/32); (f) civilian Jewish labor force, 1974 (N = 1,013,400; Israel Central Bureau of Statistics, 1975:Table xii/6); (g) Israeli Jewish population, 1974 (N = 2,890,300; Israel Central Bureau of Statistics, 1975:Table ii/19).

phardim show a closer fit to their representation in the general population, but in several of these same plants, Sephardim are up to 77% of the production workers.[5]

Historically, the proportion of Sephardim in the total Israeli population increased after 1948 when the modern state of Israel was declared. They may, therefore, have not had the opportunity to climb the status hierarchy. It should then be expected that Sephardim would have greater representation among recent cohorts of foremen. This possibility is examined in data shown in Figure 2.

The data show some evidence of a historical basis for the low representation of Sephardim in the foreman position. Among those foremen

[5] Based on four of the companies sampled in the study by de Haan (1975).

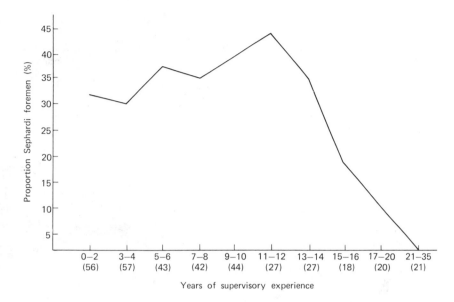

Figure 2   Proportion of Sephardi foremen in each supervisory experience cohort.
The number in each cohort is shown in parentheses.

with 21 or more years experience, no Sephardim were found in this study. The proportion of Sephardim rises in each cohort until it peaks among those with 13 years of experience (1961) and seems to have stabilized at about 33% of the foremen.[6] The higher proportion of Sephardim (44%) in the cohort with 11 to 12 years experience can be explained as either an irregularity in the trend data or a lower opportunity for Sephardi foremen to advance into higher management, resulting in an increasing proportion of Sephardim holding the foreman position after some years of experience.

The probability of Sephardim obtaining the foreman position may be reduced by achievement factors. Thus, Sephardim may be less competent to take on the tasks of a foreman (see Table 1).

Sephardim differ from Ashkenazim on background variables. Consistent with the findings in the larger Israeli society, the average Sephardi foreman has less formal education (fewer with 11 + years), was younger (under 36), and was more likely to have been born outside Israel.

In the more relevant area of work characteristics, however, Sephardim are found to be similar to the Ashkenazim. Thus, they are as likely to

---

[6] See similar conclusions in the work by Smooha and Peres (1975).

Table 1

Key Comparisons between Ashkenazi and Sephardi Foremen

	Ashkenazi	Sephardi	Gamma	Significance level (chi square)
Background attributes				
11 or more years of formal education (%)	61	46	.29	<.01
36 years or older (%)	71	53	.36	<.01
Born in Israel (%)	25	10	.51	<.01
Work characteristics				
7 or more years supervisory experience (%)	58	53	.10	n.s.
Participate frequently in occupational community (%)	50	41	.16	n.s.
Evaluated highly by their managers on their abilities to deal with workers (%)	58	61	−.06	n.s.
High on work centrality (%)	62	69	−.16	n.s.
High on importance of ethnic discrimination at work place (%)	28	42	−.29	<.05
N	250	110	—	—

have seven or more years supervisory experience and as likely to participate frequently in their occupational community of foremen. Of particular interest is the evaluation of their managers of their capabilities. In this case, the Sephardim were as likely as Ashkenazim to be evaluated highly on their technical ability and their ability to deal with workers. They were also as likely to give high centrality to their work life.

The main work-related attitude that differed between the Sephardim and the Ashkenazim was on their reporting ethnicity to be important for success at their plant. In this case 42% of the Sephardim gave it some importance in comparison to 28% of the Ashkenazim.

It can therefore be concluded that Sephardi foremen differ from their Ashkenazi colleagues primarily on the attributes associated with their low-ranked ethnicity. There is little difference in work-related items. This establishes the industrial work place as placing high value on the achievements of individuals and not on their ascriptive characteristics.[7] It is noted, however, that the Sephardim are more likely to accord some importance to ethnicity in their work place.

[7] A similar conclusion based on field work concluding that ethnicity played a minor role in an Israeli factory can be found in the work of Israeli (1979:80–89).

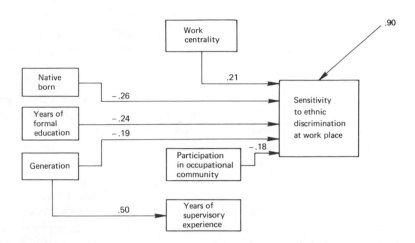

Figure 3   Path model for sensitivity to ethnic discrimination at the work place and antecedent factors among Sephardi foremen in Israel. Paths with beta of .18 or higher are included. Variance explained (R^2) = .19. Multiple correlation coefficient (R) = .43.

SENSITIVITY TO ETHNIC DISCRIMINATION

Because the Sephardim differ among themselves on background and work-related attitudes, future relationships in these plants might be predicted by knowing more about which Sephardi foremen actually perceived discrimination.[8] Key background variables, such as generation and formal education, were introduced into a path model describing the factors leading to a sense of ethnic discrimination at the work place (see Figure 3).

The generation to which the foreman belongs can be suggested as an important determinant of ethnic sensitivity. If the industrial scene is changing and placing more of an emphasis on achievement criteria, younger Sephardi foremen would be less likly to report ethnic discrimination. In the U.S. context, however, Goering reports that the younger generation of ethnics has a greater skepticism about equal opportunity in the U.S. and are more critical of the existing situation (1970:382). In the actual case it was found that the more recent generation of Sephardi foremen is less likely to perceive ethnic discrimination.

Two other background statuses, education and foreign birth, tend to

[8] A discussion of the importance of subjective evaluations of status inconsistency can be found in Baer, Eitzen, Deprey, Thompson, and Cole (1976:389–400).

become interrelated with the generation of the ethnic.[9] The younger cohort of a newly established ethnic group will usually have a higher average level of formal education and have a higher proportion of native born in comparison to older cohorts. These two factors, in turn, would be expected to reduce potential ethnic discrimination as background statuses become more similar to the dominant ethnic groups. Years of formal education and native birth were each found to make independent contributions to reducing ethnic sensitivity among Sephardi foremen. There was a beta of − .24 for the relationship between ethnic sensitivity and education and a beta of − .26 for ethnic sensitivity and native birth.

The impact of background statuses might be modified by other work characteristics of the foreman. The number of years supervising in the plant may have such an important intervening impact. With greater seniority, the foreman may find his ethnicity to be less important as he becomes more integrated into the plant. Years supervising, however, was found to be primarily related to generation and to have little independent importance.

Another factor relating to the sensitivity of the foreman may be his actual competence to do the work. Management was asked to report on the capabilities of the individual foreman, and these data were introduced into the path model. It was assumed that an ethnic who has not been able to cope with work problems might use discrimination as an excuse for his difficulties. In this case, however, little relationship was found between the foreman's competence and ethnic sensitivity, and it was dropped out of the model.

The foremen may vary in the degree to which they accord high centrality to their success at work.[10] It can be hypothesized that those who take work more seriously are those more likely to be sensitive to any form of ethnic discrimination. This was found to occur among the Sephardi foremen, and work centrality is shown to have a positive impact on work place sensitivity to discrimination in this model.

The actual involvement of a foreman with his occupational community may also be a possible mediating factor in his sense of ethnic discrimination.[11] If the foreman frequently interacts with others in the same position, his feeling of acceptance could reduce the likelihood of

[9] Among foreign born white ethnics in the United States, it was found that an inferior position in occupational achievement is largely due to their lesser educational achievement. See Blau and Duncan (1967:233).

[10] The relevance of work centrality has been discussed by Dubin (1956:131–142). A study on the relevance of this concept to Israel can be found in Mannheim, Chomsky, and Cohen (1972).

[11] For a primary source on the importance of the occupational community see Lipset, Trow, and Coleman (1956:118–159).

perceiving ethnic discrimination. This finding is established with the data and included in the model.

The path model on sensitivity to ethnic discrimination shows a number of factors that reduce the Sephardi foreman's sense of discrimination. These factors primarily point to a further decrease in the feeling of ethnic discrimination as a new generation of Sephardi foremen enter into the work world with a higher level of education and with native birth. It is of particular interest that work centrality and participation in the occupational community did not relate strongly to these background factors and will continue to make their independent contributions to a sense of ethnic discrimination.

SUMMARY

The position of production foremen in the industrial work scene in Israel is an example of the integration of ethnics through the use of achievement criteria. The proportion of Sephardi foremen comes close to their representation in the total population. This level developed fairly rapidly in the growth of the industrial system in Israel, though it has stabilized at a level still under full representation. On the other hand, the sensitivity of Sephardi foremen to ethnic discrimination would be expected to decline with the increasing level of education and native birth of new generations of Sephardim and their further integration into the national life of Israel.

REFERENCES

Baer, L., Eitzen, D. S., Deprey, C., Thompson, N. J. and Cole, C.
   1976   The consequences of objective and subjective status inconsistency. *The Sociological Quarterly* **17**(Summer):389–400.
Dubin, R.
   1956   Industrial worker's worlds: a study of the central life interests of industrial workers. *Social Problems* **3**(January):131–142.
Blau, P. M., and Duncan, O. D.
   1967   *The American Occupational Structure.* New York: John Wiley & Sons.
Derber, M.
   1963   Plant labor relations in Israel. *Industrial and Labor Relations Review* **17**(October): 39–59.
Dunkerley, D.
   1975   *The Foreman: Aspects of Task and Structure.* London: Routledge and Kegan Paul.
Goering, J. M.
   1970   The emergence of ethnic interests: a case of serendipity. *Social Forces,* **49**:382.

Goldberg, A. I., Rosenstein, E., and Weinreb, B.
   1976   *Training Needs and Motives of Foremen.* Haifa, Israel: Technion and Israel Pro-
           ductivity Institute.
de Haan, U.
   1975   Autonomy and technology: limits and optimal states. Unpublished dissertation,
           Faculty of Industrial and Management Engineering, Technion—Israel Institute
           of Technology, Haifa, Israel.
Hechter, M.
   1976   Ethnicity and industrialization: on the proliferation of the cutural division of
           labor. *Ethnicity* **3**(September):214–224.
Industrial Relations
   1970   *Industrial Relations* **9**(May).
Israel Central Bureau of Statistics
   1975   *Statistical Abstract of Israel.* Jerusalem: Central Bureau of Statistics.
Israeli, D. N.
   1979   Ethnicity and industrial relations: an Israeli factory case study. *Ethnic and Racial
           Studies* **2**(January):80–89.
Jencks, C., and Riesman, D.
   1977   Social stratification and mass higher education, in *The Academic Revolution,*
           pp. 61–154. Chicago: University of Chicago Press.
Lipset, S. M., Trow, M., and Coleman, J.
   1956   *Union Democracy.* Glencoe, Ill.: The Free Press.
Mannheim, B., Chomsky, Y., and Cohen, A.
   1972   *Work Centrality, Rewards and Role Strains of Israeli Male Occupational Groups.*
           Haifa, Israel: Technion Research and Development Foundation.
Parsons, T.
   1951   *The Social System.* Glencoe, Ill.: The Free Press.
Peres, Y.
   1971   Ethnic relations in Israel. *American Journal of Sociology* **76**:1021–1047.
Porath, Y. B.
   1973   On east–west differences in occupational structure in Israel, in *Israel: Social
           Structure and Change* (M. Curtis and M. Chertoff), pp. 215–235. New Brunswick,
           N.J.: Transaction Books.
Remba, O.
   1973   Income inequality in Israel: ethnic aspects, in *Israel: Social Structure and Change*
           (M. Curtis and M. Chertoff), pp. 199–214. New Brunswick, N.J.: Transaction
           Books.
Roethlisberger, F. J.
   1978–1984   The foreman: master and victim of double talk. *Harvard Business Review*
           43(September–October):22–37.
Smooha, S., and Peres, Y.
   1975   The dynamics of ethnic inequalities: the case of Israel. *Social Dynamics* **1**(June):
           63–79.
Teledano, H.
   1973   Time to stir the melting pot, in *Israel: Social Structure and Change* (M. Curtis
           and M. Chertoff), pp. 333–347. New Brunswick, N.J.: Transaction Books.

9

Naturalistic Categories of Ethnic Identity in Quebec*

J. Barry Gurdin

> My wish has always been to take seriously Durkheim's idea that the properties of classification systems derive from and are indeed properties of the social systems in which they are used. The questions Durkheim suggested were: how fuzzy are the boundaries of the categories? How well insulated the meanings they enclose? (1903:6–7). How many categories are there? Are the principles relating them to each other systematic? If there is a system of thought, how stable is it? (1903:35–41). These questions can be addressed to our own thought processes.
>
> [Douglas, 1975]

INTRODUCTION

The names, words, or markers of *Quebecer* and *Québécois* are examples of naturalistic categories of ethnic identity. Ethnic identity is a broad topic that raises many important questions (Bennett, 1973; De Vos and Romanucci-Ross, 1975; Glazer and Moynihan, 1975; Hraba, 1979; Isaacs, 1975; Lévi-Strauss, 1977). From the point of view of the philosophy of the rights of man, the main issue is the extent to which all groups within a politico-geographic unit are conceived of as belonging to that entity. Eschewing that question of value, the positivistic Sapir-Whorfian hypothesis asks how language in general, and therefore, how these words for ethnic groups, in particular, shape our thoughts. The more behaviorally minded ask how these glosses shape deeds. While recognizing

* The original version of this paper, entitled "Quebecer and *Québécois*: Same Meaning?" was read at the American Anthropological Association's 79th Annual Meeting in Washington, D.C., Saturday, December 6, 1980, at the session, "The Lexicon."

the importance of many other possible investigations of these terms, I will focus primarily upon these questions.

These questions could be approached from a variety of perspectives: historical, semantic, empirical, participant observatory, content analytical, and so on. In this paper I will rely on two rather different strategies and will tie together the answers of both. In this "triangulation" I will draw on Smallest Space Analysis to analyze a public opinion survey bearing on the question.[1] Besides these survey data, I will take into account my analysis of newspapers; other writings from literature, dictionaries, political science, anthropology, and sociology in English and French language publications; and eight years of residence in Quebec in various French- and English-speaking subcultural communities.

In contrast to the warning against using a dictionary that is often repeated in undergraduate linguistics, anthropology, and sociology courses, Levy and Guttman (1975) begin their study of *wellbeing* by looking it up in the dictionary and other standard references. Following their practice for my research on *Quebecer* and *Québécois*, I found that although *The Oxford English Dictionary* (*OED*, 1961) has no entry for these words, *Webster's Third New International Dictionary of the English Language* (Gove, 1961:1862) lists

quebecer *or* quebecker /-kə(r)n -s *cap* [*Quebec*, Canada +E *-er*]: a native or resident of Quebec City or province, Canada

quebecois *or* québecois\ :käːbeːkwä\ *n*, *pl*, quebecois *or* québecois\ -(z)\ *cap* [F *Québecois*, fr. *Québec*, Canada]: Quebecer

In the *Grand Larousse de la langue française* (Guilbert, Lagane, and Niobey, 1971:4805) one finds

québécois, e [Kebekwa, -waz] adj. et n. (de Québec, n. geogr.; XXᵉs.]. Relatif à la ville de Québec ou à la province du Québec; habitant ou originaire de cette ville ou de cette province.

Aware that these words were widely used in the electronic media, the printed press, literature, and in daily life, and that their usages have important overtones, I thought that it would be timely to record more accurately their usages in the wider population and to see whether or not they had any influence on behavior in daily life. Moreover, I thought it would be a project that would attract my students' attention and teach them some basic skills in social science.

My "Individual and Society" and "Sociology of Quebec" classes at the Loyola Campus of Concordia University in Montreal compiled a random,

---

[1] In his latest work Guttman (1981) encourages the researcher to design a mapping sentence; however, for the present article, I follow the precedent of Marsden and Laumann, (1978:81–111) who employ SSA without a mapping sentence.

representative sample of the personal entries in the Montreal telephone directory in the spring term of 1977. Each student had to call 80 persons on his or her list for the semester project. We compiled and checked these lists in class.

After studying identity, we decided that the definitions would be and indeed were displaying a dimension of universalism to particularism. As these were undergraduate classes, I had introduced these concepts through Broom and Selznick's (1973:38–39) discussion of them. Referring to their conceptualization of universalism and particularism, we framed an operationalization of this dimension for the definitions of *Quebecer* and *Québécois*. It stated:

1. Universalistic includes everyone legally abiding in Quebec.
2. Explicitly or implicitly includes most but excludes a few individuals or groups legally abiding in Quebec.
3. Explicitly or implicitly includes some but excludes some individuals or groups legally abiding in Quebec.
4. Explicitly or implicitly includes a few but excludes most individuals or groups legally abiding in Quebec.
5. Particularistic includes only one individual or group legally abiding in Quebec.

Toward the end of the spring term five judges independently ranked the definitions of *Quebecer* and *Québécois* from universalistic to particularistic. Then they ranked the answers to the question about a possible difference in meaning between the English word, *Quebecer*, and the French word, *Québécois*.

After eliminating data with collection errors (interviewers misunderstood instructions) or obvious coding or keypunching errors, 2371 subjects remained. Of these 308 (13%) were unavailable because they did not answer the telephone after three attempts were made to call them; 591 (25% of the total sample; that is, 29% of those contacted) refused to answer any part of the questionnaire; 390 (16% of the total sample; that is, 19% of those contacted, and 27% of those who agreed to participate in the questionnaire) were eliminated because their data contained an excessively large amount of missing data. The decision rule was that any subject who was missing more than four judges' ratings on any question or who was missing more than two reports of his or her friend's ethnicity was eliminated. Thus, 1082 subjects with adequate data remained. From this pool three samples were drawn randomly: a sample of 206 French-Canadian subjects, a sample of 206 English-Canadian subjects, and a sample of 206 subjects who were neither French Canadian nor English Canadian. The entire sample was not used because the cost of computing the monotonicity coefficients for large samples is prohibitive, and because sufficient memory to store the matrice used in computations was not available. Since the computation of monotonicity coefficients requires a separate computation for each possible pair of subjects, the central processing unit (CPU) time and memory needed to produce a coefficient escalates rapidly.

THE QUALITATIVE DATA

> But what if language speaks as much by what is between words as by the words themselves? As much by what it does not "say" as by what it "says"?
>
> [Maurice Merleau-Ponty quoted in Culler, 1975:75]

Even if Merleau-Ponty is right about the importance of implicit meaning, we should not forget that he equally stresses the significance of explicit meaning. Unfortunately, most pollsters with their positivist bias stick to surface meanings, whereas psychoanalysts tend to dwell on hidden meanings. With equally scientific pretentions, structuralists discover hidden relations between elements that generate a surface account.

Here I will begin by considering the surface meanings, what respondents actually said, and then I will proceed to discuss their deeper meanings.

Methods

The first question involving an extended open answer type of response was: "What does the word 'Quebecer' mean to you? *Que veut dire pour vous le mot 'Québécois'?*"

After the judges ranked the respondents' replies from universalistic to particularistic, responses were recorded on a separate sheet of paper bearing the judges' rank. In simple terms the answers that were ranked alike were rewritten together on another piece of paper.

Some examples of the most universalistic type of answers include the following:

1. people living in Quebec
2. six million people and we have to talk together
3. The word "Quebecer" to me means one who is a native of the

Province of Quebec or one who makes his livelihood and resides within the province.

4. *Ben, ça doit être un peu tout le monde qui vit dans la province.*
5. *tous ceux qui sont ici*
6. *un Canadien vivant au Québec*

An ethnomethodological observation is relevant now. These curt phrases and sentences are indexical expressions. They were answers given and written down when student telephone interviewers talked to randomly selected Montrealers who were chosen from their entries in the local directory. A greater number of the interviewers were bilingual English-speaking persons who speak French with an accent. However, a very large proportion were bilingual French-speaking persons who speak English with an accent. These accents might have produced a halo effect insofar as people may have toned down their responses to please the student callers; however, there is no direct evidence from this study to confirm such an influence. Furthermore, my thesis fieldwork suggests that the interviewers' ethnicity may have less of an effect on responses than is commonly thought by "conventional wisdom" in Montreal (Gurdin, 1978).

Some typical answers that the judges rated as 2 or "quite universalistic definitions" include the following:

1. *certain nombre de personnes ayant les mêmes opinions et le même endroit d'habitation*
2. *quelqu'un qui aime et veut habiter le Québec*
3. *vient du Québec*
4. born in Quebec, lives in Quebec for more than three or four years
5. person . . . makes his living, has a job in Quebec, associates with people in Quebec
6. a regional name for one who lives in a section of Canada called Quebec

Among those definitions that the judges thought to be "between universalistic and particularistic" and to which they gave a score of 3, we find the following:

1. born in Quebec and mostly one who speaks French
2. part of Canada getting to understand each other. We have a good relationship.
3. people who live in the province for many years
4. *venu au monde au Québec . . . fier de l'être . . . fier de la langue*
5. *appartenir à ce pays ici . . . d'être fort et robuste*
6. *ça peut être compliqué . . . disons que ce sont les gens qui habitent au Québec et qui parlent ou font un effort pour parler français.*

Toward the opposite end of this dimension the judges found definitions, such as the following, that they classified as being "quite particularistic" and to which they assigned the number 4:

1. *C'est vivant . . . c'est un peuple jeune.*
2. *avoir l'esprit patriotique . . . amour du pays, de la patrie celui qui travaille dans ce sens . . . qui est vrai . . . qui aide la langue française*
3. *liberté . . . parti . . . meilleure chose à être*
4. one who believes in Quebec as a nation
5. It means French Canadian most now. It is a threatening thing. I feel hostilities in the Province although I am sympathetic to the French. The word brings up things in my European background.
6. someone who is politically oriented towards separation

Finally the judges denoted the definitions that they perceived to be "the most particularistic" by the number 5. These include

1. *Si tu votes pour le P.Q., t'es Québécois.*
2. *C'est nous autres ça . . . les ouvriers pis les Indiens.*
3. *C'est un mot très français. Lorsqu'on voit le mot québécois, on voit tout en français.*
4. English persons living in Quebec
5. a French person
6. a radical

Ranking Responses

When we framed this question in class, we did not want to press the respondents to see if they distinguish between *Quebecer* and *Québécois* because it could very well bias their answer by suggesting a difference. Because this was a telephone survey, there was no way for the subject to know that there would be a follow-up question asking if, indeed, he or she makes a distinction between these terms. Once the data had been gathered, the judges ranked the responses from question 7 from universalistic to particularistic. Question 7 reads: "Do you see a difference between the words, 'Quebecer,' and its literal translation in French, 'Québécois'? If 'yes,' what is the difference? *Voyez-vous une différence entre le mot 'Québécois' et sa traduction littérale en anglais 'Quebecer'? Si 'oui,' quelle est la différence?*"

The judges found the "most universalistic difference or distinction," which they ranked as 1, to be answers like the following ones:

1. *juste une traduction*

2. *Je ne crois pas . . . c'est la même chose.*
3. *aucune différence*
4. I do not see a difference.
5. It is a difference in pronunciation only.
6. It is only natural for an English person to say the word in English, *Quebecer*, and a French person to say *Québécois*, or for a German to say it in German.

Typical of "quite universalistic differences or distinctions between *Quebecer* and *Québécois*," classified in rank 2 by the student judges, we find:

1. Yes. A Quebecer resides in Quebec. A *Québécois* resides in Quebec *plus* has ancestors from Quebec and is thus more proud and closer to Quebec.
2. Yes. *Québécois* is more French Canadian than Quebecer.
3. No. I never heard the expression, "Quebecer." It must be the same.
4. *Je ne crois pas.*
5. *non, à part la langue*
6. *Peut-être mais je ne le sais pas.*

The student judges classified items similar to the following ones as rank 3, lying "between universalistic and particularistic distinctions or differences between *Quebecer* and *Québécois*":

1. *Oui. Quebecer, je ne l'ai jamais entendu . . . sonne pas bien à l'oreille. J'ai l'habitude à l'autre.*
2. *La traduction devrait être le même mot.*
3. *Québécois . . . oui. C'est un peuple et même en anglais on emploie le mot français.*
4. Yes. French now represent a different group . . . separatists, but I don't know if all French feel this way.
5. *Quebecer*—one who resides in Quebec. *Québécois*—one whose aim is to promote French culture.
6. *Québécois*—French-speaking people. *Quebecer*—other and English.

Those differences or distinctions between *Quebecer* and *Québécois* that were judged to be "quite particularistic," ranked 4, include answers such as:

1. *Quebecer*—the people living in Quebec. *Québécois*—the people who want Quebec to get independent.
2. *Quebecer*—all people in Quebec. *Québécois*—those French people who want to separate.

3. Yes. French Canadian equals *Québécois*. I came to Canada in 1948, but now it's crazy and divided. Ottawa should send the army. Even Americans should help us run away from Communism.

4. *Oui, pas aussi précis . . . identification canadienne française . . . distinction plus vague.*

5. *Leur mot Quebecer est une expression raciste . . . il ne s'y intègre pas.*

6. *Oui, dans les deux termes il y a habituellement une petite touche d'identification et de ségrégationnisme.*

Finally, the following group of differences and distinctions are typical of those that the judges classified to be "the most particularistic" and to which they gave a rank of 5:

1. *Oui, chu [je suis] français . . . c'est mieux Québécois.*

2. *Québécois a une intonation militante tandis que Quebecer en a pas.*

3. *La différence est que ça ne se traduit pas car tout vrai Québécois est français donc traduction impossible.*

4. Yes, as a man working for Air Canada and from Winnipeg and now being in Montreal, the word, *Québécois*, means one who wants to split up the country and destroy the nation.

5. Quebecer is what the rest of English Canada calls someone in Quebec while *Québécois* is what French people are called in Quebec by other French people in other provinces.

6. Yes, *Québécois* is used by unbiased, liberal English Quebecers who respect the plight of the French, and is also used by all French Canadians [those living in Quebec and elsewhere, e.g., Manitoba].

Another point should be made to the ethnomethodologically sensitive. Because these responses were taken down by student interviewers over the telephone, many comments were written down in incomplete sentences or phrases often using a hyphen. In editing these replies I have tried to stick as closely as possible to what the students wrote down, except when an obvious misspelling, word omission, or grammatical error made a response difficult to read, and then I corrected it minimally. Also it should be noticed that some interviewers recorded the answers in *joual*, the French-Canadian patois, usually to indicate the dialect of the speaker. However, as not all interviewers did this, caution should be used in making inferences. Some of the more commonly used joual expressions found in these items are: *y* for *il*, *ils*, *chu* for *je suis*, and the omission of the negative particle *ne* in the phrase "*ne . . .* (verb) *. . . pas*," expressing negation.

Interpretations

It should be obvious that each of these items consisting of definitions of *Quebecer* and *Québécois* and the distinctions or differences or lack of them between these words could be interpreted in a myriad of ways. To an extent the items when regrouped along a continuum from universalistic to particularistic form the judges' "mirror," which is reflected back at the respondents' image. These regroupings assign a kind of meaning, namely that one's definition of and distinctions between *Quebecer* and *Québécois* exude a salient openness or closedness to others. With this interpretation in mind, I have passed from the level of surface to deeper meaning in that I am assuming that the judges perceive important degrees of difference in universalism to particularism that is read between the lines of these items.

These definitions and distinctions constitute folk opinion, and they can be more clearly understood in the wider social context in which they are located. To reach this level of deeper meaning, I must triangulate this evidence from the telephone questionnaire with other information gathered from the media, literature, and participant observation.

Literature

Literature from Quebec contains many direct and nuanced references to an awareness into which Quebec ethnic groups have been placed. Perhaps the best-known description of Quebec abroad is Louis Hémon's *Maria Chapdelaine: A Tale of the Lake St. Jean Country*. In Witt Blake's translation (1924) we find the following:

"Samuel once thought of going west," said Madame Chapdelaine, "but I was never willing. Among people speaking nothing but English I should have been unhappy all the rest of my days. I used to say to him: —'Samuel, we Canadians are always better off among Canadians.'"

When the French Canadian speaks of himself it is invariably and simply as a "Canadian"; whereas for all the other races that followed in his footsteps, and peopled the country across to the Pacific, he keeps the name of origin: English, Irish, Polish, Russian; never admitting for a moment that the children of these, albeit born in the country, have an equal title to be called "Canadians." Quite naturally, and without thought of offending, he appropriates the name won in the heroic days of his forefathers [88–89].

In a similar vein, though perhaps excluding the groups not of French or English background, Hugh MacLennan wrote in the foreword of his *Two Solitudes* (1945):

No single word exists, within Canada itself, to designate with satisfaction to both races a native of the country. When those of the French language use the word *Canadian*, they nearly always refer to themselves. They know their English-speaking compatriots as *les*

Anglais. English-speaking citizens act on the same principle. They call themselves Canadians; those of the French language, French-Canadians.

The most recent elaboration of the meaning of the words I am considering in this paper was written by Marcel Rioux in his book *Les Québécois* (1977). My translation of his text reads:

First of all, *Québécois* designated the inhabitants of Quebec City—the first permanent establishment of the French in North America—and later on the inhabitants of Lower Canada, of the old New France. Even though the term has been around for a long time, it has been only about a decade that "*Québécois*" has been revalued, to the extent of becoming a symbol of self-affirmation, of self-determination, and of national liberation. French Canadian, originally derived from English, is closer to the other axis, that of differentiating oneself from the Other.

Rather paradoxically, the term *Québécois* excludes the French-speaking minorities of Canada but includes the English-speaking minority of Quebec. One sees clearly enough the political intention with which the term of *Québécois* is laden today. It is really evident, nevertheless, that the inhabitants of Quebec being proportionally more than 80% French speaking, the name, *Québécois*, designates before all else a population of the French language [12] . . . This new man is North American, speaks French, but presents himself as *québécois*, which is to say, a being who possesses a specificity and who stops thinking of himself as being a minority. It is what he has become, what he is, more than what he is not, that he wants to prove [21].

Political Commentary and Definition

Although the mood of the items from telephone interviews is serious as is much of the discourse dealing with this subject, there is also quite a bit of interethnic joking, banter, and bittersweetness that characterizes this discussion. While I was writing this article, a friend of mine who knew of my interest in the subject clipped out the following letter to the editor, which illustrates this other mood (*The Montreal Gazette*, 17 April 1980:6):

'Voting is like fast driving'

Canadian Press reported [*Gazette*, April 17] that TV personality Dominique Michel says, "What is a Québécois? It's somebody who passes another car on a curve at 85 miles per hour, and then votes No (in the referendum) because he is afraid."

The analogy would be perfectly true if the young lady had said, "A Yes vote is like the notorious Québécois whose favorite pastime is crossing the double white line at 90 miles per hour to pass a trailer truck on an outside curve and over a blind hill."

However, in either event, the driver is not afraid, he is just dead. Sic transit gloria, what a way to go.

P. Thorpe, Westmount

A similar, though more bitingly mocking tone, was expressed by George Schwartz on *Le Devoir*'s page of commentary and opinion (8 August 1980: 7). My translation of his "Pour un nationalisme sportif" reads:

Among the adherents of sovereignty-association is found a majority of the Quebec elite, pure intellectuals, constitutional experts, political scientists, sociologists, economists, and artists. With the thrust of the young revolutionaries of the FLQ and of converted politicians, they became the spearheads of a Quebec nationalism based mainly on political affirmation and defense of culture. Yet on the 20ieth of May, the people of Quebec surprised all these beautiful people by the extent of the support that they gave to the NO. And the very evening of the election, reached by television, the great poet Gaston Miron threw out the elitist anathema upon the guilty: "It is the vote of shame."

The document that caused the greatest amount of concern to the English Canadian and other ethnic groups in Quebec regarding their legal status within the province was Chapter 5 of the "Charte de la langue française," which was approved on August 26, 1977. In a very profound tone, its preamble declared: "Whereas the French language, the distinctive language of a people that is in the majority French-speaking, is the instrument by which that people has articulated its identity [103]." This was the official translation of the original French: "Langue distinctive d'un peuple majoritairement francophone, la langue française permet au peuple québécois d'exprimer son identité."

This phraseology was changed in the preamble to the Law 101, but that it could have reached to the heights of the National Assembly produced a great fear among the minority groups as to their status. What frightened the minority groups in Quebec was that this phraseology and the sentiment that produced it excluded the achievements of English and other language groups in the arts, sciences, and everyday life. Have they not articulated their identity through instruments other than French?

Politicians' definitions of ethnicity are important because they influence the political discourse of a period and help form public opinion through wide diffusion to the mass audiences of radio, television, and the newspapers. In his book *René: A Canadian in Search of a Country*, Peter Desbarats (1976) cites Lévesque's definition of *Quebecer* contained in his nearly 6000-word "Option for Quebec." Desbarats describes this work as "disjointed and emotional, the work of a propagandist rather than a political philosopher . . . but specific enough to serve as a line of division in the years to come as individual Quebecers made up their own minds about the future of their homeland [129–130]." René Lévesque's credo began:

We are *Québécois*. What that means first and foremost—and if need be, all that it means—is that we are attached to this one corner of the earth where we can be completely ourselves: this Quebec, the only place where we have the unmistakable feeling that "here we can be really at home."

Being ourselves is essentially a matter of keeping and developing a personality that has survived for three and a half centuries.

At the core of this personality is the fact that we speak French. . . .

The struggle for survival had made Quebecers "heirs to the group obstinacy which has kept alive that portion of French America we call Quebec." Their common recollections of the past are things that made us what we are . . . enable us to recognize each other wherever we may be . . . tune in each other loud and clear, with no one else listening [129–130].

Writing of the Lesage years, the 1960s, Desbarats observes the significance of the category of "the others":

And not all of the "English" were wealthy, Anglo-Saxon and Protestant. In the previous century, when open rebellion had broken out against the British, Quebecers of Irish-Catholic origin had been among the leaders of the unsuccessful revolution. Some of their descendants were now in Westmount but many still lived in such working class districts as Verdun, St.-Henri, Ahuntsic and St.-Leonard among the Italians, Greeks, Portuguese, Germans and other members of the great non-French urban mass that French-Canadians referred to simply as "les autres"—all the rest [33].

One of the seeming truths of everyday life, something that is "common knowledge," or "what everyone knows" living in Quebec is that *Quebecer* and *Québécois* do not mean the same thing. This cognition is put up front in *Le Fait Anglais au Québec* (1979), which won the Governor General's award. According to my translation, the authors, Dominique Clift and Sheila McLeod Arnopoulos, say

Even the government of the Parti Québécois which theoretically is in favor of a pluralist society cannot help itself from making distinctions between "Quebecers of old stock" and "Quebecers of new stock." The government like the majority of the French population has difficulty abandoning this idea that to be a true Quebecer, one must be a direct descendant of one of the 60,000 colonists who lived on the banks of the Saint Lawrence in the middle of the 18th century. It is difficult to uproot some secular customs such as defining belonging to the society of Quebec by means of criteria such as language, accent, social and religious attitudes, enthusiasm shown toward folklore and traditional values or even the intensity of patriotic and national sentiments [224–225].

These author-journalists' frankness must be seen in light of a changing definition of *Quebecer* and *Québécois.* In his speech to the members of the French National Assembly given on November 2, 1977, entitled "*Nous Sommes des Québécois,*" or "We are Quebecers" in its English translation, it is clear that René Lévesque [1979/1978] used the word *Quebecer* in a primarily particularistic sense. Thus he speaks of:

We are speaking of a people that for a long time has been content to let itself be forgotten in order to survive . . .

. . . and where those whom you call "les Français du Canada," an apparently simple expression, which rejoins the essential facts, but whose meaning has nonetheless become ambiguous over the course of time, have their home. . . .

. . . More than four out of five of its inhabitants are of French origin and culture. Outside of Europe we are therefore the only large community which is of French stock [p. 155].

At last de Gaulle came . . . And this was not only, nor even particularly for his prophetic "Vive le Québec libre!" which resounded all around the world. . . .

. . . His knowledge was absolutely perfect. It was not only that of the "Canadiens" of the ancient regime, nor only that of the French Canadians of yesteryear. But also that of the Quebecers as we were then beginning to call ourselves more and more. During the 1960s, following a maturing of which nobody had taken too much notice, it was Quebec which emerged briskly, Quebec alone, and no longer "the province of Quebec," interior colony of federal Canada. It emerged moreover without hostility, without the slightest intentions of revenge, which simply indicated that along the way to self-determination, the hour of self-affirmation had sounded [p. 158].

But, addressing a political gathering of English-speaking Montrealers in a speech that was broadcast on radio and television, Prime Minister René Lévesque defined *Québécois* more universalistically. This speech was published on Monday, March 31, 1980, on *Le Devoir*'s page of opinion and commentary "Des Idées/Des Evénements/Des Hommes," in an article entitled "*Les Québécois sont des Québécois.*" My translation of that text is as follows:

Then let us come to grips, if possible, once and for all, with this question of who is a *Québécois* or Quebecer. Quebecer is a name which, for us, unites all those who are born in Quebec or who live here and it ties together their linguistic, ethnic, cultural, religious, geographic, and other diversity. It is the mark of belonging to a people and a land and the usage of the word "Quebecer" or "Québécois," two equivalent words, is in no way the exclusive property of one group, or even of one party. For those Quebecers who are tempted to believe that this name, particularly in French, tends to exclude them it can be useful to recall how it appeared in French in the beginning and how it entered into use. At the beginning of the French regime, a very long time ago, when a colony was created in Quebec, those who lived here, having taken the name from the Indians, called themselves "Canadians" and after the British Conquest, the name Canadians continued for a rather long time to designate only those who speak French. The others, after 1760 and rather long afterwards, were simply "the English." At the period of Confederation and afterwards, the expression "French Canadian" appeared and since,during the last generation, because they brought themselves into question as an ethnic group protecting their traditions in a defensive manner, and began to emerge fully as a people with a land where they could grow, the French Canadians began to call themselves "Québécois." The love of the Quebecers for their land and people largely explains the transformations of the last twenty years. Most of these transformations [have been] in the sense of self-development, self-confidence, and self-affirmation always increasing.

For their part, our English-speaking compatriots have been slower to abandon their Canadianism with a hyphen and embrace—those who do it—the name of Quebecer. At the beginning and even now in certain milieu, they refuse it all the more because the word, "Québécois," is a motor force in our nationalist movement. But now, the word Quebecer is recognized, whether it is used in English or French. Quebecers in English can do things more or less intelligently or acceptably. Québécois in French can act in a brilliant or stupid manner, but in no case their titles to their Quebec identity can be brought in doubt in any way. I hope that it is clear.[2]

[2] For commentary on this speech, see Cowan (1980:10).

Although this is clearly the most universalistic of Prime Minister Lévesque's definitions of *Quebecer* and *Québécois*, it begins with a purely inclusive statement in the first paragraph but adds a note of particularism in the last paragraph quoted here. The hinted hitch is that one must "abandon one's Canadianism" to embrace the title of *Québécois*. Moreover, the connotation that the word *Québécois* is a motor force to "our" nationalist movement is stated outright. The footwork attaching qualifications to *Quebecer* such as "in English" is immediately associated with an attitude of negative tolerance in that they are referred to as being able to do things more or less intelligently or acceptably, whereas *Québécois* in French is tied to an initial complimentary quality, acting brilliantly, which is then somewhat deflated by linking it with the possibility for stupidity. In short, an initial universalism subtly ends up being modified in a particularistic direction. Furthermore, this speech and the preceding one to the French National Assembly, given just about two years apart, starkly contrast in their degrees of universalism. On the other hand, this change could be as well interpreted as the sensitivity of a former television celebrity to the expectations of vastly different audiences.

Even though he is often depicted as being the most nationalistic member of the government in the English media, the former Minister of Cultural Development of Quebec, Dr. Camille Laurin, gives the most universalistic definition. He states that "the *Québécois* nation comprises all Quebecers, each person, whatever his ethnic origin or mother tongue who has chosen or chooses to live in Quebec among *Québécois* and to share their history [1978:6]."

The sociocultural construction of ethnic identity is not left only to political elites. Nor is formal political speechmaking the only medium through which the message of ethnic categorization is transmitted. Some commentators have asserted that the intellectual and mass media elites have replaced the priests as the most significant formers of public opinion in modern Quebec. An example of this new medium communicating ethnic identity is *Le Devoir's* usage of political cartoons to express the Liberal Party's point of view, symbolized by the sketch of Claude Ryan, that the *Parti Québécois'* position on multiculturalism, symbolized by a quotation from René Lévesque, contradicts an example of multiculturalism appreciated by René Lévesque.

Another medium conveying ethnic identity is the political tract. Sometimes these are developed by writers and poets and display varying degrees of artistic quality. The dissemination of this message is confined to political or artistic activists or persons present at rallies. Gilbert Boluleau's poem, "Peuple," associates the word *Québécois* with peoplehood onto the background of the Fleur de Lys, the symbol of Quebec. It employs the device of having the first letter of each line stand for the word it is trying to bring out, *Québécois*. Bold type makes its appearance blatant and inescapable. Its message clearly calls on the people to vote for independence in 1980.

Nor have ethnicity and ethnic identity escaped the novelist who writes on Quebec. Part of the terminology of ethnic identity consists of the pejorative glosses used by outgroups that are sometimes picked up by ingroups for use against themselves in jest or anger. Thus, English-speaking persons use the slurs "Frog," "Pea Soup," and "Pepsi" for French Canadians, and French-speaking persons employ the expressions "*Têtes carrées*" and "*Maudits blôques*," for English Canadians and a variety of expressions for other groups, such as "les Spaghett" or "Spaghettis" for Italo-Canadians. One can find these usages in the writings of Michel Tremblay, Mordecai Richler, and many others. Moreover, infrequently words like *canayen* and *habitant* may have a contemptuous sense of churl or lout (Orkin, 1967:6) and are used by French-speaking persons with a group-depreciating nuance.

Ditties and Slogans

The last medium that conveys ethnic identity is the ditty. One that was popular in the early to mid-1970s says "*Un Québécois ça frappe, ça frappe, un Québécois, ça frappe, tabernac.*" This is chanted up to as many numbers as one desires to go, with only the substitution of the first number by the following one. It is not insignificant to observe its resemblance to the words and the spirit of the songs of American cheerleaders or the chorus of "99 Bottles of Beer on the Wall." On a similar level is the slogan, "*Le Québec aux Québécois,*" which subtly excludes the Amerindians, English Canadians, and other ethnic groups, to the tune of a hockey puck.

The National Debate

The importance of the question at hand, at least to the local intelligentsia, can be seen by the frequency with which the topic of whether or not Quebecers, *Québécois*, Canadians, and/or French Canadians constitute a nation and/or a people appeared and covered a major part of *Le Devoir's* page "Des Idées/Des Evénements/Des Hommes" and the "Letter to the Editor" section, especially after the defeat of the referendum. This exchange of views was intitiated by an article written by the Prime Minister of Canada, Pierre Trudeau (1980a, 1980b, 1980c), which stimulated a series of replies and counterattacks which kept up throughout the summer of 1980 (see Boulay (1980:12); Chaput-Rolland (1980); Corbeil (1980); Hains (1980); Le Borgne (1980:7); Leclerc (1980), Lemieux (1980); Marion (1980:7); Mascotto (1980:7).

In terms of the questions addressed in this paper, this newspaper dialogue sheds light on some of the most important criteria that various writers consider essential to being included or excluded from being *Québécois*. Moreover, they touch on the major issues pertaining to the real and verbal universalism or particularism of who is considered to be a Quebecer.

The question that arises first is, can one reasonably define who is a member of the collectivity? Here we get opposing answers. Lemieux (1980) stresses that such questions and their answers are subject to a great deal of propagandizing. To support his position, he quotes Deutsch (1966) from his book *Nationalism and Social Communication*:

Consciousness is a political fact . . . The point is crucial . . . The words "German" or "Argentine" or "English" mean nothing in themselves; they mean something only if they are understood as being added to the words "persons" or "language" or "country" or "habits and customs" or "state." The importance of the things or acts so labeled . . . may well have a bearing on the rise and persistence of national consciousness, and on its power to modify the behavior of individuals and groups.

Dumont (1980) takes a similar position in one part of his article, "Their [nations'] reality escapes us when we try to qualify them by general traits which would apply to each and everyone in all circumstances." Nevertheless, his entire article and conclusion rely on making such qualifications, "In absence of anything better, let us therefore simply agree that Canada is only a state; that there exists a French nation on the continent; and that, to use the perfect expressions of Mr. Trudeau, Quebec is the 'first homeland,' the 'center of gravity' of that nation."

On the other side, Bauer (1980) bases himself on several traits, common origin, religion, and language in defining "the French Canadian people" and the "English Canadian people" and in attacking the expression, "Neo-Canadians."

Another highlight of the dialogue attacks the thesis of "two founding peoples"—the French and the English—because it grants legitimacy to only those groups while relegating the cultures of the native peoples and all subsequent immigrant groups to an inferior status vis-à-vis the governmental institutions and symbols. A related controversy is that the "Other Canadians" category, more recently called "*Québécois de nouvelle souche*" (Quebecers of new origin) or "*néo-Québécois*," (new Quebecers) see all the varying groups of national origin as ethnic groups that should have equal treatment and access to the state. Many French-Canadian intellectuals reject the idea of being one ethnic group among others and see themselves as being a nationality or a people with distinct rights as the longest settled of the colonists. This is linked to a theme that frequently comes up in various media: the abhorrence of having a mentality of a minority group and the identification with being a majority group.

This subject is coupled to the complaint that with the growth of the importance of governmental bureaucracy, non-French Canadians, constituting 20% of Quebec's population should occupy no more than an estimated 1–3% of public sector positions. Moreover, it is argued that "the present reality of Quebec" obliges "the Others" not to feel fully *Québécois* (Bauer, 1980:6). Although not in this series of articles, these charges are generally strongly denied by Quebec nationalists or are dismissed as "political blackmail" (Lévesque, 1978/1979:124–126).

The review of this qualitative data leads to a question that cannot be honestly avoided. Is a call to form an independent state a necessarily particularistic call if all groups are expressly admitted to the proposed venture?

Because no statement of any political ideology is seriously evaluated outside its material and historical reality, it would only be a speculation of theoretical abstraction to do so.

On the basis of this historicist assumption, it seems that all ethnic groups in Quebec have had a heightened sense of kind with varying degrees of outgroup rejection. This situation derived in part from a highly stratified ethnic division of labor, well depicted by Porter (1965) and Morris and Lanphier (1977).

The coolness if not overt hostility with which non-French Canadian ethnic groups have received the bid for separatism reflects to a large extent their experiences that they have not been received on an equal footing by French-Canadian Quebecers. After the Second World War the ethnic and religious minorities began to be admitted into the English-speaking, Protestant institutions (Clift and Arnopoulos, 1979:181–183), even though few French Canadians and "other Canadian ethnic" groups have been members of the upper levels of economic power (Clement, 1975:231–240). The "Other Canadian ethnics'" having made important inroads into many English-speaking institutions combines with the fact that officially pronounced definitions of *Québécois* have only recently and in many cases ambiguously or irregularly been defined to include all groups. "The Others" have interpreted these changes as mere "lip service" or "veneer." As a collectivity, they tended to perceive the call to form an independent state as a particularistic call, despite some declarations to the contrary.

THE QUANTITATIVE DATA

To find out how universalistic or particularistic the definitions of and distinctions between *Quebecer* and *Québécois* were perceived to be by the judges, a semistrong monotonicity coefficient was calculated between the first five judges' assessments of particularism to universalism (Guttman, 1981). I also wanted to know if age, sex, occupational, and ethnic groups displayed differences in the degree to which their answers to questions 6 and 7 were judged to rank on the dimension of particularism to universalism.

The background variables are (1) age, ordered from "young" to "old"; (2) sex, which can arbitrarily be ordered from "male" to "female"; (3) occupation, ordered from "low status" to "high status." These background variables are broken down by "French Canadian," "English Canadian," and "Other Canadian." Table 1 presents the correlations (semistrong monotonicity coefficients) for these three background characteristics for each of the three ethnic groupings.

When reading this table remember that the order on the variables results in a positive correlation when the same order is found on both variables and a negative correlation is found when the order is changed. Thus, because the judgments are ordered (for these particular tables) from particularistic to universalistic and age is ordered from young to old, the negative sign in the correlation, $-.05$, for judge 1, means that the younger respondents' definitions turned out to be perceived as negligibly universalistic by judge 1. It should be noted that the order is determinded by *a priori* judgments of the researcher based on knowledge of the literature and logical deductions.

Most of the correlation coefficients of judgments of particularism to universalism with background characteristics turn out to be small (less than .30). Only four out of 90 coefficients ranged between .33 and .47. In contrast interrelations among some criteria (the judges' rankings on question 6 and the ethnicity of one's closest friends) get as high as .98. Guttman has noted this often before. He and Levy (1979) write, "Indeed, this phenomenon of small correlation with background characteristics has been widely observed and is common to many research topics. Such static characteristics usually do not serve as very good predictors of attitudes and values [p. 26]."

In general, the background characteristics do not seem to have very much influence on how universalistic or particularistic a judge's rating of a subject's definition of or distinctions between *Quebecer* and *Québécois* will be.

Table 1

Judgments on the Particularism to Universalism of Definitions of and Distinctions between *Quebecer* and *Québécois* by Background Variables

Judgments (from particularistic to universalistic)	Age (young to old)	Sex (male to female)	Occupation (low status to high status)
French-Canadian subjects			
Question 6			
Judge 1	− .05	.03	− .07
Judge 2	− .08	− .19	.14
Judge 3	− .07	− .15	.14
Judge 4	− .07	− .20	.16
Judge 5	− .06	− .26	.21
Question 7			
Judge 1	− .22	− .06	− .06
Judge 2	− .11	− .11	.13
Judge 3	− .20	.01	.02
Judge 4	− .17	− .10	− .01
Judge 5	− .19	− .12	− .02
English-Canadian Subjects			
Question 6			
Judge 1	.47	.04	.29
Judge 2	.34	.09	.34
Judge 3	.29	.22	.24
Judge 4	.23	.21	.08
Judge 5	.22	.17	.15
Question 7			
Judge 1	− .05	.16	.25
Judge 2	− .13	.16	.25
Judge 3	− .04	.30	.22
Judge 4	− .01	.29	.19
Judge 5	− .10	.33	.21
Other Canadian Subjects			
Question 6			
Judge 1	− .13	− .05	− .13
Judge 2	− .05	.13	− .17
Judge 3	− .12	− .01	− .22
Judge 4	− .20	.00	− .19
Judge 5	− .26	.08	− .19
Question 7			
Judge 1	.09	− .06	.07
Judge 2	.01	− .05	.01
Judge 3	.03	− .15	.08
Judge 4	− .04	− .06	.05
Judge 5	.04	− .16	− .03

Before the data were broken down into "English Canadian," "French Canadian," and "Other Canadian," it was possible to see that the correlations ranged between .61 and .83 between the subject's ethnicity and the ethnicity of his or her six closest friends. Furthermore, substantial to very strong correlations remain among the six closest friends when the data are broken down into the three subgroupings, although the ethnicity of the respondent drops out of the martrix because it remains constant when the data are broken down by the subject's ethnicity (Figures 1–6).

There is a negligible relationship between the subject's ethnicity and the judge's ranking of his or her definition of and distinctions between *Quebecer* and *Québécois*. In a similar manner, the correlations between the ethnicity of the subject's six closest friends and the judges' rankings of the definitions of and distinctions between *Quebecer* and *Québécois* fall between no association at all to a usually low level of association. In general, neither the subject's nor his or her six closest friends' ethnicity seems to influence how universalistically or particularistically his or her definitions of or distinctions between *Quebecer* or *Québécois* will be judged to be.

As can be seen from the printouts of the SSAs (Smallest Space Analysis) in Figures 1–6, there are three distinct areas found in the three different breakdowns of the data into the ethnic subgroups. These form wedges that are evidence of a radex form. This could be verified by taking the point of a protractor at the origin and tracing in the circle around the area. The three areas that appear in this space are the area of ethnic identification, the area of the sex and occupational status of the subject, and the area of the ethnicity of the friends and age of the subject. In three dimensions age appears considerably lower in the space than the ethnicity of friends. The reader should not be concerned that on the SSA printouts the areas of ethnicity of friends, age, and ethnic identification are reversed on the surface between the "French" and "Other" Canadian categories, because "flip flopping" replicates the other groups. This can be verified by drawing the English-Canadian cutting on a sheet of transparent paper, turning it over, and then putting it over the cutting for the "Other" and "French" Canadian groupings. This exercise could be repeated in reverse fashion as well.

If both the definitions and distinctions are considered together, and they are found to be close in space, then they both deal with a semantic field having to do with the universalism to particularism of ethnic identity labels. Yet caution should be taken in inferring a lot from the intercorrelations between the definitions of and distinctions between *Quebecer* and *Québécois*. Indeed, they vary from a low positive association (.21) to

Column

	1	2	3	4	5	6	7	8	9	10	11	12	13	14	15	16	17	18	19
	Age	Sex	The ethnicity of the closest friends 1-6; friend one's ethnicity (3); friend two's ethnicity (4); etc.						The five judges' rankings of the definitions of Quebecer and Quebecois from universalistic to particularistic; judge one's ranking (9); judge two's ranking (10); etc.					The five judges' rankings of the distinctions between Quebecer and Quebecois from universalistic to particularistic; judge one's ranking (14); judge two's ranking (15); etc.					Occupation
1	0.0																		
2	-0.21	0.0																	
3	0.10	0.09	0.0																
4	0.12	0.16	0.97	0.0															
5	0.12	0.06	0.93	0.95	0.0														
6	0.20	-0.06	0.77	0.84	0.93	0.0													
7	0.30	-0.13	0.72	0.72	0.90	0.96	0.0												
8	0.33	-0.09	0.75	0.75	0.86	0.88	0.96	0.0											
9	-0.13	-0.05	-0.08	-0.13	-0.09	0.11	0.21	0.14	0.0										
10	-0.05	0.13	-0.15	-0.24	-0.18	-0.05	0.09	-0.00	0.92	0.0									
11	-0.13	-0.01	-0.13	-0.25	-0.17	-0.01	0.10	-0.04	0.90	0.96	0.0								
12	-0.20	0.00	-0.08	-0.18	-0.24	0.0	0.08	-0.04	0.90	0.95	0.98	0.0							
13	-0.26	0.08	-0.25	-0.28	-0.29	-0.07	-0.02	-0.23	0.81	0.85	0.92	0.94	0.0						
14	0.09	-0.06	-0.07	-0.12	0.07	0.09	0.22	0.07	0.61	0.37	0.30	0.40	0.31	0.0					
15	0.01	-0.05	-0.05	-0.12	0.06	0.03	0.26	0.06	0.41	0.41	0.29	0.34	0.26	0.94	0.0				
16	0.03	-0.15	-0.08	-0.09	0.12	0.15	0.31	0.11	0.49	0.36	0.27	0.37	0.30	0.97	0.98	0.0			
17	-0.04	-0.06	0.19	0.03	0.19	0.15	0.29	0.10	0.41	0.29	0.24	0.32	0.21	0.96	0.98	0.99	0.0		
18	0.04	-0.16	0.14	-0.06	0.14	0.06	0.21	0.05	0.31	0.24	0.25	0.33	0.38	0.92	0.94	0.97	0.96	0.0	
19	-0.05	-0.03	0.32	0.22	0.34	0.29	0.02	0.07	-0.13	-0.18	-0.23	-0.19	-0.19	0.07	0.01	0.08	0.05	-0.03	0.0

Row

Figure 1 Original coefficients: Other Canadian.

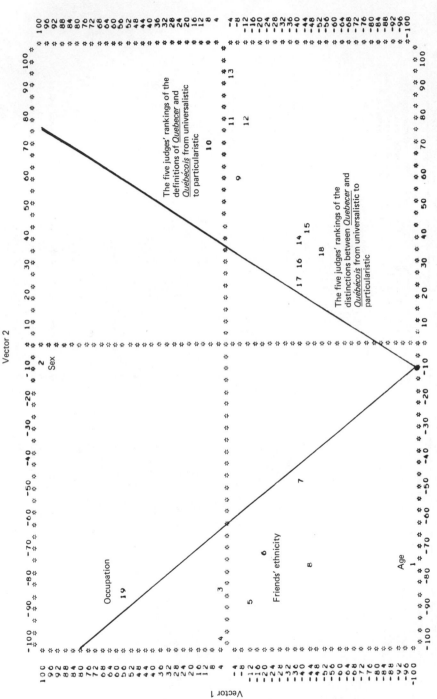

Figure 2 Vector 2 plotted against vector 1: Other Canadian. Guttman-Lingoes' coefficient of alienation = .11961 in 59 iterations; Kruskal's stress = .09918; $M = 2$ (semistrong monotonicity).

170

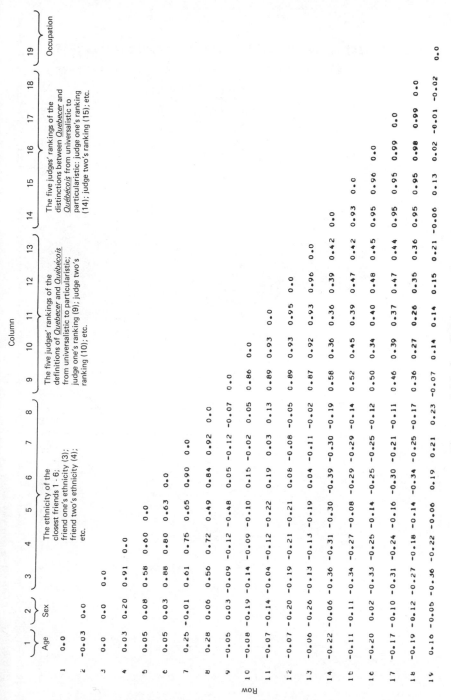

Column

Row	1 Age	2 Sex	3	4	5	6	7	8	9	10	11	12	13	14	15	16	17	18	19 Occupation
			The ethnicity of the closest friends 1-6; friend one's ethnicity (3); friend two's ethnicity (4); etc.						The five judges' rankings of the definitions of *Quebecer* and *Québécois* from universalistic to particularistic; judge one's ranking (9); judge two's ranking (10); etc.					The five judges' rankings of the distinctions between *Quebecer* and *Québécois* from universalistic to particularistic; judge one's ranking (14); judge two's ranking (15); etc.					
1	0.0																		
2	-0.03	0.0																	
3	0.0	0.0	0.0																
4	0.03	0.20	0.91	0.0															
5	0.05	0.08	0.58	0.60	0.0														
6	0.05	0.03	0.88	0.80	0.63	0.0													
7	0.25	-0.01	0.61	0.75	0.65	0.90	0.0												
8	0.28	0.06	0.56	0.72	0.49	0.84	0.92	0.0											
9	-0.05	0.03	-0.09	-0.12	-0.48	0.05	-0.12	-0.07	0.0										
10	-0.08	-0.19	-0.14	-0.09	-0.10	0.15	-0.02	0.05	0.86	0.0									
11	-0.07	-0.14	-0.04	-0.12	-0.22	0.19	0.03	0.13	0.89	0.93	0.0								
12	-0.07	-0.20	-0.19	-0.21	-0.21	0.08	-0.08	-0.05	0.89	0.93	0.95	0.0							
13	-0.06	-0.26	-0.13	-0.19	-0.19	0.04	-0.11	-0.02	0.87	0.92	0.93	0.96	0.0						
14	-0.22	-0.06	-0.36	-0.31	-0.30	-0.39	-0.30	-0.19	0.58	0.36	0.36	0.39	0.42	0.0					
15	-0.11	-0.11	-0.34	-0.27	-0.08	-0.29	-0.29	-0.14	0.52	0.45	0.39	0.47	0.42	0.93	0.0				
16	-0.20	0.02	-0.33	-0.25	-0.14	-0.25	-0.25	-0.12	0.50	0.34	0.40	0.48	0.45	0.95	0.96	0.0			
17	-0.17	-0.10	-0.31	-0.24	-0.16	-0.30	-0.21	-0.11	0.46	0.39	0.37	0.47	0.44	0.95	0.95	0.99	0.0		
18	-0.19	-0.12	-0.27	-0.18	-0.14	-0.34	-0.25	-0.17	0.36	0.27	0.26	0.35	0.36	0.95	0.95	0.98	0.99	0.0	
19	0.16	-0.05	-0.36	-0.22	-0.06	0.19	0.21	0.23	-0.07	0.14	0.14	0.15	0.21	-0.06	-0.13	-0.02	-0.01	-0.02	0.0

Figure 3 Original coefficients: French Canadian.

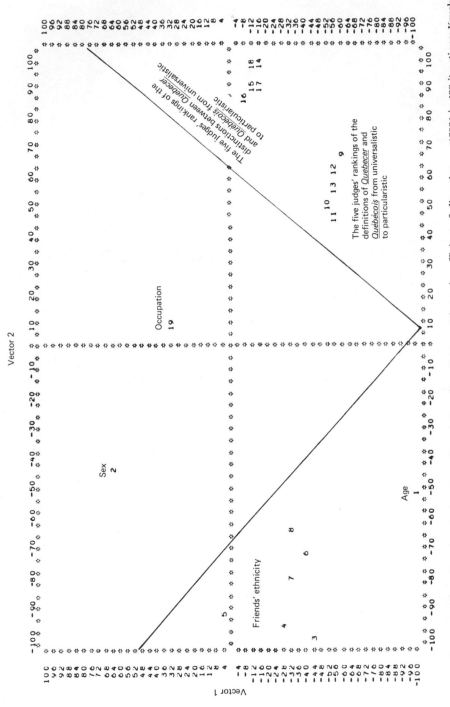

Figure 4 Vector 2 plotted against vector 1: French Canadian. Guttman–Lingoes' coefficient of alienation = .15031 in 100 iterations; Kruskal's stress = .12660; $M = 2$ (semistrong monotonicity).

Column

Row	1 Age	2 Sex	3	4	5	6	7	8	9	10	11	12	13	14	15	16	17	18	19 Occupation
			The ethnicity of the closest friends 1 - 6; friend one's ethnicity (3); friend two's ethnicity (4); etc.						The five judges' rankings of the definitions of *Quebecer* and *Québécois* from universalistic to particularistic; judge one's ranking (9); judge two's ranking (10); etc.					The five judges' rankings of the distinctions between *Quebecer* and *Québécois* from universalistic to particularistic: judge one's ranking (14); judge two's ranking (15); etc.					
1	0.0																		
2	-0.12	0.0																	
3	0.21	0.00	0.0																
4	-0.05	-0.21	0.95	0.0															
5	-0.03	-0.12	0.93	0.94	0.0														
6	0.00	0.19	0.77	0.77	0.88	0.0													
7	0.30	0.33	0.75	0.58	0.82	0.96	0.0												
8	0.24	0.37	0.58	0.54	0.74	0.92	0.95	0.0											
9	-0.47	-0.04	-0.35	-0.15	-0.28	-0.40	-0.25	-0.25	0.0										
10	-0.34	-0.10	-0.41	-0.21	-0.17	-0.27	-0.24	-0.25	0.97	0.0									
11	-0.29	-0.22	-0.26	-0.11	-0.05	-0.37	-0.35	-0.31	-0.96	0.98	0.0								
12	-0.23	-0.21	-0.33	-0.29	-0.27	-0.40	-0.27	-0.42	0.94	0.94	0.96	0.0							
13	-0.22	-0.17	-0.29	-0.18	-0.08	-0.16	-0.08	-0.21	0.84	0.92	0.89	0.93	0.0						
14	0.05	-0.16	0.32	0.26	0.03	0.01	0.06	0.01	0.61	0.52	0.60	0.55	0.41	0.0					
15	0.13	-0.16	0.26	0.22	0.00	0.05	0.11	0.13	0.40	0.48	0.44	0.37	0.40	0.97	0.0				
16	0.04	-0.30	0.47	0.43	0.27	0.16	0.18	0.13	0.44	0.52	0.59	0.50	0.50	0.96	0.97	0.0			
17	0.01	-0.29	0.41	0.43	0.17	0.06	0.22	0.15	0.38	0.50	0.49	0.55	0.61	0.93	0.96	0.97	0.0		
18	0.10	-0.33	0.52	0.52	0.36	0.25	0.22	0.17	0.36	0.42	0.43	0.51	0.59	0.93	0.92	0.95	0.97	0.0	
19	0.04	-0.11	-0.05	-0.01	-0.30	0.02	-0.13	-0.04	0.23	0.34	0.24	0.15	0.25	0.25	0.25	0.22	0.19	0.21	0.0

Figure 5   Original coefficients: English Canadian.

173

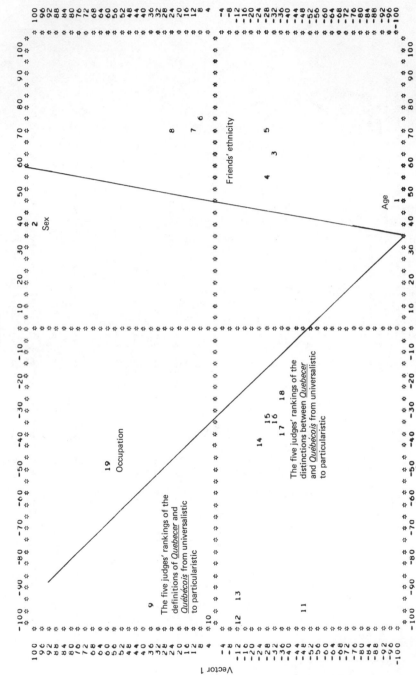

Figure 6   Vector 2 plotted against vector 1: English Canadian. Guttman-Lingoes' coefficient of alienation = .16998 in 29 iterations; Kruskal's stress = .14320; M = 2 (semistrong monotonicity).

a substantial positive association (.61), and the definitions of the words seem to be more spread out in space than do the distinctions between them. The logic of the scoring system may produce a special effect in a subset of the responses. Take, for example, the case of a person who gives a highly particularistic definition, and then for the distinction repeats the definition but adds on a highly universalistic element. This distinction would be judged to be in the middle range. Contrast that person with the individual who starts out with a highly universalistic definition, which is subsequently joined by a highly particularistic element in the distinction that gets judged as 3. Taken separately, the first individual's definition is seen as very particularistic and the second person's as very universalistic, although in the long run their intended meaning is similar. Yet even in this example, it could be argued that the definition and the distinction are different and are not influenced by language because the respondent is free to give any initial definition he or she wants, and the empirical reality reveals a highly complex field.

Although the spatial area covering the judges' rankings of the definitions from universalistic to particularistic is relatively close to the area of the judges' assessments of the distinctions between *Quebecer* and *Québécois*, it is nonetheless from distinct regions for all sets of data. This evidence suggests that the subjects' act of defining *Quebecer* and *Québécois* is distinct from the act of making or not making distinctions between these words.

The printouts in Figures 1–6 list the correlation matrices and the SSAs for all data relevant to the discussion of the quantitative data.

Conclusions

The qualitative and quantitative analyses contrast in the extent to which they depict a difference of universalism to particularism in background variables. The quantitative analysis shows that age, sex, occupational, or ethnic group affiliations do not result in their members' making *significantly* particularistic or universalistic definitions of or distinctions between the words *Quebecer* and *Québécois*. At the same time the quantitative data strongly support the observation that the English Canadian, French Canadian, and Other Canadian ethnic groupings are all highly particularistic in their choice of their six closest friends. On the other hand, the qualitative data document distinct categories that have changed in form and content over time. Although it was not an expressed emphasis of this paper, stratificational and other differences among the ethnic groups in Quebec suggest some behavioral dimensions associated with these categories. This qualitative information documents the notion that the ethnic groups in Quebec have been and still are quite particularistic in their construction of ethnic identity labels.

However, on closer examination these seemingly varying conclusions from the qualitative and quantitative data are not contradictory.

The quantitative data are people's answers to a telephone survey. The majority of individuals surveyed gave answers that were judged to be very universalistic or particularistic, although a sizable minority gave answers that were seen to be relatively neutral. No social group studied was perceived to give very particularistic or universalistic answers as a collectivity. A telephone survey is only one social circumstance, and people may employ these labels very differently when talking to intimates, colleagues, or acquaintances.

The qualitative data draw on a variety of sources, including two famous novels and on the writings and statements of political leaders for the clearest articulation of these ethnic identity labels. Although undoubtedly influencing public opinion, these highly elitist sources may have greatly exaggerated the degree of particularism expressed by different ethnic groups in Quebec.

The sources in the qualitative data document a high degree of tension in communicating across ethnic boundaries. This can very well be explained by the strong trend for ethnically particularistic close friendship choices in the quantitative data. Since all the ethnic groups in Quebec tend to recruit their six closest friends from their own ethnic group, the unfamiliarity and lack of experience in interacting on an intimate basis across ethnic lines would certainly produce a high level of anxiety when dealing with individuals whose rules of interaction, customs, and etiquette may be based on very different expectancies than those to which one is accustomed. At the same time, the world of work and the mass media bring most Montrealers into contact with individuals from outside of their own group. Yet interacting on a level of close friendship is far different from coming into contact with someone over a counter, desk, or on a TV screen or seeing someone on a relatively ethnically segregated factory floor or in a complex organization. In a society highly conscious of ethnic stratification, closest friendship may serve as a refuge from the competition of the marketplace, where outgroups are seen as possible competitors or exploiters. As long as these worlds of intimacy remain bounded along ethnic lines, a support for a particularistic construction of ethnic identity labels will exist. In this sense, my data suggest that the ethnic classification system is related to the properties of the social system of which intimate friendship is only one part.

Finally I will address the remaining questions raised in the quote by Mary Douglas in the beginning of this paper.

1. How fuzzy are the boundaries of the categories of *Quebecer* and *Québécois*? The qualitative data have shown a myriad of nuances, phrasing, expressions, and prejudices in the definitions of and distinctions between these words. Even though their boundaries are quite fuzzy indeed, judges highly agreed on the degree of universalism to particularism that they perceived in them.

2. How well insulated are the meanings they enclose? These ethnic identity labels have changed in form and content to a large extent, yet they have remained sufficiently insulated to take on new criteria for setting themselves off vis-à-vis other groups. Yet no group was empirically shown to do this to a significant extent.

3. How many categories are there? Although there have been a variety of ethnic identity labels documented historically and some of these remain around today, two main terms, *Quebecer* and *Québécois*, were pointed to as new formatives. Perhaps the only underlying principle relating these terms to one another is concatenation with or without a term relating origin. Yet for the widest part of the population, these categorizations or principles do not seem to be employed either particularistically or universalistically to any significant extent.

4. There seems to be a system of thought concerning ethnic identity. Its components appear to cover the distinct subfields discussed in this paper. The stability of this system of thought is highly dependent on major political and historical changes, which have occurred in vastly different time spans varying from 15 to over 100 years.

Do *Quebecer* and *Québécois* mean the same thing? Many people think they do, many think they do not, and many aren't sure. Yet defining *Quebecer* and *Québécois* in a particularistic, neutral, or universalistic manner is not determined by membership in a particular sex, age, occupation, or ethnic group.

Acknowledgments

This project could not have been done without the work of my students in my "Individual and Society" and "Sociology of Quebec" classes in the spring semester of 1977. I wish to thank each one of them: Philippe Williate Battet, Andrée Bourassa, Eleine Campbell, Carole Chartrand, Phil Coleman, Joan Fuller, Mike Gilbey, Michel Guay, Rena Halickman, Collen Hillock, William Dale Hoffman, Bankole A. Komolafe, Diana Kosyzycki, Claude Lafrenière, France Lalande, Sukdeo Latchman, Emanuel M. Lima, Tom Litchfield, Pamela Man-Yee Lo, Phemie London, Charles Montpétit, Colleen Moody, Bernard Nzo-Nguty, Julie Owade, Denise Paré, Greg St. Laurent, Ann Raimondo, Ana Maria Rodrigues, Claude Seris, Nancy Scholefield, Terri Sternklar, Toni Studer, Louise Sullivan, Alexander Szuba, Robert Theoret, and Renée Tyberg. Thanks go to the Department of Sociology of the Loyola Campus of Concordia University, Montreal, Quebec, Canada, for paying for the printing of the questionnaires and to Marcel Douek for helping with many hours of transcription. Many thanks go to the members of the University of Chicago's Parent Health and Infant Development Project and to Louis Guttman, who let me participate in his consultation and didactic seminar in the spring and winter of 1980. Thanks to Rita J. Jeremy for suggesting a cutting of the SSAs and for noticing a problem with the scoring system. Special thanks go to Sandy Gruba-Mc-Callister for her computer programming. Finally, I wish to express my gratitude to Eyvind Ronquist for checking my references.

References

Bauer, J.
    1980   Peuple canadien–français ou nation québécoise? *Le Devoir* **23 juin**:7.
Bennet, J. W. (Ed.)
    1973   *The New Ethnicity. Perspectives from Ethnology. Proceedings of the American Ethnological Society.* St. Paul: West Publishing.
Boulay, J.
    1980   Histoire de famille. *Le Devoir* **6 août**:12.
Broom, L., and Selznick, P.
    1973   *Sociology: A Test with Adapted Readings* (fifth ed.). New York: Harper and Row.
Chaput-Rolland, S.
    1980   Où nous mène M. Trudeau? *Le Devoir* **14 juillet**:13.
Charbonneau, J. P.
    1980   Préciser le vocabulaire. *Le Devoir* **1 août**:7.
Charte de la langue française
    1977   *Charte de la langue française.* Ville de Québec: l'Editeur officiel du Québec.
Clement, W.
    1975   *The Canadian Corporate Elite: An Analysis of Economic Power.* Toronto: Mc-Clelland and Steward.
Clift, D., and Arnopoulos, S. M.
    1979   *Le fait anglais au Québec.* Montréal: Editions Libre Expression.
Corbeil, M.
    1980   Réplique/Contre l'Etat-nation. *Le Devoir* **23 juillet**:13.
Cowan, P.
    1980   Lévesque moves to allay Anglos' fears. *The Montreal Gazette* **24 March**:10.
Culler, J.
    1975   *Structuralist Poetics: Structuralism, Linguistics, and the Study of Literature.* Ithaca, New York: Cornell University Press.
Desbarats, P.
    1976   *René: A Canadian in Search of a Country.* Toronto: McClelland and Stewart.
De Vos, G., and Romanucci-Ross, L. (Eds.)
    1975   *Ethnic Identity: Cultural Continuities and Change.* Palo Alto: Mayfield.
Douglas, M.
    1975   *Implicit Meanings: Essays in Anthropology.* London: Routledge & Kegan Paul.
Dumont, F.
    1980   Du référendum au dictionnaire. *Le Devoir* **28 juillet**:13.

Glazer, N., and Moynihan, D. P. (Eds.)
   1975   *Ethnicity: Theory and Experience*. Cambridge, Mass.: Harvard University Press.
Gove, P. B. (Ed.)
   1961   *Webster's Third International Dictionary of the English Language Unabridged*.
          Springfield, Mass.: G & M Merriam.
Guilbert, L., Lagane, R., and Niobey, G.
   1971   *Tome sixième PSO-SUR Grande Larousse de la langue française* (7 vols.). Paris,
          France: Librairie Larousse.
Gurdin, J. B.
   1978   Amitié/Friendship: the socio-cultural construction of friendship in contempo-
          rary Montreal. Unpublished Ph.D. dissertation, Department of Sociology, Uni-
          versité de Montréal.
Guttman, L.
   1981   What is not what in theory construction, in *Multi-Dimensional Data Represen-
          tations—When and Why* (Ingwer Borg, Ed.). Ann Arbor, Michigan: Mathesis Press,
          pp. 47–64.
Hains, A.
   1980   Nous, peuple(s) du Canada *Le Devoir* **28 juillet**:12.
Hémon, L.
   1924   *Maria Chapdelaine: A Tale of the Lake St. Jean Country* (Witt Blake, Trans.). New
          York: Macmillan.
Hraba, J.
   1979   *American Ethnicity*. Itasca, Illinois: F. E. Peacock.
Isaacs, H. R. (Ed.)
   1975   *Idols of the Tribe: Group Identity and Political Change*. New York: Harper and
          Row.
Laurin, C.
   1978   *Canadian Ethnic Studies*. **X**(1):6.
Le Borgne, L.
   1980   M. Trudeau a tendu une perche. *Le Devoir* **24 juillet**:7.
Leclerc, J. C.
   1980   La fête d'un pays incertain. *Le Devoir* **19 juin**:10.
Lemieux, A.
   1980   La décadence du "vrai" nationalisme. *Le Devoir*: **8 janvier**:5.
Levy, S., and Guttman, L.
   1975   On the multiple structure of wellbeing. *Social Indicators Research* **2**:361–388.
          Dordrecht, Holland: D. Reidel.
   1979   *Structure and Level of Values for Rewards and Allocation Criteria in Several Life
          Areas: Report on a Preliminary Survey in Israel designed according to "Mannheim
          II Common-Core Mapping Sentence" developed by the Working Group on Values
          and Social Problem Indicators for Contemporary Europe*. (Initiated by the Eu-
          ropean Science Foundation.) The Israel Institute of Applied Social Research
          Publication No. SL/752/E, Jerusalem.
Lévi-Strauss, C.
   1977   *l'Identité: séminaire interdisciplinaire* dirigé par Claude Lévi-Strauss. Paris: B.
          Grasset.
Lévesque, R.
   1979   *René Lévesque: My Quebec*. Agincourt, Ontario: Methuen Publications. (Originally
          published, 1978 in French under the title of *La Passion du Québec*. Paris, Editions
          Stock.)

MacLennan, H.
    1945   *Two Solitudes*. Toronto: Macmillan Company of Canada.
Marion, S.
    1980   l'Idée de nation chez les historiens anglo–canadiens. *Le Devoir* **2 juillet**:7.
Marsden, P. V., and Laumann, E. O.
    1978   The social structure of religious groups: a replication and methodological cri-
            tique, in *Theory Construction and Data Analysis in the Behavioral Sciences: A
            Volume in Honor of Louis Guttman* (S. Shye, Ed.), pp. 81–111. San Francisco:
            Jossey-Bass.
Mascotto, J.
    1980   Au coeur du problème, l'ordre politique. *Le Devoir* **24 juillet**:7.
The Montreal Gazette
    1980   Letters to the editor. *The Montreal Gazette* **April 17**:6.
Morris, R. N., and Lanphier, C. M.
    1977   *Three Scales of Inequality Perspectives on French–English Relations*. Don Mills,
            Ontario: Longman Canada Limited.
OED
    1961   *The Oxford English Dictionary VIII Poy-Ry*. Oxford: Clarendon Press.
Orkin, M. M.
    1967   *Speaking Canadian French: An Informal Account of the French Language in Can-
            ada*. Toronto: General Publishing.
Porter, J.
    1965   *The Vertical Mosaic: An Analysis of Social Class and Power in Canada*. Toronto:
            University of Toronto Press.
Rioux, M.
    1977   *Les québécois. Le temps qui court*. Bourges: l'Imprimerie Tardy Quercy Auvergne.
Robbins, E.
    1975   Ethnicity or class? Social relations in a small Canadian town, in *The New Eth-
            nicity. Perspectives from Ethnology. Proceedings of the American Ethnological
            Society* (J. W. Bennet, Ed.), pp. 285–304. St. Paul: West Publishing.
Schwartz, G.
    1980   Commentary and opinion. *Le Devoir* **8 août**:7.
Shye, S.
    1978   *Theory Construction and Data Analysis in the Behavioral Sciences: A Volume in
            Honor of Louis Guttman*. San Francisco: Jossey-Bass.
Trudeau, P. E.
    1980a   M. Trudeau et le concept des deux nations. *La Presse* **26 juin**:A6.
    1980b   M. Trudeau parle aussi au nom des Franco–Canadiens. *La Presse* **27 juin**:A6.
    1980c   Pas de pays sans notion de partage. *La Presse* **28 juin**:A6.

10

Beneath the Surface: Ethnic Communities in Phoenix, Arizona

Phylis Cancilla Martinelli

INTRODUCTION

In discussions of ethnicity and urban life in the United States, the assumption is often made that ethnic life resides in visible ethnic neighborhoods. The influential Chicago School's ecological approach of Park and Burgess (1925), Wirth (1928), Zorbaugh (1929), and others was largely predicated upon ethnic neighborhood analysis. Such subcommunity approaches continue as in the more recent work of Axelrod (1956), Suttles (1968), and Yancey and Ericksen (1979). Some researchers (Jacobs, 1963) have looked at ethnic neighborhoods as areas that foster distinctive cultures and give a city desirable diversity, whereas others (Clark, 1965; Arricale, 1977:15–18) have viewed ethnic neighborhoods as areas that result in a ghetto mentality and hold back members of a group. Traditionally, eastern cities, with New York being the most obvious example, and some midwestern cities, such as Chicago, are associated with visible ethnic neighborhoods. In contrast cities in the recently urbanizing arid Southwest, such as Phoenix, are looked upon as either having no ethnic groups or perhaps having only a few, such as Mexican Americans and Native Americans.

Yet ethnic communities do exist in Phoenix, the focus of this analysis, and perhaps in other recently urbanizing communities. Many of the self-identified ethnic communities are in the process of being formed by recent migrants from cities in other parts of the country. Phoenix has

181

CULTURE, ETHNICITY,
AND IDENTITY

grown rapidly: its population was only 65,414 in 1940; by 1980 it had increased to 764,895 (U.S. Bureau of the Census, 1981:4). The larger metropolitan area showed a definite increase in the last decade, growing from 971,228 in 1970 to 1,508,030 in 1980, a change of 55% (U.S. Bureau of the Census, 1981:4). Although it may be a leading example, Phoenix is not alone in this type of growth; in the arid region Tucson, Albuquerque, Las Vegas, and El Paso have also experienced rapid growth in recent years. This general trend of growth resulted from an expansion of market capabilities from the Midwest urban regions, the West Coast, and growth in the Northwest, Denver, Dallas, and Houston. These changes placed the arid Southwest in an ideal economic position (Gordon, 1978:105).

ETHNICITY IN THE DIFFUSE PHOENIX SETTING

Why has ethnicity in Phoenix been largely overlooked until recently? One reason is the relative invisibility of ethnic groups, because there are few areas with ethnic concentrations. Historically, there were two Chinatowns in Phoenix, but these remain only as a memory since the Chinese have scattered throughout the city (Martinelli, 1978a). Although South Phoenix does have a concentration of Mexican Americans and blacks, it is isolated and spatially large. In a city with many newcomers few people are aware that the name Indian School Road signifies a government Indian school still located in the central city. Even fewer are aware of the urban Indian neighborhood adjacent to the school.

The bulk of the other groups are scattered, and people actively involved in their ethnic groups participate through family ties, churches, voluntary clubs, credit unions, and eventful celebrations of the groups. The various groups are not, in fact, necessarily any less ethnic because they lack a geographical base. Amitai Etzioni has noted the transition from the concentrated immigrant communities to contemporary ethnic communities that are nonecologically based and do not involve the individual totally (Etzioni, 1959:255–262).

Besides being scattered, the ethnic communities of Phoenix appear dwarfed by the large concentrations in other cities. However, it can be argued that size alone does not constitute a valid criterion for an ethnic community any more than a geographic concentration does. What matters is that people choose to invest at least part of their self-identity in an ethnic group, which in a new setting like Phoenix they could often choose to discard.

Finally, many of these ethnic communities are fairly new or have gone through a transition in recent years that has brought new vitality and dimensions to the community. Some groups such as the Italians, Poles, and Greeks have been in the Phoenix area for a generation or more but have only grown in recent years. Other groups such as the Croatians, Ukranians, and Serbians only recently began arriving in numbers large enough to form a community. There has been some awareness of increasing ethnic diversity as part of the general migration to Arizona (Granger, 1973:1–2). Leonard Gordon noted that although Phoenix had not developed a Little Italy or a Greek or Jewish "town," to lump all whites in the "Anglo" category was to overlook the amount of cultural pluralism in this broad category (Gordon, 1973:3–5). Whereas Gordon looked at pluralism as evidenced in the major religious groups (Catholic, Mormon, and Jewish), the author's experience of working on the Phoenix History Project and an ethnic directory for Phoenix led to an even greater awareness of the cultural diversity of Phoenix.

Although a great deal of research still needs to be done regarding minority ethnic groups in Phoenix, such as Mexican Americans and Native Americans, there is a growing body of research regarding them (Chadhuri, 1974; Harris, 1977). The main focus here will be on the "new immigrant" people who migrated, or whose ancestors migrated, from Southern and Eastern Europe in the last great wave of migration from there to this country. In Phoenix these groups are represented by the Croatians, Czechs, Slovaks, Poles, Estonians, Greeks, Hungarians, Italians, Jews (primarily Russian), Serbians, Lithuanians, Ukranians, and Russians. Preliminary research indicates that only the Greek and Jewish communities show any signs of clustering, although more detailed research must be done (*Inside Phoenix*, 1978:15).[1] Yet there is evidence of active association among most of these groups, evident in the number and range of organizations serving these groups (see Table 1).

THE CASES OF THE ITALIAN AND POLISH COMMUNITIES

The Italians and Poles are the two largest of these groups; there were 18,915 people of Italian ancestry and 18,203 people of Italian and other ancestry, for a total of 37,118 Italians in Phoenix as of the 1980 census.

---

[1] Based on an analysis of zip codes for the Greek community done for the Phoenix History Project, 1978, and *Inside Phoenix* (1978:8).

Table 1

Associational Organizations and Activities in Phoenix[a]

	Croatian	Czecho-slovakian	Finnish	Greek	Lithuanian	Hungarian	Italian	Jewish	Polish	Russian Orthodox	Serbian	Ukranian
Service club	—	—	—	2	—	—	1	37	3	—	—	—
Veteran group	2	—	—	—	—	—	1	2	—	—	—	2
Credit union	2	—	—	—	—	—	—	1	—	—	1	1
Consular representative	—	—	Yes	Yes	—	—	Yes	—	—	—	—	—
Social club	1	2	—	1	2	1	9	—	2	—	—	2
School	1	—	—	1	—	—	—	3	—	—	—	1
Cultural group	1	—	1	3	—	—	2	1	2	—	—	2
Church or synagogue	—	1	1	1	1	1	1	5	—	1	2	2
Church or synagogue affiliated	—	—	—	1	—	—	—	6	—	—	—	—
TV, radio, or newspaper	1	—	—	—	—	—	—	3	—	—	—	—
Education	—	—	—	1	—	—	—	2	—	—	—	—

[a]Source: Phoenix Ethnic Directory.

The same census showed 9,823 people of Polish ancestry and 13,198 people of Polish and other ancestry, for a total of 23,021 Poles in Phoenix. (United States Census, 1980) These figures represent the expanded category of ancestry for European people; in previous census counts only the first and second generations were included, which meant later generations were not represented; these figures also represent the continuing migration of these groups to the Phoenix area. The two groups show a pattern that is probably typical of those groups that had historical communities in Phoenix.

The earliest Italians began moving to Phoenix in the 1880s, often arriving after giving up their search for gold or silver in Arizona's mountains (Martinelli, 1977:319–340). A loosely knit community formed primarily based on social contact and business dealings. Land records show early arrivals bought property from non-Italians; later Italians tended to buy land from the earlier Italians. Many Italians went into the saloon business either as owners or employees, until 1914 when Maricopa County went dry (Mawn, 1979:413–417). City directories also listed Italians with a wide range of skills such as barber, butcher, clerk, blacksmith, stone cutter, and music teacher. A few of the Italians operated hotels or rented rooms.

Rather than form their own societies, the Italians tended to join existing societies, often those of fellow Catholic Mexican Americans, whose Spanish was similar to Italian. The *Alianza Hispano-Americana's* lodge No. 9 as a social fraternity had services such as burial expenses and insurance. Among its members and officers were Italians, which was also the case for the Yucatec Hose Company No. 2 and the Yellow Kids Football Club, a Mexican-American athletic club.

Because the Italian community was small and scattered and lacked both a focal point to gather, like an Italian ethnic church, and a means of formal communication such as a newspaper, interaction was through frequent visiting. Since there was no one part of Italy represented, regional differences were forgotten, and "real Italian," instead of a dialect, was spoken as the common language. Besides visiting in the Phoenix area, people would drive as far as Gilbert, Superior, and Glendale to be among friends.

The community experienced a slow growth, which was generally not recognized by the larger community, with the exception of a few prominent families or individuals such as the Donofrio family, Alessio Carraro, James Minotto, and Salvatore Cudia. By 1939 the community had grown enough to support a club, after earlier efforts had failed. The club, first known as the Italo-American club, is now established as the Arizona American-Italian Club. After World War II the community continued to grow, as can be seen in the founding of a variety of organizations. The Amico Club, a service group, started in 1952, and in 1972 the Sun City American-Italian Club began. The nationally organized Sons of Italy established a Phoenix chapter in 1974 and now has six chapters in the Phoenix area as well as several others throughout the state. Besides these groups there is an Italian War Veterans group, a student club on the Arizona State University campus (located in the Phoenix suburb of Tempe), and the Fountain Hills American-Italian Club in another suburb. These groups all formed in the 1970s. In 1982 the Preservation of Italian Tradition in Arizona Foundation (PITIA) was established. The purpose of PITIA is to raise funds to support the study of the Italian language, culture, and literature at Arizona universities or in programs in Italy.

The clubs provide a focus for members of the community and involve people in social activities as well as fund-raising activities. Italian traditions such as the St. Joseph's Day Feast are practiced although there is still no Italian Catholic Church. Various churches, including St. Joseph's Catholic Church, now celebrate the feast, and so do some of the clubs (Polson, 1979). *Bocce* (Italian lawn bowling) courts are now located in various parts of the valley, and the clubs often compete against each other. There exists an active interest in finding out about the clubs on the part of people who do not belong. When an article about a course entitled "The Italian-American Experience" appeared in local newspapers (Matthews, 1979), there were many calls from people expressing an interest in finding out about the clubs, which is difficult since most are not listed in the phone book.

The Italian migration to Phoenix has also surfaced through the love of Italian food. As a recent article (Pane, 1978:49) noted, "Some Italians must be bankers, and doctors, and some must drive trucks or fix refrigerators, but it seems that mostly they feed each other—and the rest of us—in a staggering number of Italian restaurants, delis, and groceries." This is a distinct contrast to the early days in Phoenix when there were no Italian restaurants, and Italian housewives had to wait for the monthly visits from the Prescott grocer to buy cooking necessities such as olive oil (Martinelli, 1978b:325–336).

Since 1957 there has been an Italian consulate agent, and in 1982 the post was elevated to the status of a vice-consulate office for Italy. The elevation was in recognition of the growing importance of Italians in Arizona and the amount of work being done by the post.

It is now possible to speak of two Italian communities in the Phoenix area, with some overlapping membership. The early one was formed in the 1880s when foreign-born immigrants settled in the West. This group was basically static, and socializing was among the widely scattered families. Business transactions also kept people in contact. The newer migrants of the last three decades come from Italian-American communities of the East and Midwest, such as New York City and Chicago.[2] They have brought with them memories of their home communities, and many actively seek other Italian Americans. Although there is still no residential concentration (Gordon, 1977),[3] the Italians now have many organizations.

Polish families, like the Balsz brothers, also arrived in early Phoenix by the 1880s.[4] Like the Italians, Polish migrants continued to come to Phoenix in small numbers, mostly forming a small, informal community. Some individuals—such as Edward Wasielewski, Sr., a contractor—rose to prominence. The growing numbers of Polish people and their desire to keep their heritage alive resulted in the formation of the *Klub Pulaskiego* in 1939, which grew from a casual meeting of Polish people to the Pulaski Club.

By 1949 an enterprising Polish realtor named Eugene Wesolowski saw the potential for a Polish-American migration to the Phoenix area. He not only advertised Phoenix real estate in many Polish newspapers in eastern American cities, but he also listed *Polskie Biuro Realnosciowe* (Polish Real Estate Bureau) in the Phoenix phone book. He was correct in his vision; the community grew, again as shown by the organizational growth of local branches of national organizations. The Kopernik Lodge of the Polish National Alliance was formed in 1952; the Paderewski Choral Society, affiliated with the Polish Singers Alliance of America, in 1956; a chapter of the Polish-American Congress in the early 1960s; and the Arizona chapter of the Kosciuszko Foundation was formed in 1976. Another group is the Polish-American Club of Sun City.

Although there is no Polish national church, in 1980 a Polish-speaking priest was assigned to St. Louis the King parish; he has a monthly Polish mass at Brophy Chapel. A retired monsignor offers traditional Polish services at St. Joachim in Sun City for Easter and Christmas. In 1982 the Polish community commemorated the six hundredth anniversary of Our Lady of Czestochowa, the Black Madonna of Poland.

[2] Based on information from 332 obituaries and other news sources on Italian Americans moving to the Phoenix SMSA, 32% are from New York, 20% from Illinois, 8% from Ohio, and 8% from Pennsylvania.

[3] Italians are 5% of the total foreign stock, but their highest concentration in any tract is 2.2%.

[4] The following on Polish Americans is based on research done for the Phoenix History Project, G.W. Johnson director, by this researcher.

In more recent years, the Polish community in Phoenix has become more involved with the larger community and has received recognition from other Polish communities throughout the country. One of their goals, to promote Polish culture in the valley, has been accomplished by participating in concerts sponsored by the city of Phoenix. The 1977 concert was planned in connection with the unveiling and presentation of a bust of Frederic Chopin to Arizona State University by the local Polish clubs. These concerts are viewed as an important accomplishment by some members of the Polish community. As one man noted, "In the other cities, Polish concerts would be in the Polish ghetto; in Phoenix, the concerts are held downtown." Thus, the small and scattered nature of the community is seen, by some, as an asset.

The Phoenix Polish community joined other Polish communities throughout the nation in January 1982 to protest martial law in Poland. Around 300 people, many in traditional Polish dress, held a march and rally on the day proclaimed "Solidarity Day" by the governor of Arizona (*Arizona Republic*, 1982:Bl). Working with Catholic Charities, an organization within the Catholic church, the American Aid for Poland has been established in Phoenix to help refugees from Poland who settle in the Phoenix area. The Polish-American community of Phoenix is moving toward a more visible role in the city.

Research on these two groups does not exhaust the possible patterns of ethnic community development in Phoenix. For some groups historical research has been done, but there is a need for more current information. The Jewish community, for example, by the 1890s had become the nucleus of Phoenix's mercantile businesses, holding places in tailoring, banking, and other businesses. Several members of the community were active in local and state politics. Religious services began in the 1880s, although a synagogue was not built until 1922 (Lamb, 1977:299–318). However, the relationship between the early community—comprised mainly of French, German, and Polish Jews—and the later community, with many Russian Jews including recent immigrants, has not been explored.

The patterns of newer groups, such as the Ukranians, who mostly arrived in Phoenix after World War II, also need to be studied. The Ukranian community is composed of approximately 150 families who belong to the two Ukranian churches, and about the same number who are unregistered. The mission for the Ukranian Catholic church was not established until 1956, when the numbers of this group began to grow. Today this small group supports about 13 different organizations. Research is needed on other recent groups as well, such as the Czechs, Lithuanians, Estonians, Croatians, and Latvians.

THE EMERGENCE OF WHITE ETHNIC PLURALISM IN PHOENIX

The existence of growing, active white ethnic groups in Phoenix is not that surprising. Although sociologists for a long time predicted that European ethnic groups would be totally assimilated, the 1960s saw an increased recognition that ethnic group cohesion was far more durable than had been anticipated; there has been, however, a lack of agreement as to whether this is desirable.[5]

Michael Novak's *The Rise of the Unmeltable Ethnics* (1973) was one of the first books to deal with what he called the "new ethnic consciousness [p.xvi]" of European ethnics. This consciousness is evident in many areas ranging from political activity to individual self-identity. Glazer and Moynihan (1971:301) speculate that ethnic identification has grown with ethnic political appeals substituting for class appeals as traditional economic classes split along ethnic lines.

In terms of ethnic identity it should be recognized that the all encompassing identity that characterized most of the immigrant generation has been changed for later generations. As Andrew Greeley (1974) has noted, ethnicity is not a gradually eroding social force, but "a dynamic, flexible social mechanism [p. 301]." Thus, ethnicity can change as the situation changes. The term *situational ethnicity* is, in fact, used to describe an ethnic identity in modern society, such as ours, which rarely encompasses the full range of an individual's social identities (Okamura, 1981:452–465). In a similar vein Herbert Gans (1979:1–20) has described "symbolic ethnicity," which he sees as more typical of younger ethnics. Individuals are still interested in their ethnic identity, but choose various symbols and situations to express this identity.

Modern ethnic identity may be found most typically in suburban settings such as Phoenix (Yancey, Ericksen, and Juliani, 1976:391–394). Although the suburbs were once seen as capable of producing a cheerful conformity among white Americans, suburbs are now recognized as a setting for ethnic groups. In some suburbs ethnic groups are still concentrated; however, in others the ethnic groups are residentially dispersed. Even where there is not a concentration ethnic communities have formed. Gans (1951:330–339) chronicled, for example, the birth of a diffuse Jewish suburban ethnic community in Park Forest, Illinois. Within a year a community emerged complete with informal and formal contacts among people. There was no concentration of Jewish families, but people made an effort to find out who among their neighbors were

---

[5] For those who see ethnicity as undesirable, see Patterson (1977) and Stein and Hill (1977).

Jewish. The newly formed, nonecological community focused on evenings that were spent among Jewish couples who shared a feeling of relaxation and intimacy; this same feeling of closeness was not as pronounced in friendships with non-Jewish neighbors.

This seeking of an in-group intimacy is evident among ethnic people in Phoenix was well. An Estonian woman admitted she eavesdropped on people in shopping centers if she thought they were speaking Estonian, approaching them if they were and introducing herself (Cooke, 1979:32). For another person, joining an Italian club meant being "Around people who have my background; there is a sameness; there is a closeness [Martinelli, 1977:338]."

One function of ethnic organizations in the Phoenix area is to counteract the anomie and alienation that many newcomers feel in Phoenix. The ethnic group provides a person who may have left family and lifelong friends hundreds of miles away with a chance for an in-group feeling. As one member of the Polish Club said, "This place, Pulaski Hall is our Polonia." Although on one level the clubs are officially organized secondary groups, on another level there is often a feeling of informality and intimacy normally associated with primary groups.

That there is a need to combat feelings of anomie and alienation by ethnic clubs is apparent in the high divorce, crime, and suicide rates of cities in much of the West, including Phoenix. As Howard Kushner has noted (Matthews, 1982), the West has been the "least structured part of the country in family and social apparatus [p. AA5]." The ethnic neighborhoods of eastern cities, for all their problems, provided an area of transition for newly arrived immigrants; ethnic clubs and friendships with people of the same ethnic background help contemporary migrants adjust to a new setting.

Further, ethnic organizations provide a sense of cultural continuity in a new setting. According to the pastor of the Hungarian Christian Church of Phoenix, established in 1972, "Even in such a melting pot, our identity can still surface and we can share with the young like our mothers shared with us [Arizona Republic, 1980:C1].

Etizoni (1959:259–260) suggests other functions of nonecological ethnic groups. First, nonecological groups pose less of a threat to societal unity than do ecologically based groups, because an ecological group can create a power monopoly based on possessing a territory. Further, the more geographically isolated a group is, the more the group is able to avoid close contacts with outsiders. This isolation can be dysfunctional to the larger society, making the ecologically based group a threat to maintaining the overall unity of the larger group. Nonecological groups are not dysfunctional in this sense but, according to Etizoni, serve instead a positive function in preserving pluralism in a diverse soceity such as ours. They provide counterbalancing sources of power essential in maintaining an effective pluralism in a democracy, much in the way other subcultural groups, such as occupational groups, do. Additionally, ethnic groups can cut across potentially divisive class lines, contributing to solidarity in society.

There seems to be an increasing recognition and appreciation of the pluralistic nature of Phoenix. A multiethnic festival, "Hello, Phoenix!" was started in 1978. Produced by Phoenix Arts Coming Together (PACT), the festival originally involved 36 ethnic organizations; it grew to a celebration with over 50 groups active by 1982. In 1982, to accompany the festival, PACT printed a small tabloid with articles on many of the ethnic groups in Phoenix (PACT, 1982). Neighboring Scottsdale has hosted a similar, but smaller "Festival of Nations" for the last few years. Annual events sponsored by local ethnic groups, such as the Greek Orthodox Church's festival, have received increasing publicity and attendance.

Phoenix may well represent a new area in ethnic research to be more fully explored. No doubt other Sunbelt cities have ethnic diversity that has not been thoroughly studied. What is emerging in Phoenix among Italian and Polish Americans and other groups may be emerging in other cities as well. As Joe R. Feagin noted (1978:374), there is a "persistence of ethnic consciousness, ethnic identification, and ethnic impact" among European ethnic groups in the Southwest. He calls for more research, which certainly is justified.

There are many specific areas that can be studied. For example, what, if any, impact does ethnic politics have in the Sunbelt cities? What kinds of social networks have developed? Are there business ties, religious affiliations, or kinship networks? Can evidence be found of chain migration from eastern cities, similar to what characterized the migration from Europe? What demographic characteristics can be inventoried for the new migrants—for example, what are their ages, and occupational and educational levels? Perhaps most importantly, how do these people view themselves in terms of their ethnic identity, and has that perception changed since moving West?

A few more ethnic groups that have not been covered so far can also be offered for the researcher not inspired by those already discussed. A careful reading of the local newspapers supplies information of a fund raiser for the Armenian Apostolic Church, the dedication of a mosque in South Phoenix, and a mortgage-burning festival for the Serbian Orthodox Church. Other articles mention Irish, Filipino, Scandinavian, and Japanese organizations.

Phoenix has also hosted some of the newest immigrants. Since the 1930s there has been an East Indian community growing. Even more recent has been the arrival of people from Cambodia, Laos, and Vietnam.

In sum, Phoenix emerges as a multiethnic city even though much of this diversity remains beneath the sprawling surface of this Sunbelt city.

REFERENCES

Arizona Republic
   1980   Preservation of heritage binds worshipers at Hungarian church. *Arizona Republic* **January 26**:C1.
   1982   300 rally against suspension of liberty in Poland. *Arizona Republic* **January 18**:B1.
Arricale, F.
   1977   Italian americans and myths, in *Perspectives in Italian Immigration and Ethnicity* (S.M. Tomasi, Ed.), pp. 15–18. New York: Center for Migration Studies.
Axlerod, M.
   1956   Urban structure and social participation. *American Sociological Review* **21**:13–18.
Chadhuri, J.
   1974   *Urban Indians of Arizona*. Tucson: University of Arizona Press.
Clark, K. B.
   1965   *Dark Ghetto*. New York: Harper & Row.
Cooke, E.
   1979   Recipes for an Estonian Christmas. *Arizona Magazine* **December 9**:32.
Etzioni, A.
   1959   The ghetto—a re-evaluation. *Social Forces* 255–262.
Feagin, J.
   1978   *Racial and Ethnic Relations*. Englewood Cliffs, N.J.: Prentice-Hall.
Gans, H.
   1951   Park Forest: birth of a Jewish community. *Commentary* **7**:330–339.
   1979   Symbolic ethnicity: the future of ethnic groups and cultures in America. *Ethnic and Racial Studies* **2**:1–20.
Glazer, N., and Moynihan, D. P.
   1971   *Beyond the Melting Pot*. Cambridge: MIT Press.
Gordon, L.
   1973   Progress in Phoenix: a multicultural analysis, in *The Multi-Ethnic Society* (W. Noyes, Ed.), pp. 3–5. Tucson: University of Arizona Press.
   1978   Social issues in the arid city, in *Urban Planning for Arid Zones* (G. Golany, Ed.), pp. 101–121. New York: John Wiley & Sons.
Gordon, R.
   1977   1970 census tracts for Phoenix. Unpublished ms. available from Department of Geography, Arizona State University.
Granger, B. H.
   1973   The many faces of Arizona's people, in *The Multi-Ethnic Society* (W. Noyes, Ed.), pp. 1–2. Tucson: University of Arizona Press.
Greeley, A.
   1974   *Ethnicity in the United States*. New York: John Wiley & Sons.

Harris, R.
    1977   *Black Heritage in Arizona*. Phoenix: Phoenix Urban League.
Inside Phoenix
    1978   *Inside Phoenix*. Phoenix: Phoenix Newspapers, Inc.
Jacobs, J.
    1963   *Life and Death of Great American Cities*. New York: Vintage Press.
Lamb, B.
    1977   Jews in early Phoenix 1870–1920. *Journal of Arizona History* **18**:299–318.
Martinelli, P. C.
    1977   Italy in Phoenix. *Journal of Arizona History* **18**:319–340.
    1978a Phoenix ethnic directory. Unpublished ms. on file in Special Collections, Hayden Library, Arizona State University, Tempe, Arizona.
    1978b Italian immigrant women in the Southwest, in *The Italian Immigrant Woman in North America* (B. B. Caroli, R. Harney, and L. F. Tomasi, Eds.), pp. 325–336. Toronto: Multicultural Historical Society of Ontario.
Matthews, J.
    1979   Role of Italians in valley subject of ASU course. *Arizona Republic* **August 26**:FM5.
Mathews, J.
    1982   Darker side of sunny west probed in suicide study. *Arizona Republic* **January 3**:AA5.
Mawn, G. P.
    1979   Phoenix, Arizona: central city of the Southwest, 1870–1920. Unpublished Ph.D. dissertation, Department of History, Arizona State University, Tempe.
Novak, M.
    1973   *The Rise of the Unmeltable Ethnics*. New York: Collier Books.
Okamura, J.
    1981   Situational ethnicity. *Ethnic and Racial Studies* **1**:452–465.
Pane, D.
    1978   Cook's tour of the Valley's ethnic markets. *Phoenix* **May**:49.
Park, R., and Burgess, E.
    1925   *The City*. Chicago: University of Chicago Press.
Patterson, O.
    1977   *Ethnic Chauvinism*. New York: Atheneum Press.
Phoenix Arts Coming Together (PACT)
    1982   Hello, Phoenix! Phoenix: PACT, Inc.
Polson, D.
    1979   St. Joseph feast has Sicilian flavor. *Arizona Republic* **March**:RD1.
Stein, H., and Hill, R.
    1977   *The Ethnic Imperative, Examining the New White Ethnic Movement*. University Park: Pennsylvania State University Press.
Suttles, G.
    1968   *The Social Order of the Slum*. Chicago: University of Chicago Press.
U.S. Bureau of the Census
    1970   Phoenix, Arizona population and housing census tracts. *United States Census*. Washington, D.C.: U.S. Government Printing Office.
    1980   Census of population and housing, summary tape, Arizona. Washington, D.C.: U.S. Bureau of the Census.
    1981   Census of population and housing, Arizona. Washington, D.C.: U.S. Government Printing Office.

Wirth, L.
    1928   *The Ghetto*. Chicago: University of Chicago Press.
Yancey, W., Ericksen, E., and Juliani, R.
    1976   Emergent ethnicity, a review and reformulation. *American Sociological Review* **41**:391–394.
Yancey, W. L., and Ericksen, E. P.
    1979   The antecedents of community: the economic and institutional structure of urban neighborhoods. *American Sociological Review* **44**:253–262.
Zorbaugh, H.
    1929   *The Gold Coast and the Slum*. Chicago: University of Chicago Press.

11

The Politics of Jewry as a Mobilized Diaspora

Peter Y. Medding

INTRODUCTION

The politics of Jewry as an international phenomenon seems replete with contradictions. Its cultural base is varied, because wherever Jews have lived they have adopted the cultural values and characteristics of the surrounding society, as is so evident in the cultural diversity that characterizes Israel today. And, whereas there are forces in Israel that promote some cultural homogeneity, elsewhere the Jewish people remain embedded in diverse national and linguistic cultures. Yet such marked national cultural differences among Jews have not, as might have been predicted, prevented the development of shared political interests and purpose at the international level. One might also have thought that, as occurs with other groups, international and transnational political connections would threaten national integration by exacerbating existing cultural cleavages, but in fact, nowhere does Jewish communal cohesion pose a threat to national integration.[1]

How can such contradiction be explained? On the one hand, cultural diversity has not destroyed the unity of Jewish political interests. On the other hand, cleavages based upon Jewish cultural values, communality, and international political interests have not threatened the political integrity of the states within which Jews live.

---

[1] On the fragmenting and destabilizing effects of cultural cleavages cutting across national boundaries, see Geertz (1963).

CULTURE, ETHNICITY, AND IDENTITY

The Development of Jewish Political Mobilization

Applying Armstrong's (1976) concept of the "mobilized diaspora" to the international dimension can shed considerable light on these problems.[2] Over the last 100 years, Jewry throughout the diaspora underwent continuous political mobilization, its most revolutionary aspect being the establishment of a politically sovereign state within a people that remained predominantly in the diaspora. But even though the diaspora did not end with the establishment of Israel, the latter significantly influenced the political interests and outlook of Jews in the diaspora without fundamentally altering their situation.

The Jews were the archetypical diaspora people, because, as compared with others, the Jewish diaspora seemed the longest and the most complete. It was not only absence from the territory of the sovereign homeland that characterized the Jewish diaspora, like the others, but the absence of a sovereign homeland—its nonexistence except in religious and historical memory. What for others seemed transitory and remediable individually and collectively by return to the homeland, for Jews seemed permanent and irreversible. Since the middle of the nineteenth century, however, the Jewish situation has been archetypical not because of the nature of its diaspora, but because its process of continuing political mobilization became an example for many other peoples. Jewry thus reversed the usual pattern of relationship between homeland and diaspora. In the case of most other peoples, they themselves created their own diaspora by leaving their homeland; in the case of Jewry, by way of contrast, the members of the diaspora created their own homeland.

The reestablishment of the Jewish homeland was the most striking and historically revolutionary act of Jewish political mobilization over the last 100 years, but it was not the only one. From the middle of the nineteenth century onward, varying forms of international Jewish political activity mobilized various communities in philanthropic, charitable, and political activity on behalf of Jews in worse conditions elsewhere.[3] Similarly, large sections of the Jewish working classes in Eastern Europe, in particular, became politically mobilized in various socialist movements—some of which were Zionist and some ethnically based—

---

[2] As Armstrong defines the term, "diaspora" applies to any ethnic collectivity that lacks a territorial base within a given polity [1976:303].

[3] During this period the Alliance Israélite Universelle, the Anglo-Jewish Association, the American Jewish Committee, the Jewish Colonization Association, ORT, and the Hilfsverein der deutschen Juden were all founded.

seeking Jewish political or cultural autonomy within their countries of residence (Frankel, 1981).

These nationalist, autonomist, socialist, and philanthropic efforts all furthered the political mobilization of the Jewish people. In each case Jews became active as individuals and as a group in the politics of the society in which they lived, but above all, they became active as Jews in pursuit of Jewish political interests. Even when individual Jewish politicians or leaders interceded with decision makers on behalf of Jewish interests, the rest of the Jewish community was necessarily involved. It was clearly understood that these individuals spoke on behalf of the Jewish community, and this community support gave meaning and substance to their claims.

The specific historical development of Jewish political mobilization both in the diaspora and the homeland has produced a wide array of relationships. These are categorized in the following schema:

1. The activity of individual Jews and Jewish communities in pursuit of international Jewish interests
2. The activity of organized international Jewry in pursuit of these matters
3. The involvement of each individual Jewish community in the politics of its own society
4. The involvement of Israel in the internal Jewish affairs of the various Jewish communities
5. The involvement of Israel in the politics of the societies in which Jews reside
6. The involvement of Jewish communities in the internal and external politics of Israel
7. The involvement of international Jewish organizations in the internal and external politics of Israel
8. The involvement of Israel in the politics of world Jewry
9. The involvement of international Jewish organizations in the internal politics of the various Jewish communities[4]

This schema makes it clear that the politics of Jewry simultaneously take place along a number of dimensions. Jewish politics contain, at the very least, significant elements of international politics, ethnic politics, and interest group politics. Some of these elements, their interrelationships, the potential conflicts between them, and their limitations, bear further analysis in the context of the continuing process of Jewish political mobilization.

[4] Some aspects of these involvements have been discussed in Liebman (1977).

THE MOBILIZATION OF JEWISH ETHNICITY IN THE DIASPORA

Outside of Israel, Jews are distinguished from the rest of society on a communal basis. In all these societies Jewry is a primordial group separated from others on the basis of a "consciousness of kind" that fosters internal unity. But the precise nature of this sense of peoplehood and consciousness of kind varies with the different organizing and legitimating principles of these societies. The groups with which Jewry will be compared, and from which, therefore, they will be separated and distinguished, will depend in each society upon which differences are regarded as legitimate bases for group interests and demands. In recent years the primordial or ethnic basis of political claim has been accorded wider legitimacy even in societies that previously treated individuals as individual citizens and not as members of ethnic or primordial groups. Thus many societies have moved from a position of strenuously avoiding consideration of "race, religion, and national origins" in various spheres of life, to a position of specifically regarding them as part of a heightened perception of the legitimacy of ethnicity.

This universal heightening of the legitimacy of ethnic claims has had a direct impact upon Jewry. Together with Jewry's specific international and historical circumstances, it has increased their awareness of ethnic group of primordial identity and sense of belonging. Viewed against the wide range of ethnic claims in various societies, Jewish ethnic definition remains quite uniform. Despite varying stimuli, no competing conceptions of Jewish ethnicity have as yet developed. This is, in part, due to the multifaceted nature of Jewish ethnicity, which enables different groups of Jews to relate selectively to its different aspects without being obliged to accept or reject the whole.[5]

It is also in no small part due to the consensus over the role of Israel as a unifying and integrating national symbol. In previous generations, by way of contrast, the Jewish national idea constituted a major divisive force among Jews. Thus the Jewish group universally has been mobilized ethnically as well as politically. In this process, the fact of Israel has been more important to Jewry in the diaspora than any specific values it imparts. These developments have produced a distinctive set of Jewish political interests, around which Jewish political mobilization and organizational activity revolve.[6]

[5] For an analysis of these aspects, see Medding (1977a).

[6] For a slightly different and more detailed formulation of Jewish political interests, see Medding (1977b).

THE MOBILIZATION OF JEWISH POLITICAL INTERESTS

The International Scene

The paramount international or universal Jewish political interest is in Jewish survival and Jewish security, that is, in continued physical existence and cultural continuity. These have so often been in jeopardy in the past that Jewish survival is perpetually in question and not taken for granted. Politically motivated and organized physical liquidation is an ever present possibility. Political activity to prevent such a result is central in all Jewish communities.

The pursuit of this paramount universal Jewish political interest is significantly affected by organizational limitations. There are no recognized international Jewish political institutions with the capacity and authority to invoke binding commitments. Nor is there any legitimate international Jewish political leadership that is elected, representative, responsive, and accountable. Despite its common political interests and its extensive mobilization, international Jewry possesses less formal political authority and less capacity for binding collective action than, say, the Catholic church or even the head offices of large multinational corporations.

Diaspora Jewry, therefore, does not wield significant power on the international scene. It is characterized by loose, ad hoc, international coordination and by the independent activity of various Jewish communities seeking to influence their governments (Encyclopedia Judaica, 1973). With its resources and diplomatic contacts Israel sometimes acts as the coordinating or catalyzing element in such activities. But Israel cannot serve as the authoritative, legitimate political leadership welding world Jewry, homeland and diaspora alike, into a united, politically decisive body. Although on many matters homeland and diaspora agree on ends and tactics, on many issues there have been significant disagreements between them.

A fundamental disagreement exists over the question of whether the interests of Israel, as its leaders understand them, take precedence over the interests of the rest of the Jewish people, as determined by the latter. nor is there any agreement as to who decides the interests of the Jewish people: those in Israel or those outside it. This disagreement revolves around the ultimate significance for the Jewish people of the state of Israel. Is it so significant that it takes unquestioned precedence over the rest of the Jewish people? Ben-Gurion, cited in Liebman (1977), had very decided views on this question: "In considering international relations we must ask one simple question: What is good for Israel? And what is good for Israel is good for the entire Jewish people [p. 228]." This conflict has also manifested itself in actual disagreements and conflicts between Israel and the diaspora over major international questions. Israel took a softer, more conciliatory, and less public approach to the plight of Soviet Jewry during the late 1950s and early 1960s in order not to further affect its already fragile relations with the Soviet Union. World Jewry, on the other hand, favored tougher and more strident tactics. This approach was eventually adopted, and when it was, Israel actively supported it, although only after considerable pressure.

In another case, top Israeli political leaders hinted to U.S. Jews that those who sought Israel's good should tone down their criticism of U.S. involvement in Vietnam and their antiwar activities. They argued that opposition to the sending of troops, arms, and other military aid to Vietnam was not consistent with efforts to mobilize public opinion in the United States to put pressure on the administration to supply military aid to Israel or to increase it. Thus, opposing a war in Southeast Asia was seen as likely to damage Israel's interests and therefore was to be avoided.[7]

The Domestic Scene

The political interests of the Jewish communities in their respective domestic contexts are more complex and controversial than in the international context. Jewish political interests at the domestic level are also characterized by preoccupation with security and with physical and cultural continuity. These manifest themselves practically in the desire for the stable existence of a form of government that can ensure them. Such domestic concerns are further reinforced by activities to influence their governments to undertake international activity to protect and further Jewish survival and security, which was analyzed in the preceding section.

There is also a strong Jewish interest in the stability of the established order per se. This is based on the assumption that threats to order are likely to make conditions for Jews worse, and that what one knows is usually more secure and safer than the unknown (Medding, 1977b). In multicultural societies specifically these two interests come together so that Jews exhibit a strong interest in maintaining pluralism, electoral polyarchy, equality of opportunity, and political, civil, and constitutional liberties. Even if not self-regulating, these societies seem to offer satis-

[7] See the discussions of these issues in Liebman (1977).

factory institutional means to counter threats to security and survival. What is more, they are likely to facilitate the free expression and perpetuation of distinctive ethnic values, the pursuit of which in themselves constitutes a major domestic Jewish political interest.

Jews in most western societies are by and large concentrated in the metropolitan and urban middle classes, particularly in their business and professional segments. As a result, middle-class economic interests form an important element in Jewish political interests and reinforce the concern for stability, security, and order.

These domestic political interests among Jews occasionally come into conflict with each other. In the United States, for example, the Jewish interests in pluralism defined in terms of group rights have come into conflict with their interests in citizenship, liberty, and equality based upon concepts of individual rights. Seeking support for the pursuit of distinctive group identity and expression has clashed with their interest in constitutional doctrines of nonestablishment of religion, as seen in debates over state funding for Jewish day schools. Similarly, support for equality of opportunity aimed at equality of results (affirmative action or reverse discrimination) has directly conflicted with Jewish class interests, as it appeared to many that these results would be at the expense of the Jews.

This pattern of political interests differs from those of most other interest groups in western societies. There seems to be no analogue to such predominant concern with, and interest in, physical security and survival among the usual array of interest groups in pluralist political systems. Neither the average economic, professional, occupational, and trade groups nor the familiar promotional or ideological groups place the fear of extinction high on their list of priorities. Because survival is an ultimate interest, and therefore an end in itself, it is not easily given to compromise and is invested with considerable symbolic and expressive meaning. As such it is often intensely held and fought for. Nor does it ever leave the agenda for long; as soon as one issue is met, the next apprehension arises.

These international and domestic concerns with physical security and survival have recently been vividly demonstrated in the vigorous public debate in the United States over the advisability and desirability of the sale of the most advance fighter aircraft and airborne defense systems to Arab countries. On these issues the Jewish community in America generally stood strongly opposed. Many took the line, along with influential sections of the American public and leading political figures, that the sales were not in the interests of the United States, particularly after the debacle in Iran, where large supplies of sophisticated American equipment fell into the hands of a strongly anti-American regime. But beyond these considerations, much of the intensity of Jewish opposition to the sales stemmed from the fact that they increased the potential for the destruction of Israel, that is, they weakened Jewish physical security and survival. Nathan Glazer, cited in Friedman (1982:31), is reported to have written, "Israel is unique in that it is not threatened with defeat or the loss of territory or the loss of respect—it is threatened by annihilation, up to, one assumes, the massacre of its inhabitants."

The Role of Israel

This coalescence of the international and domestic elements of Jewish political interests in the focus upon Israel shares the agenda of Jewish survival with activities to secure the right to live in safety and security and/or the right of immigration for persecuted Jews in various countries (Soviet Union, the Arab states, Iran, etc.). The reactions to the plight of Jewry during the Second World War of even the most enlightened Western countries, which to many Jews constituted complicity in the Holocaust, do little to make Jews feel safe in the knowledge that if threatened with persecution they will have somewhere to go. In this regard the political mobilization of the Jewish diaspora in restoring the Jewish homeland has taken on even greater significance. Israel is not just a source of anxiety and apprehension engendering fears of another Holocaust and casting doubts about future Jewish survival. It is first and foremost regarded as a safe haven for any Jews who may need it, and its own policy of ingathering of the exiles is oriented to this eventuality. Similarly, the image of an Israel that determines its own destiny limits the dependence on others for survival, although, of course, Israel's own political and military dependency remain.

The focus on Israel has a direct and immediate effect on the nature and pattern of Jewish political mobilization on the domestic front. Because of it, Jews make no peoplehood or communal claims upon their countries of residence and no claims that might end up in demands for separation or separate identity. Its claims thus do not threaten secession, linguistic division, or territorial realignment, nor do they call into question the political or cultural integrity of the nation-state. This accords with its historical position, deriving from long-term minority status, of not seeking to have legislated for the rest of society policies that fit in with or express its particular religious values. Jewish political activity is generally particularly careful not to overstep this self-imposed limitation.

Jewry's claims for peoplehood and for broad cultural distinctiveness are thus either focused directly on Israel or on asserting the right to individual and group difference. They seek free space to enable Jews to live their own distinctive group life as they wish and as they determine. Such claims, of course, fit well with general arguments in favor of diversity, and from the overall viewpoint of society are generally easily manageable, because they involve no threats of national, cultural, or linguistic cleavages.

This focus on Israel, together with the distinctive group life that has developed in the acquired free space, has heightened Jewish political participation of all kinds. Urban, professional, and middle-class skills and political concentration in strategic electorates have facilitated this high participation. But a major motivating factor has been the political logic that ethnic political interests cannot be promoted and protected without political allies and without majority support for general political goals that benefit Jewish interests. These cannot be gained without continuous and often intense political activity, participation, and organization at the party, electoral, bureaucratic, executive, and public levels.

Organizational Aspects

The political mobilization of the diaspora in pursuit of Jewish ethnic political interests has occurred despite the always acephalous and often fragmented character of internal Jewish political organization in the various diaspora communities. An examination of their sources of leadership and authority and the processes of decision making reveals that Jewish communal organization has no binding political institutions or processes. There are no coercive sanctions, taxation (although fund raising sometimes approaches it in scope and coerciveness), or formal boundaries either within the community or between it and the outside world, and there are few formal representative processes, such as elections, relating leaders to the rest of the community.[8]

The political boundaries of the Jewish community are unclear because its general boundaries are blurred. Despite some ideological differences over conversion processes, it is possible generally to specify who belongs to the Jewish people. Yet in contrast with the past, there are today very few communities employing formal criteria for membership of the Jewish community. In the broadest sense all members of the Jewish people in a given area are ipso facto "members" of the Jewish

[8] Of course, many organizations in the communities have elections, although contestation is generally very low, except when particularly contentious issues arise. Similarly a few communities do hold or have held community-wide elections (France, Argentina, Australia), but these have been characterized by very low interest and even lower turnout. For further analysis of these phenomena, see Medding (1981).

community. Membership of the Jewish people is generally determined by self-identification and societal identification. But the Jewish community as a clearly defined corporate or autonomous political entity generally does not exist. There are, on the other hand, many Jewish organizations and institutions with which individual Jews may associate in various formal and informal ways.

Despite the absence of formal communal political order and organization, Jewish communities remain highly united, tightly knit, politically mobilized, and active, and they exercise varying degrees of political effectiveness. This is largely due to the inclusiveness of the voluntary Jewish political leadership. In many countries it is organized in a loose federative arrangement, whereby the heads of most of the important bodies and organizations cooperate in a consultative framework. This arrangement enables the Jewish community to speak with a united voice in pursuing its political interests. Moreover, this arrangement strengthens the connections between the leadership and the members of the community, many of whom are involved in voluntary, philanthropic, and charitable activities. These widely based fund-raising organizations tend to overlap with the various other organizations pursuing the whole range of Jewish activities, and so too do their leaderships. Overlapping organizations with overlapping leaderships thus facilitate communal unity and political mobilization.

Even without formal processes of representation, communal leaders and spokespersons in most Jewish communities are politically representative of, and responsive to, the political interests, attitudes, and views of the majority. Thus the process of political mobilization has resulted in considerable consensus and agreement in the Jewish communities about Jewish political interests. This was not always the case. In the earlier part of this century there were fundamental differences in diaspora communities over basic questions. Leaderships were divided, and there was considerable conflict between leaders and members of the community.[9]

That these leadership groups are significantly based upon wealth and leisure (partly due to the importance of fund raising) and tend to be self-perpetuating and renewed or replaced by cooptation does not seem to interfere with the leaderships' ability to represent the community consensus. It has, however, led to a degree of alienation among students, academics, and professionals. In recent years strenuous efforts have been made to coopt them to organizational and communal leadership, but these have met with only limited success. Some have become

---

[9] These are looked at in some detail in Medding (1981).

involved in the community, but many others have remained on the outside. In this process of cooptation Israel has served as a major focus of
unity and identification.

LIMITS TO JEWISH POLITICAL MOBILIZATION

The process of political mobilization among Jewry has limits. In those
societies in which Jews are regarded as a religious denomination, the
connection with Israel blurs the clarity of religious definition by introducing concepts of nationality and peoplehood. Moreover, where the
general basis of societal division is religious, rather than national or
linguistic, Jewish political mobilization and participation on ethnic and
national lines encounter limitations.

Policy conflicts also limit political mobilization on behalf of Israel.
These conflicts may develop because of the foreign policies of the countries of which Jews are citizens. Jews in these societies may feel under
some degree of pressure to conform to national foreign policy objectives
simply because they are national foreign policy objectives. In short, their
citizenship loyalties and their ethnic loyalties may come into conflict.
This may be muted if the society is prepared to permit democratic
opposition by its citizens to its foreign policies and does not seek to
make this an issue of loyalty. But even then, those opposed may still feel
strong pressures toward conformity to national policy interests and objectives. Because the Jewish group is so concerned about its local security
and survival, such cross-pressures will encourage withdrawal and compromise as a means of lowering the intensity of the conflict, and this
will lessen support for Israel. These pressures were clearly demonstrated
in the debate over the AWACS deal, in the success of those favoring the
deal to cast the issue in terms of "Reagan versus Begin," and in Reagan's
own statement that it "is not the business of other nations to make
American foreign policy [Friedman, 1982:29–30]."

A further limit to Jewish political mobilization may derive from Israeli
actions, policies, or demands upon Jews. This will occur if they feel that
these will compromise their status in their diaspora countries. It is not
even significant that the incapacity to enforce allegiance by coercive
means would nullify such claims by Israel on Jews outside. The crucial
point is that, if such a claim were made or thought to be made, it would
be regarded as compromising and would lead to a drawing away from
Israel. Significant developments in this direction in the United States in
the early 1950s led to an exchange of correspondence between David

Ben-Gurion and the president of the American Jewish Committee. The former, under strong pressure from the latter, specifically denied that Israel expected Jews to owe it any political allegiance.[10] Thus, Jews in the diaspora give Israel support and can be mobilized politically on its behalf only on a voluntary basis, and only if they can do so without violating their citizenship obligations.

Jewish political mobilization on behalf of Israel may be further limited by substantive disagreements with its policies or with its actions to express these policies. Thus far, care has been taken to avoid such differences, or if they occur, to keep them from becoming public. For their part, Israel's government and its leaders strenuously deny the legitimacy of any outside Jewish attempts to influence its foreign and defense policies. They expect Jewry and its leaders to give unquestioning public support to Israeli policy. There are, on the other hand, some indications that in private they are at least prepared to listen to criticism and opposing viewpoints, although the influence of such criticism cannot be documented. Similarly, Jewish leaders outside Israel feel very uneasy about opposing or criticizing Israeli policy when they do not bear its burdens and consequences. Nevertheless, some Jewish political leaders in the diaspora take the view that the Jewish people outside Israel has a deep moral, cultural, religious, and ethnic interest in the state of Israel and share in its hopes, aspirations, goals, and difficulties. This further legitimates their expression of disagreement with Israel's policies, however painful such a process may be.

These ground rules have generally held for over 30 years because Israel appeared to diaspora Jewish leaders as a democratic, liberal society, seeking to live in peaceful coexistence with its neighbors and to conclude peace arrangements with them. Should these facts or this image change, there is no guarantee that Israel will be able to rely on the same reflexive and unquestioning support of diaspora Jewry. These limits to political mobilization have been clearly tested since 1977. Thereafter prominent Jewish leaders and intellectuals in the United States

---

[10] Thus Ben-Gurion declared that

the Jews of the United States as a community and as individuals have only one political attachment and that is to the United States of America. They owe no political allegiance to Israel. . . . The State of Israel represents and speaks only on behalf of its own citizens, and in no way presumes to represent or speak in the name of Jews who are citizens of any other country.

In reply, the president of the American Jewish Committe, Mr. Jacob Blaustein, said inter alia, "Future relations between the Jewish community and the State of Israel must be based on mutual respect for one another's feelings and needs, and on the preservation of the integrity of the two communities and their institutions." Both are quoted at length and analyzed in detail in Liebman (1977:118–131).

have several times publicly declared their disagreement with the particular position of the Israeli government at the time—particularly in relation to the speed and content of the peace process and to policies
regarding settlements on the West Bank of the Jordan. Although their
views echoed those of many in Israel, in the outcry and ensuing debate
about public opposition and dissent the fact that they opposed Israel in
the *New York Times* or in other major media seemed more important
than the fact or substance of the opposition. Because the distinction
between support for Israel and support for the policies of the government
of Israel is sometimes extremely fine, opposition to the latter is regarded
by some as opposition to the former, and thus provokes a considerably
sharper reaction than mere policy opposition would generate.

If relations between Israel and her neighbors are normalized, Jewish
survival and security may come to be seen in a different light, and it
may cease to be so central a factor in Jewish life. Israel's role and its
connections with diaspora Jewry will change in character and meaning.
If these changes occur they will set in train fundamental realignments
in the pattern of Jewish political interest and in the nature of Jewish
political mobilization.

References

Armstrong, J. A.
    1976   Mobilized and proletarian diasporas. *American Political Science Review*
           LXX(June):393–408.
Encyclopedia Judaica
    1973   World Jewish associations, in *Encyclopedia Judaica, 1973 Yearbook*, pp. 351–356.
           Jerusalem: Keter.
Frankel, J.
    1981   *Prophecy and Politics: Socialism, Nationalism and the Russian Jews, 1862–1917.*
           New York: Cambridge University Press.
Friedman, M.
    1982   AWACS and the Jewish community. *Commentary* **73**(4 April):31.
Geertz, C.
    1963   The integrative revolution: primordial sentiments and civil politics in the new
           states, in *Old Societies and New States* (C. Geertz, Ed.), pp. 105–157. New York:
           The Free Press.
Liebman, C. S.
    1977   *Pressure without Sanctions: The Influence of World Jewry on Israel's Policy.*
           Rutherford, N.J.: Fairleigh Dickinson Press.
Medding, P. Y.
    1977a A contemporary paradox: Israel and Jewish peoplehood. *Forum* **1**(26):5–16.
    1977b Towards a general theory of Jewish political interests and behaviour. *The Jewish
           Journal of Sociology* **XIX**(2 December):115–144.
    1981   Patterns of political organization and leadership in contemporary Jewish com-
           munities, in *Kindship and Consent: The Jewish Political Tradition and Its Con-
           temporary Uses* (D. J. Elazar, Ed.), pp. 259–292. Ramat Gan: Turtledove Press.

12

The Role of the Family in Acculturation and Assimilation in America: A Psychocultural Dimension*

Jacqueline S. Mithun

INTRODUCTION

Recent literature on ethnicity suggests some agreement among scholars in their conceptual frameworks. First, at least with respect to the United States, the old ethnic groups are for the most part acculturated and, in part, assimilated (Gordon, 1964, 1975; Hicks, 1977). Second, the new ethnic groups are increasingly tied together symbolically, not culturally (Hicks, 1977). Third, these ethnic groups represent new forms of interest groups that have replaced to a large extent the once dominant groups centered around class or occupational interests (Glazer and Moynihan, 1975). Fourth, external factors in the political and economic arena of the welfare state, with its emphasis on equality of opportunity and the spoils system, were largely responsible for this resurgence of ethnic groups (Glazer and Moynihan, 1975; Parsons, 1975; Schiller, 1977). Fifth, the new ethnic groups serve as vehicles for communal solidarity in an age that has witnessed "the expansion of more inclusive, yet attenuated, identities" (Bell, 1975:171).

Traditionally, anthropologists had no difficulty in defining ethnic groups because ethnicity was the major focus of their studies. An ethnic group "included those who spoke a common language and shared the same cultural tradition" (Hicks, 1977:3). This notion of self-identification

* This paper was originally presented at the 77th annual meeting of the American Anthropological Association, Los Angeles, California, November 1978.

CULTURE, ETHNICITY,
AND IDENTITY

is not new (De Vos and Romanucci-Ross, 1975:9), nor is the notion of "labeling" or context (Hicks, 1977:4, 23–25), which designates a group as ethnic. All ethnic groups in the United States originally represented national, racial, or religious memberships that were diverse in region, class, religion, and/or language in their place of origin. The extent to which internal and external factors shape or foster ethnicity has not been fully documented.

In this paper I will assume that the cultural content and symbolic elements of ethnic groups have been continuously present, even though the core elements are undergoing and have undergone change. A distinction should also be recognized and maintained between cultural assimilation and structural assimilation. Although the old ethnic groups in the United States are acculturated, I would not go so far as other scholars, such as Gordon, who suggests that "for the most part cultural assimilation exists" (1964). Scholars generally agree that structural assimilation has not occurred and suggest this as one reason for ethnic resurgence in the last decade.

Numerous paradigms have been proposed for viewing ethnicity and the acculturative or assimilation process. There is no common theoretical stance. Perhaps the contributions of sociologists and social psychologists are in the forefront with four theoretical orientations: sociocultural, interactionist, group dynamics, and behaviorist (Dashefsky and Shapiro, 1974). Political scientists and economists focus on power relationships and view ethnicity within majority–minority patterns of dominance and conflict theory. Taking a broader view, historians concentrate not only on the preceding but also on time of entrance and numbers of migrants to suggest how ethnic groups might vary in their adaptations and reception by the host society.

CULTURE: ITS ROLE IN THE ACCULTURATION AND ASSIMILATION PROCESS

For purposes of this paper I will define an ethnic group as people who share a sense of tradition, be that derived from religious, physical, linguistic, aesthetic, or historical origins.[1] Members of ethnic groups may

---

[1] By introducing the Thai notion of *chat*, which, in turn, derives from the Sanskirt *jati*, meaning birth, Keyes hoped to lead us away from a Western bias in our notion of ethnicity (1976:204). The most basic notion of ethnicity as "belonging," as noted by De Vos and Romanucci-Ross (1975), and concurred in by most scholars, derives from those basic facts of birth; the given facts of sex, biological features, time of birth, place, and descent (Keyes, 1976:204–04). The extent to which persons or groups identify with these facts then depends on the individual, the ethnic group itself, and external factors.

share cultural traditions that shape values, attitudes, beliefs, and ethics on human behavior. Within the United States such ethnic groups form subcultures within the mainstream that are culturally and structurally assimilated to varying degrees, not the least important of which may be marital assimilation, as suggested by Gordon (1964).

I do not intend to discuss the social–psychological aspects of ethnic identity or ethnic stratification and structural assimilation, areas in which there is a vast literature in the social sciences. Nor will I review theories of cyclical stages in the assimilation process (Bogardus, 1930; Glick, 1955; Lieberson, 1961; Park, 1949). What I do propose to discuss is the neglected area of the psychocultural and behavioral dimensions that impede or facilitate the cultural assimilation processes.[2]

Culture is not a "total assemblage of traits" as noted by Barth (1969:12). This notion was criticized severely by Keyes (1976), who says that ethnic relations may not be reduced to purely situational phenomena either. Although the structural components are certainly important and have been discussed most frequently by conflict theorists and Marxists, this paper will not analyze group dynamics as merely power polemics between haves and have-nots; nor will the paper take the opposite perspective that analysis is impossible because "in no two instances have the interrelations of different ethnic groups run exactly the same course" (La Pierre, 1946).

This paper takes the position that the family of the culture of origin plays a predominant role in the adaptive potential of ethnic groups, even though there are other critical factors that affect the acculturation process. I would like to note some of these factors before I analyze the role of culture. One would be what Glazer has termed "the structure of opportunity" (1976:285). Laporte's succinct outline (1975) notes some relevant variables as follows:

Pertinent to this differentiation among migrants or types of migration would be such considerations as sex and age distribution, generation, country of origin, . . . pheno-typical visibility, predisposition of host society to immigrants in general and particular, economic and political conditions of host society at time of arrival, wave of entry and size of wave, initial occupational roles, literacy and socio-economic attributes [312–313].

A second element that affects the capacities of a group to achieve and adapt would be the "degree of discrimination and prejudice" encountered by the group (Glazer, 1976:285). A third element might be the

---

[2] "The psychological and cultural factors . . . are real and significant elements, elusive as they are, for nothing else will make sense of the facts" (Glazer, 1976:285). Glazer notes that few studies of adaptation and psychological adjustment under processes of acculturation, with the exception of Jews and blacks, have concentrated on ethnic groups as a research variable (1976:283).

distinction between "voluntary" and "nonvoluntary" status.[3] Other elements would be the degree of conflict with the host society and the degree of access to societal rewards as outlined by Gordon (1975:90).

I would like to take us a little closer toward measuring degrees of cultural assimilation. Utilizing Keyes's notions that "ethnic groups . . . are not mutually exclusive, but are structured in segmentary hierarchies with each more inclusive segment subsuming ethnic groups which are contrastive at another level" (1976:208),[4] one could conceivably arrive at a gradient of ethnicity similar to that in linguistics of clines or dialects that are "mutually intelligible" or of clines or grades as evidenced in racial subgroupings of men based on physical traits. We already have a convenient theoretical tool for this in the notion of segmentary lineage, which Gerlach and Hine (1970) used to analyze subcultural groups in the United States.

To view how these many cultural factors might be weighed to test the notion of "segmentary hierarchies," I have constructed a table and compared five ethnic groups in their standing on each variable with respect to mainstream culture (see Table 1). For heuristic purposes only, I have trichotimized the variables so that (1) stands for high agreement, (2) some agreement, and (3) low or little agreement with the general U. S. pattern. For each of the major cultural factors such as language, religion, family patterning, attitudes and values, one could devise a gradient of fit from most to least in terms in their fit or likeness to mainstream culture. Those ethnic groups with the lowest score stand in the highest agreement; thus, they "deviate" the least from mainstream culture (hereafter abbreviated as WASP).[5] The members of cultures who differ least would theoretically have the least difficulty in adjusting and become acculturated and eventually assimilate most rapidly, all else being equal.

[3] Voluntary status would probably not occur either without some economic or religious deprivation. There might also be "quasi-voluntary" status as a result of forced migration, explusion, or exile. "Nonvoluntary" statuses would include slavery and could arise as a result of annexation, conquest, purchase, or protector arrangement.

[4] I disagree with Keyes, who suggests that races are mutually exclusive; thus, the quote cited herein deletes "unlike races." This obviously contradicts established phenotypical evidence, genetic research, and biological fact. Glazer (1976) has also suggested that ethnic groups are not mutually exclusive. They involve the "same complexities in understanding and measurement as does social class; they merge and diverge . . . with varied consequences for consciousness and social change [282]."

[5] After I had written this paper, I noted that Milton Gordon had revised his theory of assimilation to incorporate power and conflict in his model. He suggests that his major variables be trichotomized to create a profile of the essential features of a minority group's position in the society at any given time. Thus, for example, a minority group might be high on conflict, low in degree of access to societal rewards, high on cultural assimilation, low on structural assimilation, and moderate in terms of total assimilation (Gordon, 1975:90).

Table 1

Cultural Assimilation of Mainstream Values by Ethnic Families[a]

Cultural Factors	Jewish	Chinese	Black	Puerto Rican	Mexican American
Cultural variable					
Religion	3	3	2	1	1
Language	1	3	2	2	2
Family/Type	2/B	2/A	3/C	3/B,C	2/B
Attitude toward					
Sex	1	1	3	2	2
Education	1	1	3	2	2
Work	1	1	3	2	2
Time	1	3	2	2	2
Aggressivity	1	3	1	2	2
Emotion (expression of)	2	1	3	3	3
Competition	1	2	2	3	3
Innovation	1	2	1	3	3
Self-reliance	2	3	3	3	3
Self-sufficiency	2	3	3	3	3
Individualism	2	3	1	2	2
Industriousness	1	1	2	2	2
Supernatural	1	1	3	2	2
Status seeking	1	3	1	2	2
Sobriety	1	1	3	2	3
Thriftiness	1	1	3	3	3
Authority	1	1	3	2	2
Independence	2	3	3	3	2
Intermarriage	1	1	2	3	3
Children	1	1	3	2	2
Total	31	42	55	54	54

[a]1 = high agreement.
  2 = some agreement.
  3 = low or little agreement.

THE FAMILY: ITS ROLE IN CULTURAL TRANSMISSION

As the agent of primary socialization, the family is the conduit, the shaper of the roles its members play in society, the arbiter of morality, and the maker of values, beliefs, and attitudes that determine how individuals behave in their social interactions. The cultural ideal of the family in the United States is the nuclear family with a male head of household and perhaps with some extended relations maintained with other family members, as long as these are not marked by interdependent status. The primary dyad is the husband–wife relationship within the nuclear family of procreation residing in a single independent household (Hsu, 1972).

Cultural patterns that differ from this ideal mode are "deviant" or variants, some more so than others. If an extended family resides in a single household but meets the other criteria, it would still closely approximate the ideal. Also, if the primary dyad were father–son, with or without an extended family, it would not be too deviant as that was historically the European cultural pattern, which remained the statistical, if not the ideal, norm until recently in the United States. The WASP family has been shifting over time from an authoritarian patriarchal form to an egalitarian friendship form.

The cultural content of most American families, in contrast with but not unrelated to its structure (Type B), is one of discontinuous egalitarian relations; exclusivity between husband and wife; and the independence of children, which Hsu (1972) suggests fosters self-reliance and individualism. Although family structure may influence the content, the latter is more important in determing "the pattern of thought and behavior of individuals reared in them [p. 512]." "Kinship content pertains to the characteristics which govern the tenacity, intensity, or quality of interaction among individuals related through kinship [p. 513]."

As the primary molder of culture, the family conditions attitudes, beliefs, and values toward education, work, authority, personal relations, and time orientations. WASP families, generally speaking, foster the "Protestant ethic" whose major tenets are industriousness, aggressivity, competition, speed, perseverance, goal-oriented behavior, future-time orientation, literacy, cleanliness, repression of sexuality, innovation, and self-reliance as expressed in a striving for self-sufficiency and individualism. The entire concept is aptly portrayed by Werner Herzog in his film *Kasper Hauser*, subtitled *Each Man for Himself and God Against All.* In Hsu's (1972) terms, the individual "has no inalienable place in the scheme of things except that scheme he himself initiates and contructs [p. 527]."

The extent to which different migrant groups have held WASP beliefs and values, or at least ones that were not in direct contradiction with these major tenets, has in part determined their success in acculturation and ultimately assimilation in the United States. The structure of Western European families' kinship content was basically Type B in Hsu's schema, similar to that of Americans. Eastern Europeans are the weakest example of this type in that the husband–wife dyad is "unquestionably" husband-dominated (Hsu, 1972:525).

Historically, the majority of Chinese in America were not fully acculturated because the cultural content (Type A) differed in some major elements from mainstream culture. The Chinese passivity, orientation to the past, dependence on kin, and lack of individual social mobility and recognition were detrimental to assimilation. Other factors such as their "continuity" in generations of tradition, industriousness, perseverance, and scholarly tradition fit well with concepts associated with the Protestant ethic.

The Hispanic traditions have differed on a number of these dimensions. Like the Chinese, the Spanish tradition of the extended family, the predominance of the father–son dyad, and the past to present orientation have tended to militate against the development of self-reliant individuals. In the Chinese and Hispanic tradition, obedience to authority and dependency relations were encouraged. Although this did not foster adaptation to American ways, the individuals were more sure of themselves in their own cultural context. "Individuals in such societies tend to have much less need for competition, status seeking, conformity, and hence, racial and religious prejudices [Hsu, 1972:256]."

The traditional family structure of the Jews, not unlike the Chinese, tended toward a patriarchal, patrilineal extended family whose primary dyad was the father–son relationship and which was characterized by inclusive relationships of mutual dependency within the family, continuity, respect for authority, and asexuality (Hsu, 1972:416). As Hsu notes, "People of this type of kinship pattern tend to be conservative as they are satisfied with the status quo; they have no urge toward fission, little impetus for change, and are not likely to resist subordination by violence" (1972:518–521).[6] "No society in this type is likely either to die out physically through conquest or loss of resources or even to lose the continuation of its way of life such as is found in many parts of the nonliterate world or the West" (Hsu, 1972:524).

In comparing the Jews and Chinese, both of which rank high in agreement with WASP culture and behavior, one might note that historically the demographic patterns of these groups did not differ drastically from that of other nineteenth-century immigrant groups; for example, waves peaked and dispersed as did prejudice toward them at the height of the waves. Both groups were "voluntary." The Chinese, like most immigrants, migrated for economic reasons; the Jews migrated for economic reasons, too; but many migrated to escape religious persecution as well. Both groups had negligible return migration. They also resided in segregated residential areas. Some of the migrants came from literate

---

[6] The Jews and Chinese are primary ethnic groups who strive to maintain their original identity and solidarity through their own social institutions. Hsu argues that such groups are interested primarily in maintenance of an independent identity, not assimilation, and thus do not clamor for equal treatment (1972:397).

urban backgrounds; many came from rural backgrounds. Both groups came from highly literate traditions in which education was held in high esteem. The Jews had respect for authority in the rabbi and the patriarchal heads of families; the scholarly tradition counteracted violence as a way of solving problems.

The Chinese and Jewish traditions of passivity facilitated the migrant's adaptation within American society. The WASP pattern, with an "inherent tendency to conflict between the generations" (Hsu, 1972:528), expresses itself in internal turmoil and external struggle and under conquest tends "to resist with violence either in open rebellion or in underground movement" (Hsu, 1972:530). Differing in this crucial orientation facilitated survival for the Jews and Chinese. Most of the major beliefs and values of the Chinese and Jews fit very well with the WASP norms. Respect for authority, values toward work, deemphasis on sex, and emphasis on education, sobriety, and thrift marked them in good stead for accommodation, because assimilation was never considered a goal to groups for whom religion was the basis of ethnicity.

Among black families, one significant historical type was a patriarchal, patrilineal, extended family with the father–son dyad predominant (Billingsley, 1968), but today the cultural content of Afro–American families fosters the predominance of the mother–son dyad regardless of family structure. The content of these families, Type C in Hsu's schema, is such that it fosters some exclusivity and discontinuity and creates a "one-sided dependency upon on All-answering Figure," which results in a "longing for continuity of one-sided or all-embracing dependence relationship" (1972:560).[7]

The most basic quality of this type is that the individual tends to solve life's problems not through self-reliance or mutual dependence but through dependence on the supernatural. In worshipping, the person expects

much more from the gods than they give the gods, just as the child does with the mother . . . it is all demanding, and . . . finally, unlike mutual dependence, it is loaded with diffused sexuality, an element which is at times blatant, and at other times thinly veiled, but at all times more or less present [Hsu, 1972:541].

The Hispanic family tradition, as noted earlier, was a patriarchal, patrilineal, extended family with the father–son dyad predominant, but

[7] Although Hsu's data for this type were taken from the Indian subcontinent, the characteristics that he attributes to this type seem to hold cross-culturally. Despite the fact that the Hispanic culture is male-centered, as is the Indian, adult males and females are much more segregated than is the case with Type A and B family structures. Second, fathers and sons are not as close in their relationships as they are in oriental or occidental cultures.

the mother–son dyad has become increasingly more important for Puerto Ricans, and the most basic quality of this type is that the individual tends to solve life's problems not through self-reliance or mutual dependency but through dependence on the supernatural.

The majority of Puerto Ricans are Catholics, and increasing numbers are now members of pentecostal denominations. This phenomenon, which has appeared inexplicable to many scholars (Mintz, 1960), may well be a result of the shift from a Type B to Type C family structure (Seda, 1973) and is more easily understood in this context. The majority of Afro–Americans, who have experienced the predominance of the mother–son dyad for a longer period of time, are also members of pentecostal churches, which reflect precisely the elements just outlined.

The Type C family structure of Afro–American and Hispanic cultures in its one-sided dependency indulges children and showers them with affection. They tend to live in the here and now with a present-time orientation. Personal relations are fostered, as are generosity and sharing with kindred and close friends (Mithun, 1974; Stack, 1974). Respect and *respeto* are important; there is not a rigid submission to authority.

The "faith" of blacks is analogous in many ways with the "fatalism" of Hispanic cultures. Indulgence in "playing the numbers" and the "loteria" are other facets of cultures that place dependence on the supernatural. "There is more internal dissatisfaction with the status quo" in such cultures than in Type A, but the pressures toward change are ambiguous and diffuse; "over a long period of time, there tend of be changes in appearance but not in substance" (Hsu, 1972:546).

Blacks, Puerto Ricans, and Mexican Americans all represent cases of nonvoluntary migrant status. Blacks with a long history of slavery in the United States represent such a unique situation that it is difficult to compare this ethnic group with the others, but I have included them because I believe they support the cultural argument presented here. Admittedly, race introduces another variable, but I would argue, on the basis of the Chinese alone, that it is not, in and of itself, the awesome barrier to assimilation that has been purported in the literature. For that matter, Mexican Americans and Puerto Ricans are racial subgroupings as well as cultural groups, but race does not constitute the primary identity for them.

Blacks, Puerto Ricans, and Mexican Americans, like the Chinese and Jews, have all resided in segregated residential areas. Unlike the latter groups, they do not come from a long established literate tradition. Mexican Americans and Puerto Ricans came from rural backgrounds to urban areas and had multiple hurdles to overcome in adapting to modern industrialized cities. In other words, I would suggest that for migrants of the twentieth century who move from rural to urban areas, there are more adjustments to make than there were for their counterparts in the nineteenth century. None of these ethnic groups exhibits the passivity of the Chinese. They express their emotions and warmth more openly and have a tendency to be volatile in interpersonal relations, the machismo tradition among Hispanics being but one example of this tendency.

CONCLUSION

The culture content of Mexican Americans, Puerto Ricans, and blacks is significantly different from WASPs on a number of dimensions. These ethnic groups are not marked by an adherence to the Protestant ethic. Aggressivity, competition, self-reliance, self-sufficiency, and individualism are not the primary values inculcated from birth. Thrift, sobriety, and purposeful, goal-oriented behavior directed toward the future are not the guiding tenets of people with dependence on the supernatural. And finally, the diffuse sexuality that permeates the culture is not only diametrically opposed but directly confronts the traditional tenets of mainstream culture.[8]

The Chinese and the Jews did not adhere to the Protestant ethic in terms of individual self-reliance and self-sufficiency, but they did hold other values similar to WASPs. As groups they have had perseverance and have striven for self-sufficiency. Both ethnic groups had a valued literary tradition and were marked by asexual patterns of behavior. The patriarchal extended family was similar in structure to that of the European family structure. Both the Chinese and Jewish religious traditions provided continuity and solidarity, which met American culture with passive indifference.

All the ethnic groups discussed in the paper, except blacks, have differed in terms of voluntary and nonvoluntary immigrant status, national origins, and phenotypical visibility. They differed less in terms of their occupational backgrounds, socioeconomic attributes, generations, and demographic features. The sole fact that remains constant is the host society.

[8] The ethnic group itself may impede the processes of social mobility and acculturation if an individual's progress and assimilative behavior are viewed as betrayal. Whereas the Jews, and probably the Chinese, have been able to move ahead and maintain their identity and not been suspected as traitors, blacks, Mexican Americans, and Puerto Ricans have equated social mobility or acculturation as betrayal (De Vos and Romanucc-Ross 1975:358). Thus, the culture itself may shape a psychocultural set that impedes assimilation.

The chain theory of migration suggests that most migrations begin with lone migrants—younger, single, unskilled males—who later bring their wives and children. As they become permanent residents, acquire better accommodations, and gain more secure employment, they re-create their traditional culture, which fosters greater independence and self-sufficiency for the successive waves of migrants (Price, 1963).

The cultural content of the families of the ethnic groups discussed here all differ in some respects from mainstream culture. The Chinese and Jews (Type B) more closely approximate the American family pattern (Type B) in their cultural content. The Hispanic cultures tend to fall somewhere in between with some elements of Type B and some elements of Type C. Afro–Americans are predominantly Type C with a markedly different cultural content in their family patterning. Thus, these groups can be structured in segmentary hierarchies that reflect their cultural content.

Anthropology in its tradition has long upheld the integrity of individual cultures and recognized the relativity of each culture while recognizing the uniqueness of each. In *Patterns of Culture*, Ruth Benedict (1934) introduced this notion with the principle of the cultural arc or the bell-shaped curve to point out that the variability for cultures, just as for individuals within cultures, falls along a spectrum in its distribution of traits reflecting more of some things and less of others depending upon its unique adaptive needs over time. The hypothesis of cultural adaptive potential presented in this paper does not reject the former notion of cultural relativity; it merely elaborates upon it in setting up a context in which cultures are weighed relative to the specific structure and cultural content of the American WASP family.

"Assimilation theory must, for purposes of achieving greater explanatory power, be placed in the framework of a larger theoretical context which helps explain the general processes of racial and ethnic groups" (Gordon, 1975:88). This paper suggests that family patterning may affect a migrant's adaptive potential and cultural assimilation within the host society. A preliminary weighting of relevant variables supports the concept that the psychocultural or behavioral dimensions of the family of origin are important factors to consider in the acculturation process.

Further research on ethnicity should compare groups on structural assimilation as well as the degree of conflict and degree of access to societal rewards as outlined by Gordon (1975:90). We also need research that measures the degree of cooperation and conflict between ethnic groups, as suggested by Hicks (1977). The areas of cooperation would outline the minimal and maximal lineages for the segmentary hierarchies. An area of suggested future research is systemic studies of the

220 Jacqueline S. Mithun

assimilation processes of single ethnic groups, such as the overseas Chinese, in a variety of cultural contexts to ascertain those situations in which adaptation and cultural assimilation have been more successful. Such findings could conceivably tell us more about the relative explanatory powers of the many variables involved in the total assimilation processes.

REFERENCES

Barth, F.
1969   *Ethnic groups and boundaries.* Boston: Little, Brown.
Bell, D.
1975   Ethnicity and social change, in *Ethnicity: Theory and Experience.* (Moynihan and Glazer, Eds.), pp. 141–174. Cambridge: Harvard University Press.
Benedict, R.
1934   *Patterns of Culture.* Boston: Houghton Mifflin.
Billingsley, A.
1968   *Black Families in White America.* Englewood Cliffs: Prentice-Hall.
Bogardus, E. S.
1930   A race relations cycle. *American Journal of Sociology* **35**:612–617.
Dashefshy, A., and Shapiro, H. M.
1974   *Ethnic Identification among American Jews.* Lexington: Lexington Books.
De Vos, G., and Romanucci-Ross, L.
1975   *Ethnic Identity: Cultural Continuities and Change.* Palo Alto: Mayfield.
Gerlach, L. P., and Hine, V. H.
1970   *People, Power, Change: Movements of Social Transformation.* New York: Bobbs-Merrill.
Glazer, N.
1976   American ethnic groups: identity, culture change, and competence, in *Responses to Change: society, culture, and personality* (G. De Vos, Ed.), pp. 278–293. New York: Van Nostrand.
Glazer, N. and Moynihan, D. (Eds.)
1975   *Ethnicity: Theory and Experience.* Cambridge: Harvard University Press.
Glick, C. E.
1955   Social roles and types in race relations, in *Race Relations in World Perspective* (A. W. Lind, Ed.), pp. 239–262. Honolulu: University of Hawaii Press.
Gordon, M. M.
1964   *Assimilation in American Life.* New York: Oxford University Press.
1975   Toward a general theory of racial and ethnic group relations, in *Ethnicity: Theory and Experience* (N. Glazer and D. P. Moynihan, Eds.), pp. 84–110. Cambridge: Harvard University Press.
Hicks, G. L., and Leis, P. E.
1977   *Ethnic Encounters: Identities and Contexts.* North Scituate, Mass.: Doxbury Press.
Hsu, F. L. K.
1972   *Psychological Anthropology.* Cambridge: Schenkman.
Keyes, C. F.
1976   Towards a new formulation of the concept of ethnic group. *Ethnicity* **3**:202–213.

La Pierre, R. T.
    1946   *Sociology.* New York: McGraw-Hill.
Laporte, B.
    1975   Migration and ethnicity: a commentary on inequality, power and development,
            in *Migration and Development: Implications for Ethnic Identity and Political
            Conflict* (H. I. Safa and B. M. Du Toit, Eds.), pp. 311–318. The Hague: Mouton.
Lieberson, S.
    1961   A societal theory of race and ethnic relations. *American Sociological Review*
            26(6):902–910.
Mintz, S.
    1960   *Worker in the Cane: A Puerto Rican Life History.* New Haven, Conn.: Yale Uni-
            versity Press.
Mithun, J. S.
    1974   *The Friendship Train: A Study of the Adaptive and Cooperative Networks in an
            Urban Afro-American Community.* Ph.D. dissertation, State University of New
            York at Buffalo. Ann Arbor: University Microfilms.
Park, R. E.
    1949   *Race and Culture.* New York: The Free Press.
Parsons, T.
    1975   Some theoretical considerations on the nature and trends of ethnicity, in *Eth-
            nicity: Theory and Experience* (N. Glazer and D. P. Moynihan, Eds.), pp.53–83.
            Cambridge: Harvard University Press.
Price, C. A.
    1963   *Southern Europeans in Australia.* Melbourne: Oxford University press.
Schiller, N. G.
    1977   Ethnic groups are made, not born: the Haitian immigrant and American politics,
            in *Ethnic Encounters: Identities and Contexts* (G. L. Hicks and P. E. Leis, Eds.),
            North Scituate, Mass.: Duxbury Press.
Seda, E.
    1973   *Social Change and Personality in a Puerto Rican Agrarian Reform Community.*
            Evanston, Ill.: Northwestern University Press.

13

Generational Differences in Japanese Americans' Perceptions and Feelings about Social Relationships between Themselves and Caucasian Americans*

David J. O'Brien
Stephen S. Fugita

INTRODUCTION

Since the end of World War II there have been major changes in the political, social, and economic relationships between Japanese Americans and Caucasians. The historical pattern of *de jure* discrimination, as evidenced in the Alien Land Laws and the wartime concentration camps, declined rapidly after the war. The "petit bourgeois" life-style of many Japanese prior to the war prepared them for upward mobility, and thus when new opportunities emerged, they tended to take full advantage of them (O'Brien and Fugita, 1982), moving in substantial numbers into the professions and technical fields (Fujimoto, 1975; Hirschman and Wong, 1981; Kitano, 1976). Moreover, the new economic opportunities

* This research was supported by Grant R01 MH31565 from the National Institute of Mental Health. We wish to express our gratitude to Alan Iba, Annie Iriye, Cynthia Kawachi, Cindy Rogers, Emi Takizawa, and Lynne Wada for their continuous support of the project as research assistants; to Isadore Newman for his help with statistical issues; and the University of California at Los Angeles Asian American Studies Center, the Fresno JACL/ Nikkei Service Center and Percy Masaki for providing field offices and other forms of assistance. We also wish to thank the many other interviewers and individuals who provided aid without which this project would not have been possible.

combined with the geographic dispersal created by the concentration camp experience resulted in large numbers of Japanese moving from somewhat segregated ethnic communities to more integrated settings. One indication of the social consequences of these changes is evident in the intermarriage rate between Japanese and Caucasians, which has increased from less than 10% to approximately 50% of all new marriages involving Japanese today (Kikumura and Kitano, 1973; Tinker, 1973). These facts have lent a great deal of support to the "assimilationist" position that suggests that the social boundaries between Japanese and other Americans are rapidly disappearing and that the former have become, by and large, part of "mainstream America" (Montero, 1977, 1978).

At the same time, however, there is evidence to suggest that Japanese Americans retain certain "expressive styles" and "interactional patterns" that distinguish them from the majority group. A contemporary laboratory experiment has demonstrated that Japanese American college students engage in less feedback behavior than white American students (Ogawa and Weldon, 1972). Another found that female Japanese American college students exhibit more deference in the presence of authority figures than their Caucasian counterparts, as indexed by lowered voice levels (Ayabe, 1971). This is consistent with the suggestion that the traditional Japanese "enryo" syndrome of behavioral reserve (Kitano, 1976) persists up to the present day. Johnson, Marsella, and Johnson (1974) and Johnson and Johnson (1975) have described additional verbal and nonverbal interaction differences between Japanese Americans and Caucasians.

Moreover, the development in recent years of the Asian American movement on the West Coast, and its partial institutionalization in Asian American Studies programs on a number of college campuses, indicates that among the third-generation Sansei there is an interest in examining and reconceptualizing the Japanese American experience. This movement is not only a reaction against mainstream definitions of the group (e.g., the "model minority" stereotype), but also an attempt to influence more actively political and economic processes that have an impact on Japanese Americans. Most important, although the Japanese have been geographically dispersed from the self-contained "Japantowns" and ethnic farming communities, and despite the fact that many persons in the younger generation have lost facility with the language and other cultural patterns, there remains a high degree of interaction and mutual support among members of the ethnic group. This is reflected in the preference of Japanese for one another's companionship in peer relationships (see, e.g., Johnson, 1976) as well as a high degree of identification with the Japanese community (see, e.g., Fugita and O'Brien, 1982).

The focus of the present paper is on how individual Japanese Americans in two different generations have reacted and are currently reacting to the changes just described. Specifically, we will examine how second-generation (Nisei) and third-generation (Sansei) Japanese Americans perceive and feel about their relationships with the majority Caucasian group. In this regard, we will ask, what are the similarities and what are the differences between generations with respect to perceptions and feelings about interaction with the mainstream society? In addition, the possible "mediating" effects of education and involvement in Japanese–American organizations will be examined.

GENERATIONAL DIFFERENCES AND SOCIAL BOUNDARIES

For our purposes, it is important to distinguish between (1) perceptions of differences between the "interactional and expressive styles" of Japanese and Caucasians, (2) affective reactions or feelings about interacting with Caucasians, and (3) perceptions and feelings about being discriminated against because of one's Japanese background. Each of these will be examined in turn.

Perception of Differences in Interactional Styles

The central issue here is the extent to which individuals see differences in the norms that Japanese Americans operate with in their day-to-day interactions in areas such as social activities, family life, church, and business, compared to the norms that regulate the corresponding interactions of Caucasion Americans. Hraba (1979:311) calls the latter "Anglo-American cultural styles." It is important to emphasize that there is no necessary correspondence between, on the one hand, an individual's perceptions of differences or similarities between the two groups and, on the other, the feelings that he or she has about such differences.

We find two plausible but contradictory expectations with respect to possible generational differences on this cognitive dimension of social boundaries. On the one hand, we might expect to find that the older generation Nisei will be more apt than the younger Sansei generation to see differences between their ethnic group and the larger society. The Nisei have been exposed to a more Japanese-oriented early socialization experience than the Sansei and generally have had less contact with majority group members in informal settings during their youth. This would suggest that the Nisei have a more articulated understanding of traditional Japanese American ways. Since the Nisei now have the opportunity to have more contact with persons in the dominant group, they may be in a better position to recognize differences between the two cultural systems. Consistent with this is research that has shown that Nisei see themselves as being "half Japanese and half American" (Connor, 1974).

On the other hand, one might contend that intimate social contact allows an individual to perceive differences between groups more accurately. From this perspective we might expect that the Sansei who have had more opportunity for intimate contact with majority group members will be able to see more clearly the subtle differences in interactional styles and normative processes between their ethnic group and the majority group. Moreover, the Sansei have grown up in a more secure political, economic, and social atmosphere than the Nisei, and thus differences between their ethnic group and the larger society have different implications than they had for the Nisei during the pre-World War II days of active anti-Japanese discrimination. Frequently, many Nisei, both before and during World War II, seemed to play down differences between their ethnic group and the mainstream. This is especially evident in the "100% American" symbolization and rhetoric of the Nisei-created Japanese American Citizens League (JACL) (see, e.g., Hosokawa, 1969). Alternatively, the Sansei have grown up during the period in which a number of factors in the larger society have promoted a more "positive" stereotyping of Japanese Americans, especially emphasizing their upward mobility. The generally symbiotic postwar economic and political relationship between the United States and Japan may also be a factor here. Finally, as noted earlier, the Asian American movement has created a vehicle with which younger Japanese Americans can seek out new models of ethnic identification.

We might expect that persons with higher educational levels will have exposure to a larger number of alternative frames of reference, partly as a result of contact with more persons outside of the Japanese community. Yet, here again, we find two plausible but contradictory sets of expectations. One possibility is that persons with more education will cue in on the similarities between groups, that is, have a sort of "basic humanity" viewpoint. Alternatively, such individuals may be even more sensitized to differences because of their greater exposure to different bases of comparison.

Finally, we would expect that the degree to which an individual is actually involved in an ethnic community itself would have important consequences for his or her sensitivity to differences between the group and other groups. Here we should find that individuals who are most involved in the Japanese community have the most at stake in reaffirming its uniqueness, particularly its perceived positive attributes, and thus see more differences between it and the larger society. The other possibility is that individuals who are isolated from the community are more likely to see differences between it and larger society. The latter situation might occur because an individual feels uncomfortable with the norms of the ethnic community and thus accentuates what he or she sees as its "negative" attributes. Some individuals may report, for example, that they feel constraints caused by the demanding expectations of fellow ethnics.

Feelings about Interacting with Caucasians

Overall, we expect that Nisei will feel more uncomfortable than Sansei in situations where they have to interact with majority group members. The Nisei have had less opportunity to interact with Caucasians and hence are likely to be less familiar with their norms. Moreover, persons in the older generation have had more direct experience than younger persons with unpleasant discriminatory interaction with majority group members and less opportunity to experience equal status contact.

We might expect, however, that differences in the degree to which individuals feel comfortable interacting with majority group members will be influenced by amount of education. On the one hand, individuals with more education will probably have a greater understanding of mainstream world views and norms and, overall, are likely to have more self-confidence and self-esteem. This would suggest that more educated persons should be more comfortable interacting with majority group members. On the other hand, more educated Japanese Americans are more likely to interact with Caucasians in competitive situations. This may produce a more negative effect in relating to Caucasians. The latter expectation is supported by the notion that more educated persons are more likely to be forced to deal with the pressures created by operating within two sometimes conflicting normative systems.

In addition, it is predicted that the extent to which individuals are involved in the Japanese American community will influence their feelings about interacting with majority group members in two different ways. On the one hand, individuals who are involved in the ethnic community may feel more comfortable interacting with majority group members because they have a meaningful "support group" that provides a positive subcultural "base" in dealing with the outside world (Segall, 1979:243). On the other hand, such involvement in the ethnic community may reduce interaction with the larger society and thus reduce the opportunities to develop a perceptual frame and interactional style that facilitates accommodation to majority group members.

Perceptions and Feelings about Discrimination

Clearly, the Nisei have been exposed to more direct discrimination than the Sansei. At the same time, however, the younger generation has grown up in an era of civil rights struggles, ethnic consciousness, and overall greater sensitivity to the subtleties of discrimination and prejudice. In addition, the very fact that the younger generation is more apt than the older one to move into occupations that put them into direct contact and competition with majority group members as individuals creates opportunities for new forms of prejudice to manifest themselves. Since the Nisei have experienced much greater overt discrimination than the Sansei and the current situation of the former is markedly improved over their earlier situation, we might expect the Nisei to see less discrimination in contemporary society. However, because of their lack of a reference point grounded in a earlier period of gross discrimination, along with the new types of contact and competition with majority group members, we might expect the Sansei to be more cognizant of current subtle forms of discrimination.

Certainly, educational level will be highly associated with generation, given the different educational opportunity structures available to Nisei versus Sansei. Nevertheless, we expect that this variable will have an additional effect independent of generation, either reinforcing or moderating the perception of discrimination. At least in the postwar era, persons who are more educated are more likely to have opportunities to participate in mainstream economic and social activities and thus may be more likely to see the social structure as relatively fluid and open. But, at the same time, persons with more education are also more likely to be exposed to information, perceptual frames, and ideologies, such as the civil rights or Asian American movements, which sensitize and "legitimize" one's perception of discrimination.

The relationship between involvement in the Japanese community and perception of discrimination is complex. It may "insulate" the individual from potentially discriminatory relationships with majority group members and hence reduce the perception of discrimination. On the other hand, involvement in Japanese organizations may expose individuals to information and frames of reference that encourage them to detect discrimination and respond to it.

METHOD

California was chosen as the research site to study Japanese Americans for several reasons. It contains, by far, the largest number of Japanese in the continental United States (213,277 out of 317,149 in 1970) (see, U.S. Bureau of the Census, 1973; Urban Associates, 1974).[1] In addition, the researchers are familiar with the historical and contemporary dimensions of Japanese community life in different areas of California through research on the development of "ethnic economies" and a farm labor issue involving Japanese growers (Fugita and O'Brien, 1977; O'Brien and Fugita, 1978, 1982).

The first area selected was Gardena, a three- by four-mile suburb in the South Bay section of Los Angeles. Southern California contains the largest single concentration of Japanese outside of Hawaii, and Gardena is one of the region's residential, social, and cultural centers. Japanese made up 21.5% (9144 individuals) of Gardena's residents in 1978. During the same period, blacks comprised 21.9%, whites 35.7%, and Chicanos 15.4% of the city's population.

The second area selected, Fresno and Fresno County, is markedly different from Gardena. It is located in the heart of the agriculturally rich San Joaquin Valley. Ethnically, this area is quite diverse with sizable populations of Chicanos, blacks, Armenians, Scandinavians, and various Asian groups. At the time of the 1970 census, the total number of Japanese in the Fresno Standard Metropolitian Statistical area (SMSA) was 5,640 out of a total population of 444,847 (1.27%).

The last area selected as a research site was the state capital, Sacramento. Out of a total population of 803,610, there were 11,958 Japanese living in this area (Sacramento SMSA) in 1970 (1.4%). The economy of the area is dominated by state and federal government activities, and there is little heavy industry.

Our sample was drawn from a list of all Japanese male names in the telephone directories in the three areas.[2] Telephone books were employed because Japanese are not geographically concentrated, except to some extent in Gardena, and thus any kind of cluster sampling would have been more costly than our resources would have permitted. Moreover, over 95% of all U.S. households have a telephone (Alwin, 1977). A

[1] Hawaii contained 217,175 Japanese in 1970, thus making the total U.S. population of Japanese 588,324 in 1970 (U.S. Bureau of the Census, 1973).

[2] Japanese males seldom change their surnames, and these names are distinguishable enough so that with some training they can be accurately identified (Tinker, 1973).

more serious problem encountered in using the telephone directory as a sampling frame, however, is that of unlisted numbers. Nonetheless, recent findings indicate that although there are statistically significant differences between persons who have listed versus unlisted telephones, when the number of unlisteds is around 20% (approximately the national average) the magnitude of error associated with generalizing using only listeds is between 1 and 2% (Rich, 1977). In our research site areas, the numbers of unlisteds reported by Pacific Bell Telephone were as follows: Gardena, 15%; Fresno, 24%; and Sacramento, 25%. Second, only males were selected because the universe of Japanese females who had intermarried with Caucasians or other Asians would have non-Japanese last names.[3] Thus, in order to avoid drawing a biased sample of females, we elected not to sample them. Third, we selected approximately equal numbers of Nisei and Sansei. The total sample was 634: 211 in Gardena (105 Nisei, 106 Sansei), 212 in Fresno (103 Nisei, 109 Sansei), and 211 in Sacramento (105 Nisei, 106 Sansei). Overall, our refusal rate was 26.5%. In Gardena it was 37.8%, in Fresno it was 13.8%, and in Sacramento it was 21.2%.[4]

Before interviewing in each of the three communities, an effort was made to contact community leaders and institutional sectors. Articles of varying length describing the project were published in the local newspaper and the vernacular press in each of the areas. Because the nature of the questions on the survey instrument dealt specifically with ethnic issues, we employed only Japanese American interviewers.[5] Interviewer quality and perceptions by the respondent of the interview situation were randomly checked in 20% of the sample with a callback procedure.

[3] As noted earlier, the current intermarriage rate among Japanese is approximately 50% of all new marriages involving Japanese (Kikumura and Kitano, 1973; Tinker, 1973).

[4] The higher refusal rate in Gardena is consistent with Sudman's (1976) findings that refusal rates tend to be higher in metropolitan areas. He reports about 80% overall cooperation in national samples with refusal rates up to 30% in major metropolitan areas and as low as 5% to 0% in many organizations in small towns and farms. Because the present research involved telephone screening, one would expect higher refusal rates because it is probably easier to refuse on the telephone than in the face-to-face cluster sampling procedure.

[5] Past research suggests that the racial or ethnic background of the interviewer is most likely to be relevant in cases where the interview deals with racially or ethnically specific information (Hatchett and Schuman, 1975–1976; Schuman and Converse, 1968; Sudman and Bradburn, 1974). Not only is rapport probably increased by having persons of the same ethnic group as the respondents ask the questions but the ethnicity of the interviewer seems to provide a "frame-of-reference" (see Schuman and Converse, 1968).

Table 1

Percentage of Respondents Perceiving Differences Between Japanese and Caucasian
Ways in Four Situations[a]

| | Situation | | | |
Generation	Business	Social	Church	Family
Nisei	39.9	38.3	66.0	60.7
	(121)	(116)	(200)	(184)
Sansei	50.9	46.3	82.3	70.5
	(164)	(149)	(265)	(227)
Total sample	45.6	42.4	74.4	65.8
	(285)	(265)	(465)	(411)
Zero-order and partial correlations with generation				
r, with generation	.115**	.067	.082	.183***
r, controlling for education	.121**	.094*	.080	.149***
r, controlling for Japanese organizations	.094*	.091*	.137**	.190***

* $p < .05$, ** $p < .01$, *** $p < .001$.
[a]Number of respondents is shown in parentheses.

FINDINGS

To measure perceptions of differences in interactional style, we asked
respondents to note whether or not there were differences between
"Japanese and Caucasian ways" in four different situations: business,
social affairs, church life, and family relations. The results are shown in
Table 1.

Overall, the results demonstrate that substantial numbers of Japanese
Americans still perceive differences between their group and the majority
group in the four kinds of interactional settings. There are, however,
important differences in the perceptions of Nisei and Sansei. Sansei were
more likely than Nisei to report seeing differences in all four situations,
and these generational effects were statistically significant in the case of
business and family relationships. Moreover, when the effects of education and involvement in Japanese organizations were controlled, significant relationships with generation were found in all four interactional
settings.

The next task was to measure the feelings of Japanese Americans
about their group and its relationship to the majority group. The first

item, which asked respondents to indicate their degree of agreement or disagreement with the statement "It is important for Sansei to learn something about Japanese culture" was intended to be an indicator of a minimal kind of support for the value of the ethnic group subculture. A second item, which asked respondents to state their degree of agreement or disagreement with the statement "Human relations are warmer in the Japanese community" was designed to measure feelings about the quality of interaction in the Japanese community compared with that in the larger society. Finally, the last item asked respondents to relate their feelings about the most intimate interaction between members of the ethnic group and the majority group, "Do you see more problems or benefits resulting from intermarriage?" The responses are reported in Table 2.

The vast majority of persons saw Japanese culture in a positive light, as evidenced by the fact that over 89.4% of our respondents agreed that Sansei should learn something about it. However, as we move toward issues that deal with feelings about the quality of interaction within the Japanese subculture as compared with the majority culture and the desirability of intimate interaction with Caucasians, there was greater variance of opinion. There was an approximately 50–50 split on the issue of whether the Japanese community was "warmer," and there were a wide range of responses on the intermarriage item. We should also note that there were not significant generational differences on these items even when the effects of education and degree of involvement in Japanese American organizations were controlled.

The next concern was to look at the extent to which different individuals in the Japanese American community feel uncomfortable interacting with persons in the majority group. To measure this, we asked the respondents to indicate their degree of agreement or disagreement with the statement "Socially, I feel less at ease with Caucasians than with Japanese." The responses to this item are shown in Table 3.

The zero-order correlations demonstrate that Nisei were more likely than Sansei to report feeling less at ease with Caucasians than with Japanese, but this difference disappeared when we controlled for education and degree of involvement in Japanese organizations. Moreover, there was a negative zero-order relationship between education and feeling uncomfortable interacting with majority group members $(r = -.16, p < .001)$, whereas the relationship was reversed with respect to involvement in Japanese organizations and feeling uncomfortable interacting with Caucasians $(r = .16, p < .001)$.

The questions pertaining to perceptions of discrimination dealt with three different areas. First, the respondents were asked the extent to

Table 2

Percentages of Respondents Agreeing with Statements about the Valence of the Japanese Subculture[a]

Generation	Important for Sansei to learn Japanese culture					Japanese community warmer than majority					More problems or benefits with intermarriage		
	Strongly agree	Agree	Undecided	Disagree	Strongly disagree	Strongly agree	Agree	Undecided	Disagree	Strongly disagree	More benefits	No difference, depends on individual	More problems
Nisei	45.0 (138)	45.9 (141)	4.9 (15)	3.6 (11)	.7 (2)	6.8 (21)	48.7 (150)	19.5 (60)	23.7 (73)	1.3 (4)	24.5 (72)	42.5 (125)	33.0 (97)
Sansei	43.7 (141)	44.3 (143)	9.6 (31)	2.5 (8)	—	7.8 (25)	42.9 (138)	32.3 (104)	14.9 (48)	2.2 (7)	26.0 (79)	40.4 (123)	33.6 (102)
Total	44.4 (280)	45.0 (284)	7.3 (46)	3.0 (19)	.3 (2)	7.3 (46)	45.8 (289)	26.0 (164)	19.2 (121)	1.7 (11)	25.2 (151)	41.6 (249)	33.2 (199)

Zero-order and partial correlations with generation

	Important for Sansei to learn Japanese culture	Japanese community warmer than majority	More problems or benefits with intermarriage
r, with generation	.010	.015	.011
r, controlling for education	.021	.057	.025
r, controlling for Japanese organizations	.016	.025	.011

[a]Number of respondents is shown in parentheses.

Table 3

Percentage of Respondents Agreeing with "Socially, I Feel Less at Ease
with Caucasians than with Japanese"[a]

Generation	Strongly agree	Agree	Undecided	Disagree	Strongly disagree
Nisei	5.2	33.0	12.4	43.1	6.2
	(16)	(101)	(38)	(132)	(19)
Sansei	5.3	23.3	14.9	42.2	14.3
	(17)	(75)	(48)	(136)	(46)
Total	5.2	28.0	13.7	42.8	10.3
	(33)	(176)	(86)	(269)	(65)

	Zero-order and partial correlations with generation
r, with generation	.111*
r, controlling for education	.058
r, controlling for Japanese organizations	.065

*$p < .01$.
[a]Number of respondents is shown in parentheses.

which they personally had experienced discrimination as an adult. Next, they were requested to indicate how much they agreed or disagreed with the statement "Today, Japanese Americans do not experience job discrimination." Finally, respondents were asked to indicate the extent to which they agreed or disagreed with the statement, "Japanese experience discrimination in social situations." The responses to this item are shown in Table 4.

Not surprisingly, Nisei were more likely than Sansei to report that they personally experienced more discrimination as an adult ($r = .25$, $p < .001$). Among the Nisei 31.4% reported having experienced either a "great deal" or a "considerable amount" of discrimination as compared with the corresponding percentage of 12.5 for the Sansei. Moreover, these generational differences remained when education ($r = .23$, $p < .001$) and involvement in Japanese organizations ($r = .21$, $p < .001$) were controlled.

Approximately one-half of the respondents said that they felt there was discrimination in the employment area; 55.2% disagreed with the statement that Japanese do not face job discrimination today (those agreeing with the statement comprised 36.7% of the sample, whereas

Table 4

Percentage of Respondents Agreeing with Statements about Past Experienced Discrimination and Present Social and Job Discrimination[a]

Generation	Amount of discrimination experienced as an adult				Currently, Japanese experience social discrimination					Currently, Japanese do not experience job discrimination				
	Great deal	Considerable amount	Minimal amount	None	Strongly agree	Agree	Undecided	Disagree	Strongly disagree	Strongly agree	Agree	Undecided	Disagree	Strongly disagree
Nisei	12.9 (40)	18.4 (57)	60.2 (186)	8.7 (27)	7.1 (22)	68.9 (213)	11.0 (34)	12.0 (37)	1.0 (3)	5.8 (18)	32.0 (99)	7.4 (23)	45.5 (141)	9.4 (29)
Sansei	3.1 (10)	9.7 (31)	69.9 (223)	17.2 (55)	13.6 (44)	60.7 (196)	12.4 (40)	12.4 (40)	.9 (3)	4.3 (14)	31.9 (103)	9.0 (29)	43.7 (141)	11.1 (36)
Total sample	7.9 (50)	14.0 (88)	65.0 (409)	13.0 (82)	10.4 (66)	64.7 (409)	11.7 (74)	12.2 (77)	.9 (6)	5.1 (32)	31.9 (202)	8.2 (52)	44.5 (282)	10.3 (65)
	Zero-order and partial correlations with generation													
r, with generation	.249*				.033					.036				
r, controlling for education	.227*				.019					.099				
r, controlling for Japanese organization	.219*				.031					.069				

*$p < .001$.

[a]Number of respondents is shown in parentheses.

8.2% ·were undecided). There were no significant differences between Nisei and Sansei on this item (r = .02, p = n.s.). Three-quarters (75.3%) of the sample agreed with the statement that Japanese experience social discrimination. There also was no difference between Nisei and Sansei on this item (r = .03, p = n.s.). Moreover, controlling for education and involvement in Japanese organizations did not change the relationship between generation and the perception of job discrimination (r = .02, p = n.s. and r = .06, p = n.s.) or the relationship between generation and the perception of social discrimination (r = .02, p = n.s. and r = .03, p = n.s.).

DISCUSSION

Overall, the statistical relationships obtained from the data are not very strong, but nonetheless they do reflect patterns that help in understanding variations in the way that individual Japanese Americans perceive and feel about social relationships with the majority Caucasian group. Most important, these findings provide us with some empirical referents with which to conceptualize more accurately different cognitive and affective dimensions of these relationships.

The fact that large numbers of our respondents saw substantial differences between Japanese and mainstream American interactional and expressive styles in the four areas suggests that a cross-section of the ethnic community does not see the assimilation of their group proceeding as rapidly as some researchers have proposed (see, e.g., Montero, 1978). Moreover, the very substantial numbers of Japanese who report job and social discrimination persisting against them (at least as a group) indicate that persons in this minority group continue to perceive themselves as being "apart from" the larger society in some very significant ways.

At the same time, there were significant cross-generational differences with respect to perceptions of differences in interactional style. Sansei were more likely than Nisei to see differences between the interactional style of their ethnic group and the majority, and this relationship was maintained when we controlled for education and community involvement variables.

These findings would seem to support the view that more intimate contact with majority group members and, at the same time, the development of movements and ideologies favorable to positive ethnic identity (e.g., the Asian American movement) provide individuals with more opportunities to become aware of and articulate the unique features of their own group's culture and social organization. More intriguing here is the fact that the generational differences increased when we controlled for education and community involvement factors, indicating that in this particular area there is a substantial generational effect that probably can be ascribed to differences in the historical contexts facing the respective cohorts.

As expected, Nisei were more likely than Sansei to report feeling more uncomfortable interacting with Caucasians than with Japanese. In contrast to the "generational effects" on the perception of differences items, however, the zero-order relationships between the groups on feelings about interacting with Caucasians disappeared when we introduced education and degree of involvement in Japanese organizations as controls. The fact that more educated persons were less likely to feel uncomfortable interacting with Caucasians lends support to the view that education leads to greater feelings of self-confidence and self-esteem in majority group social situations. Alternatively, the negative association between involvement in Japanese organizations and feeling comfortable interacting with Caucasians does not provide any evidence in favor of the notion that participation in an ethnic "support group" will make an individual feel more comfortable dealing with persons in the larger society. An alternative explanation is that those more involved in the ethnic community have fewer opportunities to develop diversified perceptual frames and interactional styles.

We were somewhat surprised by the lack of any significant generational differences with respect to the items pertaining to the value of Japanese culture, feelings about human relations within the community, and intermarriage. In these instances there was more generational continuity than we had anticipated. Despite the different perceptions of Nisei and Sansei with respect to social boundaries vis-à-vis themselves and the majority group, there appears to be a high degree of consensus between both generations on the positive value of the ethnic culture. This was seen, for example, in the overwhelming number of persons who agreed that Sansei should learn something about Japanese culture. At the same time, however, there was much less consensus about whether the Japanese community is "warmer" than the mainstream. Also relevant here is the fact that within the Japanese American community there are marked differences in the degree to which individuals see benefits or problems resulting from intermarriage. However, in the latter two instances we did not find any significant differences resulting from generational, educational, or community involvement factors.

The essential similarity of responses between the two generations on the job and social discrimination items suggests that most Japanese, irrespective of age or other social attributes, can relate to being treated differently as a result of their ethnicity and thus perceive a clear social boundary between themselves and the majority group. Certainly, persons in the different generations have had very different personal experiences with the two types of discrimination, as evidenced by the responses to the item measuring the degree of discrimination an individual has encountered as an adult. However, the data suggest that the more subtle forms of discrimination encountered by the younger generation, even though structural conditions have changed markedly since the Second World War, provide an experiential linkage between the two generations. Moreover, there is some indication that education "sensitizes" one to discrimination in the sense that education was positively associated with reporting job discrimination for the Nisei and social discrimination for the Sansei. Another factor that may produce similarities in the perceptions of Nisei and Sansei with respect to discrimination is the ethnic "community network," which, in effect, takes the somewhat ambiguous and subtle discriminatory situations and translates them into a similar frame of reference and makes perceptions across individuals more homogeneous.

Finally, the reader should note that despite differences in the responses of individuals on specific items, our research shows clearly that most Japanese Americans still see definite social boundaries between themselves and the majority group in American society. Moreover, there was a remarkable degree of continuity across generations on many of the items we used to measure sensitivity to these boundaries. In the most general sense, although we may expect to find continuing change among individual Japanese Americans with respect to how they relate to one another and to the mainstream society, there is likely to remain for some time to come a clear definition of ethnic group identity.

REFERENCES

Alwin, D. F.
    1977   Making errors in surveys: an overview. *Sociological Methods and Research* 6:131–150.
Ayabe, H. I.
    1971   Deference and ethnic differences in voice levels. *The Journal of Social Psychology* 85:181–185.
Connor, J. W.
    1974   Family continuities in three generations of Japanese Americans. *Journal of Marriage and the Family* 36:156–165.

Fugita, S. S., and O'Brien, D. J.
    1977   Economics, ideology, and ethnicity: the struggle between the United Farm Work-
            ers Union and the Nisei Farmers League. *Social Problems* 25:146–156.
    1982   Generational change in mechanisms of ethnic group identification. Paper
            presented at The Western Psychological Association Meetings, Sacramento,
            California.
Fujimoto, T.
    1975   Social class and crime: the case of the Japanese–Americans. *Issues in Crimi-
            nology* 10:73–89.
Hatchett, S. and Schuman, H.
    1975–1976   White respondents and race-of-interviewer effects. *Public Opinion Quar-
            terly* 39:523–528.
Hirschman, C., and Wong, M. G.
    1981   Trends in socioeconomic achievement among immigrant and native-born Asian–
            Americans, 1960–1976. *Sociological Quarterly* 22:495–513.
Hosokowa, B.
    1969   *Nisei: The Quiet Americans.* New York: Morrow.
Hraba, J.
    1979   *American Ethnicity.* Itasca, Ill.: Peacock.
Johnson, C.
    1976   The principle of generation among the Japanese in Honolulu. *Ethnic Groups*
            1:13–35.
Johnson, C. L, and Johnson, F. A.
    1975   Interaction rules and ethnicity: the Japanese and Caucasians in Honolulu. *Social
            Forces* 54:452–466.
Johnson, F. A., Marsella, A. J., and Johnson, C. L.
    1974   Social and psychological aspects of verbal behavior in Japanese–Americans.
            American Journal of Psychiatry 131:580–583.
Kikumura, A., and Kitano, H. H. L.
    1973   Interracial marriage: a picture of the Japanese Americans. *Journal of Social
            Issues* 29:67–81.
Kitano, H. H. L.
    1976   *Japanese Americans: The Evolution of a Sub-Culture* (second ed.) Englewood
            Cliffs, N.J.: Prentice-Hall.
Montero, D.
    1977   The Japanese American community: a study of generational changes in ethnic
            affiliation. Paper presented at the annual meeting of the American Sociological
            Association, Chicago.
    1978   Model minority: Japanese join mainstream America. *Human Behavior* 7:59.
O'Brien, D. J., and Fugita, S. S.
    1978   Some continuities and discontinuities in an 'Ethnic Enterprise': the Nisei Farmers
            League and the Japanese agricultural experience. Paper presented at the annual
            meeting of the American Sociological Association. San Francisco, California.
    1982   Middleman minority concept: its explanatory value in the case of the Japanese
            in California agriculture. *Pacific Sociological Review* 25:185–204.
Ogawa, D. and Welden, T. A.
    1972   Cross-cultural analysis of feedback behavior within Japanese American and
            Caucasian American small groups. *The Journal of Communication* 22:189–195.
Rich, C. L.
    1977   Is random digit dialing really necessary? *Journal of Marketing Research* 14:300–
            305.

Schuman, H., and Converse, J. M.
    1968   The effects of Black and White interviewers on Black responses in 1968. *Public Opinion Quarterly* 35:44–68.
Segall, M. H.
    1979   *Cross-Cultural Psychology.* Monterey, California: Brooks/Cole.
Sudman, S.
    1976   *Applied Sampling.* New York: Academic Press.
Sudman, S., and Bradburn, N. M.
    1974   *Response Effects in Surveys: A Review and Synthesis.* Chicago: Aldine.
Tinker, J. N.
    1973   Intermarriage and ethnic boundaries: the Japanese American Case. *Journal of Social Issues* 29:49–66.
U.S. Bureau of the Census
    1973   *Census of the Population: 1970. Japanese, Chinese, and Filipinos in the United States.* Washington, D.C.: U.S. Government Printing Office.
Urban Associates
    1974   *A Study of Selected Socioeconomic Characteristics Based on the 1970 Census* (Vol. 2): *Asian Americans.* Washington, D.C.: U.S. Government Printing Office.

14

Immigrant and Local Filipino Perceptions of Ethnic Conflict

Jonathan Y. Okamura

INTRODUCTION

The immigrant situation in Hawaii is somewhat unique compared to other terminal points of immigration in that many of the incoming groups are already represented in the host society by long-resident, substantially large populations with whom they share the same ethnic background. This state of affairs arose following the liberalization of U.S. immigration laws in 1965 with the result that Hawaii has been receiving an annual average of 7000 immigrants in recent years. Thus, Filipino, Korean, Japanese, and Chinese newcomers can expect to encounter their Hawaii-born counterparts, whose antecedents came to work on the sugar plantations in the late nineteenth century and early part of the present century. It would seem more than probable that this circumstance would tend to alleviate some of the more arduous adaptation problems that immigrants inevitably face in a new environment, because an already established ethnic community could be expected to be a source of assistance and support and a basis for interpersonal ties. Unfortunately, it has not proven to be the case for recent Filipino immigrants to Hawaii. Their adjustment process has been made more difficult due to the less than harmonious relations that have arisen between the recent immigrant and the Hawaii-born, local sectors of the Filipino community. Despite their common ethnicity, the prevailing pattern in the social relations between immigrant and local Filipinos would seem to be one of cleavage and avoidance. This paper examines one aspect of the social relations

241

between these two groups, that is, the relationships between immigrant and local Filipino students in the schools.

METHOD

Procedure

The data for this paper were obtained from a more extensive survey conducted by the Culture Learning Institute of the East-West Center for the Hawaii Department of Education in November and December of 1975. This wider study was primarily concerned with an assessment of language usage and the educational needs of Ilokano-speaking students in a number of Honolulu schools.[1] This information was to be used to formulate a set of recommendations for a model secondary bilingual–bicultural education program. Accordingly, nearly 5000 students in the three targeted schools, McKinley High and Central and Washington Intermediate schools, and in two additional schools, Dole and Kalakaua Intermediate, completed various survey instruments. One of these instruments was an attitude questionnaire that focused on conflict among students in the schools. It consisted of three open-ended questions. The first was, "Often we hear that there is trouble between local young people and young people who come here from other countries. From your own experience what groups have this trouble with each other?" The second question was "What do you think are some of the things that cause these bad feelings between groups?" The final question was "What do you think can be done at your school to solve the problems between local students and students from other countries?" It was thought that the open-ended format of the questionnaire would allow students to express their perceptions and opinions as freely as possible with a minimum of prejudgment by the researchers of the nature of the problem and of the significant categories involved.

The primary reason for inclusion of the attitude questionnaire among the survey instruments was to obtain some information on students' understanding of and explanations about ethnic conflict in their schools. Interest in this subject was generated by the occurrence in several schools of violent confrontations between immigrant Filipino and Hawaii-born, local students during the year previous to the study. Two of these affrays resulted tragically in the deaths of two students, an immigrant Filipino

[1] Ilokanos, who come from the northern Luzon region of the Philippines, represent the great majority of Filipino immigrants to Hawaii.

and a local Filipino. In fact, immigrant and local Filipino students, despite their common ethnicity, were often opponents in these encounters. This paper is concerned with a comparison of the perceptions of ethnic conflict in the schools of immigrant (Philippines-born) and local (Hawaii-born) Filipino students as expressed in their responses to the first question.

It should be stated at the outset that it is not the purpose of this paper to determine empirically the degree of fit between these subjective perceptions of ethnic conflict and actually observed or recorded incidents of conflict. Nor is the paper concerned with reconciliation of possible discrepancies between cognitive and behavioral phenomena of ethnic conflict. The task of the paper is limited to illuminating the perceptions and understandings of immigrant and local Filipino students.

Demographic Traits

The sample for this study consisted of 332 immigrant and 350 local Filipino students, who were classified into these categories according to ethnicity and place of birth. Ethnicity was based on self-identification in reply to a demographic information item on the questionnaire that asked, "What is your ethnic background?" Students of mixed parentage were encouraged to include the ancestry of all of the antecedents they knew of. The distinction between immigrant and local was based on another background information item on place of birth—the Philippines in the case of immigrants and Hawaii or the mainland United States in the case of locals. Although this use of the term "local" to refer to persons who are from the mainland is contradictory to its meaning as commonly understood in Hawaii, the number of Filipinos who were born on the mainland and who had lived only a few years in Hawaii was minimal in comparison to the size of the local Filipino sample. It is also true that the sole use of place of birth to categorize respondents as either immigrant or local has the drawback that it disregards the number of years of residence in Hawaii, particularly in the case of immigrants who have lived in Hawaii for most of their lives. However, this classification procedure avoids the assumption of acculturation processes immigrant Filipinos may undergo to be considered or to consider themselves as local.

A further breakdown of the two subsamples by ethnicity indicates that of the immigrant Filipinos, the overwhelming majority replied that their ethnic background was Filipino (97.3%), and they also replied that they were Spanish (18.4%), Chinese (4.5%), or Japanese (1.2%). The sum of these percentages exceeds 100% because students who claimed to be Spanish, Chinese, or Japanese also said that they were Filipino. It was also found that several students identified themselves as Ilokano (2.1%) or Tagalog (1.5%).[2]

Among the local Filipinos a substantial majority responded that they were of mixed ancestry (73.1); the remainder were pure Filipino. Of the former group the admixtures included Hawaiian (48.8%), Chinese (46.1%), Spanish (43.0%), Japanese (19.5%), Haole (Caucasian) (18.4%), Portuguese (14.5%), Puerto Rican (4.3%), and Samoan (3.9%). Again, the sum of these percentages exceeds 100% because of the multiethnic background of the respondents. Somewhat surprisingly, five local Filipinos stated that they were Ilokano, although none indicated that he or she was either Tagalog or Visayan.

The substantial percentage of mixed local Filipinos who stated that they were part-Hawaiian or part-Chinese is readily understandable given the relatively high rate of intermarriage between local Filipinos and Hawaiians, many of whom have Chinese antecedents. That is, local Filipino students who are part-Chinese are probably not the result of marriages between Filipinos and Chinese, but are the offspring of marriages between Filipinos (grooms primarily) and Chinese–Hawaiians. Also, the significantly large percentage of local Filipinos who stated that they were part-Spanish is noteworthy given the fact that there is no identifiable Spanish community in Hawaii. This tendency of local Filipinos to claim Spanish descent is noted by immigrant Filipinos as evidence of an ethnicity denial position assumed by their local counterparts (Jocano, 1970:155). Immigrants also contend that local Filipinos attempt to disavow themselves from their Filipino ancestry by assertions that they are Hawaiian, or if they are of mixed parentage, by invariably mentioning last that they are Filipino.

With regard to other demographic characteristics, both samples were composed of more females than males: 56.3% among immigrant Filipinos and 53.0% among local Filipinos. Immigrant males (14.2 years) and females (14.3 years) were both older on the average than their local male (13.7 years) and female (13.5 years) counterparts. Local Filipino males (13.2 years) and females (13.2 years) have lived in Hawaii for most of their lives, whereas both immigrant males (4.6 years) and females (4.2 years) have been in Hawaii less than five years.

The relatively young age of the immigrant and local Filipino students in the sample is understandable when consideration is given to the schools that they attended. The great majority of both immigrants (79.8%) and locals (81.4%) were at the intermediate schools, either Kalakaua, Dole, or Central, whereas the remainder of both groups were at McKinley

---

[2] Tagalogs and Visayans are the two largest ethnolinguistic groups in the Philippines.

Table 1

Ethnic Composition of the Schools, 1976–1977[a]

Ethnic group (%)	School				
	Central Intermediate	Dole Intermediate	Kalakaua Intermediate	McKinley High School	Total
Black	.7	0.2	0.2	0.3	0.3
Chinese	15.3	2.5	3.6	16.0	9.8
Filipino	20.2	39.8	46.8	12.1	28.1
Hawaiian	24.1	20.5	17.2	10.8	16.2
Japanese	13.9	9.0	15.2	37.5	22.6
Korean	3.2	3.7	2.7	5.4	4.0
Samoan	9.3	13.8	4.6	2.5	6.4
White	3.8	3.2	2.5	7.5	4.8
N	717	1293	1527	2373	5910

[a]Source: Hawaii Department of Education, Honolulu, personal communication, Summer 1979.

High School. Table 1 delineates the ethnic composition of the schools that students in the sample attended. This table is compiled from information on ethnicity provided by students for the Department of Education. Unfortunately, it does not indicate the proportion of immigrant students among groups that are known to have significant foreign-born populations such as Chinese, Koreans, Filipinos, and Samoans. However, in the case of Filipinos, it is more than likely that local Filipino students outnumbered their immigrant peers. Another minor drawback of this table is that it has reference to the 1976–1977 school year rather than the previous year when the survey was conducted. It was not possible to obtain valid data on the ethnic distribution of the schools for that year because up to that time this information was based on the classroom teacher's judgment of the ethnic background of his or her students. However, there is no reason to believe that the ethnic composition in the schools changed significantly during the intervening year.

It is clear that for certain ethnic groups there is a wide divergence in their proportional representation at the various schools. The reason for this discrepancy is that only students at Central Intermediate would generally move on to McKinley High upon graduation; students at Kalakaua and Dole Intermediate would attend another high school, Farrington, closer to their neighborhoods. Although it would have been more methodologically sound to have included Farrington in the sampling, the ultimate decision on which schools to include in the survey was made by the Hawaii Department of Education according to its own priorities.

It should be noted that the overall ethnic composition of these schools is not representative of the general population distribution of Hawaii. That is, in these schools Filipinos and Samoans are greatly overrepresented, Caucasians are severely underrepresented, and Japanese are somewhat underrepresented; only Hawaiians are proportionally represented. Also, the home communities of the students in these schools are primarily lower to lower-middle class in socioeconomic status.

RESULTS

Procedure

Before proceeding to a discussion of the results, we shall briefly describe the procedure that was used to code the responses. The latter were found to vary in their grammatical form; that is, some students simply listed one or more groups, whereas other students anticipated question 2 and wrote short narratives on the reasons they believed that particular ethnic groups were in conflict with each other. Because responses were generally phrased in terms of opposed pairs of groups, for example, "Portuguese and Haoles," all of the responses were recorded in such contraposed pairs for the sake of uniformity of data. This procedure posed a little difficulty with replies that were expressed as a listing of various ethnic groups, such as "Japanese, Filipinos, Chinese." Here it is not clear which pairs of groups, if any, were perceived to be in conflict with one another. The solution to this predicament was to introduce the concept of "others" so that the preceding reply was recorded as three responses: "Japanese and others," "Filipinos and others," and "Chinese and others." This coding procedure was also used when only one group was specified in an answer. However, the primary level of analysis will be in terms of the frequency with which single groups were mentioned in the responses rather than the frequency with which pairs of groups were reported. Although this mode of analysis causes some salient information on opposed pairs of groups to be disregarded, it results, nevertheless, in the least distortion or interpretation of the responses that were not originally expressed as pairs.

Another problem of interpretation that results from the specific manner in which responses were written has to do with the distinction between immigrant and local subgroupings of a given ethnic group. In

Hawaii, as a result of changes in United States immigration laws in 1965, there are several ethnic groups that include substantial numbers of recent immigrants in their population besides their Hawaii-born counterparts. Thus, a problem of elucidation of meaning arises with a response such as "Filipinos" because it is not clear if it refers to the recent immigrant, the local subgrouping, or perhaps both of these groups. Furthermore, this distinction is crucial since these subgroupings are understood by people in Hawaii to differ in varying degrees in their values, beliefs, and activities. This question of interpretation will be more fully addressed in the discussion section of the paper.

Distributions According to Ethnicity

To turn to the results, immigrant Filipino students mentioned 26 ethnic categories as involved in conflict; local Filipino students mentioned 30 such categories. To be sure, there are not that many primary ethnic groups represented among students in Hawaii's schools. The number of ethnic categories reported is somewhat large because it includes immigrant and local subsections of groups that are otherwise commonly referred to as "Chinese," "Koreans," "Filipinos," "Japanese," and "Samoans." Despite the difference in the number of ethnic groupings mentioned by immigrant and local Filipino students, there does not appear to be any category that was reported in significant numbers by one of the subsamples that was not specified in response by the other. Both subsamples had virtually the same average number of ethnic groupings mentioned per respondent, 2.48 groupings for immigrant Filipinos and 2.53 groupings for local Filipinos.

Besides responses that referred to specific ethnic groups, there were also responses that indicated that the respondent thought that "all groups" were involved in conflict in the schools or "no groups" were involved in conflict, the respondent "did not know" which groups were involved, or that he or she made "no response" to the question.

There were only a few idiosyncratic replies such as "Chicanos," "Germans," and "Indians" reported by immigrant Filipino students, and "Americans," "Spanish," and "Tahitians" reported by local Filipinos. In other words, the overwhelming majority of the groupings mentioned in response by immigrant and local Filipinos have reference to identifiable population collectivities in Hawaii, although these may not be substantially large in number. These groupings reported in response also include Vietnamese and Laotian refugees, who had arrived in Hawaii earlier in the year that the study was conducted.

Table 2a

Rank-Order Distributions of Single-Groups Responses: Filipinos

	Rank given by			
Group	Immigrants[a]	% of total responses[b]	Locals[c]	% of total responses[b]
Samoans	1	19.7	2	20.4
Filipinos	2	17.4	1	21.6
Hawaiians	3	11.5	3	8.8
Locals	4	10.2	4	8.4
Japanese	5	6.8	5	6.4
Haoles	6.5	4.5	6	6.2
Immigrant Filipinos	6.5	4.5	8	4.6
Koreans	8	4.2	7	5.3
Immigrants	9	3.8	11	2.0
Chinese	10	3.5	9	3.5
Portuguese	11	2.4	13	1.0
Local Filipinos	12.5	2.1	12	1.5
Blacks	12.5	2.1	10	2.1

[a]$N = 332$; 863 valid responses.
[b]Percentages do not equal 100 because not all groups are ranked.
[c]$N = 350$; 916 valid responses.

Noteworthy by its absence was any reference to "military" students, that is, generally Caucasian or black students whose parents are affiliated with the armed services in Hawaii. This result is not very surprising if it is noted that the schools included in the sampling are not proximate to military housing areas. However, military dependents are a salient category of interaction at other schools in Hawaii where they compose a significant proportion of the student body.

Table 2a shows the rank-order distributions of the immigrant and local Filipino student responses as to the ethnic groups they perceived to be involved in conflict in school. The number of groupings included in the rankings, 13, was extended for purposes of statistical analysis to the point at which both immigrant and local Filipinos had mentioned the same identical groups. This number of groups accounts for over 90% of the total number of single-groups responses of both immigrant and local Filipino students. Table 2b includes the rank-order distributions of the perceptions of immigrant non-Filipino and local non-Filipino students that were obtained in the original survey, although their responses will not be discussed in depth.

Regarding the rankings of immigrant and local Filipinos, for both of these subsamples the combined percentage of the first four groups that

Table 2b

Rank-Order Distributions of Single-Groups Responses: Non-Filipinos

| | | Rank given by | | |
Group	Immigrants[a]	% of total responses[b]	Locals[c]	% of total responses[b]
Samoans	1	18.8	2	16.4
Filipinos	2	17.9	1	19.4
Hawaiians	3	10.4	5	7.7
Locals	4	10.1	3	10.3
Immigrants	5	6.8	10	3.2
Japanese	6	5.9	7	5.7
Koreans	7	5.2	6	7.3
Haoles	8	5.1	4	8.4
Chinese	9	4.6	8	4.3
Blacks	10	2.6	11	1.8
Immigrant Filipinos	11	2.0	9	3.8
Immigrant Koreans	12	.6	13	1.0
Four groups tied	13	.4	—	—
Portuguese	—	—	12	1.2

[a]N = 313; 691 valid responses.
[b]Percentages do not add up to 100 because not all groups are ranked.
[c]N = 923; 2494 valid responses.

were mentioned is nearly 60% of the total single groups responses. With regard to specific groups the very high position accorded Samoans by both subsamples is striking given their relatively small proportion of the student body of the schools in the sample. It might be added that this high ranking is consistent with a common stereotype in Hawaii that portrays Samoans as prone to physical violence. The decided frequency with which Filipinos were reported as participants in conflict, besides reflecting their perceived relations with other students, may well be a function of their being the largest and thus the most visible group in the sampled schools. Filipinos were the only group with a substantial recent immigrant population for which both local and immigrant subgroupings were reported among the thirteen groups. The midrange ranking of Haoles is noteworthy given their small representation at the schools in the sample, especially at the intermediate schools that made up the bulk of both subsamples. As in the case of Samoans, the position allocated to Haoles may follow from a view of them as involved in conflict with other groups in the wider society. The middle position in the scales of Koreans is also worthy of comment in terms of their small representation in the schools. This ranking is more than likely attributable to the frequency with which immigrant, rather than Hawaii-born, Koreans were perceived to be participants in conflict. Lastly, that blacks should appear at all among the groups is extraordinary given the fact that there were only 19 black students in the sampled schools in 1976. As with Samoans and Haoles, this ranking devolves from an understanding of blacks as involved in conflictual relations in the wider Hawaii society.

The first obvious feature to note in comparison of the immigrant and local Filipino rankings is that the positions of Samoans and Filipinos are in reverse order. However, other than this reversal of priority, the two rank-order distributions show a remarkable degree of similarity. That is, five groupings occupy virtually the same postions on both of the scales, and with the exception of blacks, no grouping is more than two positions away from its ranking on the other scale. To confirm these impressions of similarity between the two distributions, the Spearman rank-order correlation coefficient (Hays, 1963) was computed, and its value ($r_s = .942$) indicates that the rank orders of the perceptions of immigrant and local Filipino students are in fundamental agreement.

It should be noted that of the immigrant Filipino responses there were actually more "no response" replies than there were replies that mentioned Portuguese, local Filipinos, and blacks. Similarly, of the local Filipino responses, there were more "no response" replies than there were replies that designated local Filipinos and Portuguese. However, since the emphasis in the analysis of the rank-order distributions is on the ethnic groupings specified rather than the overall responses, we thought it appropriate to omit this category of response from among those most frequently reported. Of the other replies of this type that do not mention specific ethnic groups, only 1.5% of the immigrant Filipino responses and .9% of the local Filipino responses indicated that "no groups" had trouble in school. The replies that denoted that "all groups" were engaged in conflict with one another, or that the respondent "did not know" which groups were involved were only a few in number for both immigrant and local Filipino students.

Comparison of the immigrant and local Filipino perceptions with those of immigrant and local non-Filipinos evidences some points of agreement and some of difference. The latter two groups also considered Samoans and Filipinos to be the groupings most involved in conflict in school, and also assigned high rankings to Hawaiians and locals and low rankings to blacks and Portuguese. However, immigrant non-Filipinos viewed immigrants as more engaged in troublesome relations in school than did the other three subsamples, but they discerned immigrant Filipinos as less engaged in troublesome relations than did the other three groups. On the other hand, local non-Filipinos allocated a higher ranking to Haoles than did the other three subsamples.

Table 3a

Rank-Order Distributions of Single-Groups Responses by Sex: Immigrant Filipinos

	Rank given by			
Group	Males[a]	% of total responses[b]	Females[c]	% of total responses[b]
Samoans	1	19.8	1	19.6
Filipinos	2	15.5	2	18.8
Hawaiians	3	11.7	3.5	11.3
Locals	4	8.7	3.5	11.3
Japanese	5	7.1	5	6.7
Koreans	6	6.3	9.5	2.6
Haoles	7	5.2	8	4.0
Chinese	8	4.9	11.5	2.4
Immigrant Filipinos	9	4.3	6	4.6
Immigrants	10	3.0	7	4.4
Blacks	11	2.7	13	1.6
Portuguese	12	2.2	9.5	2.6
Local Filipinos	13	1.6	11.5	2.4

[a]$N = 145$; 368 valid responses.
[b]Percentages do not add up to 100 because not all groups are ranked.
[c]$N = 187$; 495 valid responses.

Distributions According to Sex

Comparison of the rank-order distributions according to sex also evidences a considerable degree of agreement. Tables 3a and 3b show the rank distributions by sex of the groups perceived by immigrant and local Filipino students to be involved in conflict. Comparison of the rankings of immigrant Filipino males and females indicates that there was common agreement on the groups assigned to the first five positions and also on the low rankings allocated to blacks and to local Filipinos. However, immigrant females ranked immigrant Filipinos higher than did the males, which results in the midrange position of this grouping in the overall immigrant Filipino ratings. Females also ranked immigrants higher than did males. On the other hand, males viewed Koreans and Chinese as more engaged in conflict than did females. To compare these two rank-order distributions, the Spearman rank-order correlation coefficient was tabulated ($r_s = .845$), and it denotes that there is considerable agreement between the ratings of immigrant Filipino males and females.

Comparison of male and female local Filipino student ratings of ethnic conflict was carried out only to nine positions because the males did not include local Filipinos among their first 13 groupings most frequently mentioned. Not surprisingly, the rankings are very similar in

Table 3b

Rank-Order Distributions of Single-Groups Responses by Sex: Local Filipinos

| Group | Rank given by | | | |
	Males[a]	% of total responses[b]	Females[c]	% of total responses[b]
Samoans	1	22.1	2	19.1
Filipinos	2	20.9	1	22.2
Locals	3	8.3	4	8.5
Hawaiians	4	8.0	3	9.5
Haoles	5.5	5.8	6	6.6
Japanese	5.5	5.8	5	6.9
Koreans	7	5.3	7	5.4
Immigrant Filipinos	8	4.3	8	4.8
Chinese	9	3.8	9	3.3
Immigrants	10	1.8	11.5	2.1
Blacks	11	1.5	10	2.5
Portuguese	12.5	1.0	13	1.0
Immigrant Samoans	12.5	1.0	–	–
Local Filipinos	–	–	11.5	2.1

[a]$N = 164$; 398 valid responses.
[b]Percentages do not add up to 100 because not all groups are ranked.
[c]$N = 186$; 518 valid responses.

nature; except for the two pairs of groups Filipinos and Samoans, and Hawaiians and locals, which are both in reverse order in the scales, the remainder of the groupings have virtually the same positions. The Spearman rank-order correlation coefficient ($r_s = .963$) indicates that the two rankings are highly congruent.

The rank-order distributions of immigrant and local Filipino male students' perceptions also evidence a substantial degree of agreement. Other than the absence of local Filipinos from the first 13 groups mentioned by local Filipino males, no grouping is more than 1.5 positions away from its ranking on the other scale, and 6 groups occupy virtually the same positions on both scales. The Spearman rank-order correlation coefficient ($r_s = .973$) confirms the apparent correspondence between the two distributions.

However, comparison of the immigrant and local Filipino female rankings indicates that they are more divergent than those of the males. Although there is considerable agreement among the first five groups reported, immigrant Filipino females rated immigrants and Portuguese substantially higher than did their local counterparts, and the latter perceived blacks as more involved in conflict than did immigrant females. Thus, the Spearman rank-order correlation coefficient ($r_s = .823$) is very much lower than it is for the males.

Goodness of Fit

The next procedure of analysis was to compare the distributions of immigrant and local Filipino student perceptions of ethnic conflict in terms of their goodness of fit with each other. For this test the Pearson chi-square statistic (Hays, 1963) was used with some modification because in this case there were two observed sample distributions, instead of just one, and the samples differed in their number of responses. Thus, in order to obtain the expected frequencies for each of the 13 groups in the distributions, we multiplied the group's percentage of the total number of valid responses in one of the subsamples (A) by the total number of valid responses in the other subsample (B). This figure became the expected frequency and was then compared to the actually observed frequency for the group in subsample B in order to derive the chi-square value. Furthermore, this procedure was followed twice so that each subsample served as the observed sample. In both cases the chi-square value was sufficiently large so that it can be stated that the distributions of immigrant and local Filipino perceptions of ethnic conflict were significantly different ($p <. 001$). It was also found that the distributions of the perceptions of, on the one hand, immigrant and local Filipino males ($p < .05$), and on the other, immigrant and local Filipino females ($p < .001$) were in both cases significantly different.

The Spearman rank-order correlation coefficient and the goodness of fit tests compared the overall distributions of the perceptions of immigrant and local Filipino students and were found to have contrary results. Thus, the next step in the analysis was to compare the frequencies with which immigrant and local Filipinos perceived each of the 13 groups as participants in conflict in school. The chi-square statistic was used for this test and indicated that immigrant Filipinos perceived Hawaiians, immigrants, and Portuguese as significantly ($p <. 05$) more involved in conflictual relations than did local Filipinos; the latter perceived Filipinos as significantly ($p <. 005$) more involved than did immigrant Filipinos.

Single-Group Responses Versus Paired-Groups Responses

To clarify these results, although the principal level of analysis in the comparison of the immigrant and local Filipino responses is in terms of single groups rather than paired groups, the latter responses provide supplementary information on the students' perceptions. It was stated that immigrant Filipinos considered Samoans to be the group most involved in conflict in the schools. An examination of their paired-groups responses that include Samoans as one of the groups indicates that they reported the pair Samoans and others most frequently (11.1% of total paired-groups responses) and the pair Samoans and Filipinos second (8.5%). It would appear that although immigrant Filipinos perceived Samoans to be engaged in conflict, they did not necessarily perceive them as primarily engaged with Filipinos.

However, with regard to Filipinos, the group that was ranked second by immigrant Filipinos, the greatest number of paired-groups responses is in the previously mentioned Samoans and Filipinos category, which was followed by Filipinos and others (6.4%). In this case it might be proposed that immigrant Filipinos considered Samoans the principal adversaries of Filipinos.

The group reported third most frequently by immigrant Filipinos was Hawaiians, and it is somewhat evident here that they were not viewed as involved in conflict with Filipinos. Of their paired-groups responses that include Hawaiians, they mentioned Hawaiians and others first (5.5%) and Hawaiians and Samoans second (4.4%).

On the other hand, the fourth-ranked grouping, locals, was seen by immigrant Filipinos to be involved with Filipinos first (5.1%) and with immigrants second (3.2%).

The relation of single-groups to paired-groups responses of local Filipino students is very similar in nature to that of immigrant Filipinos. It will be recalled that local Filipinos perceived Filipinos to be most engaged in conflict in the schools. Of their paired-groups responses that include this grouping, the pair Filipinos and Samoans was foremost (9.9% of total paired-groups responses) and was followed closely by the pair Filipinos and others (8.9%). Because in the latter pair it is not apparent with whom Filipinos are thought to have troublesome relations, it cannot be stated with certainty that local Filipinos considered Samoans to be the chief antagonists of Filipinos.

The group ranked second highest by local Filipinos was Samoans, and of the paired-groups responses that include this grouping, the most frequently reported were the previously mentioned pair Samoans and Filipinos (9.9%) and the pair Samoans and others (9.6%). Again, it is not definitely clear that local Filipinos perceived Filipinos and Samoans to be one another's main opponents in conflict.

Like their immigrant counterparts, local Filipinos considered Hawaiians to be engaged in conflict with Samoans first (4.0%), but with Filipinos second (3.1%). Similarly, local Filipinos, as did immigrant Filipinos, reported locals to be participants in conflict with Filipinos foremost (5.9%), but with immigrant Filipinos and Samoans next (both 2.3%).

Further information on the perceptions of immigrant and local Filipino students can be obtained from the data on their paired-groups responses. Thus, although in terms of single groups immigrant Filipinos considered Samoans to be most engaged in conflict, a plurality of their total paired-groups responses made reference to at least one of the three categories of Filipino students used in this study. That is, 37.6% of the immigrant Filipino paired-groups responses involved Filipinos (29.6%), immigrant Filipinos (7.9%), or local Filipinos (2.9%) as one of the groups in the pair (percentages exceed 37.6% because a response such as "Filipinos and Immigrant Filipinos" was tabulated for both groups). On the other hand, 30.8% of the immigrant Filipino paired-groups responses included at least one of the three categories of Samoan students (Samoans, immigrant Samoans, or local Samoans). A partial explanation for this discrepancy between the rankings accorded the "Filipino" and "Samoan" categories in terms of single groups as opposed to paired-groups responses is that the latter type of responses include those that make reference to immigrant Filipinos, who were mentioned with much greater frequency than were either immigrant Samoans or local Samoans. This much greater use of the term "Immigrant Filipinos" would also seem to indicate that Filipino students were not perceived as an undifferentiated category by immigrant Filipinos. Another point to be noted is that the term "Local Filipino" is used with much less frequency than either of the other terms for Filipino students.

For their part, local Filipino students designated Filipinos as the group most involved in conflict in the schools. Of their total paired-groups responses, some 42.1% included at least one of the three categories of Filipino students referred to in the study—"Filipinos" (35.2%), "Immigrant Filipinos" (6.8%), or "Local Filipinos" (2.0%). This figure is to be compared with the 33.8% of the local Filipino paired-groups responses that involved one of the three categories of Samoans. Again this difference in percentage can be attributed to the greater frequency with which the term "Immigrant Filipinos" was reported. It is also apparent that local Filipinos, like their immigrant peers, did not perceive Filipino students as an undifferentiated totality, and that they used the term "Local Filipinos" with much less frequency than they did the other two terms for Filipinos.

The paired-groups responses also provide some pertinent information on conflict between immigrant and local Filipino students in the schools. Thus, of the immigrant Filipino total paired-groups responses, 3.5% related to intra-Filipino conflict; that is, both of the groups mentioned in these responses were Filipinos, immigrant Filipinos, or local Filipinos. The greatest number of these responses was in the category "Immigrant Filipinos and Local Filipinos." There were no replies for either of the categories "Immigrant Filipinos and Immigrant Filipinos" or "Local Filipinos and Local Filipinos." To place these intra-Filipino responses in proper perspective, it should be noted that their sum would rank fourth in frequency after those paired-groups responses that specify Filipinos as involved in conflict with Samoans, locals, and Hawaiians.

With regard to local Filipinos, 4.0% of their total paired-groups responses pertained to intra-Filipino conflict, but for them the most frequently reported pair was "Filipinos and Filipinos." It is not clear which Filipino categories this response refers to, but it is possible that it might have reference to immigrant and local Filipinos. Like their immigrant counterparts, there were no local Filipino respondents for the pairs "Immigrant Filipinos and Immigrant Filipinos" and "Local Filipinos and Local Filipinos." Again, to put these intra-Filipino paired-groups responses in perspective, their sum would rank third in frequency after the pairs "Filipinos and Samoans" and "Filipinos and Locals."

Thus, it would appear that both immigrant and local Filipino students did not consider other Filipino students to be their primary adversaries in school; rather, they each perceived Filipinos for the most part as engaged in conflict with other groups. It might be added that if it is recalled that the paired-groups response "Filipinos and others" actually only specifies Filipinos, and if it is assumed that this term refers generically to both immigrant and local Filipinos, then the preceding percentages for intra-Filipino conflict would increase dramatically for both immigrant and local Filipino students.

DISCUSSION

The results indicate that the immigrant and local Filipino students' rank ordering of ethnic groups in terms of their perceived involvement in conflict in the schools was in fundamental agreement. However, it was found that the overall distributions of these perceptions differed significantly in terms of their goodness of fit with one another. Further analysis at the level of single groups indicates that there were significant differences between immigrant and local Filipino perceptions of the participation in conflict of Filipinos, Hawaiians, immigrants, and Portuguese.

Meaning of "Filipinos"

Thus, significantly more local Filipino students than immigrant Filipinos considered Filipinos to have troublesome relations with their peers in the schools. The obvious question at this point is to determine the meaning of the term "Filipinos," that is, whether it refers to immigrant or to local Filipinos, or perhaps to both of these groups. The existence of intra-Filipino conflict is relevant to a discussion of this question. The results show that both immigrant and local Filipino students reported that they have conflictual relationships with each other in school. However, although local Filipino students may recognize and acknowledge that they have problems in their relations with their immigrant counterparts, they apparently perceive themselves not as the cause or the perpetrators of this conflict but as provoked in some way by the attitudes and behavior of immigrant Filipinos. Support for this proposition comes from Ponce and Lee (1975) who, as part of a consultation session, conducted interviews with immigrant and local Filipino students at a high school where a violent confrontation between these two groups occurred. The researchers reported that local Filipinos expressed a range of feelings from "shame and embarrassment to anger and repulsion" over what they (the local Filipinos) considered to be the loud style of dress and arrogant deportment of immigrant Filipino students (Ponce and Lee, 1975:14). Thus, if it is understood that local Filipinos do not perceive themselves to have the best of relations with their immigrant peers, that they are to a large extent offended by the immigrant superficial appearances, and that this resentment often results in verbal taunts and other forms of harassment of immigrant students (Alcantara, 1973:124), then it becomes plausible to conjecture that the meaning that they attribute to the category "Filipinos" may well refer to immigrant Filipinos.

Further support for this interpretation comes from the paired-groups responses of local Filipinos. Of those responses that include "Filipinos" as one of the groups, the most frequently mentioned replies of local Filipinos in descending order were "Filipinos and Samoans," "Filipinos and others," and "Filipinos and locals." The same problem of interpretation of the term "Filipinos" presents itself again. However, in the first case it is recognized in the schools that Samoans are often in conflictual relations with immigrant Filipinos, certainly much more so than with local Filipinos. Furthermore, there was only one local Filipino response to the pair "Local Filipinos and Samoans," which would imply that they did not consider themselves to have troubles with the latter group.

As for the second set of paired-groups responses, "Filipinos and others," it will be recalled that according to the data-recording procedures it refers essentially to Filipinos. Thus, at this point in the discussion it merely replicates the problem at hand of deducing the meaning of the term.

However, in the third set of paired-groups responses, contraposition of the category "Filipinos" against "Locals" would imply that the former term has reference to immigrant Filipinos in the same way that "Immigrant" and "Local" are understood to be opposed categories in Hawaii. Furthermore, the most frequently reported paired-groups response of local Filipinos that includes immigrant Filipinos was "Immigrant Filipinos and Locals," but there were no local Filipino respondents to the category "Local Filipinos and locals." These data would indicate that local Filipinos perceived immigrant Filipinos, more than local Filipinos, as engaged in conflict with locals. They thus lend credence to the interpretation of the meaning of the term "Filipinos" as having reference to immigrant Filipinos.

Blame-pinning

Another reason for this particular interpretation of the term "Filipinos" has to do with the use of ethnic categorization as a "blame-pinning" device. Parkin has noted that in situations of urban political and economic opposition (in East Africa), casting blame in tribal terms is a handy labeling system, which results in various parties having diverse explanations of the same issue (Parkin, 1969:278, 295). This aspect of ethnicity is closely related to Mitchell's notion of ethnicity as a commonsense or folk interpretation of behavior that makes people's actions plausible to ordinary observers (Mitchell, 1974:26). That is, the ethnic identity of a person dominates his or her other identities and thus serves as a valid and adequate explanation of his or her behavior to others involved in the situation (Mitchell, 1974:26). This folk explanation of behavior is to be distinguished from the analyst's abstract explanation of behavior in terms of general structural principles.

Hence, with regard to the question that was posed to the students, the content of their responses may be interpreted as denotative of more than mere specification of the groups that they perceived to "have trouble with each other," but also as indicative of a level of explanation of this conflict. That is, students "explained" or accounted for these conflictual relations with reference to the groups that they understood to be involved in them; however, involvement pertains not simply to the groups' general participation in conflict but essentially to their fault or guilt for its occurrence. Thus, the responses of students can be seen to be an expression of blame-pinning, and the decision of whom to blame is influenced by the nature of the relationship between the groups of the accuser and of the accused (Parkin, 1969:274). However, groups may still be blamed for their involvement in conflict even though it is perceived to be with groups other than that of the accuser.

To return to the original problem of deducing the meaning of the category "Filipinos," it is clear how the concept of blame-pinning is of explanatory value. If this concept is applied to an interpretation of the responses of local Filipinos, then the decided frequency with which they specified "Filipinos" as involved in conflict in the schools can be seen to be related to their view of immigrant Filipinos as responsible, by their own behavior, for the harassment that they (immigrant Filipinos) receive from other students. In other words, local Filipinos did not perceive the participation of immigrant Filipinos in these conflicts as that of faultless victims, but rather as of offending provokers. Thus, it can be proposed that the meaning that local Filipinos attributed to the term "Filipinos" in their responses has reference to immigrant Filipinos.

On their part, immigrant Filipino students mentioned the category "Filipinos" second in frequency after the category Samoans. The same problem of deduction of the meaning of the former term thus presents itself again. However, the same three paired-groups responses that were most frequently reported by local Filipinos were also those most frequently reported by immigrant Filipinos and in the same descending order: "Filipinos and Samoans," "Filipinos and others," and "Filipinos and locals." By the same reasoning that was used in the interpretation of the responses of local Filipinos, it may be conjectured that the category "Filipinos" in these paired-groups responses most likely refers to immigrant Filipinos. Furthermore, there was only one immigrant Filipino response for the pair "Local Filipinos and Samoans" and none for the pair "Local Filipinos and locals," which would imply that the groups in these two pairs were not generally perceived to be in conflict with one another. It was also found that the second most frequently reported paired-groups response of immigrant Filipinos that included themselves as one of the groups was "Immigrant Filipinos and Samoans." It would seem that immigrant Filipinos viewed themselves, more than local Filipinos, as participants in conflict with Samoans. This finding lends further support to the interpretation of "Filipinos" that was proposed earlier.

Thus, if both immigrant and local Filipino students employed the term "Filipinos" in reference to immigrant Filipinos, it remains yet to account for the finding that significantly more local Filipinos than immigrant Filipinos perceived Filipinos as involved in conflict in the schools. The concept of blame-pinning is relevant to this case. According to this concept, it is more reasonable for local Filipinos to attribute responsibility for conflict in the schools to another group—that is, immigrant Filipinos—than it is for the latter to assume responsibility for conflict themselves. Obviously, it would seem unlikely that immigrant Filipinos would find fault with themselves for the fact that they are the targets of violence from other students. Therefore, in their respective uses of the term "Filipinos," local Filipinos did cast blame upon this category (immigrant Filipinos), whereas immigrant Filipinos did not, and this differential use of blame-pinning as a commonsense explanation of behavior accounts to some extent for the greater frequency with which local Filipinos mentioned the term. Although it is true that immigrant Filipinos saw themselves to a considerable degree as involved in conflictual relations with their peers, it is probable that they perceived themselves more as victims than as instigators of conflict. However, it is certainly not the case that immigrant Filipinos did not engage at all in blame-pinning. This is clear from the range and scope of the overall distribution of their responses. The argument here is simply that in their use of the term "Filipinos" they were not casting blame upon themselves.

Significant differences also obtained between the immigrant and local Filipino perceptions of the role of Hawaiians in conflict in the schools. Immigrant Filipino students viewed them as more involved in conflict than did local Filipinos. A review of the most often mentioned paired-groups responses that include Hawaiians shows that the frequency of immigrant and local Filipino replies for the categories "Filipinos and Hawaiians," and "Samoans and Hawaiians" is virtually identical, but for the pair "Hawaiians and others" there were over twice the number of immigrant Filipino responses as there were of local Filipino. Apparently, this discrepancy accounts for much of the significance that was obtained. However, to return to the first two pairs, in terms of blame-pinning, both immigrant and local Filipinos found Hawaiians and Samoans at fault for trouble in the schools, whereas local Filipinos also attributed culpability to immigrant Filipinos. With regard to the pair "Hawaiians and others," you may recall that this response specifically refers to Hawaiians, and although it may not be possible to ascertain in this case exactly with whom Hawaiians are perceived to be in conflict, the concept of blame-pinning is still of explanatory value. That is, the greater tendency of immigrant Filipinos to cast blame upon Hawaiians is related to the former's perception of the latter as the perpetrators of abuse toward other students, probably themselves included. However, local Filipinos, who may be less engaged in conflict with Hawaiians because they are locals themselves, were not as ready to attribute responsibility to them. As was previously noted, the decision of whom to blame is affected by the social distance between accuser and accused.

The degree of participation of immigrants in conflict in the schools was discerned to be significantly different by immigrant and local Filipino students, and the former group saw them as more involved. From their paired-groups responses, it would appear that most of the divergence occurs in the category "Immigrants and locals" to which immigrant Filipinos responded with over twice the frequency of local Filipinos. In this case, the explanatory value of blame-pinning cannot be definitely established. However, one possible interpretation in terms of casting blame is that of the two groups in the preceding paired response. Immigrant Filipinos focused on locals and attributed fault to them, whereas local Filipinos did not respond to this paired response, or specifically immigrants, in terms of blame-pinning. To lay blame upon locals by mention of the paired-groups response "Immigrants and locals" has the effect of an increase in the number of single-groups responses for the former group. The end result is the greater frequency with which immigrant Filipinos, as compared to local Filipinos, reported immigrants as involved in conflict.

The concept of blame-pinning also has explanatory value for the other ethnic groups that were most frequently reported by both immigrant and local Filipinos but for which significant differences did not occur. Thus, of the immigrant Filipino paired-groups responses that involve Samoans, the three most frequently mentioned replies in descending order were "Samoans and others," "Samoans and Filipinos," and "Samoans and Hawaiians." Local Filipinos also specified the same three paired-groups responses most frequently but reversed the order of the first two pairs (although by only two replies). According to the notion of blame-pinning, the frequency with which immigrant Filipinos mentioned Samoans is related to the latter's perceived responsibility for abuse directed at the former group and to other students. Local Filipinos, on the other hand, viewed both immigrant Filipinos and Samoans at fault: the former for provocation of Samoans by their appearance and demeanor, and the latter for their harassment of immigrant Filipinos.

Locals were the fourth most often specified group of both immigrant and local Filipino students. The most frequently reported paired-groups responses of immigrant Filipinos that involve locals were "Locals and Filipinos," "Locals and Immigrants," and "Locals and others," In contrast, the three most frequently reported responses of local Filipinos were "Locals and Filipinos," "Locals and Immigrant Filipinos," and "Locals and Samoans." With regard to the responses of immigrant Filipinos, a possible explanation in terms of blame-pinning is that they found locals at fault for the maltreatment of their own group and of immigrants. On the other hand, with respect to the local Filipino responses, the notion of blame-pinning would indicate that they attributed responsibility for trouble in the schools to immigrant Filipinos and to Samoans more so than they did to locals because they belong to this group.

SUMMARY

Comparison of the perceptions of ethnic conflict of immigrant and local Filipino students shows that their rank-order distributions of ethnic groups in terms of their perceived participation in conflict were in fundamental agreement. Further comparison of these rank orderings by sex indicates that there was considerable agreement, on the one hand, between immigrant and local Filipino male rankings, and on the other, between immigrant and local Filipino female rankings. However, the overall distributions of immigrant and local Filipino perceptions differed significantly in their goodness of fit with each other. By the same test, it was also found that the distributions of the perceptions of immigrant and local Filipino males and of immigrant and local Filipino females were in both cases significantly different. Analysis at the level of single groups indicates that immigrant Filipinos discerned Hawaiians, immigrants, and Portuguese as more involved in conflict than did local Filipinos; the latter viewed Filipinos as more involved than did immigrant Filipinos. In the course of the discussion it was proposed that the meaning of the term "Filipinos" as used by both immigrant and local Filipinos has reference to the former group.

The divergent content and scope of the perceptions of ethnic conflict of immigrant and local Filipinos were interpreted in terms of the concept of blame-pinning. According to this concept, students did not simply specify in their responses the groups that they thought were involved in conflict, rather they explained or accounted for this conflict with reference to these groups. Furthermore, this level of explanation pertained to the groups' perceived responsibility or fault for the occurrence of conflict and not merely to their roles as general participants. Thus, the students' responses were an expression of blame-pinning, and the choice of whom to blame was affected by the social distance between the groups concerned. Accordingly, the differential nature of the responses of immigrant and local Filipinos is related to their differential use of blame-pinning as an explanatory notion.

REFERENCES

Alcantara, R. R.
    1973   The Filipino community in Waialua. Unpublished Ph.D. dissertation, Department of American Studies, University of Hawaii, Honolulu.
Hays, W. L.
    1963   *Statistics for Psychologists.* New York: Holt, Rinehart and Winston.

Jocano, F. L.
  1970   Filipinos in Hawaii: problems in the promised land. *Philippine Sociological Review* 18(3–4):151–157.
Mitchell, J. C.
  1974   Perceptions of ethnicity and ethnic behaviour: an empirical exploration, in *Urban Ethnicity* (A. Cohen Ed.), pp. 1–35. London: Tavistock Publications.
Parkin, D. J.
  1969   Tribe as fact and fiction in an East African city, in *Tradition and Transition in East Africa* (P. H. Gulliver Ed.), pp. 273–296. Berkeley and Los Angeles: University of California Press.
Ponce, D. E., and Lee, V.
  1975   Intra-ethnic violence in Hawaii school: a mental health consultation experience. Paper presented at the Conference on International Migration from the Philippines, East–West Center, Honolulu.

15

The Ethnic Numbers Game in Interelite Competition for Political Hegemony in Nigeria

Stephen O. Olugbemi

INTRODUCTION

Social science literature is replete with explanatory theories on the causes of ethnic conflict in culturally segmented societies. According to one group of scholars (i.e., the cultural determinists), primordialism, linguistic differences, and cultural incompatibility tend to generate conflict rather than cooperation among distinct groups in sustained social interaction. Thus Schwarz (1965) explains ethnic conflict in Nigeria in terms of "my tribe, my faith, my culture."[1] Similarly, Victor Olorunsola (1972) explains conflict among Nigerians as deriving from cultural pluralism and the attendant incompatibility of the political cultures of the Hausa, Ibo, and Yoruba cultural groups. Apart from underrating the capacity of human groups of learn and adapt to new situations, this deterministic explanation of ethnic conflict seems to posit the empirically unsupported corollary that culturally homogenous peoples tend more to engage in cooperative rather than conflictive relationships.[2] In our judgment the

---

[1] See also Wegley and Harns (1958), Kuper (1971), Geertz (1963), and Slunner (1963).

[2] The existence of a strong National Convention of Nigerian Citizens (NCNC) in the Yoruba western region competing with the Action Group (AG) for the control of the regional government is proof that conflicts do arise among culturally homogenous peoples. See Olugbemi (1978) and Wolf (1967).

CULTURE, ETHNICITY,
AND IDENTITY

lacuna in this thought process is the failure to stipulate and define the object of conflict among corporate groups and thus tending to assume that groups engage in conflict relationships for the mere fun of it.

Happily that hiatus seems to have been taken care of in the works of a second group of scholars, notably Rotberg (1967), Bamisaiye (1971), Melson and Wolpe (1971), Post and Vickers (1973), and A. O. Sanda (1974), among others, who propose that ethnic conflict arises from the attempt by a few elites to manipulate primordial loyalties to serve either their own political, economic, and social ambitions or those of the group they represent, to the detriment of other groups. Widespread historical and contemporary evidence (Olugbemi, 1978:1–38) would seem to support this alternative perspective on the origin of ethnic conflict, for wherever it has occurred, ethnic conflict seems to be more related to the competitive relationship among groups in the political, economic, and social spheres than to the mere fact of pluralism.

It would seem plausible, therefore, to hold that ethnic conflict derives from the desire for group hegemony; its objective is to secure "adequate" representation of group interests in the political, economic, and administrative leadership structures either in the direction of preserving an established hegemony and the attendant privileges or in the direction of redressing the status quo in favor of a previously disadvantaged group or groups. The close association between the desire for group hegemony and the democratic ethos of adult suffrage (one man–one vote) and majority rule are the stimulators of the "ethnic numbers game" by which groups in competition seek to adjust their numerical ratios for sectional hegemonic interests. Indeed one could go a step further than Wright (1976) to say that democracy, like socialism, has contributed to the politicization of ethnicity by replacing "might is right" and the "divine right of kings" with representative majoritarian rule and by replacing the market distribution of benefits with political allocation. In that context of zero-sum politics the privileged try to maintain their preeminent position, whereas the disadvantaged struggle to better their own chances. It is such a struggle in Nigeria that has given a new significance to numbers and to the relative population size of its numerous ethnic groups. This article examines the strategies adopted by the major actors—the Hausa–Fulani of the North, the Ibo of the East, and the Yoruba of the West—to preserve or redress their numerical ratios. We shall argue that recourse to the numbers game was necessitated, first, by the imbalance in the structure of premilitary Nigerian political system and, second, by the differential access to the system of political rewards that that structure conferred on the different groups.

THE BASIS OF ETHNIC CONFLICT IN NIGERIA

Nigeria is a conglomerate state consisting of a multiplicity of ethnic groups—what Awolowo (1947) called "nationalities"—which according to some scholars number as many as 250 (Awolow, 1968).[3] As indicated earlier, the existence of such a large number of distinct cultural groups is not a sufficient condition for ethnic conflict; other variables must intervene to create the conditions for conflict. In the Nigerian situation the two most significant factors in interethnic conflict were the lopsided structure of the polity and the differential access to the systems of rewards that that structure conferred on the different groups.

With regard to the structural frame, it is worth noting that Nigeria began its nearly smooth journey to political independence in the 1940s with the three disproportionate regions of the North, East, and West coinciding with the areas where the Hausa–Fulani, the Ibo, and the Yoruba ethnic groups, respectively, predominated. Around this hard core of dominant groups were grafted a number of other minor, though not less distinct, groups to form the constituent units of the Federation of Nigeria at independence in 1960. The point of contention, exacerbated by the introduction of adult suffrage, and parliamentary government of the Westminster model, was the disproportionate population size of the three component units of the federation, which tended to confer on one of the units and its leaders the privilege of a political "veto" over the affairs of the country. According to the 1952 national census the relative size of the three regions (Olugbemi, 1978:62) was as shown in the following table.

Region	Population size (millions)	% of national total
North (Hausa–Fulani)	16.8	55.3
East (Ibo)	7.2	23.7
West (Yoruba)	6.1	20.1
Lagos (Federal Capital)	.267	.9
Total	30.4	100.0

The effect of this skewed population spread among component units of the federal state was that in 1951 and 1954 the North claimed and got 50% of total federal parliamentary seats, and the balance of the seats

---

[3] Awolowo (1968:235–253) identified 51 "nations" within Nigeria.

were divided equally between the two southern regions. In 1959, however, the allocation of federal parliamentary seats among the units was made to reflect their relative numerical ratios. Hence the North got 174; the East, 73; the West, 62; and the Federal Capital of Lagos, 3 seats, respectively. The pattern of distribution of seats for the 1964 federal elections was not different. Despite the increased share of the southern units, the North still won 167 seats, and the East, West, Mid-West, and Lagos were allocated 70, 57, 14, and 4 seats, respectively. Given the Westminster model of political (leadership) organization, the monolithic leadership structure of northern elites and their use of the machinery of government to restrict the activities of rival political parties, the skewed population spread, and the resultant allocation of federal parliamentary seats meant that the Hausa–Fulani of the North could single-handedly rule Nigeria perpetually to the exclusion of the other two major groups. The fear of the perpetual domination of the rest of Nigeria by the Hausa–Fulani cultural group was at the root of interethnic conflict in Nigeria, and it led, invariably, to the numbers game.

With regard to differential access to the system of rewards, the possession of political authority was linked to the power to allocate rewards. It was a spoils system reminiscent of President Andrew Jackson's now classical dictum "to the victors belong the spoils of office." In that zero-sum gaming context in which the gains by one actor are a loss to the other(s), the relative share of the Yorubas and the Ibos (the two dominant groups in southern Nigeria) in central government preferments was bound to suffer (as it did in fact) progressive decline vis-à-vis their better-placed competitor. Tables 1–5 illustrate the trend.

The gains went to the Hausa–Fulani group led by the northern-based Northern Peoples Congress (NPC) which also controlled the federal government, and the share of the Yorubas and the Ibos declined. The enthusiasm of the northern group to use their new power status to benefit their group was heightened by the realization, made possible by the increasing tempo of modernization in the North, that their peoples were relatively backward vis-à-vis their southern peers and must, therefore, catch up with them. The sense of loss among the southern groups was made more intense by the knowledge (1) that the bulk of federal government resources was derived from southern Nigeria, (2) that their own progress was being retarded, and (3) that they were being impoverished in the process of helping the more backward North to develop. The urge to resist could hardly be controlled. But it was resistance only in the sense of a determination to capture control of the federal government from the northern NPC through the manipulation of the most critical variable in a democratic competitive electoral system, that is, population.

Table 1

Average Regional Share of Federal Allocations (Statutory and Grants)
for Two Consecutive Seven-year Periods[a]

Region	1951–1958	1959–1965	Change
North (Hausa–Fulani)	31.40	39.01	7.61
West (Yoruba)	40.25	31.77	−.8.48
East (Ibo)	28.03	26.64	−1.39
Mid-West (Edo and others)	—	9.30	—

[a]Computed from the approved budget estimates of the various governments.

Table 2

Regional Share of Federal Development Investments, 1962–1968[a]

Region	Value of investment[b]	As % of national totals	Public debts component[b]	As % of total public debt
North (Hausa–Fulani)	127.21	65.03	60.10	71.11
West (Yoruba)	5.88	3.00	3.75	4.44
East (Ibo	18.80	9.61	7.86	9.30
Mid-West (Edo and others)	6.95	3.55	0	0
Lagos (Fed. Territory)	36.79	18.81	12.80	15.15
Total	195.63	100.00	84.51	100.00

[a]Source: Olugbemi (1978:113).
[b]Millions of pounds.

The northern political elites, on their own part, were determined to hold
on to power at the federal center through the same means. Thus, from
1962, the three rival elite groups resorted to the numbers game using
one or a combination of the following specific strategies: (1) manipulation
of census returns, (2) intimidation of political opponents, (3) demand for
the creation of more regions particularly in the strongholds of political
rivals, and (4) intercommunal alliances or coalitions.

MANIPULATION OF THE CENSUS

Although the administration of the census in Nigeria has long been a
politically sensitive operation (Campbell, 1976:242–243), the nature and
intensity of sensitivity to it in the postindependence era differed from

Table 3

Relative Distribution of Indigenous Federal Permanent Secretaries by Region of Origin[a]

	1960		1963		1965–1966	
Region	N	% of total	N	% of total	N	% of total
North	—	—	5[c]	27.78[d]	8[d]	33.33
West	—	—	6	33.33	5	20.83
East	1[b]	100.00	6	33.33	5	20.83
Mid-West	—	—	—	—	5	20.83
Others	—	—	1[c]	5.56	1	4.17
Total	1	100.00	18	100	24	100.00

[a]Computed from (1) Federal staff list for the years and (2) Federal Ministry of Information (1976).

[b]He was Mr. F. C. Nwokedi, an Ibo.

[c]The near-parity among the three major regions is significant in view of the fact that only 6 of the 39 middle-level Nigerian administrative officers in 1953 were from northern Nigeria; the rest being indigens of the western and eastern regions.

[d]Most of these were secondments or transfers, particularly from the northern civil and Native Authority services.

[e]Sierra-Leonean/Nigeria.

Table 4

Relative Distribution of Federal Ministerial Positions By Region of Origin[a]

	1951–1954		1960–1964		1964–1966	
Region	N	% of total	N	% of total	N	% of total
North	4	33.33	13	52.17	10	45.45
West	4	33.33	4[b]	17.39	8[c]	36.36
East	4	33.33	5	21.74	3[d]	13.64
Mid-West	—	—[e]	1[e]	4.35	1	4.55
Total	12	100.00	23	100.00	22	100.00

[a]Computed from (1) Federal Government of Nigeria (1953) and (2) Federal Ministry of Information (1976).

[b]All the 10 representing the western, eastern, and mid-western regions were members of the Ibo-dominated NCNC, which went into partnership with the northern-based NPC to form the government of the Federation in 1960.

[c]Six of the eight Yoruba ministers from the western region were members of the Nigerian National Democratic Party (NNDP), and ally of the northern Northern Peoples Congress (NPC). The northern party's share thus came to 16 or 72, 73% of the total.

[d]The three from the eastern region were members of the National Convention of Nigerian Citizens (NCNC)—the senior partner in the United Progressive Grand Alliance (UPGA), the NCNC plus the Action Group, which fought the 1964 federal elections against the Nigerian National Alliance (NNA) (NPC + NNDP). The UPGA was beaten in the elections. Its three members on the federal cabinet of 1964–1966 were selected, after a compromise agreement, to represent the interests of the eastern region.

[e]The Mid-western area was part of the western region until 1963.

Table 5

Percentage Distribution of Indigenous Military
Officers by Regional Origin[a]

Region	1959–1960	1965–1966
North	14.0	33.0[b]
West	17.5	27.0
East	68.5	40.0
Mid-West	—	—

[a]Abstracted from Olugbemi (1978:66–69).
[b]Increase was aided by the introduction of the quota formula in recruitment in 1962. By it, the North was allocated 50% of all recruitment into the officer corps while the balance was shared equally among the remaining ethnic-political groups.

that of the colonial period by reason of the new connection between population, on the one hand, and parliamentary representation, control of the federal government, and the distribution of socially valued scarce resources, on the other. Whereas the census was treated with relative indifference in 1952 largely because relative population spread had little, if any, influence on the composition and control of the federal government,[4] the established connection between population size, parliamentary representation, and control of the federal government in the post 1958 period gave the census a new significance among the groups competing for power in the country. Given the lopsided structure of the federation noted earlier, one way for each of the three major contenders to national leadership (i.e., the NPC of the Hausa–Fulani North; the National Convention of Nigerian Citizens (NCNC) of the Ibo East; and the Action Group (AG) led by Obafemi Awolowo of the Yoruba West) to preserve or overthrow the status quo, was to manipulate the census for group advantage. In the 1962–1963 and 1973 national censuses this manipulation took the forms of (1) outright inflation of census figures, (2) alleged discovery of new communities, (3) a more thorough head count than in any previous census, (4) encouragement of population movements for the purpose of the count, and (5) criminal violation of established administrative procedures.

The first strategy (i.e., outright inflation) would appear to have been practiced more or less in all the three regions. From the final 1962 figures (31 million for the North; 12.4 million for the East; 10.0 million for the

---

[4] This is because the government was a sort of national coalition in which the Hausa–Fulani, the Ibo, and the Yoruba were each represented by their parties on a parity basis.

West; and .675 million for Lagos, representing an increase of 84.5%, 72.2%, 63.3%, and 152.8%, respectively, over the 1952 census figures for the areas), it would appear that the West was the least culpable. Indeed, the western region figure could be the actual figure, or verly close to the actual figure, if account is taken of its complaint about undercounting in 1952 and the fact that the region is, apart from Lagos, the most attractive of the three regions for inmigration, particularly from the North and the East. Set against the hard facts about life in Nigeria, the returns from the East and the North can hardly be justified. The case against the East is that it has the highest rate of emigration[5] as well as the highest magnitude of spinsters and bachelors of the three major ethnic groups.[6] The North, for its own part, is known to be inhabited by sparse and scattered population; its relative aridity, poor soil conditions, and low-level modernity are disincentives to immigration and permanent settlement. Thus, the wide discrepancy of 8.5 million between the pre- and post-verification figures of 22.5 million and 31 million, respectively, opened it to further suspicion.

Deliberate inflation of figures for sectional advantage was again witnessed in the decennial census of 1973, when four of the six northern states returned the incredible figure of 41.57 million people, or 52% of the national total. When the figures for the whole country were put together, the six northern states accounted for a similarly incredible figure of 51.38 million people, or 64% of the national total of 79.76 million. In these circumstances even the hotly disputed census figures of 1962 seemed insignificant.[7]

The discovery of "new communities" was a strategy adopted by the northern and eastern regional governments to prepare Nigerians for their final figures in 1962. But when pressed by their western region peers to substantiate their finding by reference to ethnographic studies of Nigeria, they explained, though without being able to convince their challengers, that "discovery" in this context meant that those communities were not identified as autonomous units in the 1952 census. The counter-explanation was that the settlements in question were enumerated in 1952 as part of the larger clan in which they belonged, rather than as self-contained units. The "discovery of new communities" was a factor in the inflation of census figures from the North and the East.

---

[5] The high pressure on land—the traditional source of wealth—in the Ibo heartland is the cause of the massive emigration of Ibos to other parts of Nigeria to seek a living.

[6] The high bride price among the Ibos is a serious disincentive to early marriage.

[7] The annual rate of growth recorded in some parts of the country was on the order of 7%, which is higher than the established United Nations annual rate of 2.5%.

Another strategy in the manipulation of the census was the subtle though intensive appeal by regional government to their peoples resident elsewhere in Nigeria to return home to be counted. Activity in this area was particularly noticeable in the eastern region whose peoples live in hundreds of thousands outside their home region. For the East, the strategy paid off as massive numbers of easterners, particularly Ibos, traveled home. But the Ibo homegoing for the census also provoked counteraction in some parts of the North and West, where the easterners were forcibly counted at motor parks, railway stations, and at mounted roadblocks. The resulting phenomenon of double counting contributed to the unreliability of census returns.

Whereas all of the foregoing strategies in census manipulation were manifest in the two decennial censuses of 1962–1963 and 1973, the last strategy—criminal violation of census administration procedures—was peculiar to the 1973 census. For instance, some northern states were alleged to have breached the 1973 census regulations for sectional advantage in three respects: (1) they exceeded the scheduled period for counting; (2) they delayed the dispatch of census data and materials to the National Census Board; and (3) they caused the census data for their states to be processed on the spot contrary to the stipulation that all processing would be done at the Lagos Secretariat of the National Census Board.

In these circumstances it is little wonder that the three postindependence Nigerian censuses generated such disruptive controversy that they heightened intercommunal conflicts. The 1962 census was cancelled in favor of a fresh one ordered for 1963. Even the result of the latter—which gave 29.8 million to the North, 12.4 million to the East, 12.8 million to the West, and .675 millin to Lagos—was hotly disputed. Although the NPC-dominated Nigerian National Alliance (NNA),[8] which was assured of its continued preeminence, welcomed and accepted the figures, the United Progressive Grand Alliance (UPGA)[9] vehemently opposed them as totally unacceptable. Indeed Dr. M. I. Okpara, leader of the UPGA and premier of the eastern region, gave several reasons why the northern returns were unacceptable, describing them as "worse than useless" [West African Pilot, 1964a]. Similarly, Chief Dennis Osadebay, the UPGA premier of the new Mid-West region, described the 1963 figures as "the most stupendous joke of our age [West African Pilot, 1964b]."

[8] The Nigerian National Alliance was a political coalition formed by the NPC, the Nigerian National Democratic Party (NNDP), and the Mid-West Democratic Front (MDF) in 1964.

[9] The United Progressive Grand Alliance was formed from a coalition of the NCNC, the AG, the United Middle Belt Congress (UMBC), and other minority parties in 1963–1964.

A similar pattern of support and opposition greeted the release of the provisional figures of the 1973 census, which showed that the six northern states accounted for 51.38 million, or 64% of the national total of 79.76 million. Against the position of civilian and military elites of northern origin that the 1973 census was the "most thorough and accurate head count ever conducted anywhere in the world [Kaufman, 1978]"[10] was Chief Awolowo's attack on the returns as unreliable, bad, and totally unacceptable. In his convocation address to the University of Ife Community in June 1974, Chief Awolowo (1974) lashed out at the census, saying that the results incredibly showed that the North grew from 54% of the national population in 1963 to 65% of it in 1973. "If the trend was repeated in 1983," he said, "74% of all Nigerians would be living in the North." "In this connection," he said further, "the results could only aggravate the entrenched fear of permanent domination of one group of Nigerians by another." He demanded the rejection of the results and the continued use of the 1963 returns, not because the latter were accurate but because they were the least disputed census results from 1931 to 1973. Wide support for Chief Awolowo's views on the 1973 census results by southern elites, civilian and military, was evidenced in the numerous critical newspaper articles, special publications (*Lagoon Echo*, 1975),[11] and public statements including one by Brigadier M. O. Johnson, Military Governor of the Lagos State, who averred that less than half the population of his state was counted and that in any case "we know how many mouths we feed in Lagos State [*West Africa*, 1974]."

POLITICAL INTIMIDATION

Whereas the census was manipulated for the purpose of increasing group populations for hegemonic interests, the intimidation of political opponents served the more limited though equally important objective of converting members of rival parties through the threat or actual employment of sanctions for the purpose of increasing electoral support for the parties in their respective regional spheres of influence. Four types of intimidation were used more or less by all the three major Nigerian parties of the premilitary rule era. One was the employment of government machinery to curtail the influence and activities of rival

[10] Attributed to General Yakubu Gowon, head of state of Nigeria from 1966 to 1975 (Kaufman, 1978).

[11] See also the *New Nationalist*, the *Daily Sketch*, and the *Nigerian Tribune* of the same period.

parties, as when the AG government of the western region harassed and later dissolved the NCNA-controlled local governments in Ibadan, Ilesha, and other centers. Other examples include the refusal to grant Dr. Okpara of the UPGA an official permit to campaign for votes at Ogbomosho, the hometown of S. L. Akintola, premier of the western region in 1964, or the use of the Native Authority police to prevent both the AG and the NCNC from canvassing freely for support and votes in northern Nigeria between 1960 and 1965.[12]

Another form of intimidation was the denial of government patronage (contracts, scholarships, public offices, social amenities, and so on) to opponents of the regional ruling parties and their strongholds. The third type of intimidation was the use of hired thugs to obstruct meetings and other activities of rival parties. Lastly, there was the wide use of native courts and other tribunals, particularly in the northern and western regions, to try and convict political opponents on trumped-up charges.[13]

The efficacy of the intimidation instrument was demonstrated in two related events—namely many people renounced their membership of rival parties in favor of the party ruling their regions under threat of penalties, and each regional ruling party gained substantial electoral successes in its region of dominance as a result. For instance, the AG's loss of the western region to the NCNC in the 1954 federal elections was reversed to victory in the 1959 federal elections. The NPC emerged from relative weakness in the federal elections of 1959 to capture all the 167 seats allocated to that region in 1964. Regional elections from 1956 to the advent of military rule in 1966 showed increased support for each of the parties in its regional sphere of influence. The regions virtually became one-party mini-states.

CREATION OF MORE REGIONS

The long-drawn demands for the further division of Nigeria into more component units (regions or states) derived from two main causes, both of which had implications particularly for the numerical ratios of the three major ethnic groups or the region where each predominated. First, the demand arose from the need, felt strongly by the AG and NCNC (two southern political parties), for redressing the lopsided structure of the Federation so that no one single unit could hold the rest to political

[12] The intention was to prevent these rival parties from reaching the electorate.
[13] The source of the charge by Dr. M. I. Okpara of the UPGA that law and order had broken down in the western region.

Table 6

Awolowo's Plan for the Creation of States in Nigeria[a]

Constituent unit	Population size (millions)	Rank order
Hausa–Fulani	13.6	1
Yoruba	13.0	2
Ibo	7.8	3
Efik–Ibibio–Annang	3.2	4
Kanuri	2.9	5
Tiv	1.5	8
Ijaw	.9	10
Edo	.9	10
Urhobo	.6	12
Nupe	.6	12
Old Adamawa, Biu, Muri, and Numa	2.7	6
Bauchi Province and Potiskum division	2.7	6
Plateau Province, S. Zaria, etc.	2.6	7
Idoma, Igala, and Igbira divisions	1.5	8
Abuja, Borgu, Kontagora, and Minna divisions	1.0	9
Old Ahoda and Ogoni divisions plus Port-Harcourt municipality	.8	11
Old Ikom, Obubra, and Ogoja divisions	.6	12

[a]Source: Awolowo (1968:235, 241–243).

ransom as the northern region appeared then to be doing. But whereas the NCNC wanted a unitary Nigerian state structured into 25 local governments along the lines of the old provinces, the AG advocated a federal Nigeria structured into 17 component states using the criterion of ethnolinguistic homogeneity or affimity.[14] To the NCNC the AG formula was motivated by "tribal" considerations; its intention was hegemonic because it would have meant the organization of all Yoruba-speaking people then divided among the West, North, and Lagos into one political unit. Although the largely Yoruba AG denied the alleged hegemonic interests, there can be little doubt that its state creation formula would have redressed the numerical ratios of the constituent units on the order shown in Table 6.

[14] This latter principle was first enunciated by Chief Awolowo in 1947 and reiterated by him in 1968 and ever since. See Awolowo (1947, 1968).

Table 6 shows that the AG formula would have moved the Yoruba region or state from being the third largest in the country to being the second largest (i.e., behind the Hausa–Fulani), and the Ibo unit would have fallen from second to third. Given the modality of politics in Nigeria prior to military rule and the fact that the Hausa–Fulani women were not yet enfranchised, it would have been very easy for the AG to gain ascendancy over other groups in any political contest.[15] This fact tended to give credence to the charge of hegemonic ambitions.

Second, the demand for more states derived from the aspiration of minority ethnic groups (for whom the AG scheme seemed to have provided) for their own separate states as an escape from the domination of the larger groups with whom they were grouped for administration.[16] Of the three dominant parties, the AG appeared the most supportive of that demand, whereas the NPC was vehemently opposed to it.[17] For its part, the NCNC appeared to be supportive only if such an exercise would not affect its eastern region as it was then constituted.

Lack of agreement among the giant sectional elites over the states issues prevented any action until the military administration took the initiative in May 1967, when it replaced the 4 existing regions with 12 states, and again in 1976, when it added a further 7 states to bring the total to 19. The relative population standing of the 19 component states of the Federation of Nigeria is shown in Table 7.

Although the new 19-state structure fairly satisfied the aspirations of agitating minority ethnic groups for self-determination within the framework of a federal Nigerian polity and in the process also evened out the population ratios among the constituent units, the strong sectional content observed in the performance of most of the five political parties— The National Party of Nigeria (NPN), the Unity Party of Nigeria (UPN), the Nigerian Peoples Party (NPP), the Peoples Redemption Party (PRP), and the Great Nigerian Peoples Party (GNPP)—in the presidential elections of 1979 did not completely justify the expectation, once widely held, that the creation of more regions or states would serve to destroy the monolithic regional political blocs of the premilitary era. Table 8, which was computed from the results of the presidential elections held on August 11, 1979, illustrates this statement.

Table 8 clearly shows that only the NPN and, to a lesser extent, the NPP were able to break out of the ethnocultural zones of their leaders.

[15] Subject to the assumption that the other groups did not unite in a political alliance.

[16] The fear of the minority groups was the subject of the Willink Commission of Enquiry in 1958.

[17] The NPC opposed the creation of state because such an eventuality would undercut a substantial portion of the northern population.

Table 7

Nineteen Component States of the Federation of Nigeria[a]

State	Region created from	Population	Rank order
Anambra	East	3,596,631	5
Bauchi	North	2,434,730	13
Bendel	Old Mid-West (No change)	3,535,839	7
Benue	North	3,041,193	8
Borno	North	2,990,526	9
Cross River	East	3,633,593	4
Gongola	North	1,585,200	16
Imo	East	3,568,125	6
Kaduna	North	4,098,297	3
Kano	North	5,774,842	1
Kwara	North	2,399,365	14
Lagos	Federal Territory	1,100,000	19
Niger	North	2,900,000	10
Ogun	West	1,448,966	17
Ondo	West	2,727,676	12
Oyo	West	5,208,944	2
Plaetu	North	1,421,481	18
Rivers	East	2,300,000	15
Sokoto	North	2,873,286	11

[a]Computed from Federal Ministry of Information (1977). pp. 37–52.

The other three parties, including Chief Awolowo's UPN, proved to be nothing more than sectional–ethnic political formations.

COMMUNAL POLITICAL COALITIONS OR ALLIANCES

In a situation of multiple competitors of unequal strength the need for survival tends to drive the underprivileged into some form of understanding and working partnership such that the combined energies of the partners can outmatch their common rival(s). Given the numerical ratios of Nigeria's major ethnic groups, working partnership among the disadvantaged was considered a worthwhile strategy to check the domination of the numerically superior Hausa–Fulani group of northern Nigeria. The first manifestation of such a combination was in 1963–1964 when the Ibo NCNC merged with the Yoruba-AG and other minority parties (such as the United Middle Belt Congress (UMBC) and the Calabar-Ogoja and River State Movement) to form the United Progressive Grand Alliance (UPGA) to oppose the Nigerian National Alliance (NNA) of the NPC, the Nigerian National Democratic Party (NNDP), and the Mid-West

Table 8

Presidential Elections, 1979: Relative Performance of the Five Parties

Political party	No. of States won or with 25% or more of votes cast (1)	No. of States in col. 2 from party leader's linguistic or regional bloc (2)	(1) − (2)
NPN	12	8	4
UPN	6	6	–
NPP	3	2	1
GNPP	3	3	–
PRP	2	2	–

Democratic Front (MDF) for the purpose of the 1964 federal parliamentary elections. The calculation of the UPGA, based as it was on the overall performance of the NCNC and the AG in the 1959 federal elections, was that the combined strength of their constituents would give them enough parliamentary seats to wrestle the control of the federal government from the NPC and its allies in the NNA. That hope was not realized; the NPC and its allies were returned to power, notwithstanding that the election results were hotly disputed.

Two recent manifestations of communal combination for the purpose of winning political power deserve mention here. The first was the emergence of Club 19, which later developed into the Nigerian Peoples Party (NPP). Embracing representatives of minority ethnic groups in the constituent assembly of Nigeria's new constitution, the objective of the Club was to pool the resources of its constituents to challenge the major ethnic groups and the party or parties that they might form for the 1979 general elections. Unfortunately, the NPP split into two factions before the elections; one faction took the name GNPP, and the other half took the name NPP. Divided they could not win the elections.

The other combination was the formation of the National Party of Nigeria (NPN) as a consociational party embracing political figures from all ethnic groups and states of the country. The consociational strategy paid off for the NPN in the general elections of 1979 in two major respects: first, it gave the party the most national outlook of the five political parties, and second, it enabled it to win the presidency, achieving here the widest national spread of votes. The lesson from the NPN plan of 1978–1979 is the basis for the current efforts by the UPN, the NPP, and the splinter groups of the PRP and the GNPP to merge or form an alliance for the purpose of the 1983 general elections.

Summary and Conclusion

Interethnic conflict in culturally plural societies like Nigeria is related to competition over the distribution of socially valued but scarce resources. The objective of ethnic politics is to secure adequate representation of group interests in the institutions of state power as a means of securing for the group an adequate share of the "national cake." Socioeconomic modernization tends to accentuate ethnic conflict by heightening awareness of the disparities in the allocation of the system's rewards among competing groups. Political modernization—defined as the diffusion of liberal democracy with its principles of adult suffrage, party government, and majority rule—tends to augment the importance of numbers such that the relative size of groups becomes a political issue to be manipulated for the purpose of redressing the balance of power in favor of one group or the other.

All these conditions were fulfilled in the Federal Republic of Nigeria, where the manipulation of group numbers for political advantage took four forms—namely, census manipulation, political intimidation, demand for the creation of more states, and intercommunal coalitions. At the center of these strategies was the control of Nigeria's federal government and its broad authority. This fact seems to be generally not understood or deliberately underplayed by foreign commentators like Michael T. Kaufman (1978:8) of the New York Times who blamed "Nigerians in dispute over census results," as if the census were no more than a statistical exercise.

References

Awolowo, O.
    1947   Path to Nigerian Freedom. London: Faber.
    1968   The Peoples Republic. Oxford University Press.
    1974   Convocation address. University of Ife, Ile. Mimeo.
Bamisaiye, A.
    1971   Ethnic politics as an instrument of unequal socio-economic development in Nigeria's first republic. African Notes 6(2):94–106.
Campbell, I.
    1976   The nigerian census: an essay in civil–military relations. Journal of Commonwealth and Comparative Politics XIV(1):242–243.
Federal Government of Nigeria
    1953   House of Representatives Debates. Lagos: Federal Government of Nigeria.

Federal Ministry of Information (FMOI)
    1976   *Unity in diversity*. Lagos: Federal Government of Nigeria.
    1977   *The Nigerian Handbook*. Lagos: Federal Government of Nigeria.
Geertz, C.
    1963   The integrative revolution: primordial sentiments and civil politics in new states, in *Old Societies and New States* (C. Geertz, Ed.). New York: The Free Press.
Kaufman, M. T.
    1978   Nigerians in dispute over census results. *New York Times* **April 20**:8.
Kuper, L.
    1971   Theories of revolution and race relations. *Comparative Studies in Society and History*. **January 13**:87–107.
Lagoon Echo
    1975   *Lagoon Echo* **1**(3 May–August).
Melson, R., and Wople, H. (Eds.)
    1971   *Nigeria: Modernisation and the Politics of Communalism*. Ann Arbor, Mich.: Michigan State University Press.
Olorunsola, V.
    1972   *The Politics of Cultural Sub-Nationalism in Africa*. New York: Doubleday.
Olugbemi, S. O.
    1978   Military leadership and political integration in Nigeria, 1966–1976. Unpublished D.PA. dissertation, Department of Public Administration, State University of New York, Albany.
Post, K., and Vickers, M.
    1973   *Structure and Conflict in Nigeria, 1960–65*. London: Heinemanu.
Rotberg, R.
    1967   Tribalism and politics in Zambia. *African Report* **December 1967**:29–35.
Sanda, A. O.
    1974   Ethnicity and intergroup conflicts. *The Nigerian Journal of Economic and Social Studies* **16**(3 **November**):507–518.
Schwarz, F. A. O.
    1965   *Nigeria: The Tribe, the Nation, or the Race: The Politics of Independence*. Cambridge, Mass.: MIT Press.
Slunner, E.
    1963   Group dynamics in the politics of changing societies: the problem of tribal politics in Africa, in *Essays on the Problem of Tribe* (J. Helm, Ed.), pp. 170–183. Washington, D.C.: American Ethnological Society.
Wegley, C., and Harns, M.
    1958   *Minorities in the New World*. New York: Columbia University Press.
West Africa
    1974   *West Africa* (London) **July 29.**
West African Pilot
    1964a   *West African Pilot* **February 29**:2.
    1964b   *West African Pilot* **March 11**:1.
Wolf, H.
    1967   Language, ethnic identity and social change in southern Nigeria. *Anthropological Linguistics* **9**(2):18–25.
Wright, T. P.
    1976   The ethnic numbers game in India: Hindu–Muslim conflicts over conversion, family planning, migration and the census. Paper presented at the 1976 Annual Conference of the American Political Science Association, Chicago, Ill.

16

Ethnic Psychology: An Approach to the Study of Race, Ethnicity, and Culture*

Albert Ramirez

Peter G. Ossorio

Introduction

The topics of ethnicity, race, and culture have received considerable attention and interest from psychologists. Unfortunately, the expression of this interest in the form of psychological investigation and discussion has all too often been extraordinarily limited in its scope and basis, and even destructive in its general effects (Caplan and Nelson, 1973). Psychology has legitimized a general approach that is narrow in its substantive scope and naive in its methodological presuppositions (Johnson, 1978). One result is that researchers have routinely conceptualized and investigated behavior from the normative perspective of one sociocultural group (Baldwin, 1979; Rappaport, Davidson, Wilson, and Mitchell, 1975). A further well-known result of such a monolithic-normative psychology is the labeling of individuals, groups, or investigations that vary from this norm as deviant, disadvantaged, or just plain inferior (Cole and Bruner, 1971). For the most part, the groups that have been labeled in

---

* An earlier version of this paper, entitled "Ethnic Psychology: Toward a Liberating Psychology," was presented as part of the Minority Fellowship Program Symposium: "Ethnicity, Race and Culture in Graduate Psychology Curricula," American Psychological Association Convention, New York City, September, 1979. As in the earlier version, the contribution of the graduate students participating in the seminars in ethnic psychology is acknowledged and appreciated.

this way are those that have been ethnically, racially, and/or culturally different from the normative group (Ryan, 1971). Unfortunately, there is little evidence to suggest that "mainstream psychology" is in the process of changing its approach to ethnicity, race, and culture or that it is making significant progress toward achieving its potential either as a field of knowledge or as a liberating discipline (Clarke, 1972). Sheltered as it is by its privileged position from many of the hard facts of intellectual and social life, it appears to be incapable of outgrowing its ethnocentrism without some help from outside (Johnson, 1978), and it is likely to be its principal victims who are most capable of providing both precept and example (White, 1972).

Consequently, there is an increasing demand that psychologists develop distinctive programs for providing training in ethnically appropriate theory, methodology, and real-world problem solving (Guthrie, 1979). The remainder of this paper describes a proposed program that focuses on the development of multiethnic-cultural approaches and perspectives in psychology. This program, a specialty graduate training program in "Ethnic Psychology" (Ramirez, 1977) has the following characteristics:

1. A conceptual framework that makes individual, group, and cultural differences an essential and systematic aspect of the general phenomenon of human behavior and development

2. A neutral, symmetric notation and vocabulary for thinking and talking across the boundaries generated by commitments to particular social groups, substantive theories, methodological ideologies, or value orientations

3. A systematic elucidation of major cultural perspectives, accomplished within those perspectives, in regard to their paradigmatic assumptions, presuppositions, outlooks, and choice principles

4. The derivation of methodological and theoretical commitments as exemplifying the corresponding cultural perspectives

5. A systematic elucidation of the correspondences among the formulations of a given cultural perspective and its derivatives, when those formulations are accomplished within a set of other cultural perspectives and their methodological and conceptual derivatives

6. The analysis and investigation of sociocultural phenomena that are distinctively associated with societies that are ethnically pluralistic or multicultural to a significant degree. Two important special cases may be noted here. The first case involves phenomena associated with cultural displacement (i.e., cases where individuals must function wholly or in important ways in a culture other than that into which they are

socialized; these cases include immigrant, refugees, and indigenous ethnic minorities). The second case involves phenomena associated with differential eligibilities, including power differentials between privileged (usually majority) groups and underprivileged (usually minority) groups.

Seminar Model for Ethnic Psychology

In the spring semester of 1974, the first graduate seminar that focused exclusively on a critical review and analysis of the psychological research conducted on minority-ethnic groups in contemporary American society was offered in the psychology department of the University of Colorado. Eleven graduate students enrolled in the seminar. Of these, four were Chicano, three black, and four Anglo. During the semester, six research areas were discussed in class. For the most part, the discussions were based on specific and representative studies conducted in a particular area. The areas were:

1. Cognitive processes—intelligence, learning, bilingualism, and achievement
2. Perceptual processes—self-perception, self-esteem, self-concept, and ethnic identity
3. Mental health—delivery systems; psychotherapeutic approaches; social pathology models; and problem behavior such as alcoholism, drug addiction, crime, and delinquency
4. Attitudes and personality—attitudes toward education (police, other groups, etc.) and personality characteristics and types
5. Values—assimilation, acculturation, and family–cultural values
6. Group processes—intergroup conflict, cooperation, and separatism, group identity, ethnic group relations, intra-group conflict

The discussions not only dealt with research design and methodology but also encompassed the areas of ethnic and social and professional responsibility. A number of important questions and issues were raised by our class discussions concerning the research that had been conducted on ethnic minorities. Some of the questions that we attempted to deal with were the following:

1. The concept of "inferiority" was first attributed to minority peoples on a principle of biological determinism; then the cultural determinism model became more popular. Since reviewing the research literature in

class, we have become increasingly aware of the necessity of moving away from the cultural determinism model and the associated concept that minorities are inferior. How can we begin to accomplish this as social scientists?

2. How can we, as psychologists, deal with the problems involved in psychometric testing? Are there alternative methods other than testing that are appropriate in assessing an individual's learning ability, success in school, level of aspiration, and so on?

3. As minority researchers or educators being educated primarily in traditional institutions, which encourage and reinforce the Anglo values and concepts that we have seen resulting in research on ethnic minorities, how can we avoid this "molding" process and begin to influence graduate training programs in psychology?

4. How can minority research approaches, as opposed to research on minorities, take into account the questions of (a) who determines how it should be done, (b) who determines what research should be done, (c) who evaluates what is done, and (d) what is done with the results?

5. Does psychological research based on ethnicity serve any useful function, or does the risk to ethnic group members outweigh any possible scientific gains that might result from such study?

6. What responsibility does psychology have as a profession for preventing the misapplication and misinterpretation of research findings? What steps can psychology take in this direction?

7. Under what circumstances should studies concerning a certain minority group be done by only members of that group? Under what circumstances can such studies be done by nonminority researchers?

Since 1974, the seminar in ethnic psychology has been offered every other year. Student enrollment in this course has been high and diverse, the course attracting students not only from the six graduate training programs in the psychology department (clinical, social-personality, quantitative, developmental, experimental, and biopsychology), but from other departments as well.

SPECIALTY GRADUATE TRAINING IN ETHNIC PSYCHOLOGY

A proposal to initiate a specialty training program in ethnic psychology has been approved by the psychology department at the University of Colorado. As presently proposed, the program would consist of a six-course, two-year sequence integrated with the training received in one of the six doctoral programs in the department. It should be emphasized that students interested in the speciality training program of ethnic psychology would be admitted to a graduate training area—one of the six mentioned earlier—and would have to complete the requirements of that area in order to receive a degree. The program, therefore, would function within the existing departmental structure, not as a separate entity. The specialty work in ethnic psychology will broaden and strengthen the students' methodological and theoretical perspectives, irrespective of the specific graduate program in which the student is enrolled. Thus, for example, a student might graduate from the graduate training program in social-personality psychology, but with specialization in ethnic psychology.

The specialty training program in ethnic psychology will begin in the spring semester of the student's first year of graduate study. The first course, "Introduction to Ethnic Psychology," would be taken at that time. This course will deal with general issues, specific problems, and conceptual tools, including the following:

1. The problems of diversity to which ethnic psychology is addressed
2. Areas where diversity considerations are relevant (e.g., schools, industrial organizations, civil service organizations, political units, health service, and other social service delivery systems)
3. Models for dealing with diversity: (a) formal or conceptual models—monolithic, relativistic-pluralistic, internal colonalism, multiplex, and displaced person models; (b) experimental models—the contributions of value orientation and cognitive orientation to experimental paradigms. Varieties of experimental paradigms.
4. Ethnic psychologies: what we (they) are like; the relation of value and outlook aspect to conceptual, methodological, and experimental models.

The second course, "Research Practicum," will be taken during the summer following the first year. This course will provide a review of the first-year statistics course and a formulation of ethnically relevant research problems, and will focus on

1. A review of ethnic diversity problems, formulating them as research, treatment, and political problems
2. A review of quantitative and experimental paradigm considerations in relation to these research problems

The third course, "Multiple Approaches in Ethnic Methodology," will be taken in the fall semester of the second year. This course will deal with the ethnic research literature and research procedures for field research in a variety of real-world settings and communities. The course will focus on

1. A review and critique of ethnic research literature
2. Survey and development of research methods and procedures appropriate to ethnic diversity and ethnic specificity
3. Research designs and proposals for ethnically relevant topics
4. Ethnic psychologies: more advanced work

The fourth, fifth, and sixth courses would be a year-long sequence covering the spring, summer, and fall sessions of the second and third years, respectively. This sequence will involve a combination of field placements and biweekly seminars. The emphasis here will be on understanding ethnic communities, formulating realistic and significant research problems, and designing or implementing research and/or service activities. This series of courses, "Fieldwork in Ethnic Psychology," will consist of

1. Seminar on treatment, action programs, and field research: (a) literature review; (b) design of changes, interventions, data gathering; (c) evaluation; (d) problems and observations in field placement
2. Field placement: participation in governmental or other organizations, mental health delivery systems, or community decision-making systems
3. Practicum: teaching courses or giving colloquia or workshops to students in the program

The history of psychology has clearly shown us that broader and more diverse perspectives are necessary if we are to advance our understanding of the human condition. The profession and the discipline of psychology need the type of perspective embodied in ethnic psychology, a perspective in which the dominant group's values, beliefs, and life-styles do not serve as the standard of comparison and point of reference (Ramirez, 1977). Ethnic psychology deserves to have a vital place in our discipline, approaches, theories, and social action policies. We need a liberated and liberating psychology.

REFERENCES

Baldwin, J. A.
    1979   Theory and research concerning the notion of Black self-hatred: a review and
            reinterpretation. *Journal of Black Psychology* **5**:51–77.

Caplan, N., and Nelson, S. D
    1973   On being useful: the nature and consequences of psychological research on social problems. *American Psychologist* **28**:199–211.

Clarke, C.
    1972   Black studies or the studies of Black people, in *Black Psychology* (R. L. Jones, Ed.), pp. 3–17. New York: Harper & Row.

Cole, M., and Bruner, J. S.
    1971   Cultural differences and inferences about psychological processes. *American Psychologist* **26**:867–876.

Guthrie, R. V.
    1979   Graduate psychology curricula and Black communities. Paper presented at American Psychological Association Convention, New York City.

Johnson, D.
    1978   A metatheory of Chicano psychology: the case for a minority based metatheory. *Atisbos: Journal of Chicano Research* **Summer–Fall**:36–60.

Ramirez, A.
    1977   Chicano power and interracial group relations, in *Chicano Psychology* (J. Martinez, Ed.), pp. 87–96. New York: Academic Press.

Rappaport, J., Davidson, W. S., Wilson, M. N., and Mitchell, A.
    1975   Alternatives to blaming the victim or the environment: our places to stand have not moved the earth. *American Psychologist* **30**:525–528.

Ryan, W.
    1971   *Blaming the Victim*. New York: Random House.

White, J.
    1972   Toward a Black psychology, in *Black Psychology* (R. L. Jones, Ed.), pp. 43–50. New York: Harper & Row.

17

Community Control and the Black Political Agenda

Paul Ritterband

INTRODUCTION

The call for community control of schools among blacks arose as part of the shift in emphasis from integration to black power. From the early 1950s black educational reformers in New York City had been struggling with the Board of Education to develop and implement a plan for the integration of the schools. By 1966, after repeated failure and disappointment and particularly after the Board had reneged on its promise to build a new model integrated intermediate school, the leadership within the black educational reform movement announced a program of community control. The group called for a "radical redistribution of power" in the school system (Goldberg, 1966–1967:3). Although the earliest demand for community control seems to have been expressed in New York, the doctrine of black control of the black community schools rapidly became a national issue. It was proclaimed as a goal by the National Association of Afro–American Educators (Hamilton, 1968:670) and was a key item on the political agenda of the Black Power Conference in Newark, New Jersey (see also Carmichael and Hamilton, 1967:43).

It is reasonable to assume that much of the support for community control was based on concern over the academic failure of large numbers of black pupils. The extent to which (if at all) community control would result ultimately in higher levels of achievement among black pupils was not known. Community control as an educational strategy was based

291

more on hope than hard evidence. Perhaps what is important in understanding support for community control is not so much its hoped for results in improving education, but rather the likely benefits that might accrue to some of its proponents. Some supporters of community control in New York City linked quality education for black pupils with increased hiring of black teachers and the promotion of black teachers already in the system to supervisory positions.

In New York City, the African–American Teachers Association (A.T.A.) played a central role in the struggle for community control. In presenting its platform and demands the A.T.A. linked improved educational achievements for black children with enhanced employment opportunities for black teachers generally and its organization in particular. The Vice-President of the A.T.A., Leslie Campbell (1968), wrote in *Forum*, the A.T.A. journal:

Less than 2% of the administrators of New York City schools are black. Only 8% of the teachers employed by the devil's board are black. Only 10 schools of 950 have black custodians. The unions and companies holding fat contracts for goods and services in the schools are all owned and operated by devils. Conclusion: only a minute percentage (1%) of all monies spent for education ever finds its way into the black community. . . . Outsiders reap the benefits ($) and privileges (pensions and other goodies) of this system and all the colony receives is a yearly flow of functionally illiterate youth . . . some of you often cry about "Good, well-meaning" devils. Well, I have been in the system for eight years and for each "Good" devil that I have encountered I have seen 100 murderers of our children's minds. I am not willing to gamble with that kind of odds against me [p. 1].

A less emotional, more reasoned statement was made in the same issue of the *Forum* by Albert Vann (1968), then President of the A.T.A.:

Basically, we are dedicated to guaranteeing a meaningful education to children in the black community because they have been denied this opportunity. A second related concern is to fight for equality of opportunity for black teachers and to continue to remind ourselves that our roots are in, and our responsibilities to, the black community. It is, therefore, understandable that A.T.A. was in favor of community-control of schools long before the Bundy Report or any of the others [p. 2].

A later statement (ATA, 1970) was even more explicit in outlining the benefits of community control for the A.T.A.: "We demand that the African–American Teachers Association, Inc. be granted the authority not only to recruit, but also to test and then assign successful candidates directly through local community boards [p. 5]."

Nationwide there was significant variation in support of community control among blacks. In part, support for community control can be explained in terms of the objective conditions and subjective attitudes of individual blacks in the cities under study. The first part of my analysis will briefly examine some aggregated individual correlates of commitment to community control. For the second and major part of the analysis I shall examine the relationship between support for community control and local political structure with particular reference to the ways in which the local political structure frames self-interest and thus support for community control.

The analysis is based in part on a reanalysis of data from a Kerner Commission supplemental study reported in Campbell and Schuman (1968) and Schuman and Gruenberg (1970). The measure of community control sentiment is an index created by Schuman and Gruenberg, which they call "Favor Black Control of Black Institutions." The indices of subjective sentiment and housing integration are taken as well from the Kerner Commission data. The sources of other data are presented in the appendix.[1]

PERSONAL CORRELATES OF COMMITMENT TO COMMUNITY CONTROL

Community control generated a complex social movement, interweaving elements of resentment, felt deprivation, and political tactics. The response to the movement by individual blacks reflected in part a more general malaise and discontent with their lives, which did not necessarily reflect their particularly depressed objective state. The demand for community control (as the demand for many if not most social changes) was not expressed by those who were objectively most deprived and downtrodden. Support for community control was strongest among individual blacks and within black communities that had supported other expressions of black militancy.[2]

Demand for community control was correlated with dissatisfaction with housing or income but was weakly associated both with a higher median black income and relatively higher ratio of black to white median income. Where blacks *believed* there was police abuse, community control sentiments were stronger; however, the actual *experience* of police abuse was negatively (albeit weakly) correlated with support for com-

---

[1] The Kerner Commission studies were based on data collected in 15 cities. Of these, Washington, D.C., was excluded because it has no elected local government. The structure of local government in California is not really comparable with the rest of the country. I have, therefore, excluded San Francisco, which was part of the original sample. We are left with 13 cities. See Appendix for list and sources of variables.

[2] For detailed discussion on this issue, see Marx (1967:49–33).

Table 1

Aggregated Individual-Level Correlates of Support
for Community Control

Item	Product-moment correlation
Dissatisfaction with own housing or income among blacks	− .71
Median income of blacks	.11
Ratio of black to white median incomes	.27
Belief in the existence of police abuse among blacks	.49
Personal experience of police abuse	− .14
Dissatisfaction with level of neighborhood services among blacks	.49

munity control. Support for control was correlated with dissatisfaction with the level of neighborhood services; however, these were cities that had the highest per capita expenditure on municipal services ($R = .23$). The evidence suggests that support for community control was to be found among those blacks who felt most aggrieved, whereas their objective condition was probably better than that of most blacks (see Table 1).

POLITICAL ORGANIZATION, POLITICAL PATRONAGE, AND COMMUNITY CONTROL

Political agendas in so far as they are realistic, reflect political facts that transcend individuals or aggregates of individuals. The existence and strength of the party organization (i.e., the "machine")[3] is one of the key elements in determining the policies and platforms of various groups in

[3] For the sake of simplicity, I have termed the political variable "machine–nonmachine." In some cities (e.g., New York) there was a political reform movement exhibiting the standard reform characteristics. In others (e.g., Newark) the issue was not so much the positive implementation of political reform as it was the collapse of a traditional political machine. For our purposes reform and collapse of machines have similar consequences. For further elaboration of the logic of this indicator, see Greenstone and Peterson (1968:278–286).

the cities. Machine administration is one in which a professional organization dominates the governance of the city and controls access to elective offices. In machine cities one party rules and is largely unchallenged by the opposition party or by good government groups. As long as the machine is functioning well, elections ratify decisions taken within the party caucus. The party decides who will run for office—that is, in cities run by machines, the party decides who will be elected. When there is a large number of contenders for elective office, it usually means that the party has not been able to impose its will. It is a sign that the machine has broken down (or perhaps, never emerged.) Therefore, to measure the extent to which a city was dominated by a political machine, I looked at the municipal election immediately prior to the collection of the Kerner Commission data in the spring of 1968. For each city I noted the number of seats in the city council and the number of candidates for the seats. The higher the ratio (that is, the more candidates per seat), the weaker the political organization—the further the city departs from the machine model.

The ratios largely correspond with one's intuitive sense of the extent to which given cities are dominated by machines. Seven out of the 13 cities had two candidates for each seat in accord with the textbook version of electoral politics. Of the other 6, Chicago and Cleveland (particularly the former) were clearly machine cities; New York and Newark were cities in which the machines had collapsed; Cincinnati and Philadelphia showed signs of trouble for the machine. Chicago was, for all intents and purposes, a one-man city. Of the 50 seats in the city council, only 7 were contested in the election of April 4, 1967. In New York City, by contrast, in the election of November 2, 1965, there were 114 candidates for 32 city council seats. In 1965 New York elected its fourth reform administration since the turn of the century. The mayor was supported by a Republican–Liberal coalition, which was successful in electing only one man to citywide office (the mayor). The other citywide offices were captured by Democrats. Even in the halcyon days of machine politics in New York City, the organization was fragmented: each of the five counties in the city had its own machine with its own leadership. No one political organization was ever able to dominate New York the way the Daley machine had been able to dominate Chicago.[4]

---

[4] The decline of machine government has been associated with the rise of various manifestations of substantive liberalism, such as housing integration. Both blacks and whites in nonmachine cities are more likely to live in mixed neighborhoods (blacks, $R = .32$; whites, $R = .80$). There is probably a reciprocal link between machine government and

Black communities in nonmachine cities were far more likely to want community control (see Table 2). That is, the more candidates per seat in the municipal election, the more likely were blacks to favor community control. The political life of nonmachine cities supplied both the "motive" and reasonable prospects of success for community control advocates. The motive inhered in a desire to create new forms of patronage in cities in which patronage declined along with the decline of the machine. The prospects of success for a program of community control were suggested by the demonstrated success of other groups in asserting their influence at city hall.

During the course of this century, political machines declined in importance as the governance of the cities became bureaucratized. The great migration of blacks to the cities of the North coincided with the period of decline of some of the municipal machines. Just at the point where their numbers would have given blacks the political resources to permit them to demand their share of patronage, the patronage system fell into disrepute in "progressive" cities. Describing New York City, Wilson (1960:35) reports that "Negros broke into Tammany (the New York Democratic Organization) just as the posts for which they were fighting were rapidly decreasing in value."[5]

In the 1920s and 1930s when their political position was still weak, the interests of blacks in New York City (and presumably in other machine cities) lay in a nonpolitical merit system. The early black appointments to cabinet positions within New York City government were largely to the civil service commission (Lowi, 1964:42). Because employment discrimination was widespread in the private sector and blacks were still weak in machine politics, their access to opportunity lay in a meritocratic

housing segregation. Machines depended upon ethnic bloc voting for gaining and maintaining power; thus, cities that were highly segregated at an early date would have the natural base for the machine. Once established, the machine would not feel constrained to integrate housing; on the contrary, its self-interest would dictate maintaining segregated housing in order to maintain its electoral base and political control. It is likely that the breaking up of segregated neighborhoods through antidiscrimination statutes would be more likely to come out of reform political administration, which would further contribute to the higher level of housing integration in reform cities. I take the correlation of housing segregation with machine government as partial validation of my measure of machine administration.

[5] The Alfred C. Chapin Democratic Club (founded 1889) in Brooklyn and the United Colored Democracy (founded in 1897) did manage to secure some patronage for Negroes. The amount of patronage was small, and both clubs have long since disappeared (Morsell, 1951:12–13, 26–32).

Table 2

Correlates of Nonmachine Local Government

Favor black rule of black institutions (community control)	.78
Per capita expenditure for all municipal services	.60
Expenditure on education per student enrolled	.57

civil service. By the mid-1960s New York and other progressive cities had gone a long way toward eliminating discrimination in the private sector, making the nondiscriminatory public sector relatively less attractive. The private sector had begun to engage in compensatory positive discrimination, opening up opportunities for blacks. Although earlier, government employment offered blacks "opportunities for the non-discriminatory employment . . . closed to them in so many private economic sectors" (Lowi, 1964:43), the situation more recently had changed significantly. Black electoral strength had risen to the point where black political leaders would have been in the position to demand a large number of jobs from the patronage system if the system were still working. However, few patronage positions were left. District leaders had less and less to say about public employment. Black interests, no longer served by an apolitical civil service, would be served by the spoils system in which employment and government contracts reflected electoral resources. If community control were to be instituted, then the local community would be able to let contracts and hire personnel. The call for community control was strongest in those cities in which the civil service system held down the number of black municipal appointees and blocked patronage for blacks.

One would expect that mass political programs not only reflect belief in the desirability of the end sought (as has been suggested), but are conditioned as well as by a sense of the realistic probability of achieving those ends. Where the goals are desirable but there seems to be little chance of reaching them, few people will invest their energies in the struggle. Thus, two conditions have to be met in order to gain widespread support for a political program: belief in the value of the end and realistic hope of achievement. Nonmachine government contributes to the meeting of the second of these conditions as it does the first. Nonmachine government, constantly seeking electoral support, cannot afford to alienate importants blocs of voters by ignoring or rejecting their petitions.

There is no buffer between city hall and the various pressure groups in the city. As Banfield and Wilson (1963:214) put it, "Where a party organization is strong, the city's administration is in a relatively good position to resist the demands of the organized employee (or for that matter any other pressure group). On the other hand, where party organization is weak or altogether absent, the political weight of the employees is relatively large and maybe decisive." The weakness of nonmachine government means that municipal unions are in a strong bargaining position, which, in turn, leads to higher salaries and thus to greater expenditure for municipal services (see Table 2). Although we have no direct objective measure of the quality of most municipal services, we do know that expenditure per pupil is unrelated to achievement in schools (Coleman, Campbell, Hobson, McPartland, Mood, Weinfeld, and York, 1966:314). Yet nonmachine cities spend much more on education. Nonmachine cities spend more on municipal services (see Table 2) with less citizen satisfaction with the quality of services rendered ($R = .39$). The greater spending on the part of nonmachine cities is as likely or more likely to be the consequence of interest group pressure that city hall cannot withstand, rather than a thrust toward quality in government. Other groups in the nonmachine city (including community control advocates), following the lead of municipal unions, press their case where there is a demonstrated likelihood of success. In both machine and nonmachine cities, many want a piece of the action. Where the machine does not exist, alternative forms of patronage will be sought to make up for the lack of a spoils system.

SUMMARY AND CONCLUSIONS

Political agendas in black communities (as in white communities) arise out of a mixture of fancy, moral concern, and material interests. As the objective conditions of blacks undergo change, interests change and the political agenda is reformulated to take into account the new conditions and interests. The black power movement emerged out of a discrepancy between hopes and reality. Community control as a political goal was a means of filling the gap. It was at least in part an expression of black self-interest, just as the opposition to it on the part of some teachers was an expression of their self-interest. The political forms of cities played a central role in determining the interests, and thus the political agendas, of the various constituencies in the city.

APPENDIX

Table A.1

Sources for Variables Used

Variable	Source
Blacks "favor black rule of black institutions (community control)"	Schuman and Gruenberg (1970)
Black "dissatisfaction with own housing and/or income"	Schuman and Gruenberg (1970)
Black median income	U.S. Bureau of the Census (1960)
White median Income	U.S. Bureau of the Census (1960)
Blacks "believe there is police abuse"	Schuman and Gruenberg (1970)
Blacks "have experienced police abuse"	Schuman and Gruenberg (1970)
Blacks "living in a racially mixed neighborhood"	Schuman and Gruenberg (1970)
Whites "living in a racially mixed neighborhood"	Schuman and Gruenberg (1970)
Expenditure on education per student enrolled	National Center for Educational Statistics (1967)
Service expenditure by city (per capita)	U.S. Bureau of the Census (1976)
Black "dissatisfaction with neighborhood services"	Schuman and Gruenberg (1970)

REFERENCES

Afro American Teachers Association (ATA)
    1970   Platform of A.T.A. Presented at the annual meeting of the ATA, November 1, 1980.
Banfield, E. C., and Wilson, J. Q.
    1963   *City Politics.* New York: Vintage Books.
Campbell, A., and Schuman, H.
    1968   *Racial Attitudes in Fifteen American Cities.* Washington, D.C.: U.S. Government Printing Office.
Campbell, L.
    1968   The devil can never educate us. *Forum* **November**:1.
Carmichael, S., and Hamilton, C. V.
    1967   *Black Power.* New York: Vintage Books.
Coleman, J. S., Campbell, C. Q., Hobson, C. J., McPartland, J., Mood, A. M., Weinfeld, F. D., and York, R. L.
    1966   *Equality of Educational Opportunity.* Washington, D.C.: U.S. Government Printing Office.

Goldberg, G. S.
    1966–1967   A Summary of the Controversy at I.S. 201. *IRCD Bulletin* **2**(5), **3**(1)
Greenstone, J. D., and Peterson, P. E.
    1968   Reformers, machines and the war on poverty, in *City Politics and Public Policy*
            (J. Q. Wilson, Ed.), pp. 267–292. New York: John Wiley & Sons.
Hamilton, C. V.
    1968   Race and education: a search for legitimacy. *Harvard Educational Review* **38**(4):669–
            684.
Lowi, T. J.
    1964   *At the Pleasure of the Mayor.* New York: The Free Press.
Marx, G.
    1967   *Protest and Prejudice.* New York: Harper and Row.
Morsell, J. A.
    1951   The political behavior of Negroes in New York City. Unpublished Ph.D. disser-
            tation, Department of Sociology Columbia University, New York.
National Center for Educational Statistics
    1967   *Statistics for Local School Systems—Finances 1967.* Washington, D.C.: U.S. De-
            partment of Health, Education, and Welfare.
Schuman, H., and Gruenberg, B.
    1970   The impact of city on racial attitudes. *American Journal of Sociology* **76**(2)213–
            261.
Vann, A.
    1968   Goals of A.T.A. *Forum* **November**:2.
Wilson, J. Q.
    1960   *Negro Politics.* New York: The Free Press.
U.S. Bureau of the Census
    1960   *U.S. Census of Population: 1960 Detailed Characteristics.* (Final Report PC (1) 6-
            D–53-D). Washington, D.C.: Government Printing Office.
    1967   *County and City Data Book, 1967* (A statistical abstract supplement). Washington,
            D.C.: Government Printing Office.

18

Israel as a Latent Plural Society

Ofira Seliktar
Lee E. Dutter

INTRODUCTION

Focusing explicitly on Israeli Jews, this paper examines the applicability
to Israel of some extant theoretic ideas about the nature of politics in
plural societies. Four theoretic frameworks are relevant to our discussion:
(1) the theory developed by Rabushka and Shepsle (1972), subsequently
referred to as the RS theory; (2) pluralist (PL) theory, developed and
applied by a number of scholars; (3) consociational democracy (CD)
theory, developed and applied by Lijphart (1969, 1975, 1977); and (4)
mobilization (MO) theory, modified and applied to Israel by Peleg and
Peleg (1977).

The RS Theory

Rabushka and Shepsle (1972) define a plural society as one which "is
culturally diverse and . . . its cultural sections are organized into cohesive
political sections [pp. 8–10, 21]." Their key assumption is that individuals'
political preferences are "well-defined," that is, citizens know what they
want out of the collective decision process. These preferences may concern matters such as the constitutional organization of the polity; the
form and operation of political and governmental institutions; political
parties or candidates; the status of economic and social groups within
the society; and/or specific issues of public policy.

301

The logical structure of these well-defined preferences is specified by three additional assumptions (Rabushka and Shepsle, 1972:66–74).

A.1 *intracommunal consensus*: the members of an ethnic community perceive and express preferences about political alternatives identically. Thus all members may be represented by identical "ethnic preference functions."

A.2 *intercommunal conflict*: communities are in disagreement on all issues that face the collectivity.

A.3 *perceptual consensus*: alternatives are viewed according to a perceptual frame common to all actors.

A.1 and A.2 are interpreted to mean that one community's preference ordering on political issues is the inverse of the other's. A.3 means that every individual knows the nature of the available political alternatives and the impact of each on his or her community.

In this context three subsidiary assumptions are made. First, the law of contradiction, which states that the adoption of one community's most preferred policies as the collective choices precludes adoption of the other's most preferred, is operative. Second, collective decisions are made through the mechanism of elections in which candidates and parties compete for votes. Third, and most important, ethnic preferences are intensely held. This goes beyond the simple assertion that each ethnic community cares a great deal about the realization of its goals. Intense preferences mean that individuals value their most preferred alternative greatly when it is compared to all others.[1]

Other, less crucial assumptions are that only one dimension (issue) of conflict is operative; the society is divided into only two ethnic groups; and group size is relevant to the pattern of politics. The RS theory then presents a paradigm of political behavior in the plural society (Rabushka and Shepsle, 1972:74–78). Its five "steps" are

(1) preindependence ethnic cooperation;
(2) postindependence ethnic cooperation: ambiguity;
(3) demand generation and the increased salience of ethnicity;
(4) outbidding and the decline of the multiethnic coalition; and
(5) electoral machinations and mistrust.

To illustrate how these steps play themselves out in the abstract, suppose we are examining a society that is culturally diverse and has passed through step (1), that is, colonial rule has ended, but ethnicity has not yet emerged as the salient political issue. Let us further suppose that the society has two distinct cultural groups, roughly equal in size, with intensely held, mutually exclusive policy preferences. The problem

[1] The mathematically inclined reader who desires a formal explanation of intense preferences should consult Rabushka and Shepsle (1972:43–55).

facing incumbent, "multiethnic" politicians is to adopt an electoral strategy that will attract sufficient votes to win elections. In this situation they would likely opt for a "strategy of ambiguity," subsumed under step (2) of the paradigm, on relevant issues. In fact, Rabushka and Shepsle (1972:62–92) have shown that, if a multiethnic candidate wishes to secure votes from both ethnic groups, thus maximizing his chances of election, he or she must adopt such a strategy.

Multiethnic candidates are not expected to go on winning elections indefinitely. Specifically, given that all candidates are free to adopt any issue positions, an ambiguous, multiethnic candidate can be outflanked at the extremes—a process subsumed under steps (3) and (4) of the paradigm. For instance, if in a subsequent election a candidate, who can be called a "political entrepreneur," adopts the policy alternatives that are the most preferred of one ethnic group, voters in that group vote for him or her. Thus, the ambiguous, multiethnic candidate loses votes in this group and likewise in the other, if a second entrepreneur adopts its most preferred alternatives. Gradually, the multiethnic candidate loses votes, and, depending on the strength of desire to remain in power, he or she may adopt extralegal means to do so, subsumed under step (5) of the paradigm. Similarly, if political entrepreneurs fail to achieve their goals legally, they and their followers may do the same. As a result, the initially "democratic" political system may lose the characteristics that allow its classification under that adjective.

The PL Theory

The PL theory can be summarized in three propositions regarded by students of pluralism as relevant to the survival of stable democracy: (1) plural societies pose grave obstacles to viable democratic government; (2) the existence of numerous secondary groups contributes to stable democracy by providing checks and balances against governmental authority and preventing the atomization of society; (3) cross-cutting affiliations make an additional contribution to stability by attenuating the salience of any one cleavage (Lijphart, 1975:1–15).

The CD Theory

Lijphart has noted that there are a few societies that ought to be subsumed under the first proposition of the PL theory but cannot be (e.g., the Netherlands). He resolved these apparent anomalies by formulating the CD theory (Lijphart, 1969, 1975, 1977). Its key explanatory element is the mode of behavior of political elites. These elites may promote ethnic conflict or make "deliberate efforts to counteract the immobilizing and unstabilizing effects of cultural fragmentation [Lijphart, 1969:212]."

The MO Theory

The MO theory, as modified and applied to Israel by Peleg and Peleg (1977), consists of a series of preconditions necessary for the appearance of ethnic politics: (1) identification, that is, the amount of ethnic political activity depends on the intensity of ethnic identification in a society; (2) issue relevance, that is, the amount of activity depends on the issues involved; (3) economic stratification, that is, disadvantaged ethnic groups must have made some economic gains in order to become politically active; (4) leadership, that is, ethnic leaders are crucial in the "ethnic mobilizatory process"; (5) reinforcement, that is, individuals in an ethnic group maintain loyalty to organizations that give them their initial success; (6) defense, that is, groups will go to great lengths to hold the power and status they possess; (7) demand, that is, if differences between groups persist, then the probability of "forceful ethnic mobilizatory politics" increases, and diversified ethnic demands and extremist leadership are more likely to emerge.

To recapitulate, the RS theory initially focuses on the "masses"—that is, a society's ethnic groups and group attitudes, beliefs, perceptions, and preferences. It then turns to elite behavior, the steps of the paradigm, and argues that that behavior will eventually reflect politically relevant ethnic divisions. On the other hand, the CD theory gives primary attention to elite behavior, which is assumed to be crucial in keeping the ethnic masses under control. However, it has been shown that the elite behavior aspects of the CD theory closely parallel the RS theory's paradigm (Dutter, 1978).

The PL theory deals with more general, thus less focused, aspects of politics in plural societies. Since the RS theory is basically a detailed elaboration of the first pluralist proposition, these propositions receive no additional, independent attention. By contrast, the MO theory contains elements of all three theories, but the overlap is such that it can also be included within the RS theory. Specifically, the identification, issue relevance, and economic preconditions parallel the RS theory's definitions and assumptions epitomized by A.1, A.2, and A.3. The leadership precondition corresponds to the RS theory's focus on the political entrepreneur. The reinforcement, defense, and demand preconditions parallel the steps of the RS theory's paradigm. Thus, it is not necessary to assess the applicability to Israel of each theory in turn. Instead, the RS theory serves as our operational framework.

ISRAEL AND THE RS THEORY: PREREQUISITES

The RS theory has two prerequisites that must be satisfied before it can be directly applied. First, the society must be culturally or ethnically diverse. Second, this diversity must be politically relevant. Regarding ethnic diversity, a number of scholars have documented ethnic cleavages among Israeli Jews. (See Alport, 1967; Bar-Yosef, 1970; Ben-David, 1970; Cohen, 1972; Dutter, 1977; Eisenstadt, 1967, 1968, 1970; Etzioni-Halevy and Shapira, 1977; Friendly, 1973; Iris and Shama, 1972; Katz and Zloczower, 1970; Peleg and Peleg, 1977; Peres 1971; Shumsky 1955; Shuval, 1963.) Discussion has typically focused on an Eastern–Western dichotomy. *Eastern* refers to Israelis born in or descended from Jews born in North Africa, Middle East, and Far East. They are sometimes called Oriental or Sephardic. *Western* refers to Israelis born in or descended from Jews born in Europe (including the USSR), North America, South America, and English-speaking countries. They are sometimes called Occidental or Ashkenazi.

However, until recently, relatively little attention has been paid to the potential and real political relevance of these divisions. The main reason for this neglect appears to have stemmed from the lack of significant ethnic political activity prior to 1971. Although minority lists have competed in most elections to the Knesset (parliament) and were occasionally successful in winning seats (e.g., the Sephardic party), they consistently disappeared (Arian, 1968). Furthermore, given the cooperative spirit mainfested by many post-1948 immigrants, some observers presumed that interethnic harmony would persist until these mostly Eastern arrivals were "absorbed" into Israel's dominant, Western-oriented culture (Ben-David, 1970:368).

These optimistic expectations were not warranted. Significant economic, political, and social differences between Eastern and Western Jews have persisted, and the former have generally fallen into disadvantaged categories. These differences did not originate through overt discrimination. Rather, they can be attributed to the lower educational and economic standards of Eastern immigrants (Friendly, 1973; Shuval, 1963:32). Their persistence can be partially explained by the slow response of the

Israeli government, both in recognizing the special problems of Easterners and implementing remedial policies.

Of greater importance, differences have been found between the Israeli-born of both groups (Katz and Zloczower, 1970:398; Weingrod, 1962), and the differences are clearly perceived. In a study of Israeli high school students, Peres (1971) found that many respondents of Western background displayed attitudes toward Easterners similar to those of race prejudice found in other countries. However, he also found that these attitudes were not reciprocated; nonetheless, many of Eastern background felt themselves to be victims of discrimination. Similarly, Yinon, Abend, and Chirer (1976) found attitudes of prejudice in a sample of adult Westerners. (See also Brichta, 1972; Etzioni-Halevy, 1975a, 1975b; Katz and Zloczower, 1970; Nachmias, 1973).

In summary, the first prerequisite for application of the RS theory is satisfied. Regarding its second, the theory draws attention to the importance of observed differences between a society's ethnic groups in political attitudes, beliefs, perceptions, and preferences. Despite the plethora of evidence on ethnic differences between Israeli Jews, little evidence, especially survey data, deals directly with these political matters. For instance, Burstein (1978:96) notes the lack of such data on the relationship between ethnicity and party choice. Our data consists of selected questions from the 1969 Israeli Election Study.[2] Since the data were not gathered with any particular theory of ethnic political activity in mind, two problems qualify our analysis.

First, the samples ($N = 380, 1314, 1825$) were not representative of the Israeli population at the time of the surveys. Although 25% of the samples were Easterners, 37% of the population could be so classified. In addition, Westerners (50% of the samples, 46% of the population) and Israeli-born (25% of the samples, 16% of the population) were overrepresented.[3] Furthermore, Israelis living in small towns and rural areas, those with low levels of education, and those lacking proficiency in the Hebrew language were also underrepresented. These factors magnified the underrepresentation of Easterners because many of them resided in disproportionate numbers outside Israel's principal urban areas and possessed low levels of education. The effect of this underrepresentation was to introduce some bias against finding statistically significant dif-

[2] The data utilized here were made available by the Inter-University Consortium for Political Research. The data for the "Israeli Elections Study-1969" were originally collected by Alan Arian, Michael Gurevitch, Emanuel Gutmann, and Louis Guttman. Neither the original collector of the data nor the Consortium bear any responsibility for the analysis or intrepretations presented here.

[3] *Statistical Abstract of Israel*, 1969 (Jerusalem: Central Bureau of Statistics), 42–43.

ferences between Easterners and Westerners, but not enough to invalidate our findings.

Second, we had to decide on the disposition of Israeli-born respondents. Although too large a proportion to delete, it was not immediately clear how their presence affected the survey results. For instance, after examining the same data, Arian (1973) found that the Israeli-born sometimes responded like Easterners, sometimes like Westerners, and sometimes in a pattern distinctly their own. Because this problem has not been conclusively resolved, it was decided to include the Israeli-born. They were assigned to the Eastern and Western categories depending upon father's place of birth. This is justified by the widely accepted propositions that there is a modicum of cultural continuity from generation to generation; that most Israeli families are patriarchal, that is, mixed parentage assignment followed father's origin; and that Israeli culture is Western oriented, that is, if the respondent's father was Israeli-born, then assignment was Western.[4] The division of the samples then became 30% Easterners and 70% Westerners, which, to some extent, redressed the original underrepresentation of the former.

Our first finding complements that of others on economic differences between Easterners and Westerners by use of the Elections Study's questions on education and income.[5] A multiple regression analysis, displayed in Table 1, was performed with income as the dependent and education and ethnic group as the independent variables.[6] These results clearly indicate that, after controlling for education, the income of an Easterner was significantly lower than that of a Westerner.

The first set of political questions concerned respondents' information and interest. These are displayed in Table 2. In question 2.a, a clear pattern is evident. Westerners read public opinion polls to a greater extent than Easterners; both rarely read polls to about the same extent; Easterners never read polls to a greater extent; and almost four times as

[4] Other assignments, including a "mixed" category of Israeli-born respondents of Israeli-born parents, were made and analyzed. However, these variations had a negligible impact on our statistical results.

[5] On economic differences, see Cohen (1972); Friendly (1973); Iris and Shama (1972); Nachmias and Rosenblum (1978); Peleg and Peleg (1977); Weingrod (1962b). The education question included eight categories ranging from 1 (respondent did not study at all) to 8 (respondent completed some higher education beyond the B.A.). The income question included nine categories ranging from 1 (respondent earned 0 to 199 lira per month) to 9 (respondent earned more than 1750 lira per month).

[6] Here and in subsequent tables, the N's vary from 1000 to 2000 depending on the questions and subsamples selected for analysis. Ethnic group is a dummy variable, which is 0 if the respondent is a Westerner and 1 if an Easterner.

Table 1

Regression of Income on Education and
Ethnic Group[a]

Independent variable	Coefficient
Education	.54
	(.03)
Ethnic group	− .27
	(.09)
Constant	2.68
R^2	.16

[a]The numbers in parentheses are the standard
errors of each regression coefficient.

many Easterners had never heard of polls. Question 2.*b* was asked only of those respondents who knew of polls. Here group differences are less and no pattern is evident. In 2.*c*, more Westerners expressed great interest in Knesset voting results; both groups indicated mild interest to about the same extent; and Easterners were more likely to express little or no interest. We would expect education to be related to political information and interest, and the regression results of Table 3, which treat the questions of Table 2 as ordinal variables, bear out this expectation. Specifically, the more educated a respondent, the more likely he or she was to know about polls and read their results, but Easterners less so. However, the pattern of 2.*c* disappears, that is, the more educted a respondent, the greater his or her interest in Knesset results regardless of ethnic group. Last, the nonpattern of 2.*b* is confirmed by the nonsignificant coefficients for education and ethnic group.

Related to information and interest is efficacy: Do individuals feel that they actually have an impact on politicians when public policy is made? Table 4 displays four such questions. A cursory examination reveals only small differences between groups, and the corresponding regression results (not reported) support this finding. These nonsignificant results can apparently be explained by the relatively stable pattern of Knesset voting results before the May 1977 elections. Namely, the major parties received roughly the same percentage of votes in each election, party leadership was stable with only small changes in ideological outlook, and each governing coalition had the same basic composition as its predecessor (Nachmias, 1974). Thus, voters might be likely to feel that their attitudes and behavior made little difference.

Table 2

Survey Questions on Political Information and Interest[a]

2.*a*. Do you usually read the results of public opinion polls
which appear in the newspapers?

Ethnic group	Often	Rarely	Never	Does not know of existence of polls
Western	42	31	23	4
Eastern	27	27	31	15

2.*b*. In your opinion, can you believe these polls?

Ethnic group	Yes, always	In general, yes	No answer	In general, no	Never
Western	14	62	2	16	6
Eastern	17	57	2	15	9

2.*c*. To what extent are you interested in the Knesset voting results?

Ethnic group	Very interested	Interested	Irrelevant	Not so interested	Not at all
Western	37	43	0	13	6
Eastern	25	42	0	18	14

[a]Table is read horizontally. Numbers are percentages of each group giving that response. Each row totals 100%.

Next, we examined respondents' attitudes on important political issues. Table 5 displays these questions and some clear patterns emerge.
For instance, in 5.*b* Easterners reported themselves to be more "religious"
than Westerners and the latter more secular. In 5.*c*, more Easterners
endorsed government intervention in religious affairs, whereas more
Westerners were opposed to this idea. In 5.*e*, more Easterners than
Westerners endorsed an "aggressive" policy toward the Arabs. These
patterns are clarified by the regression results of Table 6, and ethnic
group is significant in five of nine equations. Thus, we can conclude that
Easterners to a significantly greater extent than Westerners (1) observed
religious traditions, (2) endorsed government intervention in religious
affairs, and (3) supported adoption of "aggressive" policies toward the
Arabs.

Regarding political participation, Table 7 displays questions on Knesset voting behavior in 1965 and 1969. To simplify the presentation, we
focus only on undecideds, abstainers, and supporters of major parties.
In 7.*a* and 7.*b*, roughly equal percentages of both groups supported one

Table 3

Regression of Questions Concerning Political Information and
Interest on Education and Ethnic Group

Independent variable	Dependent variable		
	2.a	2.b	2.c
Education	.15	.03*	.19
	(.02)	(.02)	(.03)
Ethnic Group	− .19	− .03*	− .10*
	(.06)	(.06)	(.08)
Constant	2.68	1.50	1.87
R^2	.04	.01	.06

*Not significant at the .05 level.

of the religious parties, did not vote in 1965, did not plan or had not decided to vote in 1969, or did not answer the questions. However, more Easterners than Westerners indicated support for Gahal, the forerunner of Likud; fewer supported the Alignment, but the differences were not statistically significant. By contrast, using some later survey data, Burstein (1978) found significant differences.

Questions 7.c and 7.d probed the reasons behind a respondents' 1969 voting decision. In 7.c, no clear pattern is manifest, but in 7.d a pattern does emerge. Westerners placed greater emphasis on identification with a party and its stand on issues. On the other hand, Easterners gave greater emphasis to a party's position in government or opposition and identification with its candidate(s) and were twice as likely to say that none of the listed factors was important. Thus, in the sense of identification with a specific party and its stand on issues, Westerners were more "ideological" and Easterners more "pragmatic" in their rationales for voting.

Another dimension of voting involves the relationship between participation in Knesset and local elections. Local elections in Israel are, in many ways, extensions of national politics. The same parties operate at both levels, electoral ground rules are similar, and coalition politics is practiced. Regarding voters, Arian and Weiss (1969) noted that interest and turnout in these local elections has been as high as in Knesset elections. The reasons are that the same parties compete; often local issues appear and heighten interest; and, prior to 1977, both elections were held on the same day.

In analyzing voting patterns, several authors have found a significant amount of "split-ticket" voting, that is, individuals who voted for one

Table 4

Survey Questions on Political Efficacy[a]

4.a. In your opinion, to what extent do these (public opinion) polls influence *the voting public?*

Ethnic group	Have great influence	Have some influence	Have little influence	No answer	Have no influence
Western	9	36	28	4	23
Eastern	13	33	25	4	25

4.b. In your opinion, to what extent do these polls influence *the politicians?*

Ethnic group	Have great influence	Have some influence	Have little influence	No answer	Have no influence
Western	26	29	19	6	20
Eastern	26	26	19	8	21

4.c. What are the chances that the party you plan to vote for will be influential and important in the next Knesset?

	Very great chance	Great chance	Mediocre chance	Small chance	No answer	No chance at all
Western	34	35	19	7	5	1
Eastern	31	38	21	5	4	1

4.d. Some people say that elections do not actually affect policy. What's your opinion?

	Absolutely agree	Agree	No answer	Have reservations	Absolutely disagree
Western	15	23	2	31	30
Eastern	17	21	5	27	30

[a]Table is read horizontally. Numbers are percentages of each group giving that response. Each row totals 100%.

Table 5

Survey Questions on Political, Security, and Social Issues[a]

5.a. Some people say that a few strong leaders could be more useful for the State than all the debates and laws. Do you agree with this opinion?

Ethnic group	Absolutely agree	Agree to some extent	No answer	Have reservations	Absolutely disagree
Western	35	27	3	18	18
Eastern	40	24	5	15	16

5.b. Do you usually observe the religious tradition?

Ethnic group	Yes, absolutely, in detail	To a great extent	Observe a little	Don't observe it at all
Western	10	10	47	33
Eastern	15	20	50	15

5.c. In your opinion, should the government see to it that public life is conducted according to the Jewish religious tradition?

Ethnic group	Absolutely	Perhaps	No answer	Perhaps not	Absolutely not
Western	20	14	1	14	51
Eastern	34	18	1	14	34

5.*d*. Concerning the economic structure of the country—do you support the socialist approach or the capitalist approach?

Ethnic group	Absolutely capitalist	More capitalist than socialist	No answer	More socialist than capitalist	Absolutely socialist
Western	7	27	7	43	17
Eastern	10	18	17	31	25

5.*e*. To what extent would you support an aggressive policy towards the Arab states?

Ethnic group	To a great extent	To a certain extent	No answer	Do not support	Absolutely not
Western	32	35	3	18	12
Eastern	53	27	2	11	7

5.*f*. With what political trend do you identify?

Ethnic group	Left	Moderate left	Center	Right–Religious
Western	5	23	49	23
Eastern	6	13	55	26

5.*g*. If you were asked to use one of the following terms to indicate your social position, would you say that it is

Ethnic group	Upper	Upper middle	Middle	Lower middle	Worker
Western	2	10	75	4	9
Eastern	2	5	73	10	11

[a]Table is read horizontally. Numbers are percentages of each group giving that response. Each row totals 100%.

Table 6

Regression of Questions Concerning Political, Security, and
Social Issues on Education and Ethnic Group

Independent variable	Dependent variable								
	5.a	5.b	5.c	5.c	5.d	5.e	5.e	5.f	5.g
5.f	− .04*	—	− .10	− .11	− .14	− .10	− .13	—	—
	(.04)		(.03)	(.03)	(.02)	(.03)	(.03)		
5.b	.03*	—	.90	.99	.06	.07	—	− .24	—
	(.04)		(.03)	(.04)	(.03)	(.03)		(.02)	
5.g	− .11	—	.05*	—	.12	.03*	—	− .08	—
	(.03)		(.03)		(.03)	(.03)		(.02)	
Education	− .13	− .05	− .09	− .09	− .05	− .11	− .12	.05	− .11
	(.03)	(.02)	(.02)	(.03)	(.02)	(.02)	(.02)	(.02)	(.02)
Income	.01*	− .08	.03*	.03*	.05	− .01*	—	.03	.07
	(.02)	(.01)	(.02)	(.02)	(.01)	(.02)		(.01)	(.01)
Ethnic group	− .03*	.22	.14	.15	− .01*	.40	.45	− .07*	− .05*
	(.08)	(.05)	(.07)	(.07)	(.06)	(.07)	(.07)	(.05)	(.05)
Constant	.68	2.38	− .55	− .61	2.80	1.02	1.25	3.80	3.11
R^2	.02	.07	.32	.35	.05	.05	.06	.05	.05

*Not significant at the .05 level.

party at the national level and a different one at the local. Three correlates of such behavior have been identified. First, whenever the local Mapai organization was unstable or ineffective, split-ticket voting was more likely to occur (Arian and Weiss, 1969). Second, ticket splitting was more likely in communities that had experienced the emergence of a popular, charismatic ethnic leader or local, usually ethnic, issues (Arian and Weiss, 1969:379), and Deshen (1972:288) notes the importance of ethnic appeals in local election campaigns. Third, the less populous a community, the greater the incidence of split-ticket voting (Arian, 1973:188; Torgovnik and Weiss, 1972:310).

Table 8 contains questions of split-ticket voting. Table 9, derived from Tables 7 and 8, delineates ethnic differences. Ignoring nonresponses, fewer Easterners than Westerners indicated that their votes were identical in 1965. In 1969 this gap shrank. Regarding ticket-splitters, slightly more Easterners indicated that they would do so in 1965, and in 1969 this gap grew.

Table 7

Survey Questions on Voting and Voting Rationales[a]

7.a. What party did you vote for, for the Knesset, in 1965?

Ethnic group	Did not vote, no answer	Alignment: Labor Ahdut Haavodah	Gahal	Religious party
Western	30	50	11	9
Eastern	34	44	16	6

7.b. Do you plan to vote in the Knesset elections of this next election (1969)?

Ethnic group	Have not decided, will not vote, no answer	Alignment: Labor–Mapam	Gahal	Religious party
Western	27	52	11	10
Eastern	27	48	17	8

7.c. Among the following factors, does any one stand out as the most important one in determining your vote for the Knesset? Identification with the party (including: habit or emotional and historical ties of the person with the party); the party's candidate; the party's stand on various issues; the party's position in the government or in the opposition.

Ethnic group	None of the factors is important	One factor is somewhat more important	One factor is much more important	All the factors are equally important
Western	6	20	53	21
Eastern	13	19	45	23

7.d. Which is the most important factor, in your opinion?

Ethnic group	Identification with party	Party's position in government or opposition	Party's candidate	Party's stand on issues	None of factors is important
Western	21	9	19	44	7
Eastern	16	14	26	30	14

[a]Table is read horizontally. Numbers are percentages of each group giving that response. Each row totals 100%.

Table 8

Survey Questions on Voting in National and Local Elections[a]

8.a. What party did you vote for, for the municipality in 1965?

Ethnic group	Did not vote, no answer	Alignment: Labor–Ahdut Haavodah	Gahal	Religious party
Western	34	45	12	9
Eastern	43	37	13	7

8.b. Which party will you vote for in the municipal election (1969)?

Ethnic group	Have not decided will not vote, no answer	Alignment: Labor–Mapam	Gahal	Religious party
Western	36	43	12	10
Eastern	37	39	17	8

8.c. Do you plan to vote for the same party for the Knesset and the municipality (1969)?

Ethnic group	Will vote same in both	Will vote different	Have not decided on vote in one or other	Won't vote in local	Won't vote in Knesset
Western	59	17	16	6	2
Eastern	55	19	14	9	4

8.d. Among the following factors is any one the most important in determining your vote for the muicipality? Identification with the party; the party's candidate; the party's stand on various issues; the party's position in the government or in the opposition.

Ethnic group	None of the factors is important	One factor is somewhat more important	One factor is much more important	All factors are equally important
Western	10	21	51	18
Eastern	17	17	45	21

8.e Which is the most important factor, in your opinion?

Ethnic group	Identification with party	Party's position in government or opposition	Party's candidate	Party's stand on issues	None of factors is important
Western	16	6	35	33	11
Eastern	14	9	34	24	19

[a]Table is read horizontally. Numbers are percentages of each group giving that response. Each row totals 100%.

Table 9

Split-Ticket Voting in 1965 and 1969

Ethnic group	Same vote	Split ticket	No answer in one or other	No answer in both
			1965	
Western	59.9	4.3	6.7	28.6
Eastern	49.6	6.3	10.3	33.6
			1969	
Western	55.8	4.6	15.5	23.6
Eastern	52.8	9.1	12.8	25.3

On rationales for local voting, the pattern of 8.*d* is similar to that of 7.*c*. In 8.*e* we observe three interesting results. First, fewer Easterners than Westerners cited a party's stands on issues as an important factor, complementing 7.*d*. Second, also complementing 7.*d*, more Easterners cited none of the factors as important. Third, both groups cited a party's candidate at roughly the same frequency; that is a notable difference from 7.*d*, which suggests that the emergence of local ethnic leaders has been relevant to voting in both groups.

Another dimension of participation is membership in political organizations. Table 10 gives the ethnic breakdown of Histadrut, the Israeli labor federation, and party membership. Easterners were slightly more likely than Westerners to belong to the Histadrut (10.*a*). On the other hand, in 10.*b*, official membership and performing some official function in a political party were roughly equivalent activities for both groups, but Easterners were less likely to support any one political party. This complements our earlier finding from Tables 7 and 8 that Easterners were more pragmatic in their voting decisions, that is, less attached than Westerners to a single party. (See also Brichta, 1972; Etzioni-Halevy, 1975a, 1975b; Nachmias, 1973).

ISRAEL AND THE RS THEORY: ELITE BEHAVIOR

We have uncovered evidence that, at the mass level, Israel largely satisfies the prerequisites of the RS theory. However, Israel diverges from the theory's predictions in the sense that its divisions have led to relatively

Table 10

Survey Questions on Membership in Political Organizations[a]

10.a. Are you a member of the Histadrut?

Ethnic group	Yes	No
Western	63	37
Eastern	69	31

10.b. Do you support any party, or are you a member or an official in a party?

	Member and salaried official	Member and unsalaried official	Member, holds no office	Supporter	Does not support any one party
Western	1	4	15	40	40
Eastern	1	3	11	35	50

[a]Table is read horizontally. Numbers are percentages of each group giving that response. Each row totals 100%.

little ethnic conflict. For instance, the appearance in 1971 of the Israeli Black Panthers, a loosely knit protest organization of young Moroccan Jews, which engaged in demonstrations and occasional violence, was short-lived (Cohen, 1972; Etzioni-Halevy, 1975a, 1975b; Iris and Shama, 1972). This disparity between Israel's potential and the limited scope of such conflict thus far can best be understood in the context of the RS theory's paradigm.

Step (1) of the paradigm is "preindependence ethnic cooperation." As formulated, it is of little relevance to relationships among Israeli Jews after 1948. However, if "overt, external threat to the physical survival of the nation and its inhabitants" is substituted for "preindependence," it can be reformulated as "external threat to physical survival: ethnic cooperation" and becomes applicable.

Though not fully articulated, the theoretical and empirical relevance of external threats to the mitigation of domestic ethnic conflict in plural societies has been noted. Rabushka and Shepsle observed that "the force of exogenous events may affect ethnic politics in unpredictable ways . . . grave economic crises, *external aggression* [italics added], or natural catastrophies may, at times, alter the course of politics in plural societies [1972:92]." Lijphart (1969:217) also emphasized the role of the external threat factor. "In all cases [examined], the external threats impressed on the elites the need for internal unity and cooperation. *External threats can also strengthen the ties among the subcultures at the mass level and the ties between leaders and followers within the subcultures* [italics added]."

In a later work, Lijphart (1975:66–70) argued that the potential threat posed by Germany during World War I was a contributing factor in establishment of the "politics of accommodation" by the elites of Holland's three cultural–ideological groups. Nordlinger (1972:61) pointed out the relevance of external threats to the formation and preservation of the Swiss Confederation. Esman (1977:376) found a relationship between the Soviet threat to Western Europe and the frequency and intensity of ethnic political activity in some of those nations.

Regarding Israel, a few authors have noted the relevance of the perceived and real threats to its survival posed by its Arab neighbors to the mitigation of all internal political dissension (Alport, 1967; Amir, Sharan, Ben-Ari, Bizman, and Ribner, 1978; Beit-Hallahmi, 1972; Etzioni-Halevy, 1975a; Etzioni-Halevy and Shapira, 1977; Iris and Shama, 1972; Nachmias, 1973; Peres, 1971; Peretz, 1974). That the national security issue is uppermost in Israeli thinking is often illustrated by the statements, not to mention actions, of Israeli political leaders. Because Easterners, the potentially dissident group, have been more "hawkish" than Westerners toward the Arabs, such statements have been singularly effective in defusing ethnic conflict.

This discussion implies that the magnitude of the threat is related to internal cohesion—that is, the greater the perceived or real threat, the greater the solidarity within and between a society's ethnic groups. Although we do not directly test this proposition, Etzioni-Halevy and Shapira (1977:179–204) have found evidence that tends to support it in the Israeli case. On the question of how a declining threat may "stimulate" ethnic conflict, we suggest that it is not coincidental that Israel's worst ethnic disturbances and tensions have occurred during periods of relative external peace. For instance, Etzioni-Halevy and Shapira (1977:189) found a noticeable drop in group solidarity between 1970 and 1973, one such period.

Continuing in the paradigm, it is implicitly assumed that a plural society "evolves" through subsequent steps. In other words, although there will be some overlap between steps, they are intended to describe a relatively straightforward temporal process. However, given our reformulation of step (1), this is no longer the case. Because an external threat may continue indefinitely and vary in severity, its impact on ethnic politics can result in greater overlap between steps and the simultaneous appearance of events originally classified under separate steps.

Step (2) is "postindependence ethnic cooperation: ambiguity." Reformulation is again necessary, and we make three changes. First, "post or varying external threat" is substituted for "postindependence." Second, "ethnic cooperation" is reinterpreted as "elite cooperation" in the CD theory sense of the term. Third, "conflict management" is substituted for "ambiguity." Thus, step (2) now reads "post of varying external threat: elite cooperation, conflict management" and has direct relevance to Israeli politics.

Elite cooperation has manifested itself in two principal ways. One has been the building of a modern, industrial state, which, it was presumed, would benefit all Israelis and eventually close the economic and social gaps. However, although the standard of living has improved in both groups, the relative disparity has changed little. Second has been the handling of the Arab threat. Ironically, this threat, although promoting ethnic cohesion, has absorbed resources that could have been devoted to improving the lot of Easterners. Thus, there has developed a phenomenon of *latent ethnicity*, that is, a situation in which unsatisfied ethnic grievances are sublimated to other concerns.

In the management of ethnic conflict Israeli leaders have been aided by background characteristics of Israeli society, and they have employed specific techniques. Among background characteristics four stand out. First is the ideological factor: the strong commitment to Zionism and the high degree of national identification among most Israelis, regardless fo their origins. Alport (1967:158) summarized well the relevance of this factor by emphasizing that Jewish nationalism is the "most powerful unifying force . . . [which goes] beyond the multitude of local differences." That this is indeed the case has been established in a number of empirical studies (e.g., Etzioni-Halevy and Shapira, 1977).

Second is the practical factor: Israel as a refuge for Jews. Although important to both groups, it was especially so to Easterners. To many of them, residence in Israel presented an opportunity to worship without hindrance and to advance economically without hostility from the host society. Moreover, as the Arab–Israeli conflict escalated after 1948, threatening the physical security of Jews residing in Arab countries, Israel became their only refuge (Friendly, 1973:7; Iris and Shama, 1972:39: Nachmias, 1973;457–458).

Third is the symbolic rewards factor, especially symbolic representation. For instance, Czudnowski (1970, 1972) found ethnicity to be an important variable in legislative and leadership recruitment within Israel parties. However, Eastern Jews have been proportionally underrepresented, and even those who hold top positions have often been relegated to secondary roles. In an examination of the Seventh Knesset, Brichta (1972) found that the Afro–Asian born, who accounted for 28% of the population, constituted only 12% of the membership. In addition, he labeled several Afro–Asian members "pseudo-representatives" because their presence appeared to be aimed at "appeasing" and attracting ethnic voters, rather than "genuine" representation of those voters' interests. Complementing Brichta, Nachmias (1973) found that leaders of the Israeli Moroccan community felt underrepresented in decision-making circles. More recently, Nachmias and Rosenblum (1978) found that, except for the lower ranks, Afro–Asians are proportionally underrepresented in the national bureaucracy.

Fourth is the split-ticket factor. As noted, split-ticket voting is quite widespread and related to ethnicity. In our view, ticket-splitting has served as a "safety-valve" for ethnic tensions. It allows Easterners to voice ethnic issues and/or support ethnic candidates at the local level without carrying these divisions to the national arena.

When open protest has developed (e.g., Black Panthers, the 1979 antiinflation demonstrations), specific conflict-management techniques have been employed. These have included: (1) restraint in suppressing protest activities, even if illegality is involved; (2) issuing public statements assuring the aggrieved parties of the sympathy, understanding, or commitment of the authorities to the problems raised; (3) promising extended funds for the solution of problems; (4) taking measures, such as the establishment of investigative committees, to postpone actual confrontation with the problem(s); (5) decreasing activists' involvement in the protest, for example, by their cooptation into the political establishment and/or granting personal benefits; (6) selectively satisfying some of the aggrieved parties' demands (Etzioni-Halevy, 1975a:305–308). However, the recurrence of ethnic lists in Knesset elections and occasional protest demonstrations indicate that these techniques and factors have their limitations.[7] This leads to step (3).

Step (3) is "demand generation and the increased salience of ethnicity," which means that political entrepreneurs are likely to appear and base their political appeals on issues related to ethnic cleavages. Eventually, "ethnicity" dominates political discourse. In Israel no such politicians have, as yet, become firmly entrenched. In other words, although Israel displays developments subsumed under earlier steps, it has only the potential for the appearance of those under (3). Namely, ethnicity is salient in local elections and is increasingly important in national politics (Burstein, 1979; Peleg and Peleg, 1977). Thus, although the theory indicates that these are preconditions for the appearance of political entrepreneurs and ethnic parties, the external threat may again interfere with the steady progression of this process.

---

[7] On the varying effectiveness, see Etzioni-Halevy (1975a:292); Friendly (1973:3–5); Iris and Shama (1972:39); Nachmias (1973:457–458).

Step (4) is "outbidding and decline of the multiethnic coalition." "Outbidding" means that the political entrepreneurs are eventually successful in winning significant electoral support and polarizing a society along ethnic lines. "Decline of the multiethnic coalition" means that multiethnic candidates and parties experience a gradual loss of electoral support and consequently their power base. As with (3), step (4) has some, though limited, applicability to present Israeli politics. Specifically, developments subsumed under (4) are a major part of what Peleg and Peleg (1977) call the "ethnic mobilizatory process," which has begun in Israel.

Step (5) is "electoral machinations and mistrust." This means that, upon seeing their electoral support and power base erode, multiethnic candidates and parties will likely use extralegal means to check that erosion and remain in power. These means vary from the gerrymandering of electoral districts and tampering with voting registers or election returns to assassinations and coup d'etats. If political entrepreneurs and ethnic parties respond in kind, the society may quickly lose its democratic characteristics and, in extremis, degenerate into civil war. Of course, events such as these have not occurred in Israel, and, although we cannot unequivocally rule them out, they appear highly unlikely to occur in the foreseeable future.

However, if a less stringent interpretation of (5) is adopted, that is, less severe forms of ethnically related disruptions than those originally predicted, then the step is applicable. For instance, ethnic tensions reached an unprecedented level in the June 1981 Knesset elections campaign, during which Oriental supporters of the incumbent Likud coalition engaged in acts of verbal and physical violence against the "Ashkenazi" Labor party. Thus, depending principally upon the course of the Arab–Israeli conflict, we expect a growth of ethnic politics but not an immediate erosion of latency.

CONCLUSION

The thirty-five-year-old Arab–Israeli conflict has thus far generated sufficient consensus among Israeli Jews to prevent a serious breach between the Eastern and Western groups. As long as this conflict persists, Jewish ethnic divisions are likely to remain latent and Israel will continue to be a latent plural society. Thus, the most important contribution of this study is the development, within the RS theory, of the concept of *latent ethnicity*. This concept helps explain why Israeli society has not experienced worse consequences of its ethnic divisions.

One important question remains: What effects may the Middle East peace process have on Israel's latent ethnicity and future ethnic politics? The Egyptian–Israeli peace treaty raises the possibility that Israel and its Arab neighbors may move in stages toward a comprehensive peace settlement. If peace were established, it is reasonable to assume that the perceived and real external threat to Israel's survival would significantly decline, if not disappear. This decline would result in greater political salience of all domestic issues, especially the ethnic one. In the latter case, it is likely that economic issues would provide a focus for dissension. Such dissension would likely be aggravated, at least in the short run, by the lack of an measurable "peace dividend," which could be devoted to raising Easterners' standard of living. On the other hand, it is, of course, possible to argue that the underlying national consensus would persist and prevent the society from fully evolving into what Bar-Yosef (1970:428) described as a "forum of struggling national minorities; with no political vision other than the preservation and fostering of their own ethnic interests."

REFERENCES

Alport, A.
    1967   The integration of Oriental Jews into Israel. *World Today* **23**:153–159.
Amir, Y., Sharan, S., Ben-Ari, R., Bizman, A., and Ribner, M.
    1978   Asymmetry, academic status, differentiation, and the ethnic perceptions and preferences of Israeli youth. *Human Relations* **31**:99–116.
Arian, A.
    1968   *Ideological Change in Israel*. Cleveland: Case Western Reserve University Press.
    1973   *The Choosing People, Voting Behavior in Israel*. Cleveland: Case Western Reserve University Press.
Arian, A., and Weiss, S.
    1969   Split-ticket voting in Israel. *Western Political Quarterly* **22**:375–389.
Bar-Yosef, R.
    1970   The Moroccans—background to the problem, in *Integration and Development in Israel* (S. N. Eisenstadt, R. Bar-Yosef, and C. Adler, Eds.) pp. 419–428. New York: Praeger.
Beit-Hallahmi, B.
    1972   Some psychological and cultural factors in the Arab–Israeli conflict: a review of the literature. *Journal of Conflict Resolution* **16**:269–280.
Ben-David, J.
    1970   Ethnic differences or social change, in *Integration and Development in Israel* (S. N. Eisenstadt, R. Bar-Yosef, and C. Adler, Eds.), pp. 368–387. New York: Praeger.
Brichta, A.
    1972   The social and political characteristics of members of the seventh Knesset in *The Elections in Israel–1969* (A. Arian, Ed.), pp. 109–131. Jerusalem: Jerusalem Academic Press.

Burstein, P.
   1978   Social cleavages and party choice in Israel: a log-linear analysis. *American Political Science Review* **72**:96–109.
Cohen, E.
   1972   The Black Panthers and Israeli society. *Jewish Journal of Sociology* **14**:93–109.
Czudnowski, M.
   1970   Legislative recruitment under proportional representation in Israel: a model and a case study. *Midwest Journal of Political Science* **14**:216–248.
   1972   Sociocultural variables and legislative recruitment. *Comparative Politics* **4**:561–587.
Deshen, S. A.
   1972   "The business of ethnicity is finished!"? The ethnic factor in a local election campaign, in *The Elections in Israel—1969* (A. Arian Ed.), pp. 278–302. Jerusalem: Jerusalem Academic Press.
Dutter, L. E.
   1977   Eastern and Western Jews: ethnic divisions in Israeli society. *Middle East Journal* **31**:451–468.
   1978   The Netherlands as a plural society. *Comparative Political Studies* **10**(4):555–588.
Eisenstadt, S. N.
   1967   *Israeli Society.* New York: Basic Books.
   1968   Israeli society—major features and problems. *Journal of World History* **11**:313–328.
   1970   The process of absorption of new immigrants in Israel, in *Integration and Development in Israel* (S. N. Eisenstadt, R. Bar-Yosef, and C. Adler, Eds) pp. 341–367. New York: Praeger.
Esman, M. J.
   1977   Perspectives on ethnic conflict in industrialized societies, in *Ethnic Conflict in the Western World.* (M. J. Esman Ed.), pp. 371–390. Ithaca N.Y.: Cornell University Press.
Etzioni-Halevy, E.
   1975a   Patterns of conflict generation and conflict absorption: the cases of Israeli labor and ethnic conflicts. *Journal of Conflict Resolution* **19**:286–309.
   1975b   Protest politics in the Israeli democracy. *Political Science Quarterly* **90**:497–420.
Etzoini-Halevy, E., and Shapira, R.
   1977   *Political Culture in Israel, Cleavage and Integration among Israeli Jews.* New York: Praeger.
Friendly, A.
   1973   *Israel's Oriental Immigrants and Druzes.* London: Minority Rights Group.
Iris, M., and Shama, A.
   1972   Black Panthers: the movement. *Society* **9**:37–44.
Katz, E., and Zloczower, A.
   1970   Ethnic continuity in an Israeli town: relations with parents, in *Integration and Development in Israel* (S. N. Eisenstadt, R. Bar-Yosef, and C. Adler, Eds.), pp. 397–418. New York: Praeger.
Lijphart, A.
   1969   Consociational democracy. *World Politics* **21**:207–225.
   1975   *The Politics and Accommodation: Pluralism and Democracy in the Netherlands.* Berkeley: University of California Press.
   1977   *Democracy in Plural Societies, A Comparative Exploration.* New Haven: Yale University Press.

Nachmias, D.
   1973   Status inconsistency and political opposition: a case study of an Israeli minority
           group. *Middle East Journal* **27**:456–470.
   1974   Coalition politics in Israel. *Comparative Political Studies* **7**:316–333.
Nachmias, D., and Rosenbloom, D. H.
   1978   Bureaucracy and ethnicity. *American Journal of Sociology* **83**:967–974.
Nordlinger, E. A.
   1972   *Conflict Regulation in Divided Societies.* Cambridge: Center of International Af-
           fairs, Harvard University.
Peleg, I., and Peleg, S.
   1977   The ethnic factor in politics: the mobilization model and the case of Israel.
           Ethnicity **4**(2):177–187.
Peres, Y.
   1971   Ethnic relations in Israel. *American Journal of Sociology* **76**:1021–1047.
Peretz, D.
   1974   The war election and Israel's eighth Knesset. *Middle East Journal* **28**:111–125.
Rabushka, A., and Shepsle, K. A.
   1972   *Politics in Plural Societies, A Theory of Democratic Instability.* Columbus, Ohio:
           Charles E. Merrill.
Shumsky, A.
   1955   *The Clash of Cultures in Israel.* Westport, Conn.: Greenwood Press.
Shuval, J. T.
   1963   *Immigrants on the Threshold.* New York: Atherton Press.
Torgovnik, E., and Weiss, S.
   1972   Local non-party political organizations in Israel. *Western Political Quarterly*
           25:305–322.
Weingrod, A.
   1962a   Reciprocal change: a case study of a Moroccan immigrant village in Israel.
           American Anthropologist **64**:115–131.
   1962b   Two Israels. *Commentary* **April**:313–319.
Yinon, Y., Abend, A., and Chirer, A.
   1976   Prejudice towards Israelis of Oriental origin among Israelis of Western origin.
           Journal of Social Psychology **99**:171–178.

19

The Jewish Identity of Soviet Immigrant Parents and Children

Rita J. Simon

INTRODUCTION

Between 1966 and 1975 some 125,000 Jews emigrated from the Soviet Union. About 111,000 of them settled in Israel, about 11,000 came to the United States, and practically all of the others immigrated to Canada, Australia, and New Zealand (Edelman, 1977:157). From 1975 on, an increasing number of Soviet Jews opted to come to the United States rather than settle in Israel. Whereas earlier in the decade over 75% went directly from Vienna to Israel, since 1975, Leimsidor, of the Hebrew Immigrant Aid Society (HIAS) estimates that 65% have immigrated to the United States, Canada, Australia, and New Zealand. The remaining 35% have gone to Israel. Of the 65% opting for resettlement in countries other than Israel, approximately 85% have chosen to come to the United States. Since 1975 about 90,000 Soviet Jews immigrated to the United States. Over 50,000 arrived in 1978 and 1979 (Leimsidor, 1980:35–36).

In the following paragraphs, Leimsidor describes the complicated, expensive, and often painful procedures that the Soviet Jews must undergo in order to gain an exit visa.

They must ask permission to leave from parents and employers, which generally results in being fired and some times in denunciations at public meetings. Frequently pressure is placed upon other family members who have not applied for exits. The potential refugee also must prove that he or she has no outstanding debts, and in many cities this proof entails getting written statements from all retail establishments in the city. The individual must take these risks without any assurance that he or she will, in fact, be permitted to

327

CULTURE, ETHNICITY, AND IDENTITY

leave. After permission is given to leave for family reunion in Israel, the refugee must renounce Soviet citizenship, a process which is expensive and cuts off any possibility of return.

Practically the only way that a Jew can leave the Soviet Union is by claiming desire for reunion with family in Israel. The ability of the refugees to exercise the option of going to countries other than Israel is a result of the strong position taken by the American Government and the Jewish community that refugees fleeing from oppression must have the freedom to immigrate to any country which is open to them [1980:35].

Once the Soviet Jews have arrived in the United States, the costs of resettling them have been borne largely by the American Jewish community.[1] One of the motivating forces in the American Jewish community's commitment to resettle the Soviet Jews is its hope that they will develop a strong Jewish identity and participate actively in American Jewish communal life.

This article discusses the response of 200 Soviet Jews living in Chicago to a series of questions about their Jewish identity and practices. The information has been culled from a larger study of recent refugees and immigrants that was prepared for the Select Commission on Immigration and Refugee Policy (Simon, 1980). The major thrust of the larger study was to understand how the Soviet, Vietnamese, and Mexican familes who arrived in the United States between 1975 and 1980 were adjusting to their new lives. They survey focused on the expectations and aspirations that the parents had for their children and the plans and hopes that the children had about their own futures. It asked the parents about their economic situation and about their expectations concerning the kind of life they hoped to live in their new environment. In addition, the Soviet questionnaire contained a series of items about the respondents' Jewish identity and their observances of Jewish practices. The design called for interviews with 50 mothers and 50 adolescent daughters between the ages of 15 and 20 in the same families, and 50 fathers and 50 adolescent sons in the same families. All of the respondents were located in Chicago.[2]

Before discussing the responses to the items about Jewish identity and practices, I shall provide a brief profile describing some of the respondents' demographic and social–psychological characteristics.

---

[1] With the passage of the Refugees Act of 1980 the United States government acknowledged its responsibility for assisting "state and local communities and voluntary agencies in resettling refugees by authorizing generous and flexible federal support for domestic resettlement programs [Kennedy, 1980:5–6]."

[2] We obtained our sample frame of refugee families from the consortium of agencies in Chicago that helped to settle them. Everyone who participated in the survey did so voluntarily and with the assurance that anonymity would be maintained. The interviewers spoke Russian; some were themselves refugees who had arrived earlier, some were not.

Table 1

Parents' Occupation in Soviet Union

Occupation in the Soviet Union	Father (%)	Mother (%)
Engineer	48	36
Other professions (architect, doctor, dentist)	11	18
Teacher	7	6
Technician or skilled worker	20	22
Clerical	—	10
Laborer	7	—
Housewife	—	4
Retired	7	4

COLLECTIVE PROFILE

The Soviet parents are well educated and technically skilled. Most of them opted to leave the Soviet Union and come to the United States because of anti-Semitism, which they believed hurt their own chances for a successful life and would limit their children's opportunities. Most of them came in family units of a father, mother, and one child. About 20% also came with a grandparent. They came mostly from the larger cities in the Ukraine: Kiev, Kharkov, and Odessa. Practically all of them, with the exception of 4%, waited less than a year for their exit visa: two thirds waited six months or less.

The fathers' average age is 46; the mothers' is 43. All of the fathers had at least the equivalent of 4 years of college; another 13% had between 17 and 18 years of schooling, and still another 17% had more than 18 years of schooling. Among the mothers, 60% had completed at least 4 years of college, and 10% had more than 18 years of schooling.

The work the parents did in the Soviet Union is described in Table 1. Except for 7% of the fathers who said they worked as unskilled laborers, all of the other respondents in the labor force, male and female, worked as professionals or in skilled occupations.[3] All of the mothers, except for 4%, had held full-time jobs outside their homes.

[3] We also examined the occupations, the years of schooling, and the cities from which the respondents came by their year of arrival in the United States between 1975 and 1980 and did not find that there were any noticeable differences.

Among the parents who were employed at the time of the survey, (62% of the fathers and 44% of the mothers), almost all were working as engineers, computer programmers, draftsmen, or mechanics or in clerical positions. Forty-four percent of the fathers and 50% of the mothers had studied English in the Soviet Union; and according to their own assessments, their English was already more than serviceable.

In the course of the interview we asked the parents to think ahead and try to imagine what their economic situation might be 5 years hence. By that time they would have been in the United States 6 to 10 years. We found that both the fathers and the mothers were optimistic about their futures. The large majority expected to hold important and prestigious jobs that will provide them with a comfortable, above-average living. They also expected to be fluent in their new language.

The portion of the parents' interview that focused on their son or daughter asked the mothers and fathers to describe their child's current activities and to comment on the quality of the relationship they have with each other. It also asked the parents about their expectations and aspirations for their son's or daughter's future. The parents told us whether their son or daughter is in school, working, a combination of both, or neither; and if in school or at work what it is they are studying or where they are working. The adolescents were asked the same questions. The parents' and children's responses were almost identical, except for 9% of the fathers who said that their sons are going to school full-time, but according to the sons they are enrolled in an "English as a second language" course and looking for work the rest of the time.

Seventy-three percent of the sons and 96% of the daughters are full-time students. Almost all of the sons who are not attending school said that they had completed the equivalent of four years of high school before they left the Soviet Union. On the average the sons are a year and a half older than the daughters; their mean age is 17.6 years and the daughters' mean age is 16 years. Half of the sons are in their last two years of high school, and the others are enrolled in junior and community colleges. Those who are not in school are working as laborers; but three quarters of them claim that they plan to enter a community or other college next year. Among the daughters, 38% were still in the 9th and 10th grades.

On the quality of the relationship between parents and adolescents, both were asked if during the past year they had had any disagreements or conflicts about the following issues: How the son or daughter spends his or her time when he or she is not at school or working; the son's or daughter's choice of friends; how well the son or daughter is doing in school; his or her use of liquor and/or drugs; his or her willingness to listen to the mother's or father's advice; and current work or work plans in the future. The highest percentage of disagreements were reported by both the mother and the father to the item about how hard their son or daughter is working at his or her studies. Twenty-two percent of the fathers and 20% of the mothers described conflicts between themselves and their son or daughter on that issue. Eighteen percent of the fathers also reported conflicts with their son on how he spends his leisure time. They expressed dissatisfaction with their son's activities mostly because he was "out of the house too much." On all of the other items, over 90% of both the fathers and the mothers reported no disagreements or conflicts with their children.

In the main, the adolescents shared their parents' views about the level and areas of conflict between them. Sixteen and 18% of the sons reported disagreements between themselves and their fathers on how they spend their leisure or spare time and how much effort they put into their schooling. Whereas only 7% of the fathers reported conflict between themselves and their sons on the matter of listening to parental advice, 22% of the sons mentioned that this issue had been a source of conflict between them. None of the other issues solicited more than 5% acknowledgment that there had been conflicts or disagreements about them. Thirty percent of the daughters shared their mothers' perceptions that they have had disagreements about how much studying they do or whether they work hard enough at their schooling, and 20% reported that they and their mothers disagreed about their "American style of dress" and choice of clothes. Only 6% of the mothers claimed that they had disagreements about clothes. For the other issues, less than 10% of the daughters reported any conflicts between themselves and their mothers.

When we shifted from the present to the future and asked both the parents and the adolescents about how much schooling they expect their sons and daughters to have, their fields of study, and future work plans, there was a good deal of consensus about these matters. All of the fathers expect their sons to complete four years of college; 20% expect them to acquire a masters degree, and another 20% expect they they will finish medical school or obtain a Ph.D. They anticipate that their sons will study computer science, medicine, and engineering. A few thought they would major in business or law. All of the sons who were in school at the time of the survey plan to finish at least four years of college and 28% expect to go on to graduate school. The most popular courses of study are computer science, medicine, and engineering. Twenty-three percent of the boys who are not full-time students and who are working mostly as laborers said that they expected to return to school in a year.

The mothers' expectations about their daughters' education and future careers sounded much like the plans and hopes the fathers had for their sons. Seventy-eight percent of the mothers expect their daughters to complete at least four years of college. Of those, almost half also expect that their daughters will continue on and obtain a masters, Ph.D., or medical degree. The areas of study that most of the mothers expect their daughters to major in are medicine, computer science, and the natural sciences. By and large the daughters' plans reflect their mothers' expectations. Most of them said that they expected to complete at least four years of college; and 52% expect to continue on and obtain a masters degree (20%), Ph.D. (7%), or medical degree (25%). Their most popular choices of majors are computer science, medicine, and the natural sciences.

On more personal matters, such as when the sons and daughters expect to marry, the type of person they are likely to marry, and the number of children they want, we found that the parents and children saw eye to eye on these issues as well. Two thirds of the fathers want their sons to marry when they are between 25 and 29 years old. All of them want their sons to marry a Jew; 40% specified a Russian Jew. Seventy-one percent want their sons to have two children; 19% said three; and the others said as many as they could afford. The son's expectations match the fathers' hopes on each of these matters, except that one third of the sons said that a persons' ethnic or religious background would not be an important consideration in whom they chose to marry. The majority expected to marry a Russian or American Jew.

The mothers were less willing than the fathers to commit themselves about their daughter's futures. For example, a third of the mothers would not guess how old their daughter would be when she married or the type of person she would be likely to marry. Among those who expressed an opinion, half thought she would marry when she was 20 or 21 years old, the others when she was less than 29. All of the mothers thought their daughters would marry a Jew, and a Russian Jew was preferred over an American or any other ethnic background. Seventy-two percent of the mothers hope that their daughters will have two children, 10% said one, and 12% said three. The others would not express an opinion.

A comparison between the mothers and daughters' responses of these issues reveals a good deal of consensus. For example, 40% of the daughters think they will marry when they are 21 years old; 46% when they are between 22 and 24, and only 14% when they are between 25 and 29. Although 24% of the daughters claim that ethnicity or religion will not be an important consideration in their choice of spouse, all but 10% of the others said they expect to marry a Jew; some specified a

Table 2

Responses to Questions about Jewish Identity and Strength of Identity[a]

Question	Respondent	%	Target	%
Do you consider	Fathers	96	Sons	91
yourself Jewish?[b]	Sons	96	Fathers	96
	Mothers	88	Daughters	90
	Daughters	88	Mothers	90
How would you define the	Fathers	44	Sons	44
strength of your Jewish	Sons	22	Fathers	42
identity?[c]	Mothers	46	Daughters	42
	Daughters	48	Mothers	42

[a]For the first question, percentage answering "yes" is reported; for the second question, percentage with strong identity is reported.

[b]All, except one respondent who did not answer yes, said they considered themselves to be partially Jewish.

[c]With the exception of about 10% of the respondents in each category, all of the others who did not answer "strong" said "fairly strong."

Russian Jew, others said an American Jew. Two thirds of the daughters want to have two children (for 40% of them that is one more child than their mothers had), 10% want to have three or four children, 14% one child, and the others did not want to speculate.

JEWISH IDENTITY, ATTITUDES, AND PRACTICES

We began this section by asking each respondent, "Do you consider yourself Jewish?" The parents were then asked, "Does your son/daughter consider him/herself Jewish?"; and the adolescents were asked, "Does your father/mother consider him/herself Jewish?" Responses to these items and to the question that followed, which asked the respondents to rate the strength of their identity, are shown in Table 2.

Among the four sets of responses only the sons' and fathers' assessments of the strength of the sons' identity differ. A smaller percentage of the sons believe they have a stronger Jewish identity than the fathers attribute to them (22 vs. 42%).

When asked "Do you consider yourself a religious Jew?"[4] less than 10% of the respondents in each category said yes. Generation made no difference. As many parents as adolescents do not consider themselves

[4] The parents were also asked to answer for their children and the children for their parents.

religious and are not perceived as being so by the other. In response to a question about how often they go to the synagogue, between 40 and 50% said two times a year "on the high holidays" (the Jewish New Year and the Day of Atonement), and not at any other time. Almost all of the others said they never go to the synagogue.

A set of rituals that are part of traditional Jewish life were read to the respondents, and they were asked, "Do you or your spouse [The adolescents' questionnaire read 'family'] practice any of the following in your home? (1) light Friday night candles, (2) have a special family Sabbath, (3) light Hanukkah candles, (4) do not eat bread on Passover, (5) fast on Yom Kippur, (6) do not eat ham or bacon, (7) have separate dishes for meat and milk foods, (8) have some Sabbath observance other than candles, or (9) say daily prayers." Sixty percent of the fathers and 48% of the mothers do not practice any of these rituals. Twenty-three percent of the fathers and 38% of the mothers practice between one and three of the rituals. The ones most often cited by either parent are not eating bread on Passover (38% of the fathers and 22% of the mothers), fasting on Yom Kipper (29% of the fathers and 20% of the mothers), and lighting Hanukkah candles (25% of the fathers and 20% of the mothers).

The sons' and daughters' responses were similar to those reported by their parents: 53% of the sons and 58% of the daughters said they do not practice any of the rituals. Forty-one percent of the sons and 30% of the daughters observe between one and three of the rituals. Among those who observe any, the most popular ones are not eating bread during passover, lighting Hanukkah candles, and fasting on Yom Kippur.

Table 3 presents responses to a question we asked the parents about the hopes they had for their children's future ties to Jewish life. Note first that the mothers and fathers share much the same hopes for their sons' and daughters' futures, except that the mothers feel more strongly than the fathers (note the higher percentages for the mothers in the actively encourage category). The one issue about which most of them have negative reactions, and want to discourage their children from doing, is settling in Israel. They themselves made the choice not to immigrate to Israel once they were out of the Soviet Union.

The behaviors that the parents are most anxious to encourage are marriage "within the faith," Sabbath observance, and Jewish education. It is worth noting, however, that although two thirds of the parents said they would encourge their sons or daughters to receive a good Jewish education, only 11% of the sons and 24% of the daughters are enrolled in Jewish schools. The others attend public or nonsectarian high schools or colleges.

Although 91% of the fathers and 82% of the mothers said that they

Table 3

Parents' Responses to Question on Their Hopes for Children's Future[a]

Respondent		Actively encourage (%)	Encourage (%)	Makes no difference (%)	Discourage (%)	Actively discourage (%)	No answer (%)
Get a good Jewish education	Fa.	13	50	31	4	—	2
	Mo.	34	38	26	2	—	—
Settle in Israel	Fa.	2	13	36	42	—	7
	Mo.	2	8	32	50	2	6
Marry a Jew	Fa.	27	64	9	—	—	1
	Mo.	40	48	12	—	—	—
Believe in God	Fa.	4	47	40	7	—	2
	Mo.	12	34	48	6	—	—
Observe the Sabbath	Fa.	11	80	9	—	—	1
	Mo.	26	56	18	—	—	1
Have mostly Jewish friends	Fa.	9	22	63	4	—	2
	Mo.	14	18	64	4	—	—

[a]Respondents were asked, "People want different things for their children. Please tell us what you would like your children to do with regard to the following items."

Table 4

Responses to Questions about Religious Feelings[a]

Respondent	%	Target	%
Fathers	32	Sons	26
Mothers	48	Daughters	48
Sons	31	Fathers	20
Daughters	64	Mothers	36

[a]Respondents were asked, "Since you arrived in the United States have there been any changes in your religious feelings or beliefs?" Percentage answering "Feelings have changed in the direction of making me more religious" is reported.

would encourage their child to observe a Sabbath, only 4 and 6% of the fathers and mothers said they themselves observe a Sabbath. Less than 8% said they light candles on Friday evening or have a special family Sabbath dinner. Less than 10% defined themselves as "religious." Indeed, only when we asked, "Since you arrived in the United States have there been any changes in your religious feelings or beliefs?" did we observe any positive feelings about religious identity. Forty-eight percent of the mothers and 32% of the fathers said there had been a change in their feelings and beliefs in the direction of making them more religious.

The parents were also asked to speculate whether there had been any change in their childrens' beliefs, and the children were asked to do the same about their parents. Table 4 shows that the woman's responses (mothers and daughters) have changed more then the men's, and that the mothers perceive the daughters' beliefs as matching their own. What is perhaps more interesting about these responses is that only 36% of the daughters believe their mother's religious feelings or beliefs have changed in the direction of making her more religious, and only 20% of the sons think that their father has changed his beliefs about religion. In other words, the parents claim greater changes in their own religious beliefs than their children perceive, and the parents underestimate the changes that have occurred in their children's beliefs.

The last item on the questionnaire asked, "If you were to start your life over and had a choice would you want to be Jewish, not care whether you were Jewish, or not want to be Jewish?" On this issue there was consensus. As shown by the percentages in Table 5, a large majority of the parents and children said that if they had to do it over again they would want to be Jewish.

Table 5

Responses to Question about Starting Life over
as Jew or non-Jew[a]

Respondent	%[b]	Target	%[b]
Fathers	96	Sons	89
Mothers	92	Daughters	84
Sons	89	Fathers	91
Daughters	84	Mothers	88

[a]Respondents were asked, "If you were to start your life
over and had a choice, would you want to be Jewish, not
care whether you are Jewish, or not want to be Jewish."
Percentage answering "As a Jew" is reported.
[b]Only 2% in each category said they would not want to
be Jewish; the others said it would not matter.

CONCLUSION

To review briefly, the Soviet respondents arrived in the United States well
educated. Most of them worked as technicians and professionals in large
cities in the Ukraine. In the short time that they have been in Chicago
(for most of them it was less than two years) they have adapted well.
Over 60% of the fathers and 40% of the mothers are in the labor force
full time, working mainly as engineers, computer programmers, draftsmen, and mechanics. The parents are ambitious for themselves and for
their children. They want their children to follow in their footsteps and
to exceed them in educational and occupational prestige. Many of them
left the Soviet Union because their children's educational and occupational opportunities would be limited by their being identified as Jews.
The United States offers not only a relative absence of anti-Semitism but
occupational and educational opportunity, a larger horizon, and a bright-
er future.

Practically all of the adolescents are enrolled in school. Those who
are not in school claim they are working temporarily for about a year
and plan to enter college the following year. The girls as well as the boys
plan, or have already begun, to study computer science, engineering,
and medicine. Language acquisitions does not seem to be an overwhelming obstacle for either the parents (about half of whom had studied
English in the Soviet Union) or the adolescents.[5]

[5] Their vocational interests are in areas that do not involve as much proficiency in
their new language; this would not be true of careers in law, the humanities, or the social
sciences.

On the whole, the respondents are optimistic about their futures. They believe they will succeed economically, professionally, and socially in American society. But what about their Jewish identity and their ties to the American Jewish community? First, almost all of the respondents consider themselves Jewish. But less than half claim that they have a strong Jewish identity, and less than 10% consider themselves religious. They rarely attend the synagogue (about 45% go on the High Holidays), and most of them do not observe traditional practices and rituals in their homes. On the other hand, the parents appear to want their children to attach themselves to Jewish life. Specifically, they want their sons and daughters to marry Jews, to receive a Jewish education, and to observe a Sabbath. Since they have been in the United States, the mothers and daughters especially, but a third of the fathers and sons as well, claim that their religious identity has changed in the direction of making them more religious. The strongest affirmation of their Jewish identity was made when 90% of them said that if given a choice they would want to start their life over again as a Jew.

What do these data tell us about how the Soviet Jews are likely to relate to the American Jewish community, and what do they tell us about the strength of the Soviet Jews' commitment to their Jewish identity? For many Soviet Jews, professional and economic recognition and success will be all-important; and the Jewish connection will fade or disappear. For others, the Jewish identity will be strengthened. It will manifest itself by their having Jewish friends, their children marrying Jews, their occasional attendance at the synagogue, and their participation in Russian–Jewish cultural, intellectual, and social activities. Perhaps most important, the majority of Soviet Jews will find that in the United States there are few costs and even some benefits to being identified with a Jewish community. The absence of social and economic costs, the lack of political barriers between the Jewish community and the larger society, and the positive incentives that both the Jewish community and the larger society offer are likely to enhance and strengthen the ties that a large proportion of the Soviet Jews will have to the American Jewish community.

REFERENCES

Edelman, J.
    1977   Soviet Jews in the United States: a profile. *American Jewish Yearbook* **77**:157.

Kennedy, E.
    1980   Expanded "survey" much needed. *World Refugee Survey.* Washington, D.C.: Government Printing Office.
Leimsidor, B.
    1980   Refugees leave Soviet Union. *World Refugee Survey.* Washington, D.C.: Government Printing Office.
Simon, R. J.
    1980   Russian, Vietnamese, and Mexican immigrant families: a comparative analysis of parents' and adolescents' adjustment to their new society. Report to the Selection Commission on Immigration and Refugee Policy. Unpublished.

20

Social Ties and Ethnic Settlement Patterns*

Bryan Thompson

INTRODUCTION

For many years the model of American society shared by most people
was that of the melting pot. The melting pot assumes that the many
ethnic groups that flocked to America would "by a process of accommodation, acculturation, and assimilation become one people, one ethnic group, the American (Feinstein, 1973:3).[1] In recent years increasing
numbers of social scientists are supporting a pluralistic view of society
in which groups, even though changes occur, are able to maintain separate and distinct identities (Greeley, 1969, 1974; Laumann, 1973; Novak,
1971).

The different groups coming to America did not settle uniformly
throughout geographic space. Time of departure from source areas,
opportunities in America at time of arrival, trade ties, immigrant skills,
and environmental preferences all influenced the initial settlement patterns of new immigrants (Ward, 1971). These early settlement patterns
are still evident today. The Irish, for example, are disproportionately
represented in New England, Germans in the Midwest, blacks in the

* The writer is indebted to Carol Agócs, Karl Raitz, Robert Sinclair, and Leo Zonn for
their comments on an earlier draft of this paper, and to Tina Humphrey for cartographic
assistance.
[1] Throughout this article "ethnic group" refers to any group defined or set off by race,
religion, or national origin, or some combination of these categories. The group shares
similar patterns of values, beliefs, norms, and a tendency to maintain generational continuity by certain-group marriages. See Gordon (1964) and Singer (1962).

South, and Scandinavians in the Upper Midwest. There are also marked contrasts in the ethnic composition of urban areas both interregionally and intraregionally. Milwaukee has large concentrations of people of German and Polish background, whereas Providence, Rhode Island, has a large Italian population. At the intraregional scale, Philadelphia has a relatively small Polish population, which contrasts with the large Polish populations of many other Pennsylvania cities. The traditional pattern of settlement in urban areas has been for each ethnic group to lay claim to its own particular parcel of land. Even with growth and change, there is evidence to suggest that some groups have maintained spatial or territorial integrity as they move upward socially and outward geographically.[2] Ethnic populations still are segregated from each other in metropolitan areas in North America, and suburban space has not become the spatial melting pot that many suggest (Agócs, 1977; Balakrishnan, 1976; Guest and Weed, 1976; Kantrowitz, 1973; Sinclair and Thompson, 1977).

STUDY OBJECTIVES

Much of the geographic literature dealing with the migration and settlement patterns of ethnic groups has emphasized description at the expense of process and theory. Furthermore, little attention has been given to the relationships between the ties that bind family and friends and the effects that these ties have had on the nature of migration and settlement. This article presents and analyzes a deductive schema outlining these relationships (Figure 1).

The schema developed out of research on ethnic settlement in North American cities that is still in progress, and it is viewed as preliminary and suggestive of further elaboration and refinement. The research timeframe varies from late 19th- and early 20th-century settlement of Italians in Worcester, Massachusetts, to more recent settlement patterns of ethnic groups in the metropolitan Toronto and Detroit areas (Thompson, 1973, 1980). Parts of the schema are more appropriate to 19th-century settlement, other parts to the 20th-century, and others are appropriate to both. Most of the suggestions apply more to working-class migrants than to migrants of higher socioeconomic ranking. Finally, the applicability of the schema varies from group to group. However, the schema does

---

[2] Spatial and territorial integrity refer to concentrations of ethnic groups in certain parts of an urban area.

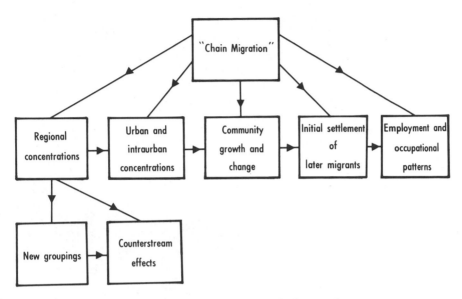

Figure 1   Social ties and patterns of ethnic settlement.

provide a framework for thinking about settlement patterns and processes—a move toward bridging a socio-temporal-spatial gap.

The schema's main theme centers on the role of kinship and friendship ties, and the consequences these ties have had on patterns of ethnic
settlement. In the sociological literature these ties are referred to as
"social networks" (Barnes, 1954; Bott, 1957; Craven and Wellman, 1973;
Graves, 1979; Laumann, 1973; Mitchell, 1969). In the context of international migration, the process whereby early immigrants, usually friends
and relatives, influence the migration decisions of later migrants has
been termed "chain migration" and is defined as the process by which
prospective immigrants learn of opportunities, are provided with passage money, and have initial accommodation and employment arranged
through immigrants who preceded them (Choldin, 1973; MacDonald and
MacDonald, 1972, 1964; Price, 1963). This paper suggests that similar
processes influence interregional and intraurban migration patterns and
have influenced the ethnic spatial structure at these scales.

The major components of the framework outlined in Figure 1 are
derived from the fact that social ties, that is, interaction and communication patterns, are maintained during and after the migration process
and have an effect upon: (1) *regional differences* in the distribution of
ethnic groups; (2) the nature of *international and interregional* flows of
people; (3) the *ethnic makeup of cities* both in terms of how many people

from particular groups live in any one city as well as where they live in the city; (4) the nature of *ethnic spatial change in cities*; and (5) ethnic *occupational patterns.*

REGIONAL PATTERNS

Chain migration has been recognized as an important form of migration in the settlement of North America (Tilly, 1974:226). Similar findings are documented by Price (1963:109; 1966) in his definitive studies of southern Europeans in Australia. He concluded that only a small proportion of the southern Europeans came to Australia outside of the chain migration process. Richmond (1972) in his study of ethnic settlement in Toronto also points out the importance of the "chain migration" process.[3] This distinct mode of migration has important consequences on the process and form of settlement in both regional and urban settings.

In the period before 1850 many Irish immigrants settled in New England. Often they came by way of British America; Portland, Maine, and Boston, which traded frequently with the Maritime Provinces, served as major ports of arrival (Ward, 1971:63). The destination choices of later migrants from Ireland were influenced by·earlier immigrants, resulting in an Irish identity that was perpetuated and maintained even to this day. At a metropolitan level Philadelphia has a smaller proportion of Poles relative to its size than many cities in Pennsylvania. This phenomenon is largely explained in terms of the economic opportunities available to Poles at their time of arrival in America. The Poles were preempted from the unskilled labor market by earlier migrants, namely, the Irish and blacks. However, opportunities in newly developing industrial and mining centers in other parts of Pennsylvania provided work for new Polish immigrants, resulting in higher proportions of Poles in cities like Pittsburgh (Golab, 1977). Work is not the only factor determining immigrants' destination choices. Migrants also moved to urban areas under the auspices of kinship and friendship ties, causing disproportionate representation of some groups in certain urban areas (Tilly and Brown, 1967). The concern and search for work for many does not begin until residence is established, with the choice of city dictated by social ties. It should be kept in mind that factors other than work and social ties also have influenced patterns of ethnic concentration, including:

---

[3] The importance of chain migration for Italians moving to Toronto in the post-war era is discussed in Ziegler (1977).

(1) the nature of trade ties between American ports and other world ports; (2) the financial resources of immigrants at their time of arrival in America; (3) regional transportation networks; and (4) ethnic preferences for certain social and geographic environments.

THE MOVE TO THE CITY: INTERNATIONAL AND INTERREGIONAL MIGRANTS

Migrants follow in the paths established by earlier migrants in what have been referred to as channelized migration flows (Roseman, 1971). The result has been that migrants from highly localized source areas regroup in localized destination areas throughout urban space. This process has characterized the history of urban America and is understandable considering the different physical and cultural environments that migrants enter. Newcomers are culturally alienated, suffer from job insecurity, and are subject to discriminatory practices. Urban villages provide sociopsychological cushions during a period of adjustment in alien and frequently hostile settings.

Oscar Handlin (1959:35), commenting on the emergence of numerous "Little Italies" in New York City, states, "By 1928 there were some twenty communities . . . the population of which were 50 to 90 percent Italian, often concentrated in terms of province of origin." Research by the MacDonalds (1962; 1964) documents the role of kinship and patron–client relations in their analysis of Italian settlement patterns in American cities. Similar findings are documented by Barton (1975) in a study of settlement in Cleveland, where the Italian community originated largely from two regions, Sicily and the Abruzzi, and where more than half of the immigrants came from 10 villages. A study of migration from the Yemen Arab Republic revealed that one village near Yerim was found to have concentrated on migration to the Sudan, and another village near Rada sent most of its emigrants to Chad (Swanson, 1978). Recent movement of Indians and Pakistanis to Britain and of Algerians to France reveal similar channelized flows. Southall, for example, has a large fraction of its population from India, and Bradford, Yorkshire, is the most Pakistani of British towns (Cox, 1972:80).

Studies on interregional migration reveal similar patterns. A study of the out-migration of people from communities in eastern Kentucky over a 20-year period found LePlay's "famille-souche" or "stem-family" concept useful in understanding the functions of the kinship structure in the migration process and the adjustment of individuals within a migration system (Brown, Schwarzweller, and Mangalam, 1963; Schwarzweller,

Brown, and Mangalam, 1971). It was shown that "stem-family" and "branch-family" networks resulted in: (1) channelized flows to the towns and cities of Ohio; (2) donor cultures that provided "havens of safety" during times of crisis and failure; (3) societal transplants that maintained and perpetuated a way of life through time and over space; and (4) new communities that provided a sociopsychological "cushion" for the migrant during the transitional phase.

Roseman's (1971:140) study of migration out of selected State Economic Areas in the South revealed destination patterns that concentrated in a limited number of medium-sized metropolitan areas of the Midwest and were attributed, in part, to the channelization of information flow. He concludes by stating, "This channelization may have begun with a small community in the South establishing ties with a Midwestern city, only to have the word spread gradually to neighboring communities, then on to a broader region via inter-personal communications" (Roseman, 1971:143).

Some researchers refer to this process of new community formation as clone colonization (Bylund, 1960; Hudson, 1969). Personal observation of Chaldean settlement in Detroit reveals similar patterns. Many of the Chaldeans in the Detroit area originated in the village of Telkaif, in northern Iraq (Sengstock, 1974). Now a new community is being spawned in San Diego, California, as Chaldeans leave Detroit in search of new economic opportunities.

Channelized migrations also characterized black migration out of the South. During the period 1940–1960 blacks from the West South Central region tended to move to the West Coast, with Los Angeles being the most important destination. Blacks moving out of the East South Central region overwhelmingly moved to urban centers in the Midwest, while those leaving the South Atlantic region moved to cities along the northeastern seaboard (Davis and Donaldson, 1975; Rose, 1969). There is abundant documentation that biases in information flow and family and friendship ties have had a strong influence in channelizing migration.

Rochester, New York has been one of the stops along the East Coast migrant labor stream. With time and demand for the labor decreased, but the flow of migrants did not stop. From 1950 to 1970 the black population in Monroe County grew over 550 percent, from 8,000 to an estimated 45,000. By far the largest proportion of these migrants came from two points of origin on the stream: Sanford, Florida, and Williamsburg County, South Carolina [Davis and Donaldson, 1975:39].

Another study by Goldstein (1958:38) noted "that high proportions of Negroes resident in Norristown, Pennsylvania in 1950 had come from Saluda, South Carolina where a small contingent of Negroes had been recruited by the Pennsylvania Railroad as laborers and sent to Norristown during World War I."

Details of the influence of family, friends, letters, and newspapers on the form of migration are outlined by Davis and Donaldson. Migrants to the North, after they were established, usually wrote back to family and friends urging them to follow:

My dear Sister: . . . . The people are rushing here by the thousands and I know if you come and rent a big house you can get all the roomers you want. You write me exactly when you are coming. I am not keeping house yet. I am living with my brother and his wife. . . . I can get a nice place for you to stop until you can look around and see what you want. I am quite busy. I work in Swifts Packing Co. in the sausage department. My daughter and I work for the same company. . . . Well I am always glad to hear from my friends and if I can do anything to assist any of them to better their condition. . . .

P.S. My brother moved the week after I came. When you fully decide to come write me and let me known what day you expect to leave and over what road and if I don't meet you I will have someone there to meet you and look after you [Davis and Donaldson, 1975: 87–89].

Letters were not the only sources of information about the North. The *Chicago Defender* printed numerous ads for job opportunities, served as a symbol of defiance against southern racism, and reproduced letters and poems enticing blacks to move North.

Friends and relatives have had a great influence on the location of the new homes of black migrants. Apparently there is a saying in the Fort Green neighborhood of New York City that "if you stand on a street corner long enough you will see somebody you know from South Carolina" (Davis and Donaldson, 1975:89).

THE COUNTERSTREAM

Discussion up to this point has centered on migration streams from origins to certain destination areas. Another aspect of the migration process is the counterstream, meaning the return flows of remittances and people to source areas.[4] Many immigrants view migration as a temporary sojourn. However, for some there is movement back and forth over a period of many years, others return permanently, and some never return. One illustration of the back and forth movement is found in Detroit's Cass Corridor, an area with large numbers of people from Kentucky. A local bus company operates a daily service with pickups in areas

---

[4] For a discussion of the "counterstream" see Lee (1966).

Bryan Thompson

having concentrations of Kentuckians. The ultimate destinations of what is affectionately called the "Paducah Express" are Paducah and Fulton, Kentucky. Many North American Indians, who are also residents of the Cass Corridor, move freely between Detroit and reservations.

If the sources of out-migration are highly localized, then the impact of the counterstreams also will be localized. Return flows may be in the form of cash, ideas or attitudes, and skills.[5] Cash flows to the families of emigrants usually make up a significant proportion of their total income (Philpott, 1973; Watson, 1975). Just how the money is spent is not clear. The overall effects generally are not in capital generating activities. For the most part money is used to improve the material quality of life. Foerster (1919) describes how cash from South America and the United States raised the standard of living in Italian peasant villages. Many returnees spend their money on improving their housing situation (Paine, 1975; Watson, 1975). Swanson's (1978) study revealed a penchant for investment in land and property that resulted in highly inflated prices.

Returnees may introduce new ideas and attitudes. Lopreato (1968) says that returning migrants think of themselves as vehicles of social change. Patel (1972) indicates that certain variations were introduced that had a profound influence on the village, particularly in connection with home renovation. There is little evidence to suggest that skills learned abroad can be usefully adapted following the return home. Usually workers are unable to find jobs to utilize their skills, or they return to villages where their skills are inappropriate.

COMMUNITY GROWTH AND CHANGE

An important aspect of the history of America has been the way in which newcomers have adjusted to urban living. Many of these newcomers, particularly in the 19th century and early part of the 20th century, originated in Europe. Family ties and ties extending to village and even regional network systems resulted in the emergence of socially and physically homogeneous enclaves within cities. Similar ties have influenced the settlement of other migrants, for example, whites and blacks moving from rural areas of the South to the cities of the North and West, as well as the development of Spanish-speaking neighborhoods in urban areas throughout America. Many of the older European ethnic neighborhoods in American cities, allowing for constraints imposed by ability-to-pay

---

[5] References to the "counterstream" literature are from Swanson (1978).

and discrimination, developed as spatial expressions of voluntary choices related to systems of values and ways of life rooted in traditional societies. For blacks and other minority groups, segregation has resulted largely from discriminatory constraints imposed by society.

Rapid growth brought successive waves of immigrants to the cities of America. Different groups came at different times. For example, the first Europeans came from western and northwestern Europe, later from central Europe and northern Europe, and finally, before restrictive immigration laws were passed in the 1920s, from southern and eastern Europe. How did these groups arrange and rearrange themselves in physical urban space during periods of growth? Park (1936) in a seminal essay talks of competition between groups for space and the idea of "invasion" of a natural area by one group leading to "succession" and dominance of the area by a new group. These urban ecological processes, Park says, derived their energy from the expansion of the city's population and the city's area grew in a concentric ringlike fashion over time. As earlier groups improved their economic position, they were able to move to the newly developing housing stock on the city's periphery. New arrivals moved to the city center, occupying housing made available by those who were moving upward socially and outward geographically in what has been referred to as a "filtering down" or "housing filtration" process.[6] The distinctive spatial pattern of activity and residence zones that emerged generally is referred to as Burgess' (1925) Concentric Zone Model.

Another model of the changing spatial structure of the city was advanced by Homer Hoyt (1933, 1939). Using a study of 142 cities, Hoyt stated that high and low rent neighborhoods occupied distinct subareas of the city, and that these were not aligned concentrically about the city center but were distributed sectorally. In Hoyt's opinion the spatial pattern was determined by those who could afford the highest rents. The more affluent preempt the land along "the best existing transportation lines," "high ground-free from the risk of floods," and "land along lake, bay, river and ocean fronts where such water fronts are not used for industry" (Hoyt, 1939:118–119).

There has been considerable debate over the relative merits of the classical models of urban structure. Recent research suggests that the models are not mutually exclusive but "independent, additive contributors to the total socio-economic structuring of city neighborhoods" (Berry, 1965:115). In other words, a city might vary sectorally along certain

---

[6] For discussion of "housing filtration" refer to Berry (1975), Kristof (1965, 1973), and Smith (1971).

dimensions but exhibit concentric variation with respect to other dimensions.

In the late 19th and early 20th century, ethnic settlements surrounded the city core because

The central tenement districts . . . possessed the advantage of convenient accessibility to the growing employment opportunities of the emerging central business district . . . many immigrants were employed in occupations with long and awkward hours and, therefore, preferred a short pedestrian journey to work. The tenure of unskilled employment was also characteristically uncertain, and daily hiring was the common procedure in general laboring and portering. Consequently, immigrants not only faced the problems of numerous changes in the location of their work, but also suffered from frequent spells of unemployment. . . . Under these circumstances, employment in the central business district had the advantage of a wide range of alternative opportunities when regular work was abruptly terminated [Ward, 1968:346].

As more and more immigrants poured into urban areas, and as the second generation and the earlier immigrants moved upward socially, neighborhood expansion usually occurred along the main transportation corridors away from the city core.[7] This pattern is particularly true in cities with large expanses of land to accommodate unrestricted expansion, as for example, in midwestern cities like Detroit and Chicago. If growth had been simply a function of natural increase, then a series of ethnic sectors (wedges) would develop with concentric variation according to stage in the life cycle and socioeconomic status dimensions. Children of the foreign-born moved outward from the communities surrounding the core into newer and contiguous residential areas along the major arterials. Intraurban migration typically is short distance because social networks (ties to family, friends, parish, church, etc.), shopping, recreational and other activity patterns, and even a knowledge of the housing market are all geographically localized. Also, moves to other sectors of the city frequently necessitate a longer journey to work. As an ethnic group expands sectorally, spatial cohesion is maintained over time and through space. The significance of the ethnic dimension alone is by no means clear in explaining the evolving and somewhat predictable sociospatial form of cities. Ethnic factors do appear to act in concert

[7] There is some evidence to suggest that in the very early phases of settlement improvements in transportation may have resulted in community consolidation rather than dispersal. Early Italian settlement in Worcester, Massachusetts, was centered around a number of factories. The form of settlement could be described as dispersed clusters dictated by the journey to work in a pedestrian city. Later as more Italians moved in and as the intraurban transportation system improved, the community became more consolidated. This consolidation is explained either by: (1) Italians choosing to use their improved mobility to travel greater distances to work in order to live in the same neighborhood as their compatriots or (2) increasing discrimination against Italians as the community increased numerically. See Thompson (1980).

with other variables in building on a foundation established during an earlier period in the history of cities.

Urban growth has not simply resulted from natural increase but also from net in-migration as immigrants are attracted by expanding opportunities for employment. Newcomers generally start at the bottom socioeconomically. Spatial pressure is applied on the older housing stock of the city, and what typically has happened could be thought of as a socialspatial filtering process. Those who can afford new housing move outward as pressure is applied through the sector. This is made possible by new construction on the urban periphery and results in "filtering-down" of older housing to other groups (Figure 2). Ethnic community growth in metropolitan Detroit has produced a series of ethnic sectors with concentric variation according to family-status and socioeconomic-status variables.[8] The growth of Detroit's Polish community typifies a general pattern of ethnic community extension throughout the area (Figure 3).

There are examples of socioeconomic mobility resulting in noncontiguous spatial expansion to suburban communities. In the postwar period Italians from a village outside of Rome moved to a neighborhood in the western part of Toronto. After a few years there was a channelized flow of people from central city to suburban Downsview (Fred Pariselli, personal communication, summer 1975). In this case an efficient freeway system enabled economically mobile Italians to live in a culturally and economically homogenous suburb ("high" social status) but at the same time maintain social and family ties with "lower" social status areas in central-city neighborhoods.

Family and group ties have influenced the evolving residential spatial structure of American cities. As ethnic communities extend outward toward the suburbs, the pattern of initial residence of newer migrants becomes more dispersed as new arrivals join relatives and friends who preceded them. Recent Italian settlement in Melbourne, Australia, has followed the overall change in the distribution of the Italian community (Lee, 1969). Whitelaw (1969:3) in a study of migration to Auckland, New Zealand, states that "with a marked increase in both Maori and Island families in the outer suburbs . . . new urban arrivals will perhaps make as much use of kin in that area as those in the Inner City before finding suitable accommodation and employment." Similar findings are reported in Detroit, where the pattern of initial residence for new immigrants follows the overall pattern of settlement for each of the groups (Carlson, 1977).

[8] Note that an ethnic wedge does not mean ethnic homogeneity but rather an ethnic concentration that is two or more times the metropolitan average. See Agócs (1977).

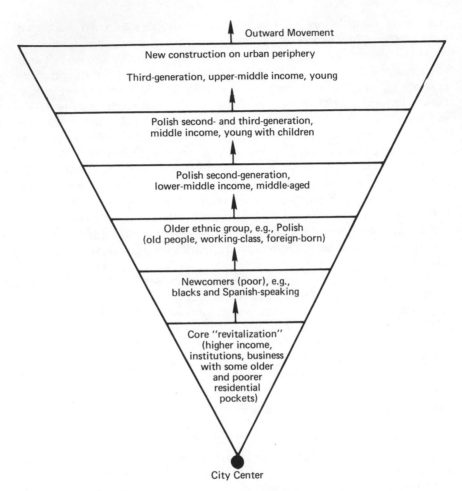

Figure 2 Ethnic sector: sorting, filtering, and outward movement.

URBAN RENEWAL

During the 1950s and 1960s many central-city neighborhoods were torn down and replaced by upper-middle class housing; institutional complexes of various types including medical, cultural, and educational facilities; and elaborate freeway systems. The tragedy of urban renewal has been that communities with sound housing and a strong sense of community identity often were erased from the map. Ethnic and racial communities have borne the brunt of renewal with disastrous human

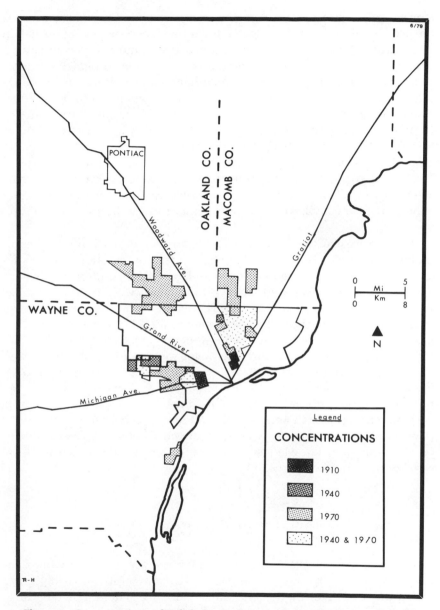

Figure 3   Concentrations of Polish foreign-born in the Detroit area. Adapted from Agócs (1977).

consequences. In what has become a classic study, Gans (1962) records the process of renewal as it affected the lives of second-generation-Italian Americans in Boston's West End. He concluded that the behavior patterns and values of working-class subcultures should be recognized, understood, and taken into account by planners. Later research in working-class neighborhoods comes to similar conclusions concerning the positive role neighborhoods have for their residents, and the importance of community ties and community identification (Fried and Levin, 1968; Hartman, 1974; Suttles, 1968). Recent research on peripheral settlements around cities of the Third World rejects a blanket "culture of poverty" thesis and suggests that these settlements may exhibit differing characteristics in different parts of the world and that in many cases they play a positive role as rural migrants adapt to life in an urban setting (Berry, 1973).

In America we have had the ability to tear down inner city communities but little ability or will to plan for their re-creation. The impact of forced relocation on people has been devastating, resulting in physical and mental disorders (Fried, 1963, 1973). Clearly, we did not recognize, understand, or care about the significance of social ties on the lives of people. Yet, despite the difficulties, and on an ad hoc basis, partial regrouping occurred. In the cities where reconsolidation did occur, it was the exception rather than the rule. Relocation out of a Toronto urban renewal area that was primarily Italian and Jewish did reveal a regrouping pattern for both groups (Gad, Peddie, and Punter, 1973). Tilly (1974), quoting another Toronto study, points out that Portuguese immigrants were able to reestablish and even consolidate their community following relocation. This was possible because low cost housing was available in nearby areas and knowledge of housing opportunities was spread by word-of-mouth procedures.

EMPLOYMENT AND OCCUPATION PATTERNS

Family and friendship ties are key elements in determining where immigrants settle (Tilly and Brown, 1967). For immigrants arriving under the auspices of kin or friends, the initial residence is determined because most newcomers move in with their sponsors. Once residence is established, an immigrant's concern turns to work. The search for work occurs in a variety of ways. In many instances it begins in areas close to home with the chance of finding a job decreasing with increasing distance from home. In a sense, initial residence, over which most immigrants have no control, is an important determinant of the initial employment field. Thus, residence in the initial phase of urban settlement affects the emergent work pattern, rather than work placing constraints on where one will live. Subsequent patterns of intraurban migration follow a somewhat predictable pattern because of: (1) the desire to maintain social ties (family and friends) and functional ties (shopping, work, etc.); and (2) an information field about new housing opportunities that decreases with increasing distance from home. At later stages work does place constraints on the changing residential pattern.

Social ties influence employment patterns through the development of occupation and employment chains. In an "occupational chain" immigrants do the same kind of work as their predecessors, whereas in an "employment chain" newcomers are employed at the same place of work but not the same type of job. The literature is replete with documentation of the overrepresentation of some ethnic groups in certain professions or businesses. One outstanding example in Detroit is the overwhelming majority of Chaldeans who are involved in the running of party stores (Sengstock, 1967). A few years ago contacts with Detroit's Albanian Catholic community revealed tht many newcomers became employed at the Dodge Main plant simply because an earlier immigrant who had acquired a familiarity with English was able to fill out application forms for would-be employees.

Another aspect of the employment picture concerns the pattern of intergenerational mobility.[9] Frequently, sons followed in the footsteps of their fathers, whether it was working in the same factory or moving into the family business. In many instances intergenerational socioeconomic mobility patterns were tied to the same type of work. Early Italian immigrants may have started out as modest fruit vendors, but their descendants, in turn, now manage large supermarkets and wholesale fruit operations (Thompson, 1980).

In a study of Slovaks, Italians, and Rumanians in Cleveland, Barton was able to show that there were marked differences in patterns of social mobility for the second generation:

The Slovaks, for whom the ethnic community provided a pattern of stability and continuity, remained largely in the working-class. Although the fathers gained skills and property which they were able to pass on to their sons, their social mobility and education served not as avenues to the middle-class but rather as a means of gaining a stable working-class life. . . . The Italian settlement shared the Slovak emphasis on continuity, but the basis lay in particularistic cultural values rather than in an amalgam of religious and associational loyalties. . . . the working-class families developed a stable work orientation, a coherent pattern of family structure, education, and mobility, which gave the sons a decided edge

[9] For a discussion of social mobility see Lipset and Bendix (1966) and Strauss (1971).

in the urban labor market. Italian fathers who gained middle-class status . . . consistently failed to pass on their status to their children. As a result, the second generation started out in the thirties with no better chance than those with which the immigrants had begun.

It is the Rumanians who present the classic rise of an immigrant group. . . . The cumulative advantages of small families, extended schooling, and upwardly mobile fathers provided a middle-class competence for most of the second generation [Barton, 1975:172–173].

SUMMARY

This chapter has examined the effects, largely spatial, that social ties have had on the pattern of settlement during and after migration. In the migration literature this process is referred to as "chain migration." I suggest that social ties between family and friends and "chain migration," in part, explain:

1. Regional concentrations of certain ethnic groups
2. The emergence of new regional concentrations as migrants travel the paths established by those who preceded them
3. Ethnic concentrations within urban areas
4. The localized impact of remittances and returnees (the "counterstream")
5. The possibility, where a strong sense of ethnic identity is present, for spatial consolidation following improvements in transportation
6. Maintenance of spatial cohesion (ethnic concentrations) as: (a) a community grows; (b) those that are socioeconomically mobile move outward from the core of the city; (c) communities are broken up because of urban renewal, institutional expansion, and other spatial-changing forces
7. The direct move to suburban locations of recent immigrants, whose settlement patterns follow the overall pattern of community growth
8. The initial employment patterns of newcomers to the city
9. The development of occupation and employment chains
10. The nature of intergenerational occupation patterns.

REFERENCES

Agócs, C.
    1977   Ethnic neighborhoods in city and suburbs: metropolitan Detroit, 1940–1970.
            Unpublished Ph.D. dissertation, Department of Sociology, Wayne State University, Detroit.
Balakrishnan, T. R.
    1976   Ethnic residential segregation in the metropolitan areas of Canada. *Canadian Journal of Sociology* 1:481–498.

Barnes, J. A.
    1954   Class and committees in a Norwegian island parish. *Human Relations* **7**:39–58.
Barton, J. J.
    1975   *Peasants and strangers: Italians, Rumanians, and Slovaks in an American city,
            1890–1950.* Cambridge, Mass.: Harvard University Press.
Berry, B. J. L.
    1965   Internal structure of the city. *Law and Contemporary Problems* **30**:111–119.
    1973   *The Human Consequences of Urbanization: Divergent Paths in the Urban Ex-
            perience of the Twentieth Century.* New York: St. Martins' Press.
    1975   Short-term housing cycles in a dualistic metropolis, in *The Social Economy of
            the City* (G. Gappert and H. M. Rose, Eds.), pp. 165–182. Beverly Hills, Calif.: Sage
            Publishers.
Bott, E.
    1957   *Family and Social Networks.* London: Tavistock.
Brown, J. S., Schwarzweller, H. K. and Mangalam, J. J.
    1963   Kentucky mountain migration and the stem-family: an American variation on
            a theme by Le Play. *Rural Sociology* **28**:48–69.
Burgess, E. W.
    1925   The growth of the city, in *The City* (R. E. Park, E. W. Burgess, and R. D. McKenzie,
            Eds.), pp. 47–62. Chicago: University of Chicago Press.
Bylund, E.
    1960   Theoretical considerations regarding the distribution of settlement in inner
            North Sweden. *Geografiska Annaler* **42**:225–231.
Carlson, A. W.
    1977   A map analysis of recent european immigrants settling in metropolitan Detroit
            based upon petitions for naturalization. *The East Lakes Geographer* **12**:71–89.
Choldin, H. M.
    1973   Kinship networks in the migration process. *International Migration Review* **7**:163–
            175.
Cox, K. R.
    1972   *Man, Location, and Behavior: An Introduction to Human Geography.* New York:
            John Wiley & Sons.
Craven, P., and Wellman, B.
    1973   The Network City. *Sociological Inquiry* **43**:57–88.
Davis, G. A. and Donaldson, F. O.
    1975   *Blacks in the United States: A Geographic Perspective.* Boston: Houghton Mifflin.
Feinstein, O.
    1973   *Ethnic Directory I: The Heritage of America.* Detroit: Southeastern Regional
            Ethnic Heritage Studies Center.
Foerster, R. F.
    1919   *The Italian Emigration of Our Times.* Cambridge, Mass.: Harvard University
            Press.
Fried, M
    1963   Grieving for a lost home, in *The Urban Condition* (L. J. Duhl, Ed.), pp. 151–170.
            New York: Basic Books.
    1973   *The World of the Urban Working Class.* Cambridge, Mass.: Harvard University
            Press.
Fried, M., and Levin, J.
    1968   Some social functions of the urban slum in *Urban Planning and Social Policy*
            (B. J. Frieden and R. Morris, Eds.), pp. 60–83. New York: Basic Books.

Gad, G., Peddie, R., and Punter, J.
    1973   Ethnic differences in the residential search process, in *The Form of Cities in Central Canada: Selected Papers* (L. S. Bourne, R. D. MacKinnon, and J. W. Simmons, Eds.), pp. 168–180. *The University of Toronto, Department of Geography Research Publications*, No. **11**. Toronto: University of Toronto Press.
Gans, H. J.
    1962   *The Urban Villagers: Group and Class Life of Italian–Americans.* New York: The Free Press.
Golab, C.
    1977   *Immigrant Destinations.* Philadelphia: Temple University Press.
Goldstein, S.
    1958   *Patterns of Mobility, 1910–1950: The Norristown Study.* Philadelphia: University of Pennsylvania Press.
Gordon, M.
    1964   *Assimilation in American Life: The Role of Race, Religion, and National Origins.* New York: Oxford University Press.
Graves, F. W., Jr.
    1979   Social interaction, size, and problem-specific helping: the dynamics of informal social networks. Unpublished Ph.D. dissertation, Department of Sociology, Wayne State University, Detroit.
Greeley, A. M.
    1969   *Why Can't They Be Like Us? America's White Ethnic Groups.* New York: American Jewish Committee.
    1974   *Ethnicity in the United States: A Preliminary Reconnaissance.* New York: John Wiley & Sons.
Guest, A. M., and Weed, J.
    1976   Ethnic residential segregation: patterns of change. *American Journal of Sociology* **81**:1088–1111.

Handlin, O.
    1959   *The Newcomers: Negroes and Puerto Ricans in a Changing Metropolis.* Garden City, New York: Doubleday.
Hartman, C.
    1974   *Yerba Buena: Land Grab and Community Resistance in San Francisco.* San Francisco: Glide.
Hoyt, H.
    1933   *One Hundred Years of Land Values in Chicago.* Chicago: University of Chicago Press.
Hoyt, H.
    1939   *The Structure and Growth of Residential Neighborhoods in American Cities.* Washington, D.C.: U.S. Government Printing Office.
Hudson, J. C.
    1969   A location theory for rural settlement. *Annals, Association of American Geographers* **59**:365–381.

Kantrowitz, N.
    1973   *Ethnic and Racial Segregation in the New York Metropolis.* New York: Praeger.
Kristof, F. S.
    1965   Housing policy goals and the turnover of housing. *Journal of the American Institute of Planners* **31**:232–245.
    1973   Federal housing policies: subsidized production, filtration and objectives: part II. *Land Economics* **49**:163–174.

Laumann, E. O.
    1973   *Bonds of Pluralism: The Form and Substance of Urban Social Networks.* New
            York: John Wiley & Sons.
Lee, E. S.
    1966   A Theory of Migration. *Demography* **3**:47–57.
Lee, T.
    1969   The role of the ethnic community as a reception area for Italian immigrants
            in Melbourne. Paper presented at the first Institute of Australian Geographers
            Urban Studies Group Symposium, Adelaide, Australia.
Lispet, M., and Bendix, R., Eds.
    1966   *Class, Status, and Power* (second ed.) New York: The Free Press.
Lopreato, J.
    1968   *Peasants No More.* San Francisco: Chandler.
MacDonald, J. S., and MacDonald, L. D.
    1962   Urbanization, ethnic groups and social segmentation. *Social Research* **29**:433–
            448.
    1964   Chain migration, ethnic neighborhood formation and social networks. *Millbank
            Memorial Fund Quarterly* **42**:82–97.
Mitchell, J. C., Ed.
    1969   *Social Networks in Urban Situations.* Manchester: University of Manchester Press.
Novak, M.
    1971   *The Rise of the Unmeltable Ethnics: Politics and Culture in the Seventies.* New
            York: Macmillan.
Paine, S.
    1975   *Exporting Workers: The Turkish Case.* London: Cambridge University Press.
Park, R. E.
    1936   Human ecology. *American Journal of Sociology* **42**:1–15.
Patel, N.
    1972   A passage from India. *Transaction* **9**:25–29.
Philpott, S. P.
    1973   *West Indian Migration: The Montserrat Case.* New York: Humanities Press.
Price, C. A.
    1963   *Southern Europeans in Australia.* Melbourne: Oxford University Press.
    1966   Post-war migration: demographic background, in *New Faces: Immigration and
            Family Life in Australia* (A. Stoller, Ed.), pp. 11–29. Melbourne: F. W. Cheshire.
Richmond, A. H.
    1972   *Ethnic Residential Segregation in Metropolitan Toronto.* Toronto: Institute for
            Behavioral Research, York University.
Rose, H. A.
    1969   *Social Processes in the City: Race and Urban Residential Choice. Resource Paper*
            No. **6.** Washington, D.C.: Association of American Geographers.
Roseman, C. C.
    1971   Channelization of migration flows from the rural south to the industrial mid-
            west. *Proceedings, Association of American Geographers* **3**:140–146.
Schwarzweller, H. K., Brown, J. S., and Mangalam, J. J.
    1971   *Mountain Families in Transition: A Case Study of Appalachian Migration.* Uni-
            versity Park: The Pennsylvania State University Press.
Sengstock, M.C.
    1967   Maintenance of social interaction patterns in an ethnic group. Unpublished
            Ph.D. dissertation, Department of Sociology, Washington University, St. Louis,
            Mo.

1974   Iraqi Christians in Detroit: an analysis of an ethnic occupation, in *Arabic Speaking Communities in American Cities* (B. C. Aswad, Ed.), pp. 21–38. Staten Island, New York: Center for Migration Studies.

Sinclair, R., and Thompson, B.
1977   *Metropolitan Detroit: An Anatomy of Social Change.* Cambridge, Mass.: Ballinger.

Singer, L.
1962   Ethnogenesis and Negro–Americans today. *Social Research* **29**:419–432.

Smith, W. F.
1971   Filtering and Neighborhood Change, in *Internal Structure of the City* (L. S. Bourne, Ed.), pp. 170–179. New York: Oxford University Press.

Strauss, A. L.
1971   *The Contexts of Social Mobility: Ideology and Theory.* Chicago: Aldine.

Suttles, G. D.
1968   *The Social Order of the Slum: Ethnicity and Territory in the Inner City.* Chicago: The University of Chicago Press.

Swanson, J. C.
1978   The consequences of emigration for economic development in the Yemen Arab Republic. Unpublished Ph.D. dissertation, Department of Anthropology, Wayne State University, Detroit.

Tilly, C.
1974   *An Urban World.* Boston: Little, Brown.

Tilly, C., and Brown, C. H.
1967   On uprooting, kinship, and the auspices of migration. *International Journal of Comparative Sociology* **8**:139–164.

Thompson, B.
1973   Newcomers to the city: factors influencing initial settlement and community growth patterns: a review. *The East Lakes Geographer* **8**:50–78.
1980   *Cultural Ties as Determinants of Immigrant Settlement in Urban Areas.* New York: Arno.

Ward, D.
1968   The emergence of central immigrant ghettoes in American cities: 1840–1920. *Annals, Association of American Geographers* **58**:343–359.
1971   *Cities and Immigrants: A Geography of Change in Nineteenth Century America.* New York: Oxford Univ. Press.

Watson, J. L.
1975   *Emigration and the Chinese Lineage.* Berkeley and Los Angeles: University of California Press.

Whitelaw, J. S.
1969   Residential patterns of new non-europeans in Auckland. Paper presented at the first Institute of Australian Geographers Urban Studies Group Symposium, Adelaide, Australia.

Ziegler, S.
1977   The family unit and international migration: the perceptions of Italian immigrants' children. *International Migration Review* **11**:326–333.

21

Affirmative Action in Quebec: Middle and Upper Management in the Private Sector

Morton Weinfeld

INTRODUCTION

The French–English conflict in Canada is waged on two fronts; one national, the other focused within the province of Quebec itself. The former is concerned with issues like Quebec's position vis-à-vis the federal government or the other provinces, and the fate of the francophone (French-speaking and/or French origin) minorities outside Quebec; the latter is concerned primarily with the political, economic, and cultural development of the francophone collectivity in Quebec, the Québécois. Of special concern has been the historic dominance of the anglophone (English-speaking and/or British origin) minority in Quebec over business life in the province, particularly regarding large corporations in the areas of natural resources, manufacturing, and finance. This economic issue, largely internal to Quebec, forms the context of this paper. (Readers interested in a broader overview of Quebec's recent social and political history might consult McRoberts and Postgate [1980]).

Beginning in the early 1960s, the government of the province of Quebec has played an active and expanding role in the economic development of the province, and in the modernization of its institutions. The state apparatus has served as a vehicle to achieve "ratrappage," or catching up, with the more developed regions of Canada (Guindon, 1971). Through investment in education and the expansion of the provincial

361

public sector, many francophones have benefited from increased economic opportunities. Yet these general initiatives had little immediate impact on ethnic inequalities experienced by francophone Quebecers in the private sector in the province, where middle and upper echelons were dominated by anglophones (Vaillancourt, 1978).

It became apparent that the predominance of English as the language of work in these areas served as a barrier to the mobility of aspiring francophones, independent of any active discrimination. Thus, language policies of successive governments designed to make French the language of work in the province emerged as a strategy to overcome this obstacle and increase the representation of francophones in the higher levels of the corporate world.

These policies can be treated as examples of "affirmative action" on behalf of francophones in Quebec. The distinctions have not always been clear between objectives such as "francization"—promoting the use of the French *language*—and "francophonization"—promoting the employment of francophone *persons* in the private sectors. At times, each has been considered as means to achieve the other as end; in either case, the end result is some form of preferential treatment.

In this chapter I present an analytical history of the policies of francization and/or francophonization of the workplace in Quebec.

I begin with a brief review of actual and perceived economic inequalities of francophones, followed by a delineation of the legislative evolution of the current policy, with a concern for civil libertarian issues. I conclude by noting some limits of the affirmative action model suggested by the Quebec case.

THE EVIDENCE OF ECONOMIC INEQUALITY

Two sets of data form the empirical basis for the affirmative action case in the private sector in Quebec. The first concerns francophone underrepresentation in the elite corporate sectors, not only in Quebec but in Canada as a whole. There are roughly 6 million francophones in Canada, of whom roughly 5 million live in Quebec; francophones comprise roughly 25% and 80% of the populations of Canada and the province of Quebec, respectively. Clement (1975) has shown that francophone representation in the Canadian corporate elite has risen from 6.7% in 1951 to only 8.4% in 1972. Another study based on names of executives of 2400 companies listed in the 1971 *Directory of Directors* (a sample far broader than Clement's elite) found only 9.5% to be French Canadian (Presthus, 1973). Similar underrepresentation can be found within the province of Quebec, where one study found that only 15% of persons working in Quebec head offices and earning over $22,000 were francophone (Québec, 1972, 1:125). Another recent study found that although anglophone and francophone members of Quebec's economic "establishment" shared most views on ideological and economic questions, far greater power rested with the anglophone sector of the elite; the French elite often found itself relegated to a public relations function, mediating between the English-controlled business world and the government and consuming public (Fournier, 1976).

Yet the trend has been one of steady increases in francophone representation in recent years. One study by the Montreal Board of Trade found significant progress over 10 years. For 413 head offices, francophones participating in top management increased from 19% in 1967 to 31% in 1977; the middle-management gain was from 25 to 39%. For 147 regional offices sampled, the top-management gains rose from 42 to 77% (Montreal Board of Trade, 1977). Other data cited by Allaire and Miller (1980) reveal an increase between 1971 to 1978 from 68 to 75% in the proportion of Quebec's managers who are francophone; moreover, francophone managers are younger than anglophone managers, suggesting a future narrowing of the gap (Allaire and Miller 1980:16–17). Assessment of the current situation will depend on whether one stresses the current underrepresentation of francophones, or the trend toward more proportional representation.

The debate continues. A recent feature story in *La Presse* (Jannard, 20 June 1981:D1) reported a survey of the private sector with the (translated) headline "Very Slow Penetration in Large Corporations." The report cited in the article claimed that from 1964 to 1979, francophone representation in senior management rose only from 18 to 27%, and in middle management from 22 to 45%. Yet presentation of data in this way masks the effect of annual increments in recruitment of francophones, which had been rapid. Certainly, a cumulative change at middle-management from 22 to 45% must involve *annual* proportions of new francophone recruits well in excess of 45%. (This would be no surprise to any reader of the business sections of Montreal dailies.) Indeed, the same article documented that an average of 18 years is required for accession into upper management positions. Thus expansion of the pool of francophone junior executives through 1964–1979 would only begin to show dramatic impacts in the 1980s and 1990s. It should be noted that these changes refer to management, not ownership. Firms owned or controlled by French-speaking Quebecers have constituted a very small part of the overall provincial production; most corporations in Quebec are under American, Anglo-Canadian, or Anglo-Quebec control (Rayauld, 1967).

The second area of inequality was the low francophone incomes compared to those of other Quebecers. (The income gap between the provinces of Quebec and Ontario is another matter (see Armstrong, 1970:Chap.2; Faucher and Lamontagne, 1964).) Research for the Bilingualism and Biculturalism Commission (Raynauld, Marion, and Beland, 1967) found that the 1961 average incomes of English-origin Quebecers, whether unilingual or bilingual, were substantially higher than the incomes of unilingual or bilingual French-origin Quebecers. In a separate analysis of the income of salaried males in Montreal in 1961, the authors further clarified the dismal position of francophone workers. In a rank order of 14 ethnic origin categories by average annual income, French workers ranked 12th, ahead only of Italians and native Indians. A regression analysis of these incomes found that variables such as unemployment, age, years of schooling, and occupation could explain only a part of the variance in individual incomes. "Ethnicity" conceived as a residual variable, explained both $606 of the $1319 advantage (above the average) enjoyed by those of English–Scottish origin, and $267 of the $330 disadvantage of the French.

The Raynauld *et al*. study is an important example of the use of social science findings in influencing public discourse and political behavior. The findings confirmed the nationalist claim of anglophone exploitation of francophones in Quebec and were used as support for the need for the Quebec government to intervene actively to eliminate perceived linguistic discrimination against francophones, notably in the private sector. Subsequent studies using 1961–1971 comparisons seemed to confirm the image of unchanging inequalilty in income and were reported in the press (*Montreal Gazette*, 2 May 1977).

Even as such findings were being publicized in the 1960s and 1970s, they had declining applicability. First, the data drawn from the 1961 census reflected that period in Quebec history in which French workers clearly had lower educational attainment, lower occupational levels, and hence lower income levels than their English counterparts. Quebec was still emerging, belatedly, from the strict supervision of the Church and its self-image as a largely rural society; the substantial educational reforms of the 1960s and the ensuring upgrading of the Quebec labor force had not yet had much visible effect. Francophone opportunities were thus limited by a degree of antibusiness traditionalism, discrimination based on prejudicial stereotyping by anglophones, and the dominant role of English as the language of business. Given the changes underway in Quebec by the end of the 1960s, the findings of such studies were of more historical than contemporary accuracy.

Linguistic comparisons for 1961 and 1971 based on provincewide data were also flawed. The provincewide gaps were substantial. Yet anglophone Quebecers were and are concentrated overwhelmingly in Montreal, whereas the vast majority of francophone Quebecers are found outside the Montreal metropolitan area. The population in Quebec's smaller cities and in the farm and nonfarm rural areas is overwhelmingly French. Independent of any ethnic factor, metropolitan incomes in 1971 were significantly higher than incomes for smaller cities and for rural areas. Any fair comparison of ethnic income differences must control for the ethnic differences in rural and urban residence in Quebec.

The choice of the geographic unit of comparative analysis continues to affect recent research (and thus may have policy implications). Two recent studies have both confirmed substantial narrowings of the income disparities of the two groups by the late 1970s. Yet the study focusing on male incomes in Montreal (Boulet, 1979) found a greater reduction than that focusing on provincewide earners of both sexes (Bernard, Demers, Grenier, and Renaud, 1979); the remaining gaps were 15% (down from 51% in 1961), for the former study, and 20% for the latter. This remaining income gap may be explained by disparities in educational attainment. A *Montreal Star* survey (Clift, 30 March 1976) of the Montreal work force, which anticipated Boulet's results, found 19.3% of the English respondents, compared to 8.4% of the French, were university graduates.

These findings suggest that the salience of French origin, whether as discrimination on the part of the anglophones or as autonomous cultural factors characteristic of francophone Quebecers, plays far less a role in the process of income attainment today than in the past. The data offer testimony to the strides taken in the two decades since the "Quiet Revolution" was launched in the early 1960s. Still, some caution is needed in interpreting these findings. The narrowing of the income gaps may simply reflect greater wage increases in the province's public sector compared to the private, along with a more rapid expansion of the public sector work force, where francophones predominate. A recent comparison of salaries for similar work in the public and private sector in Quebec found the former between 7 and 16% higher than the latter (Vennat, 9 January 1979).

The image of francophones as underrepresented in private sector management and as comparatively victimized in terms of income has long been accepted by Quebec's intellectual and political elite and by the population at large. Recent francophone gains are seen as due both to natural social forces, including the upgrading of the labor force, and to the multidimensional effects of the francization policies (Allaire and Miller, 1980; Vaillancourt, 1978).

The foregoing discussion on trends in French–English income disparities parallels American debates on the trend with regard to black–white income gaps. Interpretation of the gap will depend, apart from other factors, on the units of comparison. In the United States, focusing on black–white gaps for the entire population will tend to obscure any progress made through the 1960s and 1970s. The incidence of high unemployment, low education, family disorganization, and low wage work for ghetto youth and for southern, rural, and older blacks would lower income levels and minimize progress over time.

However, a focus on that black subgroup in the population that has reaped the benefits of progressive legislation, in the form of expanded educational and occupational opportunity, and residence in high wage areas, paints a different picture. Looking at black family income of two-person families in the Northeast—for younger, educated blacks—reveals incomes as great as those for comparable whites (Glazer, 1975:41–42; Sowell, 1978). This controlled comparison indicates that income gaps in the U.S. are less the result of racial discrimination, as in unequal pay for equal work or unequal work for equal qualification—though that still persists—and more the result of structural factors producing a bifurcation in the black community itself (Wilson, 1977). Part of the community finds itself mired in poverty and low wage conditions, notably in the case of ghetto youth and female-headed families on welfare; whereas the young and college-educated enjoy career opportunities that some analysts have found surpass those for comparable whites (Freeman, 1976). In Quebec the rate of increase of francophone participation in postsecondary education is comparable to the gains registered for American blacks; for this reason incomes of younger, educated francophones approximate more closely the incomes of their anglophone counterparts in Quebec.

The Roots of Affirmative Action in Quebec

The foundations for affirmative action thinking in Quebec can be found in the federal Report of the Royal Commission on Bilingualism and Biculturalism and Quebec's Gendron Report. This is not surprising, given the reports' role in providing social scientific support for claims of francophone inequality. The Commission advocated a linguistic strategy to increase the number of French Quebecers in the business community through making French the language of work in the private sector in the province.

However, one thing is clear; the proportion of Francophones among recent recruits (to private firms) was much below the proportion of Francophones in the province of Quebec. . . . Clearly, some intervening factor, such as language difficulty or Francophone reluctance to join Anglophone companies, is hindering the development of Francophone participation in private industry [Canada, The Royal Commission, 1969:484].

Most of the recommendations made by the commissioners were specifically related to the objective of making the use of French widespread in private industry in the province through the use of French in internal communications, in published material, and so on. One recommendation, however, departed from the formally linguistic nature of the others to advocate an ethnic strategy more directly.

We recommend that the firms make every effort to interest Francophone students on [sic] business careers, by providing full information on career opportunities to the appropriate officials in French language educational institutes, by sending recruiting teams to these institutes both within and without Quebec [Canada, The Royal Commission, 1969:561].

As worded here, we have affirmative action in the sense of recruitment efforts, though the procedures suggested are less linguistic than "ethnic." Ethnic policies simply make explicit what is an implicit objective in linguistically framed policies—to increase the numbers of French Quebecers working in middle and senior positions in private industry. In one of the Commission's recommendations of an expressedly linguistic nature, designed to strengthen the position of the French language, we find one other element of affirmative action programs—that of a rigorous plan with goals and timetables, and the setting up of a mechanism for monitoring the performance of firms and institutions with regard to fulfilment of the goals. These proposals are set forth in recommendation 44, which called for the creation of Quebec task force to

design an overall plan for establishing French as the principal language of work in Quebec and to set a timetable for this process. . . . And to make recommendations to the provincial government for the achievement of the goal and for the establishment of permanent machinery of co-ordination [Canada, The Royal Commission, 1969:559–560].

The "permanent machinery" exists now in L'Office de La Langue Française, which has been responsible for implementing the provincial government's language legislation.

With the release of the provincial *Rapport de la Commission d'enqûete sur la situation de la langue française et sur les droits linguistiques au Québec* (Gendron Report) in December, 1972, the idea of affirmative action became further entrenched.[1] The section dealing with the language of

[1] The central theme of the Gendron Report was the demographic threat to the future survival of the French language in Quebec. The evidence from the mini-census of 1976 suggests that the "gloom and doom" predictions of the Gendron Report, have not materialized. In Montreal, and certainly in the province of Quebec, the French language is no longer threatened. It is not yet clear what role the language legislation of the Liberals and the Parti Québécois, and other Quebec government initiatives as in the field of immigration, have played in this development. Over the past few years the volume of immigration has abated, and the source of immigrants has shifted to include large numbers from French-speaking areas, such as France, Haiti, Morocco, Vietnam, and so on. For further evidence on the security of the French language in Quebec, see Joy (1978).

work refers to the overrepresentation of anglophone Quebecers and underrepresentation of francophones in the corporate hierarchy. As a strategy for resolving the dilemma, the Gendron Report placed far greater emphasis than did the Commission's Bilingualism and Biculturalism Report on the process of "francophonization" as an optimum means of "francization." It was argued that rather than simply making the workplace more linguistically attractive to francophones by increasing the use of French, increased use of French could be achieved by increased hiring of francophones. It is this logic, (which had a secondary place in the Commission's report), which is elevated to prominence in the Gendron Report.

In other words, the use of French as the language of work and the bilingualization of English-speaking senior personnel will become truly possible only when there are larger numbers of French-speaking individuals working at all administrative levels (*francophonisation*). The overrepresentation of the English-speaking element and the segregation of the two groups on the basis of language, constitute obstacles which, if not removed, will prevent any change in language usage within enterprises. [Québec, 1972, **1**:158].

The Gendron Report's central recommendation concerning the language of work is a straightforward enuciation of affirmative action objectives, endorsing statistically derived criteria to define proper objectives. The goal is to increase the proportions of francophones in the private sector at the various levels of administration—to levels commensurate with the francophone population proportions in Quebec, noting the different proportions in Montreal and in the remainder of the province.

We recommend that the Government propose, to the enterprises, a policy of "*francophonisation*" whereby, competence being equal, the number of French-speaking employees at intermediate and senior levels of the administrative hierarchy would be increased to an average rate which, in most establishments, would appreciably approach that existing in the Québec labor force, according to the two regions defined in this report [Québec, 1972, **1**:160].

Following this commitment to francophonization, the report then presents estimates of acceptable goals and a realistic timetable, given the constraints of labor supply and institutional change. As an example, the report suggested a plan whereby francophone representation among corporate personnel earning over $20,000 per year would increase from 30 to 40%, those earning $15,000–$20,000 would increase from 30 to 50%, and those earning less than $15,000 would increase from 50 to 60%, all by 1981, or roughly ten years from the release of Volume 1 (Québec, 1972:167–168).

Our objective here is not to summarize the full range of argument and recommendation proposed by the Gendron Report; rather it is to recognize the groundwork laid from the perspective of affirmative action.

The essence of the report is its espousal of a joint policy of francization and francophonization. Little attention was paid to civil libertarian issues arising from such policies.

Affirmative action plans as envisaged in the report are constrained solely by the limits of the supply of trained francophone personnel—given the desire of the planners to make certain that francophonization proceeds "*a compétence égale*," that is, without a dilution of the quality of the personnel recruited to private enterprise. In a section recapitulating the steps recommended to the government, one finds ethical and legal issues subsumed in a subordinate clause:

and, on the other hand (d) persuade firms in the private sector not only to encourage the recruitment and promotion of French-speaking employees, which presupposes a certain initial discrimination in favor of that group . . . [Québec, 1972, **1**:176].

In short, the Gendron Report endorsed legislative intervention to increase the proportion of francophones in the private sector.

THE LEGISLATION

Following the release of the Gendron Report, the provincial Liberal government initiated the legislative basis for affirmative action in Quebec.[2] As in the report, the distinctions between francophonization and francization in the corporate world were often blurred. Which was to be considered the primary aim of policy, and which means to that aim? Civil libertarians and anglophones were particularly concerned that the emphasis remain as much as possible on language rather than origin. The Liberal government's 1974 Bill 22, known as the Official Language Act in Quebec, made French *the* official language in the province, and also the language of work. The thrust of Bill 22 in the private sector was the concept of the francization program, designed to make French the working language.

Section 29 c. 6 of Bill 22 stated:

The francization programs which must be adopted and applied by business firms wishing to obtain the certificates mentioned above must . . . relate especially to:
a) the knowledge that the management and the personnel must have of the official language
b) the francophone presence in management

Bill 22 provided no definition of the term *francophone*. Thus, interpreters of the law were left to their own devices to puzzle out the meaning of

[2] I am indebted to Rosenstein (1977) of the Quebec Bar for his analysis dealing with possible legal interpretations of the different terminologies used in Bill 22, Bill 1, and Bill 101.

the term. Could a francophone be someone who spoke French—in which case any French-speaking Quebecer, regardless of ethnic or linguistic background, could qualify? From the text of the law, it would seem that the emphasis was on an ethnic definition of the term, implying far more than simple French-speaking ability. Subsection *a* of section 29 already referred to the French linguistic aptitude of management. Obviously the expression "francophone presence in management" was not intended to be redundant under subsection *a* and must have meant something other than linguistic competence. In short, the term was used as was "francophonization" in the Gendron Report, that is, aimed at increasing the numbers of French origin Quebecers in management positions.

Just at the time the Quebec government was legislating its language laws endorsing francophonization of the workplace, it was enacting a new antidiscrimination bill. In June 1975, the government of Quebec passed its Charter of Human Rights and Freedoms, the central antidiscrimination and civil rights document of the provincial administration. This act (henceforth the charter) did not endorse affirmative action programs designed to favor minority groups. Indeed, section 10 of the charter, its central antidiscrimination article, might be intrepreted as prohibiting affirmative action programs:

Every person has a right to full and equal recognition and exercise of his human rights and freedoms, without distinction, exclusion, or *preference* based on race, colour, sex, civil status, religion, political convictions, language, ethnic or national origin, and social conditions. (Emphasis added.)

Use of the term *preference* might well form a basis for ruling against the legality of affirmative action programs, based either on ethnic origin or on language. At any rate, one can ask what is envisaged by inclusion of language as a proscribed category. Certainly, one interpretation might well be that job seekers cannot be penalized in the seeking of employment because of their language. Does the inscription of language bias call into question the very basis of francization programs, which very clearly favor one group, the speakers of French, over another group, the speakers of English or other languages? Francophonization might well be prohibited not only by the language criterion, but by that of ethnic or national origin as well. It would seem that section 10 could pose serious judicial obstacles toward the development of affirmative action policies as envisaged in Bill 22 (and subsequent legislation), if some preference could not be shown to French-speaking persons over English-speaking persons.

Following its provincial election victory in 1976, the Parti Québécois produced its White Paper on Language, which appeared in 1977 (C. Laurin, 1977). The White Paper continued in the Gendron tradition by advocating affirmative action strategies as the optimum means for increasing francophone participation in business management:

To avoid becoming embroiled in quarrels over words [here referring to the controversy over *francization* and *francophonization*] business firms should set themselves the following definite objective: to reflect at every level and in every function of their personnel, the *ethnic make up of the population of* Quebec. There is nothing revolutionary about this; it is such an elementary principle of social justice that the United States, that paradise of private enterprise, has adopted it as the basis of its social hiring policy. [C. Laurin, 1977:99; emphasis added].

The statement here reaffirms the thinking expressed earlier in the Gendron Report—that francization in the workplace is optimally achieved through a process of francophonization—and at any rate the latter remains the ultimate objective of policy.

Bill 22 was never tested in the courts. The Parti Québécois's first attempt at language legislation was the short-lived Bill 1, introduced on April 27, 1977. In the relevant "affirmative action" section 112(*b*), the legislation departed from the previous text in Bill 22 by introducing the ambiguous term *Québécois* to substitute for the previously ambiguous term, *francophone*.

The francization programs adopted and applied by business firms in accordance with the foregoing sections must provide for the attainment of the following objectives:
a. a satisfactory knowledge of the official language of the part of both managament and personnel;
b. an increase on the number of Quebecers (Québécois) at all levels of the business firm, including the board of directors and the senior executive levels so as to generalize the use of French.

In this formulation we have for the first time the introduction of specific target areas, such as the board of directors, indicating that the goals of corporate francization are as much the regaining of economic control from anglophone hands as the broadening of economic opportunity for francophones. In quantitative terms corporate directorships would have little effect on increasing francophone representation, compared to opening up management at middle levels. A situation in which middle management was predominantly francophone whereas senior executives and directors were predominantly anglophone would be unacceptable.

The perplexing introduction of the term *Québécois* signaled a clear departure from the definition of both the Gendron Commission and that expressed by Parti Québécois officials. Once again from the legal text it is clear that more is meant than simply a linguistic reference, given the content of 112 (*b*) (item *a*), which spells out linguistic requirements. Moreover, the ethnic meaning of the term *Québécois* is expressed clearly in the preamble to Bill 1 in such phrases as "the French language has always been the language of the Quebec people (*peuple Québécois*" or by the statements in other sections of the law that Quebecers have the right to demand communication and instruction in French (section 2 and 6).

In its brief submitted to the government on Bill 1, the Quebec Human Rights Commission expressed its worry about the use of the term *Québécois* in a nationalistic sense, rather than in a civic sense denoting all residents of the province of Quebec. The commission also addressed the possible conflicts between the individual rights based on language in section 10 of the Human Rights Charter, and the very basis of language legislation as in either Bill 22 or of the Liberals or Bill 1. The commission affirmed the tension here between the collective rights of the majority expressed in the language legislation and the nondiscrimination rights defended for the minority (or individual) in the charter. However, the commission argued that the intention of section 10 was clearly not to guarantee the right of every Quebecer to work in their own language, and that realistic interpretation of the charter must take into account the primacy of the French language in Quebec.

Bill 1 was permitted to die on the order paper and was replaced by a new "Charter of the French Language," or Bill 101, which has been passed and which was still in force in 1983. Although the opposition of the anglophone community to Bill 101 remains substantial,[3] as was the case for Bill 22 and Bill 1, there is a shift *away* from francophonization to francization in the text of the bill dealing with employment in the private sector. The reversal can be seen in section 141 of Bill 101, which provides that

The francization programme is intended to generalize the use of French at all levels of the business firm. This implies:
a. the knowledge of the official language on the part of management, the members of the professional corporations, and the other members of the staff;
b. an increase at all levels of the business firm including the board of directors, in the number of *persons having a good knowledge of the French language* so as to generalize its use. (Emphasis added)

[3] Bill 101 has been subjected to a variety of legal challenges. The section defining French as the sole language of record for authoritative texts of the bills of the National Assembly has already been overturned by the Supreme Court. The Charter of Rights and Freedoms of the new Canadian Constitiution, adopted in 1982, established minority language education rights that differ slightly from those in Bill 101. The Canadian Constitution, which supercedes any provincial legislation, would permit Canadian citizens who had received their primary education in English anywhere in Canada to send their children to English language public school in Quebec. Bill 101 limits this right to citizens who had received their primary schooling in English in Quebec. The Supreme Court will have to adjudicate this conflict.

Gone are the ambiguous categories of *francophone* or *Québécois*; in their place is the nonethnic phrase "persons having a good knowledge of the French language." As a result, anyone who masters the French language is theoretically entitled to any "preferential treatment" that may emerge in the pattern of corporate hiring. Section 141, carefully drafted as a language measure, contains no references to percentage goals or quotas, though timetables are outlined for the receipt of francization certificates. It is sufficient to demonstrate that the working language of the firm, including management, is French, with no reference to either the ethnic or linguistic composition in the staff. Thus, although the long-term objective may remain that of increasing francophone participation in management, the legislative strategy is that of francization.

THE RIGHTS OF ANGLOPHONES

Notwithstanding the clear linguistic nature of the policy, there may well remain powerful incentives for Quebec firms to adopt a shortcut to francization by the hiring of francophone employees, that is, Quebecers who already had the requisite knowledge of French (Vaillancourt, 1978:300). Other firms might still sense—rightly or wrongly—that the end goal of government intervention remains francophonization, meaning the hiring of French Canadians.

Francophonization is perhaps an expedient, but certainly not the only, way for firms to francize their operations. In theory, francization could proceed through the provision of language training for all anglophone employees, particularly those older employees most likely to be unilingually English, or in providing French language training to new anglophone recruits, in much the same manner of the federal government's language programs for the public service.

Anglophone job-seekers might seek legal recourse in the protections under section 10 of the Quebec Human Rights Act, since Bill 101 must conform to its provisions. Thus anglophones claiming linguistic discrimination could test the legality of selective hiring procedures against the antidiscrimination provisions (which include language) of section 10 of the Human Rights Charter.

It is doubtful that section 141 of Bill 101 would be tested against the Charter of Human Rights in the courts, let alone overturned. Section 20 of the Quebec Human Rights Charter permits the suspension of non-discrimination strictures when there does seem to be a clear job-related function: "A distinction, exclusion or preference based on the aptitudes or qualification required in good faith for an employment . . . is deemed nondiscriminatory."

Here we have the merit loophole found in most civil rights legislation,[4] which poses the question of whether knowledge of French can be considered as a "qualification required in good faith for an employment" in the area of middle or senior management in Quebec. If the courts so ruled, the application of section 10 would be suspended, and that at least with regard to language of work, Bill 101 could stand.

In the absence of legal precedents, one can develop scenarios "ad absurdum." One ironic such scenario would have Quebec courts follow an "American model" in defense of victimized groups. The courts may well interpret a requirement (French-speaking ability) to be legal, while recognizing a possible discriminatory impact of such a requirement. Is there equal opportunity for all citizens to achieve the specific qualification required? Are there any protective obligations that the courts might mandate (short of explicit preferential hiring) toward non-French speakers from either firms or the provincial government? Should at some future point anglophones become underrepresented in middle management in the private sector, might the courts then mandate some form of affirmative action, such as language training, on behalf of unilingual anglophones?[5] English school systems might then be held accountable, even sued, for failure to provide French fluency and for thus contributing to unequal opportunity. Even in the present situation, one wonders whether the court might not differentiate for reasons of equity between categories of non-French speakers: for example, an anglophone born and raised in Quebec who speaks little French versus a recent immigrant who never had any opportunity to learn French?

Although it is true that the vast majority of persons having a "good knowledge of French" are francophone Quebecers, the proportions of young anglophones with a working knowledge of French has been increasing steadily. In times of economic recession limited positions in Quebec firms will be sought both by bilingual anglophones as well as by francophones (many of whom will also be bilingual), and the supply of candidates may exceed the demand. In such conditions it is hoped that any employment clauses of Bill 101 will be administered in accord-

---

[4] The equivalent in the federal Human Rights Act of 1977 is found in section 14a, which stipulates that a distinction based on a "bona fida occupational requirement" cannot be considered as discriminatory.

[5] Such speculations may be less farfetched than seems the case at first glance. A lead article in *The Montreal Gazette* (Stewart, 23 September 1980) reports on a *"plan d'action"* to be proposed to the Quebec cabinet suggesting increased government services to Quebecers in languages other than French, along with affirmative action initiatives to increase nonfrancophone respresentation in the provincial public service.

ance with the letter and the spirit of Quebec's Charter of Human Rights and Freedoms.

In both its first and second annual reports, the Quebec Human Rights Commission has urged amendment of the charter to permit the introduction of affirmative action programs. This recommendation has been accepted by the Parti Québécois government, which introduced amendments to Quebec's Human Rights Charter in 1982 that were designed to legalize voluntary and mandated affirmative action programs. It should not be assumed that such a recommendation is rooted solely in the desire to promote the interests of francophones more effectively. Quebec has a number of growing racial and ethnic minorities—including native peoples, blacks, Orientals, other immigrant groups—as well as women, who suffer from discrimination in Quebec as elsewhere in Canada. Affirmative action may be seen by the Quebec Human Rights Commission as an effective remedy. Moreover, the existence of enabling legislation for affirmative action in Section 15.2 of the Canadian Charter of Rights and Freedoms of the new Canadian Constitution passed in 1982, as well as the earlier (1977) Canadian Human Rights Act, and in legislation of other provinces, has prodded the Quebec Commission to demand similar powers.[6]

CONCLUSION: LIMITS OF THE AFFIRMATIVE ACTION MODEL IN THE QUEBEC CASE

The emergence of the policy of francization as applied to the use of French in the workplace has reflected in its various stages what may be called a conventional model of affirmative action: A group is defined as disadvantaged due to past and present discrimination (established by deviations from expected proportional representation in desired social categories). Members of this group (more or less precisely defined) are therefore eligible for preferential, compensatory treatment. The Quebec case raises specific issues that deserve discussion.

What criteria or definitions are used to delimit the group categories, which will avoid the injustice of excluding the deserving and including the nondeserving? Perhaps in no area of public policy is the task of determining eligibility for benefits as difficult as in affirmative action programs. In Quebec the confusion is multiplied by the intersection of linguistic and ethnic objectives of the policy. Unfortunately, social group-

---

[6] Most provincial Human Rights Acts do permit affirmative action programs in one form or another.

ings whose boundaries are clear and nonoverlapping are rare. The Gendron Report (Québec, 1972, **3**:1–7) provides a long list of ascriptive categories of citizens of Quebec and definitions of each. The terms include: "*majorité, minorité, francophone, anglophone, allophone, allogène, bilingue, unilingue, Québécois, autre origine, néo-Canadien, Canadien français, Canadian anglais, immigrant.*" One questions the value of such a proliferation of categories as a guide to equitable, efficient policymaking.

Under the new Canadian Constitution passed in 1982 there is no doubt that affirmative action programs, including those advocating preferential treatment, are legal (Hogg, 1982; Tarnopolsky, 1982). Ironically, many of the earlier debates about the ethnic versus linguistic basis of affirmative action in Quebec are rendered obsolete; section 15.2 explicitly permits programs aimed at "the amelioration of conditions of disadvantaged individuals or groups including those that are disadvantaged because of race, national or ethnic origin, colour, religion, sex, age or mental or physical disability." Thus programs or laws aimed at benefitting people who are by origin French Quebecers are legal, once we define French Quebecers as a disadvantaged group with regard to employment in Quebec's private sector.

One might note for comparative purposes that no legislative text of similar clarity exists in the United States, where the case for affirmative action programs and/or preferential treatment has relied on executive order or heroic judicial interpretation of statutes such as the 1964 Civil Rights Act or the Fourteenth Amendment to the Constitution.

Ironically, "language" is not mentioned in the list of suspect categories in the Canadian legislation. Language rights are dealt with in other sections of the Constitution (see footnote 3). It seems that the term *including* in section 15.2 signifies that the list is not exhaustive, and perhaps language might be added through subsequent amendment or judicial intrepretation. Until that time, however, the affirmative action clauses of Bill 101, in its character as a purely linguistic measure, may not as yet have clear constitutional protection.

Even if groups could be fairly and consistently defined, it is not clear why every member of the group ought to be eligible for preferential treatment. In the Quebec case, clearly not all francophones are (or have been) disadvantaged. Thus in Quebec, as elsewhere, variation in need or circumstance within a group is ignored.

Although the problem of equitable categorization plagues any affirmative action plan, the Quebec case offers other important characteristics that suggest limits to the extension of the model. We note first that the group targeted for special help constitutes the numerical majority (in Quebec), comprising roughly 80% of the population; in most other societies the targeted groups are numerical minorities as well as minorities in terms of power and the distribution of societal resources. Economically, the French in Quebec have been a minority group, with the English controlling industrialization; politically and culturally, however, French Quebecers have controlled their own institutions at least since Confederation and have enjoyed formal equality of opportunity in both public and private life. Where formal democracy exists, so that a majority group can exercise formal political power through the principle of majority rule, any assumption of economic victimization of the majority group by a minority, reflected in statistical disproportion, and any assumed notion of culpability (of the minority) and redress (for the majority) must be made with caution. It is this absence of democratic control of political power that differentiates the South African from the Quebec case, though in both cases the majority group has suffered economic inferiority.

It is the group that holds political power—the French—that is devising policies from which it will benefit. This contrasts with American affirmative action, where theoretically, the white majority legislates benefits for a nonwhite minority. In the U.S. not only are nonwhites a numerical minority, but the majority of the persons issuing the executive orders, passing congressional legislation, implementing these through the bureaucracy and upholding affirmative action through the courts have been white.

These characteristics may carry implications for an assessment of Quebec's initiatives from the standpoint of liberal, democratic practice. In most cases of affirmative action a majority group in a society, not without some needed prodding, recognizes the problems persisting after the achievement of formal equality of opportunity by minority groups. Affirmative action programs for "small" minorities mean that for the vast majority the process of status allocation remains unchanged—a rough amalgam of merit, ascriptive advantage, connections, personality, and luck. Nothing restricts the numerical minority from developing its human resources to a point where a quota may not be necessary, and in fact a minority may even become naturally overrepresented in various desired categories, as has happened to groups such as Jews and Orientals, without serious impact on majority opportunities. Though the notion may grate on certain members of minority groups who have fought long against oppression, there may be something altruistic, at least attractive, about a society in which the majority group finally makes a decision, articulated through a variety of its institutions, to restrict its own opportunities in order to help—and compensate—minority group members.

This contrasts with the Quebec case, where a numerical majority legislates benefits—perhaps long overdue—to its own members. French control of Quebec's political institutions and the absence of legal restrictions on francophone business activity make the case for extreme discrimination in the past weaker than that for American blacks, who have the legacy of slavery and Jim Crow. Indeed, historians of Quebec still debate the degree to which the evolution of Quebec's French population reflected natural cultural forces, disinclining French Quebecers from entrepreneurial endeavor and scientific training, or subtle oppression and manipulation by the British. Assertions of historic antipathy toward business and business careers by French Canadians are not the fictional creation of anglophone historians (P. Laurin, 1978).

Thus, I would argue that although the modalities of Quebec's language legislation, as they impinge upon corporate hiring, are those of "affirmative action," the philosophical underpinnings are diametrically opposed to those underlying affirmative action; they reflect the values of economic self-determination and economic nationalism, complements to the political nationalism that has infused political expression in all provincial political parties, but most intensively, the Parti Québécois.

Societies can be evaluated in terms of how well they treat minorities. Quebec's leaders have argued correctly that the status of its anglophone minority, in terms of the acquired language rights enjoyed by the group, contrasts favorably with the historic experience of francophone minorities in the rest of Canada who have been deprived of language rights. The comparison has been used to demonstrate Quebec's tolerance of its minorities and its democratic predisposition. Yet affirmative action on behalf of a French majority, legislated and enforced by a French majority, lacks the check of political backlash or public opinion operative in cases of preferential treatment for numerical minorities. Restraint and caution are thus crucial. Historically, numerical minorities have suffered more often and more intensely than majorities, and have thus been the main beneficiaries of antidiscrimination legislation and an unfolding tolerance; for this reason legislative restrictions on minorities—even minorities perceived to be privileged—have become rare in liberal–democratic societies.

REFERENCES

Allaire, Y., and Miller, R. E.
    1980   *Canadian Business Response to the Legislation on Francization in the Workplace.*
           Montreal: C. D. Howe Research Institute.
Armstrong, D. E.
    1970   *Education and Economic Achievement* (Documents of the Royal Commission
           on Bilingualism and Biculturalism). Ottawa: Information Canada.

Bernard, P., Demers, A., Grenier, D., and Renaud, J.
  1979   L'Evolution de la situation socioeconomique des francophones et des non-fran-
          cophones au Québec (1971–1978). Montreal: Office de la langue française.
Boulet, J.
  1979   L'evolution des disparités linguistiques de revenues de travail dans la zone me-
          tropolitaire de Montréal de 1961 à 1977 (Document 127). Ottawa: Conseil Econ-
          omique du Canada.
Canada, The Royal Commission
  1969   The Royal Commission on Bilingualism and Biculturalism (Vol. 3) The Work World.
          Ottawa: Information Canada.
Clement, W.
  1975   The Canadian Corporate Elite. Toronto: McClelland and Stewart.
Clift, D.
  1976   French elite suffers most in salary scale. The Montreal Star **March 30**:1.
Faucher, A. and Lamontagne, M.
  1964   History of industrial development, in French Canadian Society (M. Rioux and
          Y. Martin, Eds.), pp. 257–270. Toronto: McClelland and Stewart.
Fournier, P.
  1976   The Quebec Establishment. Montreal: Black Rose Books.
Freeman, R. B.
  1976   The Over Educated American. New York: Academic Press.
Glazer, N.
  1975   Affirmative Discrimination. New York: Basic Books.
Guindon, H.
  1971   Social unrest, social class, and Quebec's bureaucratic revolution, in Canadian
          Society (B. R. Blishen, Eds.), pp. 469–477. Toronto: Macmillan.
Hogg, P. W.
  1982   Canada Act 1982 Annotated. Toronto: Carswell.
Jannard, M.
  1981   Tres lente percée dans les grandes enterprises. Le Presse **June 30**:D1.
Joy, R.
  1978   Canada's Official Language Minorities. Montreal: C. B. Howe Research Institute.
Laurin, C.
  1977   Quebec's Policy on the French Language. Québec: Éditeur officiel du Québec.
Laurin, P.
  1978   The businessman: Quebec's public enemy no 1? A speech given in Montreal,
          Chambre de Commerce, February 14.
McRoberts, K and Postgate, D.
  1980   Quebec: Social Change and Political Crisis. Toronto: McClelland and Stewart.
Montreal Board of Trade
  1977   Questionnaire to Member Firms. **June.** Montreal: Montreal Board of Trade.
The Montreal Gazette
  1977   Unilingual francophones get lowest pay in 1971: study. The Montreal Gazette
          May 2:3.
Presthus, R.
  1973   Elite Accommodation in Canadian Politics. Toronto: Macmillan.
Québec, Commission d'enquête (Gendron Report)
  1972   La Situation de la langue française au Québec. Rapport de la Commission
          d'enquête sur la situation de la langue française et sur les droits linguistiques
          au Québec, Québec: Editeur officiel du Québec. vols. 1–3.

Raynauld, A.
    1967   *La Propriété des entreprises aux Québec* (a study for the Royal Commission on
            Bilingualism and Biculturalism), Ottawa.
Raynauld, A., Marion, G., and Beland, R.
    1967   *La Répartition des revenus selon les groupes ethniques au Canada* (a study for
            the Royal Commission on Bilingualism and Biculturalism), Ottawa.
Rosenstein, M.
    1977   Bill 101 and affirmative action: francization vs. francophonization, in *Language
            Regulations of Business* (Meredith Memorial Lectures), pp. 151–159. Toronto:
            Richard de Boo.
Sowell, T.
    1978   Are quotas good for Blacks? *Commentary* **65**(6):39–43.
Stewart, J.
    1980   Quebec eyes boost to Anglos. *The Montreal Gazette* **September 23**:1.
Tarnopolsky, W. S.
    1982   The Equality Rights, in *The Canadian Charter of Rights Freedoms: Commentary*
            (W. S. Tarnopolsky and G. A. Beaudoin, Eds.), pp. 395–442. Toronto: Carswell.
Vaillancourt, F.
    1978   La Charte de la langue française du Québec. *Canadian Public Policy* **4**(3):284–
            308.
Vennat, P.
    1979   Le publique paie mieux. *La Presse* **January 9**:1.
Wilson, W. J.
    1977   *The Declining Significance of Race.* Chicago: University of Chicago Press.

22

The New Asian Immigrants*

Morrison G. Wong
Charles Hirschman

INTRODUCTION

Following the communist victory in Vietnam in the spring of 1975, more than 130,000 Vietnamese and Cambodian refugees entered the United States. Subsequently, the Indochina exodus continued, and by the middle of 1979, the United States had admitted over 200,000 refugees. With the continuing human tragedy of the "boat people" in Southeast Asia these numbers will surely increase. Behind the headlines of the Vietnamese refugees, there is an equally significant process of new immigration to the United States from other Asian countries, including Korea, China (including Taiwan and Hong Kong), the Philippines, and India. In the early 1960s, only about 7% of all immigrants, about 20,000 per year, came from Asia. But by the middle 1970s, more than one-third of all legal immigrants to the United States, almost 150,000 per year, were arriving from Asia. These figures exclude the Indochina refugees because they were admitted under "parole status" outside of the normal immigration process. In this paper we will review the background of the new Asian immigration to the United States during the last decade and describe the changes in the numbers and characteristics of immigrants from

* This research was made possible by a U.S. Public Health Service Grant (MH 15497-01) and a Duke University Biomedical Research Support Grant. The authors wish to thank Linda Gordon and Steven Schroffel of the Immigration and Naturalization Service, Stephen Couch of the Smithsonian Institution, and Monica Boyd of Carleton University for their valuable assistance.

specific Asian countries relative to other immigrants. Finally, we will speculate on the possible consequences of this new Asian immigration on American society.

UNITED STATES IMMIGRATION POLICY TOWARD ASIA

As a flow between nations, international migration has almost always been subject to legal restrictions of one kind or another. Both the historical barriers that limited Asian immigration to the United States and the turnaround of the last decade arose from shifts in United States policies. Although the reforms of the Immigration Act of 1965 put all countries on a relatively equal footing, previous United States immigration policy favored whites above other races, and northwestern European groups above all.

United States immigration policy toward Asia is a classic case of racial exclusion, predating the restrictive legislation of the 1920s by several decades. Immigration to the United States from China reached significant levels in the middle of the 19th century, with most Chinese immigrants settling on the West Coast (Lyman, 1974). After several decades of anti-Chinese agitation inspired by real or imagined competition with white workers and racist propaganda (Sandmeyer, 1973; Saxton, 1971), Congress passed the Chinese Exclusion Act of 1882, which sharply curtailed further labor immigration from China. Originally intended to be terminated after 10 years, the act was renewed in 1892 and made a permanent feature of the United States policy in 1904 (Kung, 1962). Small numbers of Chinese immigrants, usually around 1000–2000, continued to arrive in the United States during the first several decades of the 20th century under special provisions (U.S. Bureau of the Census, 1975:107).

A similar fate was experienced by Japanese immigrants a few decades later. Japanese immigration was encouraged by West Coast business as a source of cheap labor during the last decade of the 19th and first decade of the 20th century. But anti-Japanese sentiments were fanned by white workers whose wage levels were undercut by the new immigrants. Thus, Japanese immigration was reduced to much lower levels with the "Gentlemen's Agreement" of 1908, whereby Japan limited migration to the United States to only nonlaborers (Daniels, 1970).

Filipinos were the third major Asian group to immigrate to the United States. Like the Japanese before them, many first immigrated to Hawaii to work on the sugar and pineapple plantations. During the 1920s Filipino migration to the United States (mainland) gained momentum, coming directly from the Philippines or indirectly through Hawaii (Burma, 1951; Daniels and Kitano, 1970). Because Filipinos were nationals of the United States, there were no legal restrictions placed on them and they were not subject to quota restrictions. However, in 1934, the Tydings–McDuffie Act (Filipino Exclusion Act) was passed, this placed an "alien" status on Filipinos and hence restricted Filipino immigration to 50 persons per year. In 1946, an immigration quota of 100 persons was established for Filipino immigrants (Christiansen, 1979).

The Immigration Act of 1924 reinforced the racist and exclusionistic immigration policies of the United States toward all immigrants, especially those of Asian ancestry., (For a more detailed review of Asian immigration, see Hune, 1977).

The Immigration and Nationality Act (McCarran–Walter) of 1952 was more of a rationalization of existing immigration policy than a reform. For the Eastern Hemisphere, including Asia, there were two routes of immigration through the "quota" or the "nonquota" system. Nonquota immigration was only for immediate relatives (spouses, children, parents) of United States citizens and other selected cases. Wives of United States servicemen stationed abroad were a typical case of immigration exempt from the quota system. The quota system followed the national origins restrictions of the 1924 legislation with only token quotas for Asians: 105 for China, 185 for Japan, and 100 each for India and the Philippines (the minimum).

The Immigration Act of 1965 provided the first real reform of immigration policy in the 20th century. The national origins quotas, which favored immigrants from northwestern Europe, were abolished, and each country was put on an equal footing. The principle of family reunification and the emphasis of scarce occupational skills became the major criteria for the admission of immigrants. The preference system of the 1965 Act (see Table 1) was used to select the 170,000 immigrants allowed under the numerical ceilings. Aside from a limit of 20,000 immigrants annually from any single country, no country was given preference under the new system. In addition to the 170,000 spouses from the Eastern hemisphere under these preferences, immediate relatives (parents and children below the age of 21) of United States citizens were exempt from numerical limitations. The new preference system of the 1965 Act was phased in from 1966 to 1968, providing for an adjustment period from the old McCarren–Walter period. During this transition period, unused visas from undersubscribed countries were allotted to other countries with a large waiting list. Beginning in 1969, immigrant visas were to be distributed without preference to any country.

Table 1

Preference System, Immigration Act of 1965[a]

Preference category	Limit
1. First preference: Unmarried sons and daughters of U.S. citizens.	Not more than 20%
2. Second preference: Spouse and unmarried sons and daughters of an alien lawfully admitted for permanent residence.	20%, plus any not required for first preference
3. Third preference: Members of the professions and scientists and artists of exceptional ability.	Not more than 10%
4. Fourth preference: Married sons and daughters of U.S. citizens.	10%, plus any not required for first three preferences
5. Fifth preference: Brothers and sisters of U.S. citizens.	24%, plus any not required for first four preferences.
6. Sixth preference: Skilled and unskilled workers in occupations for which labor is in short supply in U.S.	Not more than 10%
7. Seventh preference: Refugees to whom conditional entry or adjustment of status may be granted.	Not more than 6%
8. Nonpreference: Any applicant not entitled to one of the preceding preferences.	Any numbers not required for preference applicants.

[a]Source: Reports of the Visa Office, 1968, Bureau of Security and Consular Affairs, Department of State, p. 68., in Keeley (1975a).

THE IMPACT OF THE REFORM IMMIGRATION ACT OF 1965

The reforms of the 1965 Immigration Act have had important consequences for American society at large and especially for specific ethnic or nationality communities in the United States (Keely, 1971, 1974, 1975a, 1975b). Perhaps the most significant consequences were the sharp increase in the number of Asian immigrants to the United States and the corresponding decrease in the number of European immigrants. Under previous legislation, including the McCarran–Walter Act of 1952, the number of Asian immigrants was limited to a small trickle. But with the passage of the 1965 Immigration Act, the number of Japanese, Chinese, Koreans, Indians, and Filipinos rose dramatically (Boyd, 1971, 1974). "The Asian Pacific triangle was immediately abolished and, with it, the last vestiges of a policy which discriminated against those of Asian birth or ancestry (Keely, 1975b)."

Figure 1 graphically illustrates the impact of the 1965 Immigration Act of annual immigration for selected European and Asian countries.

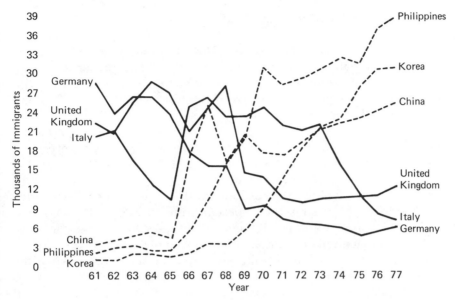

Figure 1   Annual number of immigrants from selected European and Asian countries,
1961–1977.

Using these countries as representative of European and Asian migration
trends, we note a reversal of roles of Europe and Asia as contributors
to the immigrant flow of the United States. During the McCarran–Walter
period, European countries were the major contributors of immigrants
to the United States (42%). However, in recent years (1975–1977), only
about 17% of the immigration came from Europe. Note that the recent
annual number of immigrants from Germany, the United Kingdom, and
Italy is lower than before the enactment of the 1965 Immigration Act.
Asian immigration, on the other hand, has experienced a phenomenal
increase since the McCarran–Walter days. Though limited to a small
trickle in the early 1960s, present Asian immigration accounts for about
35% of the total legal immigration to the United States.

   Except for the period 1975–1976, when more than 130,000 Vietnamese
were admitted to the United States under the conditional status (as
refugees), Asian immigration to the United States has largely gone un-
noticed by the larger society. This may be partly due to the small proportion of Asians in the United States (about 1% of the total United States
population in 1970) and their geographical segregation in certain West
Coast cities (U.S. Bureau of the Census, 1973). However, in terms of sheer
numbers, the influx of migrants from Korea, China, and the Philippines
for the 1975–1977 period has been equally as high as that of the Vietnamese.

The Number of Asian Immigrants

In order to measure the impact of the 1965 Immigration Act on the sources of immigration to the United States, Table 2 presents data on the numbers of immigrants by region of birth (specific countries with Asia) and percentage change between five time periods: (1) the last five years under the McCarran–Walter (Immigration and Naturalization Act of 1952) regulations (1961–1965); (2) the three-year transition period[1] in which the quota system was phased out (1966–1968); (3) the three successive three-year periods (1969–1971, 1972–1974, 1975–1977) when the policies of the act were fully in effect.

The annual number of immigrants to the United States has steadily increased with each subsequent period (from 290,000 to 416,000 immigrants). (The annual average figure of 380,000 persons for the 1966–1968 period is actually inflated due to the inclusion of 99,312 Cuban refugees who had their parole status adjusted to immigrants in 1966. When the Cubans are excluded, the average annual immigration for 1966–1968 was about 347,000 persons.) But most significant has been the relative and absolute decline in the number of European immigrants and the phenomenal increase of Asian migration to the United States. In the early 1960s an average of 21,000 Asians immigrated to the United States annually. Currently, about 150,000 Asian immigrants are admitted to the United States annually, an increase of about 600% (Asians comprised 35% of the recent total immigration to the United States). With the exception of Japan, the impact of the 1965 Immigration Act was to increase substantially immigration from all Asian countries, though numbers and percentages differ for each country and time period. The upward trend in Asian immigration has continued throughout the 1970s. Immigration from North America and South America, though showing a numerical increase, decreased in relative terms from their 1961–1965 figure. Lastly, we note slight increases of immigrants from Africa and Oceania, though these increases are numerically small.

Changes in the Distribution by Type of Visa among Asian Immigrants

In addition to the abolition of the infamous national origins quota system, the changes in immigration priorities dictated by the Immigration Act of 1965, with emphasis on family reunification and scarce oc-

---

[1] The transition period lasted from December 1965 to June 1968, a period of 31 months. But the data are only published for fiscal years (July 1 to June 30), so our figures are for the 36-month period.

Table 2

Number and Percentage of Legal Immigrants Admitted to the United States by Region of Birth for Selected Periods, 1961–1977[a,b]

	Average annual number of immigrants (in thousands)					Percentage distribution for each period				
	1961–1965	1966–1968	1969–1971	1972–1974	1975–1977	1961–1965	1966–1968	1969–1971	1972–1974	1975–1977
Europe	122	133	110	88	72	42	35	30	22	17
Asia[c]	21	54	89	125	147	8	14	24	32	35
China[d]	5	20	19	22	24	23	38	21	18	16
India	1	4	10	14	17	3	8	11	11	12
Japan	4	4	4	5	4	18	7	4	4	3
Korea	2	3	10	23	30	9	7	11	18	20
Philippines	3	11	27	31	36	15	22	30	25	24
Other Asia	7	10	19	30	36	32	20	21	24	24
Africa	3	4	7	6	8	1	1	2	2	2
Oceania	1	2	3	3	4	1	1	1	1	1
North America	119	165	134	150	159	41	44	37	38	38
South America	24	21	22	21	26	8	6	6	5	6
Total	290	380	367	393	416	100	100	100	100	100

[a]Source: U.S. Department of Justice, (1961–1977).
[b]The sums of the subtotals are slightly different from the totals due to rounding error.
[c]Percentages are based on total Asian population.
[d]Includes Taiwan and Hong Kong.

cupational skills, has affected the regional distribution of immigration by changing the criteria under which persons are granted immigrant status.

Prior to the reforms of the 1965 Act, only those exempt from the quota system (except for the token quotas of a few hundred) by being an immediate relative of a U.S. citizen were eligible for entry to the United States. It is, therefore, not too surprising that most of the small numbers of Asian immigrants came from countries where U.S. armed forces were stationed (Taiwan, Korea, Philippines, Japan). In such places, marriages between American soldiers and Asian women were not uncommon.

After 1965, there were two channels of immigration: those exempt from numerical limitation (immediate relatives, spouses, parents, and children below age 21 of U.S. citizens) and those subject to the 170,000 annual maximum of the preference system. Of the latter there were four basic categories: Relatives (Preferences 1, 2, 4, 5), Occupational (Preferences 3 and 6), Refugees (Preference 7), Nonpreferences (Preference 8). Table 3 shows the total numbers of immigrants by type of visa for both transition period (1966–1968) and three subsequent three-year periods (1968–1971, 1972–1974, 1975–1977) for the Eastern hemisphere as a whole and for Asia by specific countries.

In every period the numbers of immigrants from the Eastern hemisphere who were immediate relatives of U.S. citizens (those exempt from the numerical limitations) substantially outnumbered those arriving through the preference system. For instance, in the most recent period, 1975–1977, three-quarters of a million immigrants were in the "exempt" category, but less than one-half million arrived through the preference system (maximum of 170,000 per year). The ratio of 60% "exempt" to 40% "preference" has been fairly consistent for the entire period since 1965.

In contrast, over 70% of Asian immigrants during the 1970s have been admitted under the preference system. In fact, the proportion of immigrants arriving under the "immediate relative of U.S. citizen" criteria has declined for several countries, including China (mostly from Taiwan), Japan, and Korea. The reason for this relative decline, notably for Japan and Korea is the lesser importance of GI brides as a source of Asian immigrants. For the Philippines, there has been a faster growth under the "immediate relatives of U.S. citizens" criterion than for the preference system. This would indicate an advanced stage of a family process of immigration, with a large number of Filipino immigrants having already achieved U.S. citizen status.

In the early years after the 1965 Act, occupational preferences were less frequently used for Asian immigrants than relative preferences under the preference system. However, occupational preferences were the key methods for Korean, Indian, and Japanese immigration. But as the 1970s progressed, more Asians from all countries became eligible for family reunification immigration as immediate relatives of resident aliens or as brothers and sisters of U.S. citizens. By the late 1970s, more Asian immigrants arrived under the relative preference criterion than the occupational preference criterion for every single country. More than any other Asian group, Koreans have been able to develop this family-chain pattern of migration and fully utilize the Relative Preference category. Whereas in the transition period only 10% of Korean immigrants (under the Preference System) entered the United States under the Relative Preference category, now about 50% of the Koreans fall under this category. One aspect without any clear explanation is the large number of nonpreference immigrants from India (25%) and Japan (15%)—applicants not entitled to any other preferences but admitted because the 170,000 overall maximum for the Eastern hemisphere was not reached.

Demographic Composition of Asian Immigrants

With the enormous increase in Asian immigration during the last decade, it seems that the composition of immigrants has changed, and therefore their likely impact on U.S. society. In particular, we might ask whether there has been a shift from a small influx of dependents, such as wives of servicemen and their relatives, to greater numbers of young and older dependents both male and female. One way to address this question partially is to examine changes in the demographic composition of Asian immigrants over the past 17 years. This inquiry is sharply limited by the availability of published data in the Immigration and Naturalization Service (INS) reports. Marital status, a key variable in the immigration process, is not cross-classified by age, nor is it available by country of origin. Age and sex are the only two demographic variables that are available for a trend analysis by specific countries. Additionally, the 10-year age categories include the 10–19 age group, a most unfortunate category that includes young adolescent dependents and 18- and 19-year-olds, who are old enough to marry and enter the labor force.

With these limitations Table 4 presents the age composition and percentage of females of each age category for all immigrants, all Asian immigrants, and specific Asian countries, for selected intervals from 1961–1965 to 1975–1977. The age categories were grouped into a functional classification of 0–9, youthful dependents; 10–29, young adults; 30–49, middle-age adults; and 50 and above, older dependents.

For all immigrants and Asia as a whole, there has been remarkably little change in age composition from the early 1960s to the middle 1970s,

Table 3

Number and Percentage of Immigrants by Type of Visa for Eastern Hemisphere and Asian Countries (Birthplace or Country of Chargeability) for Selected Regions, 1966–1977[a,b]

	Total number (in thousands)				Percentage of all immigrants			
	1966–1968	1969–1971	1972–1974	1975–1977	1966–1968	1969–1971	1972–1974	1975–1977
Eastern Hemisphere								
Exempt From Num. Limit	704	614	690	750	62	56	58	60
Preference System	436	488	490	497	38	44	42	40
Relative	203	267	270	316	18	24	23	25
Occupation	63	100	89	77	6	9	8	6
Refugee	20	26	29	30	2	2	2	2
Nonpreference	150	95	102	73	13	9	9	6
Asia								
Exempt From Num. Limit	61	82	114	134	39	30	30	30
Preference System	95	192	262	306	61	70	70	70
Relative	48	86	121	200	31	31	32	45
Occupation	38	64	66	58	24	23	18	13
Refugee	6	1	10	11	4	—	3	2
Nonpreference	3	40	64	37	2	15	17	8
China[c]								
Exempt From Num. Limit	21	16	12	15	36	28	18	21
Preference System	38	41	54	58	64	72	82	79
Relative	22	22	26	44	38	39	39	60
Occupation	9	10	7	7	16	18	11	10
Refugee	6	1	8	4	10	2	12	5
Nonpreference	1	8	13	4	2	14	20	5

India								
Exempt From Num. Limit	2	1	4	3	15	3	9	6
Preference System	10	29	39	49	85	97	91	94
Relative	2	5	16	22	15	17	37	42
Occupation	8	9	10	14	70	30	23	27
Refugee	—	—	—	—	—	—	—	—
Nonpreference	—	14	14	13	1	47	33	25
Japan								
Exempt From Num. Limit	8	13	9	6	71	72	60	46
Preference System	3	5	6	7	29	28	40	54
Relative	1	2	3	3	11	11	20	23
Occupation	2	2	2	2	17	11	13	15
Refugee	—	—	—	—	—	—	—	—
Nonpreference	—	1	2	2	—	6	13	15
Korea								
Exempt From Num. Limit	6	13	21	31	63	43	30	34
Preference System	4	17	48	59	37	57	70	66
Relative	1	6	23	46	10	20	33	51
Occupation	3	5	10	11	27	17	14	12
Refugee	—	—	—	—	—	—	—	—
Nonpreference	—	6	16	3	—	20	23	3
Philippines								
Exempt from Num. Limit	12	22	35	48	34	27	38	44
Preference System	22	59	58	60	66	73	62	56
Relative	12	27	27	41	36	33	29	38
Occupation	10	31	31	19	30	38	33	18
Refugee	—	—	—	—	—	—	—	—
Nonpreference	—	—	—	—	—	—	—	—

[a]Source: U.S. Department of Justice (1961–1977).
[b]The sums of the subtotals are slightly different from the totals due to rounding error.
[c]Includes Taiwan and Hong Kong.

Table 4

Age and Sex Composition of All Immigrants and from Asian Countries (Birthplace) for Selected Periods, 1961–1977[a,b]

Age	Percentage distribution[c]					% female of distribution				
	1961–1965	1966–1968	1969–1971	1972–1974	1975–1977	1961–1965	1966–1968	1969–1971	1972–1974	1975–1977
All immigrants	100	100	100	100	100					
0–9	17	17	18	17	15	49	49	49	50	50
10–29	49	44	46	49	47	59	60	56	55	54
30–49	25	27	28	25	25	52	54	50	51	51
50+	9	12	9	9	13	59	59	57	59	60
N	1450	1139	1102	1180	1247	55	56	53	53	53
All Asia	100	100	100	100	100					
0–9	14	15	16	17	17	54	50	50	51	51
10–29	49	44	47	49	47	65	58	61	61	57
30–49	28	32	31	27	24	63	49	48	50	51
50+	9	10	6	8	11	50	58	57	60	60
N	108	156	270	376	440	62	54	55	56	55
China[d]	100	100	100	100	100					
0–9	10	14	13	12	12	53	48	48	48	47
10–29	40	39	43	46	48	65	54	59	58	54
30–49	28	32	32	28	25	55	44	44	45	48
50+	22	15	12	15	15	45	59	57	58	56
N	24	59	56	66	73	57	51	52	53	52
India	100	100	100	100	100					
0–9	9	11	14	16	14	56	51	49	51	50
10–29	51	51	51	53	53	45	46	46	55	51

30–49	33	35	34	28	28	32	26	27	36	38
50+	6	2	2	2	5	51	46	46	55	57
N	3	12	30	43	52	42	40	40	49	48
Japan	100	100	100	100	100					
0–9	10	9	9	10	10	50	55	50	52	47
10–29	50	43	50	51	48	89	79	79	74	64
30–49	35	41	36	34	36	91	79	75	72	65
50+	5	7	5	5	6	52	66	66	73	75
N	19	11	13	15	13	84	76	74	71	64
Korea	100	100	100	100	100					
0–9	30	19	20	25	28	66	64	59	57	56
10–29	54	50	49	43	44	87	83	78	70	66
30–49	15	28	28	27	22	71	55	52	50	52
50+	1	2	3	5	6	67	72	62	64	62
N	10	10	30	70	90	78	71	66	61	60
Philippines	100	100	100	100	100					
0–9	12	16	19	19	14	49	50	49	49	49
10–29	52	42	44	45	45	65	62	63	63	61
30–49	31	35	31	26	21	72	56	58	62	62
50+	5	7	6	10	20	68	56	58	64	63
N	16	34	80	93	108	65	58	59	60	60

[a]Source: U.S. Department of Justice (1961–1977).
[b]The sum of the subtotals are slightly different from totals due to rounding error.
[c]N is shown in thousands.
[d]Includes Taiwan and Hong Kong.

in spite of the major changes in the numbers of immigrants. In fact, except for a slight increase in older dependents, there have only been minor fluctutations in the age composition of all immigrants. For Asia as a whole, there have been slight gains of a few percentage points among youthful (0–9) and older (50 and above) dependents, and a slight relative reduction among middle-age adults. But the changes are so small that we are reluctant to attach any strong interpretation.

For specific countries, it is possible to detect some clearer trends. There has been a small but steady trend toward a higher proportion of young adults (age 10–29) from China (Taiwan, Hong Kong). This might reflect an increasing number of foreign students who "adjust" their visas to immigrant status.

Increases in proportions of young dependents (India, Korea since 1966–1968) and older dependents (India since 1966–1968, Korea, and especially the Philippines) suggest an increasing process of family immigration and reunification—one of the major objectives of the 1965 Act.

Sex composition, measured by the percentage of females of each age group, is shown in the second panel of Table 4. Around 53–55% of all immigrants to the U.S. are women, and this figure has not changed from before the 1965 reforms. Within age groups, women outnumbered men among the young adults (10–29) and among older dependents (50 and above). The same general patterns hold for the all Asia immigrant populations, except that the proportion of females in the young and middle-age categories has declined about 10 percentage points from the early 1960s.

The drop in female dominance among young and middle-age adults is most notable for immigrants from China, Japan, and Korea, though women are still the majority of immigrants in this age category. In contrast, the fraction of women from India has increased over the years. Unlike other countries in East Asia, immigration from India has been primarily male, especially in the middle-aged adult category. But the trend toward increasing numbers of Indian women immigrants suggests that a family process of immigration is becoming more typical.

Both the absolute rise in Asian immigrants and the increasing fraction of males in the adult years are indicators of growing participation of Asians in the U.S. labor force. It also seems reasonable to assume that a greater fraction of female immigrants will enter the labor force. Asian women married to ex-American soldiers would seem less likely to be employed than single women or women married to immigrant husbands. This interpretation is based not upon the attitudes of husbands but the fact that family enterprises, very common among immigrants, provide employment opportunities for many immigrant women. In the next section we consider the occupational patterns of Asian immigrants.

Table 5

Percentage of Immigrants with Occupation, Occupational Distribution, and Ratio of Occupational Distribution from Asia and Selected Asian Countries, 1961–1977[a,b]

	Percentage of all immigration					Ratio of occupation distribution of each country to total				
	1961–1965	1966–1968	1969–1971	1972–1974	1975–1977	1961–1965	1966–1968	1969–1971	1972–1974	1975–1977
All immigrants										
% with occupation	46	43	42	39	40					
% of total with occupation										
Professional	20	25	29	27	25					
Manager	5	5	4	6	8					
Clerical/sales	21	15	10	10	13					
Blue collar	33	32	37	36	36					
Service	7	8	7	11	9					
Private household	7	11	8	6	4					
Farm	6	5	5	4	4					
Asia										
% with occupation	31	35	43	38	37					
% of total with occupation										
Professional	40	52	62	54	44	2.0	2.1	2.1	2.0	1.8
Manager	9	6	5	8	11	1.8	1.2	1.2	1.3	1.4
Clerical/sales	17	10	8	10	13	0.8	0.7	0.8	1.0	1.0
Blue collar	18	22	12	14	17	0.5	0.7	0.3	0.4	0.5
Service	12	11	6	8	7	1.7	1.4	0.9	0.7	0.8
Private household	2	3	3	3	4	0.3	0.3	0.4	0.5	0.8
Farm	2	4	3	2	3	0.3	0.8	0.6	0.5	0.8

(Continued)

Table 5 *(Continued)*

	Percentage of all immigration					Ratio of occupation distribution of each country to total				
	1961–1965	1966–1968	1969–1971	1972–1974	1975–1977	1961–1965	1966–1968	1969–1971	1972–1974	1975–1977
China[c]										
% with occupation	36	41	41	41	41					
% of total with occupation										
Professional	31	35	47	37	31	1.6	1.4	1.6	1.4	1.2
Manager	17	9	7	11	17	3.4	1.8	1.8	1.8	2.1
Clerical/sales	13	11	11	12	15	0.6	0.7	1.1	1.2	1.2
Blue collar	16	19	16	18	21	0.5	0.6	0.4	0.5	0.6
Service	21	22	15	12	12	3.0	7.8	2.1	1.1	1.3
Private household	2	3	4	1	1	0.3	0.3	0.5	0.2	0.2
Farm	1	2	—	1	2	0.2	0.4	—	0.2	0.5
India										
% with occupation	58	59	58	50	48					
% of total with occupation										
Professional	68	67	89	84	73	3.4	3.5	3.1	3.1	2.9
Manager	4	2	2	4	8	0.8	0.4	0.5	0.6	1.0
Clerical/sales	16	5	4	5	8	0.8	0.3	0.4	0.5	0.6
Blue collar	5	3	3	4	7	0.2	0.1	0.1	0.2	0.2
Service	4	1	1	2	2	0.6	0.1	0.1	0.2	0.2
Private household	1	1	—	1	—	0.1	0.1	—	0.2	—
Farm	3	1	1	—	2	0.5	0.2	0.2	—	0.5
Japan										
% with occupation	10	23	26	29	35					
% of total with occupation										

	1	2	3	4	5	6	7	8	9	10
Professional	44	50	45	37	28	2.2	2.0	1.6	1.4	1.1
Manager	7	7	8	11	19	1.4	1.4	2.0	1.8	2.4
Clerical/sales	22	15	17	16	15	1.0	1.0	1.5	1.6	1.2
Blue collar	11	10	9	11	11	0.3	0.3	0.2	0.3	0.3
Service	8	9	12	21	24	1.1	1.1	1.7	1.9	2.7
Private household	2	6	5	2	2	0.3	0.5	0.6	0.3	0.5
Farm	6	4	4	1	1	1.0	0.8	0.8	0.2	0.2
Korea										
% with occupation	11	25	28	27	26					
% of total with occupation										
Professional	71	75	70	51	38	3.6	3.0	2.4	1.9	1.5
Manager	4	4	5	12	13	0.8	0.8	1.2	2.0	1.6
Clerical/sales	14	8	7	4	14	0.7	0.5	0.7	0.7	1.1
Blue collar	4	5	10	20	25	0.1	0.2	0.3	0.6	0.7
Service	6	5	4	7	6	0.9	0.6	0.6	0.6	0.6
Private household	—	3	3	2	1	—	0.3	0.4	0.3	0.2
Farm	—	—	—	1	2	—	—	—	0.2	0.5
Philippines										
% with occupation	25	45	46	41	42					
% of total with occupation										
Professional	48	60	70	63	47	2.4	2.4	2.4	2.3	1.9
Manager	3	2	2	5	7	0.6	0.4	1.2	0.8	0.9
Clerical/sales	12	7	7	10	14	0.6	0.5	1.0	1.0	1.1
Blue collar	13	11	8	7	12	0.4	0.3	0.2	0.2	0.3
Service	15	6	3	3	4	2.1	0.8	0.4	0.3	0.4
Private household	5	5	4	8	11	0.7	0.5	0.5	1.3	2.8
Farm	4	10	6	4	6	0.7	2.0	0.8	1.0	1.5

[a] Source: U.S. Department of Justice (1961–1977).

[b] The sums of the subtotals are slightly different from totals due to rounding error.

[c] Includes Taiwan and Hong Kong.

Occupational Distribution of Asian Immigrants

This discussion of the occupational distribution of the Asian immigrants is severely constrained by the lack of detailed tabulations of the occupational composition of immigrants. The INS reports do not publish occupational distribution of immigrants by sex or age. Unfortunately, without basic demographic controls, trends in the data must be subject to modest interpretation.

Table 5 presents data on the proportion of immigrants who report having a job and a summary occupational distribution *only* for those who report having a job. These data are reported for all immigrants, for all Asian immigrants, and for selected Asian countries for selected periods from 1961–1956 to 1975–1977. For ease of comparison, adjacent panels present the ratios of the occupational percentages of each country to the percentages for all immigrants.

From the early 1960s to the middle 1970s, the proportion of immigrants reporting an occupation dropped from 46% to 40%. The obvious interpretation would be that this represents an increase in nonworking dependents as a result of the new emphasis on family reunification. This may be true, but it must be qualified that previous data (Table 4) showed little change in the age and sex composition of all immigrants. For all Asian immigrants, there was an increase of more than 10 percentage points in those reporting an occupation from the prereform days of the early 1960s to the postreform period of 1969–1971. From this level, the proportion of Asian immigrants reporting an occupation has declined a few points in the 1970s. It seems that the reforms in immigration law allowed Asians to be considered for occupational preferences and thus raised the proportion of immigrants destined for the labor force, but as family ties led to further immigration, the proportion with stated occupations decreased. It should be noted that these data are measured in the visa applications for immigration and do not necessarily represent postimmigration labor force status.

Considering specific Asian countries, there were great differences in the proportion reporting an occupation in the early 1960s, ranging from almost 60% among Indians to only 10% among Koreans and Japanese. During the late 1960s, the proportions with labor force attachments rose significantly (for the Philippines from 25 to 45%). Then during the 1970s, the proportion of dependents increased (except for China, which held steady). At the present time, the only Asian countries that are distinctive from all immigrants are India with a higher than average labor force participation and Korea with a substantially lower figure.

Turning to the occupational levels of those with an occupation, we note that the occupational distribution of Asian immigrants are quite different from the general population. Compared to other immigrants, Asian immigrants are about twice as likely to be professional and technical workers. The most extreme case is India, which had almost 90% professionals (of those reporting an occupation) in the 1969–1971 period. The figure is down to 75% in 1975–1977, but this is still triple the average proportion. The proportion of immigrants who reported professional occupations has declined for all Asian countries during the 1970s but still remains very high for the Philippines and Korea.

As large-scale immigration from Asia continues, the occupational composition appears to have become more broadly based and to include proportional increases among managerial workers, sales or clerical workers, and even blue-collar workers (especially for Korea). There is also a shift toward service workers in the relatively small Japanese stream and to private household workers among Filipinos. Asian immigrants are still very selective compared to all immigrants, but the wide gap has narrowed somewhat in the mid to late 1970s.

Discussion and Conclusions

As past studies (Boyd, 1971, 1974; Keely, 1971, 1974, 1975a, 1975b) have shown, the major impact of the 1965 Immigration Act was to open the door to Asian immigration. In updating the results of these earlier studies, we note that trends through the late 1970s indicate a continuing increase of Asian immigration to the United States—especially of immigrants from Korea and the Philippines. Currently about 35% of all immigration to the United States is from Asia, an increase of 500% in the relative share and more than 700% in absolute numbers.

Asian immigrants have made good use of both the preference system, which has emphasized family ties and occupational skills, and also the exemption from numerical limits channel for immediate relatives of U.S. citizens. A greater percentage of Asian immigrants in the preference system are now utilizing the "relative preference" category than during earlier periods. A family-chain pattern of migration among Asian immigrants seems to be developing. Underscoring this trend is the increase in recent figures from previous time periods in the percentage of Asian dependent children and dependent adults immigrating to the United States.

The occupational status of the immigrants has become more diverse over the years. Though the percentage of Asians who were entering the labor force in a professional capacity are still about twice as common as in the general immigrant population, there is an increasing share of other white-collar and blue-collar workers. This seems understandable as the base of immigration becomes broader and family ties are used to bring in additional relatives.

Reviewing the background of the new Asian immigration to the United States during the last decade and describing the changes in the numbers and characteristics of immigrants from specific Asian countries relative to other immigrants, especially since 1965, raise a number of significant questions for future research on Asian immigration and the new Asia immigrants.

One area of research concerns the hypothesis that this recent influx has resulted in the expansion or growth of Asian American neighborhoods or settlements. Impressionistic observations indicate that this may be the case. Within the last 10 years, we have noted the development of several new Asian enclaves or communities—the Koreans in Los Angeles and Chicago and the Vietnamese in certain midwestern towns—and also a resurgence of growth of indigenous Asian communities (i.e., the expansion of the original Chinatown and the development of a "new Chinatown" in another sector of San Francisco). But because Asian immigrants are largely white collar, especially in the professional occupations, they may be less concentrated into immigrant enclaves and more geographically dispersed than other recent immigrant communities. This an important question that will undoubtedly have a great effect upon subsequent assimilation or segregation of Asian immigrants. Future research should consider the following issues:

1. Is the population of various Asian communities actually expanding, or is this visible expansion more a product of differential modes of socioeconomic advancement (i.e., the development of ethnic restaurants in other parts of town to attract a wider range of customers and lessen the economic competition within the ethnic community)?
2. What are the characteristics of the new immigrants residing in the ethnic enclave? How do they differ from Asian immigrants living outside the ethnic enclaves?
3. Are Asian professional immigrants different from other immigrants in the residence patterns and their adaption to American society?
4. What sort of involvement (if any) do these new Asian immigrant professionals have with the ethnic enclaves? Are they a source of leadership, or are they uninvolved?

Another related question is whether the increase in the influx of Asian immigration will promote the development and expansion of ethnic organizations—organizations that cater to the needs and specific problems of these new immigrants. Such organizations may take the form of English and citizenship classes, career and employment centers, occupational training centers, and legal aid services, especially those dealing with legal aspects of immigration and government bureaucracies. Traditional ethnic organizations, such as the clan organizations, whose power and influence in the past have declined, may undergo a revitalization in their influence and power as new immigrants attempt to construct some sense of order, identity, and community in this strange land. However, if Asian immigrants are dispersed because of their occupational status, then it is quite possible that the revitalization process of traditional ethnic organizations may not be occurring. It would be interesting to know answers to the following:

1. Are ethnic organizations being developed to cater to the needs of the immigrants, and if so, what types of organizations are being developed?
2. Are traditional ethnic organizations undergoing a revitalization process, or are immigrants utilizing different mechanisms for adjustment?

A third area for further research concerns the occupational status of Asian immigrants. Because of the emphasis on scarce occupational skills in the 1965 Immigration Act, a disproportionate amount of Asian immigrants are entering the labor force as professionals. The question is, Is the Asian professional distribution similar to that of the general population, or do they occupy special occupational niches in specific sectors of the American economy? A related issue is the employment patterns of other family members, especially those who had not planned to work outside the home. The maintenance of a middle-class lifestyle may dictate labor market activity. The impact for the larger society of Asian immigrant participation in the secondary labor market would be an area worth investigating.

Another area of investigation may be the impact this tremendous influx of Asian immigrants may have on racial and ethnic relations in the United States. It may be hypothesized that, because of the high degree of professionalism among Asian immigrants, there may be a fading (though not an elimination) for past stereotypes of Asians as coolie laborers, laundrymen, restaurant workers, houseboys, and gardeners. On the other hand, Asian professionals may be seen as "pseudoprofessionals"—employed in institutions that American professionals avoid (inner city hospitals). Further research is needed to ascertain if as a result of the changes in the characteristics of recent Asian immigrants, there has been changes in Asian stereotypes. The sheer influx of Asian immigrants within recent years will increase their visibility within American society. Further research is needed to ascertain the response of the dominant American society to this new Asian influx and visibility, noting any variation in the race relations situation between Asians and whites, especially during recent times of economic instability. Such areas of study may deal with (1) cases of conflict between Americans and immigrants as a result of economic competition, (2) current stereotypes of Asian Americans, and (3) interaction patterns between Asians and whites in selected cities or states.

A last area of future research may deal with traditional social problems that continue to plague Asian American communities (Kim, 1978; Owan, 1975; Wong, 1977). In both West and East Coast cities, housing shortages, substandard and crowded living conditions, and the lack of adequate medical care and facilities are characteristic of many Asian ghettos. No doubt, many of these social problems existed before the tremendous influx of Asians. The following questions may be entertained:

1. How extensive, relative to the general population, are the social problems among the various Asian American communities?
2. Are there any underlying themes that tie the various Asian communities together in terms of consequences of the social problem?
3. Are the social problems in Asian American communities (as documented by recent research) a product of the new Asian influx, were they excerbated by the Asian influx, or did they exist before the Asian influx but were made more public as more studies on the Asian communities were conducted?

With the limitations of the published data, we have measured a very real revolution in Asian migration to the United States as a result of the 1965 Immigration Act. It remains for future research to investigate the processes of adaptation, acculturation, or ethnic segmentation that these new Asian immigrants encounter in American society during the 1970s and 1980s.

References

Boyd, M.
  1971   Oriental immigration: the experience of the Chinese, Japanese, and Filipino population in the United States. *International Migration Review* **5**(Spring): 48–60.
  1974   The changing nature of the central and southeast Asian immigration to the United States: 1961–1972. *International Migration Review* **8**(Winter):507–520.
Burma, J. H.
  1951   The background of the current Filipino situation. *Social Forces* **30**(October): 42–48.

Christiansen, J.
  1979   The split labor market theory and Filipino exclusion: 1929–1934. *Phylon* **50**(March
          1):66–74.
Daniels, R.
  1970   *The Politics of Prejudice*. New York: Antheneum.
Daniels, R., and Kitano, H.
  1970   *American Racism: Exploration of the Nature of Prejudice*. Englewood Cliffs, N.J.:
          Prentice-Hall, Inc.
Hune, S.
  1977   *Pacific Migration to the United States: Trends and Themes in Historical and
          Sociological Literature. Research Institute on Immigration and Ethnic Studies,
          Bibliographical Studies* No. **2**. Washington, D.C.: Smithsonian Institution Press.
Keeley, C.
  1971   Effects of the Immigration Act of 1965 on selected population characteristics
          of immigrants to the U.S. *Demography* **8**(May):157–169.
  1974   The demographic effects of immigration legislation and procedures. *Interpreter
          Releases* **51**(April 3):89–93.
  1975a   Effects of U.S. immigration laws on manpower characteristics of immigrants.
          Demography **12**(May):179–192.
  1975b   Immigration composition and population policy in *Population: Dynamics, Eth-
          ics, and Policy* (P. Reining and I. Tinker Eds.), pp. 129–135. Washington, D.C.:
          American Association for the Advancement of Science.
Kim, B. L.
  1978   Problems and service needs of Asian Americans in Chicago: an empirical study.
          Amerasia **5**(2):23–44.
Kung, S. W.
  1962   *Chinese in American Life*. Seattle: University of Washington Press.
Lyman, S.
  1974   *Chinese Americans*. New York: Random House.
Owan, T.
  1975   *Asian Americans: A Case of Benighted Neglect. Occasional Paper* No. **1**. Chicago:
          Asian American Mental Health Research Center.
Sandmeyer, E. C.
  1973   *The Anti-Chinese Movement in California*. Chicago: University of Illilnois Press.
Saxton, A.
  1971   *The Indispensible Enemy: Labor and the Anti-Chinese Movement in California*.
          Los Angeles and Berkeley: University of California Press.
U.S. Bureau of the Census
  1973   *Census of the Population, 1970* (Vol. 1). *Characteristics of the Population* (Part 1).
          U.S. Summary. Washington, D.C.: U.S. Government Printing Office.
  1975   *Historical Statistics of the United States. U.S. Bureau of the Census*. Washington,
          D.C.: U.S. Government Printing Office.
U.S. Department of Justice
  1961–1977   *Annual Report: Immigration and Naturalization Service*. Washington, D.C.:
          U.S. Government Printing Office.
U.S. Senate, Committee on the Judiciary
  1979   *U.S. Immigration Law and Policy: 1952–1979*. Washington, D.C.: U.S. Government
          Printing Office.
Wong, M.
  1977   Asian Americans: a case of benign neglect. Paper presented at the Pacific So-
          ciological Association Convention, Sacramento, California.

23

The Ethnic Numbers Game in India: Hindu–Muslim Conflicts over Conversion, Family Planning, Migration, and the Census*

Theodore P. Wright, Jr.

INTRODUCTION

One of the causes of conflict between ethnic groups[1] in the course of political development is that modernization may make their relative numbers politically significant more quickly than it can erase ethnic differences. If there was any common denominator to what have been called "traditional polities," it was that power was not distributed within them at all evenly among the population, especially in multiethnic empires, but was concentrated in small, often religiously or linguistically distinct elites that enjoyed a monopoly of weapons and military–administrative skills. Their rule had often originated in conquest (Kautsky, 1962; Huntington, 1968). The effects of this political specialization of labor were sometimes mitigated, as in the Ottoman millet (peoples) system, by the devolution of many functions now regarded as governmental to semiautonomous minority religious communities. Numbers were no more

* I wish to thank Professor W. H. Morris-Jones for his hospitality at the Institute of Commonwealth Studies, where I did the initial research for this paper, and the Social Science Research Council and American Council of Learned Societies for their South Asia research grant in 1974–1975.
[1] I am using the term *ethnic group* in the broad sense employed by Glazer and Moynihan (1975:4): "Any group of distinct cultural tradition and origin, even if it is the majority ethnic group within a nation."

405

relevant to this system than in the parliamentary "estates" of medieval Europe.

Concern over the relative size of the component class and ethnic groups in such a state waited upon the ideas and institutions of equal citizenship, popular suffrage, and national self-determination. This is not to imply that sheer numbers are anywhere the sole or even the principal determinant of political power, but only that an ideology of majority rule in itself increases the potential strength of what Richard Schermerhorn calls "mass subjects" (Cobban, 1944; Schermerhorn, R. A., 1970). If the ethnically distinct ruling elite lacks a majority in the total population, it is likely to become conscious of this defect and begin playing the numbers game to forestall its own displacement.

Whether democratic or totalitarian, modern regimes have felt obliged to prove their legitimacy by going through at least the forms of popular elections on the basis of some approximation of one person–one vote. The predicament of the white rulers of South Africa representing at most 16% of the population is that they can neither democratize the state without losing control nor play the numbers game with any hope of success, because apartheid, their version of the millet system, lacks legitimacy outside their own circles.

Liberal democrats as well as Marxists have expected and hoped that voters in mass democracies would align themselves according to economic class interests, but in practice many citizens of even the most developed states, when given a free choice, have expressed a preference for being represented by parties or politicians with "primordial" group identities (Gordon, 1975). Socialism itself, by replacing the market distribution of benefits with political distribution, has contributed to the politicization of ethnicity.

In British India the paradox of increasing "communalism" (as ethnic conflict is called is South Asia) with modernization is said to be traceable to the open competition for government jobs introduced by the colonial rulers (Gopal, 1959:Chapter VI; Zakaria, 1970:Chapter 8). The Indian National Congress, organized in 1885, hoped to rally support from all religious communities, but in 1906 some leaders of the Muslim minority founded the Muslim League. Since this communally defined party could never hope to attract a majority of the voters and was therefore condemned to exclusion from office except as a member of a coalition government (Wright, 1966), the question naturally arose how to change the proportions of the majority and minority groups to the advantage of the latter. This would be especially the case where one or both sides perceived politics as a "your gain my loss" ("zero-sum-game") situation. A minority like the North Indian Muslims, whose leaders think of themselves as a declining former elite, is most likely to have that view (Wright, 1972).[2] This and the colonial context in which the issue became salient, help explain why the numbers game came to be played in India, where the Hindu majority even before Partition had an apparently insurmountable three-to-one advantage. The Muslim League sought to solidify its control over its community through the device of separate electorates and to ensure its proportionate or even more than proportionate representation in nascent legislatures through reserved seats and "weightage,' but it could not well justify preponderance over or even equality with Hindus to the British rulers as long as the Muslim community lacked numbers.

Logically, the following methods suggest themselves for reversing majority and minority power and status positions by exchanging their numerical ratio: (1) religious conversion, where the chief criterion of differentiation is faith; (2) differential fertility rates, especially from different responses to family planning; (3) immigration–emigration ratios of majority and minority; (4) manipulation of the census; (5) language differentiation or aggregation; (6) political boundary changes—cession or accession of territory the population composition of which is different from that of the country as a whole; (7) changes in the definition and procedures for obtaining citizenship or other changes in a group's legal status; (8) exogamy where the partner from outside the community can be brought in; (9) exchange of populations with other countries or explusion; (10) genocide.

I shall discuss only the first four of these, about which there is adequate material regarding India. Number five has been extensively covered by other authors (Brass, 1974).

RELIGIOUS CONVERSION

Where majority and minority are distinguished by religion and one or both is universalistic, the conversion of unbelievers to the true faith is the natural method of reversing their ratio. By and large Hinduism is not a proselytizing religion; Islam is. But even missionary religions tend to lose their dynamism over time. Although its followers are doctrinally committed to spread its message by *Jihad* (the Muslim version of cru-

---

[2] Both Hardy (1972) and Frykenberg (1975) have concluded that neither Muslims nor Hindus were sharply defined, mutually exclusive communities before the nineteenth century.

sade), Islam failed to convert the bulk of Hindus in South Asia in the way it did most Zoroastrians in Iran or Hindus and Buddhists in Indonesia.[3] Nor was the immigration of Muslim Arabs, Persians, Pathans, or Turks sufficient to tip the balance in the already heavily populated subcontinent.

Of all the ways in which the ethnic ratio in a population may change, conversion until recently has been the least discussed in the literature, probably because modern, rationalist scholars find the whole process incomprehensible and distasteful. Those specialists who do investigate "conversion to Islam" (Levtzion, 1978; Hardy, 1972:8) now stress that in the Christian sense of a sudden, individual change of faith resulting from the efforts of a self-conscious missionary, it was a misnomer in South and Southeast Asia. Rather, the process has usually been a gradual one, extending over several generations and involving stages of progressive Islamization to a new culture and fellowship that ranges from the most nominal adherence to the fervid devotion of the revivalists.

The actual facts concerning the expansion of Islam in South Asia, that is, how much was achieved by coercion and how much by persuasion, as well as the proportions of immigrant-descended and convert-descended among present-day Muslims are probably irretrievably lost to history.[4] What is significant for contemporary politics is that these questions became in the course of the nineteenth century matters of controversy, answers to which served as weapons in the polemics among "Nationalist" Muslims, Hindu Nationalists, and Muslim Separatists. The two latter agreed upon the predominance of conquest and other coercive measures in the establishment of a Muslim community in South Asia and opposed the Nationalist historians, who emphasized peaceful conversion by Arab merchants and Sufi mystics.[5] On the other hand, the alignment among these schools of interpretation shifts on the issue of

[3] The closest I have found to an explanation (Nizami, 1961) is that "The Turks who established the Sultanate of Delhi were . . . singularly free from all religious bigotry . . . They treated the Indian Muslims (converts) and the Hindus with equal nonchalance. They were concerned more with the maintenance of their political power and prestige than with the religious problems or prejudices of their people [p. 312]."

"Since conversion to Islam meant loss of *Jiziya* (tax) on the one hand and additional expenditure, in the form of pensions on the other, [perhaps they, like the earlier Ummayad Caliphs] discouraged conversions [p. 316]"

[4] A beginning attempt has been made by Richards (1974). He concludes, "Despite the frequent emphasis upon peaceful forms of Muslim settlement in South Asia by traders and Sufi missionaries, it is clear that the most substantial Muslim *settlement* was achieved by conquest. . . . Political control encouraged internal expansion or Islamization [pp. 92, 102]." (My emphasis)

[5] The varying social functions and methods of the Sufis are revealed in a case study by Eaton (1978).

the proportions of indigenous and alien-descended Muslims in the population, with Hindu and Muslim Nationalists stressing the former, though with different resultant prescriptions (reconversion and pluralism, respectively) and with Muslim separatists exaggerating the proportion of the immigrants because of the prestige of foreign origin in their community.[6]

It has been argued by Lal (1973) that the rate of increase has been steady both absolutely and apparently relatively throughout the medieval and modern periods. He attributes this trend largely to forceful conversion and then concludes rather illogically that since "the vast majority of Muslims of India and Pakistan are converts from indigenous elements, the 'two nation theory' has no historical basis. [p. 204]." Peter Hardy records that "to most British officials it was a revelation in the first census of 1871 (to find) that Muslims were 22.8 percent of (British India) and that a preponderance of them were not of immigrant descent (1977:177)," thus implying a large amount of successful conversions in the past. Each decennial census thereafter revealed a slight increase in the Muslim percentage of the population from 19.9% in 1881 to 24.27% in 1941 (Davis, [1951] quoted in Khan, [1974]).

This rate of increase became politically salient only when the British rulers of India instituted elective representation of Indians and related it to communal proportions of the population (Mason, 1971:63; Smith (1963:166). No wonder that some of those scholars as well as politicians who defined "Indian" as Hindu in culture if not religion became alarmed at the changing ratio and began to search for its cause so that various political and social actions could reverse the trend. On the other side, Hardy found, surprisingly, that

Those Muslims who brought themselves to the attention of the British rulers . . . were late in showing interest in conversion and converts . . . [but] by the mid-1930's converts to Islam in India had become of conscious interest to Muslim historians of the period of Muslim political supremacy and has remained so to the present in both India and Pakistan [1977:177–206].

Previously, the Muslim elite had argued on behalf of the Urdu language, for instance, that Hindus and the Hindi language should not be allowed to prevail in official use by reason of numbers alone because they did not have the same social importance as Muslims and Urdu (*A Defense of the Urdu Language* [1900:38] cited in Brass [1974:133].).

If the rate of Muslim expansion before 1871 is subject to nothing better than educated guesses like Lal's, at least we can examine the explanations offered for the period since then. Those who view the up-

---

[6] For examples of social hierarchy by place of origin, see Ahmed (1973a).

ward trend favorably now cite the attraction of the egalitarian Islamic community for oppressed, low-caste, or untouchable Hindus (and former Buddhists in the case of Bengal). Those like Lal who regard Muslim conversion as coercive stress the penalties of discriminatory taxation (the *Jizya*) against non-Muslims under Muslim rule, the fear of expropriation on the part of Hindu landlords, and the desire by artisans for royal patronage.

There is a difference of opinion among experts over whether there has been much if any outright conversion to Islam from Hinduism during the two centuries since the decline of Muslim rule set in. Certainly immigration dried up as a source of Muslim increase. The last wholesale attempt to employ state power for the purpose of conversion was apparently during Tippu Sultan of Mysore's invasion of Malabar in 1788, although the Moplah rebellion there in 1921 produced enough such incidents to revive Hindu fears throughout India (Thursby, 1975; Dale, 1980). However, conversion went on quietly and without official patronage under British rule. Thomas Arnold, writing in 1896/1935[7] reported that, "In more recent years there have been abundant witnesses for Islam seeking to spread this faith in India and with very considerable success; the second half of the nineteenth century especially witnessed a great revival of missionary activity [p. 282]." Hardy (1977) suggests that the fourfold increase in the absolute number of Muslims during a century of British rule could have had a lot to do with the efforts of the Deobandi ulema.[8] Titus (1959), too, notes a "widespread revival of Islam all over India since the middle of the nineteenth century and annual conversions estimated anywhere from 10,000 to 600,000 [p. 49]" with missionary activity most notable on the Malabar coast and in East Bengal due to the Faraizi movement. Imtiaz Ahmad (1973b) has recorded the typical group conversion of the Siddiqui Sheikhs from the Kayastha caste in Allahabad.[9]

The shadow zone of the half-converted became an arena of Hindu–Muslim conflict first, significantly, in the Punjab, a province with a virtual balance in numbers between Muslims on the one hand and Hindus and Sikhs on the other. In the 1890's, the Arya Samaj, a Hindu revivalist organization, devised the *shuddhi* or purification ceremony to reconvert Christians and Muslims whose ancestors had been Hindus (Barrier, 1968; Jones, 1968, 1976). Soon, as Thursby remarks, "The controversial ex-

---

[7] For earlier material on Malabar, see Dale (1974).

[8] Curiously, Faruqi (1963:73) refers to this only in connection with the *tabligh* movement of the 1920s and then, as a nationalist, deplores it for deepening the already existing antagonism between the two communities.

[9] Another contributor, D'Souza (1973:50), also refers to contemporary conversions among Hindu fishermen in Malabar.

changes surrounding the *shuddhi* practices became a more disruptive factor in Hindu-Muslim relations than the activities themselves [1975:155]." Theretofore, Hinduism had been a nonproselytizing religion. Muslims responded to *shuddhi* in 1924 by founding the *tabligh* (education) and *tanzim* (organization) movements. The rivalry reached its peak in competition for the allegiance of the Malkana Rajputs of Agra District (Sharma, 1968).[10]

After Partition in 1947 and the involuntary exchange by migration of about 5 million Hindus, Sikhs, and Muslims, the Muslim minority in the new Republic of India was reduced to 9.61% of the population, whereas Pakistan was overwhelmingly Muslim, especially in its western half. Despite adverse conditions, the Muslim minority in India soon resumed its demographic march upward to 10.69% in the 1961 census and 11.21% in 1971 (Visaria, [1974:363] citing censuses of India, 1951, 1961, and 1971). Hardy (1977:205) takes the position that "Politics have probably put paid to any prospect of researchers investigating conversions to Islam in either the republic of India or of Pakistan and Bangla Desh."[11] Nevertheless, Partap C. Aggarwal's (1971) work on the Meos, another part-Hindu tribe of North India, shows that despite all of the pressures in the direction of the dominant majority's religion, which followed the trauma of partition, Islamization among them has proceeded apace.[12]

The most ardent, if not necessarily the most successful of evengelists among Muslims since 1947, except when the organization was banned in 1975 to 1977, seems to have been the revivalist body, *Jama'at-i-Islami.* It appears to hope that by cleansing Muslims of unorthodox beliefs and practices and by leading pious, exemplary lives, its followers will attract non-Muslims, particularly low caste Hindus, to the fold and eventually tip the balance of numbers in favor of Islam. The Jama'at's founder, Maulana Abul Ala Maudoodi, has written:

The movement should take the field against the wrong system of life . . . Its torch-bearers should furnish proof of their moral strength and sincerity by facing adversities . . . By means of such a struggle all those elements in society (whose nature is not entirely devoid of truth and justice) will become attracted to the movement [1975:17–18].

A Nationalist Muslim critic of Maudoodi's, Professor Moin Shakir, charges that:

[10] On the *shuddhi* vs. *tabligh* movements in 1923, see Mathur (1972:31–44); for Hyderabad in 1946, see Elliot (1974).

[11] Dr. S. L. Sharma of the Panjab University, Chandigarh seemed to be the only Indian scholar working on this subject. In addition to his article previously cited (1968), see Sharma (1966:194–197).

[12] Less sympathetic studies of the Meos have been done by Amir-Ali (1970:33–45) and Sharma and Srivastava (1967:69–80); for Muslim missionary organization, see Haq (1972).

To him the considerations of minority and majority are absurd. There was a time when the Prophet was in the minority of one. Islamic society does not rely on the strength of population but on the strength of faith . . . Maudoodi favours an Islamic movement for domination . . . The goal of the Muslims should be an Islamic state where there will be no Muslim majority or minority, but only Muslims and non-Muslims [1970:24, 26, 34].

That the Jama'at's chiliastic hope is not as unreasonable as it would appear to be to a rationalistic secularist is indicated not only by the historical record of rapid expansion of Islamic power, but also by the startling success of various other Asian sects and pseudoreligions in the West during the past decade.

Since Indian Independence, Hindu communal parties like the Hindu Mahasabha have pushed for laws forbidding the proselytization of converts from other faiths, which in any case is repugnant to the mainstream of Hindu philosophy (Devaseṅapathi, 1966; Smith, 1963:211).[13] Although aimed in the first instance at Christian missionary activity among tribals and scheduled castes, they clearly would affect Muslim efforts too. Part of the orthodox Hindu fear is that if these groups peripheral to the main body of caste Hinduism were to be formally detached by conversion, as happened to Dr. Ambedkar's followers among the Untouchables in 1956, when they were converted by their own leader to Buddhism, the prospects for the Hindu majority community being reduced to a minority "in its own country" would become much more credible at 61% than its present nominal 81% would indicate (Franda, 1972a).[14] One might even elaborate an additional minority tactic for reversing the numbers ratio: divide and conquer the majority, or at least so split it up that the erstwhile minority would enjoy a plurality position.

Some caste Hindus do perceive themselves as already a minority. The reasoning or calculation is exemplified in an article by Prakasa in *Bharat Jyoti*:

The question of majorities and minorities (implies) the desire of looking after the welfare of minorities and to protect them from the alleged tyranny of majorities . . . It is taken for granted that the Hindus are the majority . . . [but] to say [so] is totally wrong. The vast mass of people that are called Hindus are a vast congeries of (sub-caste) minorities . . . [whereas] the Muslims form the actual majority . . . as much after the Partition as they did in undivided India . . . Some persons feel very worried about conversions to Christianity,

[13] *Radiance*, the newspaper of the Jama'at-i-Islami, reported a bill in the Gujarat legislative to prevent conversions September 4, October 15, and November 11, 1972. The legislation was said to be aimed at preventing conversion of Harijans to Islam and Christianity, and was attempted at the national level in 1979 during the Janata Party rule.

[14] *Organiser*, the Jan Sangh paper, apparently charged that B. Shamsunder, a Scheduled Caste leader in Hyderabad, was really Shujaat Ali, a Muslim agent (*Radiance* 29 August 1971).

but they dare not interfere with Muslims for they are actually a powerful and well-knit majority [quoted in *Organiser*, 17 May 1969:15].

Another way of answering the question, Are Indian Muslims really a minority? (Jain, 1970) is to weigh the total number of Hindus against the larger world population of Muslims. In either case, the foe is seen typically as monolithic and the author's group as weak and subdivided.

The Jan Sangh party newspaper, *Organiser*, evinced a continuing apprehensiveness about Muslim missionary activity by quoting aggressive passages from the Muslim Urdu press such as "Propagation and spread of Islam is sacred duty of the Muslims in the world [*Organiser* 2 September 1972:3, quoting the August 22, 1972 *Jamiat*, organ of the Nationalist Muslim *Jamiat-ul-Ulema*]," and "If all the Hindus [would] embrace Islam there would be an end to communalism, nepotism, untouchability and riots [*Organiser* 2 September 1972:3, quoting the June 20, 1972 *Tarjuman-e-Millat*,"[15] Other *Organiser* articles have attributed the "Muslim Dominance in Bengal" to the zealotry of Brahmin renegades, desire to retain estates, and abduction of Hindu girls (Gupta, 1968; Mukherjee, 1967). The journal even elicited an article from its favorite Muslim, Dr. S. Jeelany, (1969) in which the author urged anyone contemplating apostasy for material or marital reasons to stick to his own religion, study it well, and live up to its teachings.

For all of this agitation about conversion in communal circles, the actual amount of crossing over since Independence seems, from whatever bits of evidence are available, to have been miniscule. That any attention at all is paid to it stems from the perennial fear that a reversal of the ratio in any part of India will create more Pakistans to demand secession. Since the boundaries were drawn at Partition on the basis of which religion had a majority of the population in each district (except, of course, for Kashmir and for Murshidabad in West Bengal, which controlled the headwaters of the Hooghly River and was given to India) a not unreasonable fear of further territorial losses was implanted in Hindu minds. It was for this reason that the carving of a Muslim majority District of Malappuram out of Malabar in Kerala state at the behest of the Muslim League when it was a partner in the state's United Front Ministry created such a furor and brought charges that this "Moplahstan" was only the opening wedge for seccession.[16]

[15] Another article in *Organiser* (22 March 1969) is entitled "Al-Jamiat Wants Muslim Majority in India," and cites the *Aljamiat*, March 13, 1969.

[16] For a lone example of a notification of conversion by a Hindu, Vikrama Tripathi, to Islam as Tareef Hasan, see *Radiance* (30 July 1972). For the struggle over creating Mallapuram District, see Malik (1969:154–155).

With the tremendous increase in wealth of oil-producing Arab states after 1973, Hindu fears were rekindled that "foreign money" would buy the conversion of India's 15% Untouchable population to Islam. During the Janata Party rule, a "Freedom of Religion" Bill was introduced in Parliament, which actually would have limited the constitutionally guaranteed right to propagate one's religion by prohibiting the use of "force, threat and inducement." The hopes of Muslims and fear of Hindus for a reversal of ratios by conversion reached a climax in 1981 when the bulk of the Harijans in the village of Meenakshipuram in Tamilnad accepted Islam. Alarmists among Hindus concocted a global conspiracy to turn the tables on the Hindu majority. Hindu revivalist organizations rushed to reconvert the defectors and prevent further losses by eliminating residues of untouchability. The chief consequences of all this furor seems to have been the spread of communal tensions and riots to heretofore peaceful South India. All observers agree that it was the educated young Harijans who initiated the conversion movement in order to achieve the equality of social status to which the constitution and their attainments both entitled them (Wright, 1982).

FERTILITY DIFFERENTIALS

If conversion has in fact had little effect on the proportions of the two communities, how then are we to explain the small but steady rise in the Muslim percentage of India's population at each census? With the growing awareness by educated circles in the 1960s of the Indian population explosion has also come knowledge of the connection between contrasting religious group attitudes toward family planning and the fertility differentials between them. If the death and marriage rates of two groups are the same, then varying birthrates must explain their different rates of increase. Thus there has been a shift of attention among Hindu militants from changing of peoples' subjective identities by conversion to changing their objective numbers by procreation. Their Muslim counterparts in the *Jama'at-i-Islami* claim not to have undergone this reorientation, if one can accept at face value an editorial in *Radiance* that ascribes the rising Muslim percentage in the population to conversion rather than to rejection of birth control (*Radiance* 2 July 1972).

More broadly speaking, Wriggins and Guyot (1973) have alerted their fellow political scientists to the political significance of comparative ethnic demography:

In multi-ethnic societies, differences in growth rates and age structures among ethnic groups are likely to be perceived as affecting the distribution of political power for the future . . . Accordingly, short-run demographic changes may loom large in the minds of competing political leaders of groups fearful of losing their positions . . . [which] may precipitate ethnic group conflict [p. 6].

As a policy issue, this is a question primarily of varying group responses to contraception. Thus in India, some Hindu writers have charged that Muslims are gradually increasing their proportion of the population by not practicing birth control when more and more Hindus do, as well as by perpetuating traditional customs like polygamy and *purdah*, which isolate Muslim women from antinatalist modern influences.[17] This accusation was most bluntly stated by Hendre (1971):

The 10.7 percent of Muslims in 1961, in union with other religious groups, will numerically overtake the Hindus in A.D. 2051 so decisively that the Hindus will be at the mercy of the non-Hindus . . . Indian Muslims do not want monogamy and/or family planning. They are directly encouraged by our democracy to multiply at a fast rate with a view to eventually overcome the Hindu majority. Hindus therefore must oppose family planning and either impose monogamy on the Muslims or amend the present Hindu code to enable Hindus to follow polygamy [pp. 45, 87].[18]

The generally negative position of the *Jama'at-i-Islami* on birth control as reflected in the pages of its journal, *Radiance*, (Mufakkir, 5 December, 1971; Vasfi, 2 April, 1972; *Radiance*, 8 October, 1972) and in Maulana Maudoodi's book, *Birth Control* (Hussain, 23 March 1969)[19] lends some plausibility to Hendre's charges, though they do not prove that the purpose for that position is merely a tactic in the numbers game, any more than does the comparable position of the Vatican on the same issue for Catholic Christians.

Variations on Hendre's thesis have appeared in the Jan Sangh paper, *Organiser*, under provocative titles like, "Polygamy for Muslims and Birth Control for Hindus Would be National Suicide" (October 22, 1967); "Family Planning or Death Wish?" (November 11, 1972); "Hindus Must Wake Up or They Will be Gone" (January 14, 1968); "How Family Planning Lost us our Lahore" (August 8, 1965); "In India That is Bharat Birth Control Means Only Hindu-Control" (April 19, 1965); "Mr. Chandrasekhar—Minister for Death" (May 14, 1967); and "When We Will Need to Import Our Soldiers" (November 27, 1966).

[17] The same kind of fears are present among blacks and whites in the United States. See Hallow (1969:535–536).

[18] But for Muslims alone to have an overall majority would take 383 years. See Agarwala (1974:17). A more sophisticated version of the Hendre position is taken by Davies (1976: 19–32).

[19] Maudoodi argues that birth control produces sexual anarchy.

A whole battery of demographers and doctors, both Hindu and Muslim, have rushed into print to refute the analysis and predictions of Hendre and his followers (Agarwala, 1974; Hoque 1970; Khan, 1975; Khan, 1974; Pethe, 1973; Owaisy and Kapur, 1970). Their arguments are essentially alike:

1. It is incorrect to assume that present fertility differentials between religious groups can be projected indefinitely into the future. Long before Muslims or even non-Hindus as a whole have become a majority of India's population, the same factors causing a decline in the Hindu birthrate will affect the minorities in the same way. Franda (1972a), for instance, notes that the increase in Muslim percentage between 1961 and 1971 was already lower than that in 1951–1961. If these social and economic considerations somehow did not intervene, Malthusian natural limitations would set in before the astronomical projected total population figure of 4 billion Indians was reached. In somewhat contradictory fashion, however, several of the authors assert, ignoring low Parsi and Jewish birthrates, that it is characteristic of minorities to increase more rapidly than the majority.

2. The differences in fertility that do exist (more urban than rural) between Hindus and Muslims are not correlated with religion as such but with lower average education and income level of the latter group compared to the former. Bring Muslims up to the Hindus in these social respects, it is argued, and the gap in growth rates will disappear. This contention seems to be belied by the growth rates of the Sikh and Christian minorities, which are even greater than that of the Muslims, but who are more advanced educationally and economically than they are. This inconsistency is explained away by reference to a high rate of conversions to the other two minority faiths.

3. Regarding Islam itself, several Muslim writers go to great lengths to demonstrate that the *Quran*, properly interpreted, is not incompatible with family planning and that *muftis* in many Muslim majority countries, including Egypt and Pakistan, have issued *fatwa* (decrees) to this effect. Even the *imam* of the Delhi Jama Masjid is reported to have done so. What this argument neglects, as does the analogous movement for the reform of the Muslim Personal Law in India (Wright, 1970a), is the resistance of Muslims to state interference in the Shariat when they are in a minority and that the change would be legislated by a parliament with a non-Muslim majority.

4. Specifically, it is pointed out by the demographers that the practice of polygamy does not alter a group's fertility as long as the proportion of females in the reproductive age bracket remains stable. Given the

normal 50:50 ratio, for every polygamous marriage, some other Muslim male is deprived of a wife. Anyway, the ratio of polygamous marriages among Indian Muslims (8.6 per 1000) is not significantly higher than among Hindus (6.7 per 1000), despite the changes in the Hindu Code forbidding multiple marriages to Hindus.

5. Widow remarriage, and possibly also easy divorce among Muslims, does, on the other hand, affect lifetime fertility per female, but the Hindu prohibition on both is not the Muslims' "responsibility" and in any case is breaking down among Hindus.

6. More indirectly, the practice of purdah (veiling) is associated with higher fertility for Muslim women because they are less "liberated," less likely to work outside of the home. The practice too is declining among Muslims (Raza, 1976).

What emerges from this debate is that Muslim attitudes toward and behavior regarding family planning are probably influenced by their perceptions of the ethnic numbers game and by their position as a minority only as one among many factors. Militant Hindu awareness of the discrepancy in growth rates produces the demands for a common civil code to replace or modify the Muslim Personal Law. Resistance to this demand by elements of the majority community is one of the few causes, in addition to preservation of the Muslim character of Aligarh Muslim University and an end to communal riots, around which orthodox, revivalist, and modernist Muslims have been able to rally, for instance in the Muslim *Majlis-i-Mushawarat* (Wright, 1970b).

The Government of India, under the Emergency proclaimed in June 1975, banned the principal Hindu and Muslim organizations and journals that had agitated the differential fertility issue. So this source of communal conflict was for a while greatly reduced. On the other hand, the Emergency Government itself increased both the positive and negative incentives for the populace to practice birth control. Special emphasis in the new campaign was placed on sterilization, which is regarded as un-Islamic by orthodox Muslims.[20] Resistance to sterilization was one cause of a Muslim riot against the police in Old Delhi on April 19, 1976, which more than any other single factor precipitated the defeat of Mrs. Gandhi's government in 1977.[21] Family planning has been a lower priority for succeeding governments.

[20] Agarwala (1976:11) fails to make the distinction between Muslim acceptance of family planning and opposition to sterilization.

[21] For the new government policy, see *Hindustan Times* (December 22, 1975). For a partial account of the riot see Deputy Home Minister F. H. Mohsin's statement in the *National Herald* (1976) and Wright (1977:1207–1220).

MIGRATION

Differences between majority and minority migration patterns, internal as well as international, and provincial distribution may both threaten to cause a reversal in their population ratio. Although the all-India Muslim proportion of the population is only a little over eleven %, which makes hopes and fears for a future Muslim majority chimerical, the minority is very unevenly distributed among Indian states and districts, rendering somewhat more realistic militant Hindu fears of further secessionist demands. For instance, Jhangiani wrote the following about the Jan Sangh before the Bangladesh separation from Pakistan in 1971:

The party is convinced that the aim (of Pakistan) is to sustain the faith of Indian Muslims in the ultimate objective of establishing Muslim domination over the rest of India as well . . . The party is exercised over the continued infiltration of Muslims from East Pakistan into Assam and Tripura and reads a sinister purpose in this movement: . . . to convert these states into Muslim majority areas to facilitate the realization of Pakistan's designs of grabbing them [1967:48].

Assam has the third highest Muslim percentage (24.03%) among Indian states and territories after the Laccadive Islands (94.4%) and Jammu and Kashmir State (65.9%) (Khan, 1973). Just before Partition, it was governed by a Muslim League ministry, which reportedly permitted encroachments on government lands by Muslim immigrants (Weiner, 1973:213). Assam is followed in rank order of Muslim population strength by West Bengal (20.46%) and Kerala (19.5%). But Kerala and the Laccadives are remote from Pakistan. Rather it is the border states and districts that arouse more credible Indian anxieties. Six of the eight Indian districts with Muslim majorities (and one more among those with 40 to 50% Muslims) are in Jammu and Kashmir state, the chief bone of contention between India and Pakistan through three wars in the postindependence period. Besides Malappuram District in Kerala, the others with over 40% are Murshidabad and Malda in West Bengal (55.4% and 43.13%, respectively) and two in Assam: Goalpara (42.25%) and Cachar (43.25%). None of these now border on Pakistan. The demographer, S. N. Agarwala (1976), asserts flatly:

Barring those districts where the Muslim population at present is above 32 percent or so, the possibility of other districts becoming Muslim majority districts by the turn of the century when India's population would exceed one billion . . . does not exist . . . During the period 1961–71, the percentage of the Muslim population in all these districts (i.e., as a whole) did not increase [1974:19].[22]

[22] But Chand (1972:337) retorts that "the possibility of the number of Muslims exceeding that of the Hindus in the state (Assam) cannot be ruled out."

Be that as it may, the long-term trend has been one of massive Bengali migration into Assam, Manipur, and Tripura, and this has been heavily comprised of Muslims from the densely populated former state of East Pakistan, now Bangladesh. This movement has been going on at least since the 1911 census and therefore seems much more likely to be caused by peasant land hunger than by any conscious campaign of either Indian Muslims or Pakistan.[23] The pre-Partition Muslim League did claim Assam for the future Pakistan in 1940, so Hindu suspicions are not groundless. After Partition, the new Congress party ministry in Assam declared squatter settlement illegal, and the Indian Parliament passed the Immigrants (Explusion from Assam) Act of 1950 to remove those "infiltrators" who had come in since 1946 (Franda, 1972b).

From the Pakistani point of view, this act was a "systematic campaign of forcible eviction of long-resident and even native born Indian Muslims . . . on the pretext that they were Pakistani infiltrators [Mujahid, 1970:130]." Al Mujahid ascribes to India, "The aim of reducing the number of Muslims by fair means or foul." By contrast, he asserts, the largely Hindu refugees from East Pakistan in 1950 were met with open arms. During the Bangladesh War of 1971 there were proposals by the Hindu Mahasabha for a massive population exchange of Indian Muslims for the East Pakistan Hindu refugees (Gauba, 1973).[24] Bhatia (1971) in the *Organiser* asked, "Now that every Hindu is being denied a right to live in Pakistan, will the Muslim communalists, who supported Pakistan and who are always feeling uneasy here, pack up and go [p. 3]?" The Indian Government did not heed these demands but insisted that the refugees return to Bangladesh after the war. A less drastic proposal was made by the Jan Sangh in 1971 that the Muslim population be removed from border areas in Assam, Rajasthan, the Punjab, and Kashmir (Bhatia, 1971). (For information on the border clearance, see Wright's [1978] discussion of articles published in the *Organiser* (September 25, 1971).

In general, the separation of Pakistan into two parts has quieted fears about migration as a source of ethnic reversal in India. But another flareup over immigration to Assam culminated in a major national crisis in 1980. Ostensibly aimed at all non-Assamese immigration to the state (be it Hindu Bengali, Muslim Bangladeshi, or Nepali), to Hindu militants the rapid change in the composition of the state's population had clearly communal implications. At the height of the Assam agitation, the *Organiser* (Goswami, 1980) published an article that accused "designing

---

[23] Apte (1966) illustrates the Jan Sangh charge.
[24] Coincidentally, Gauba is himself a convert from Hinduism (Kanhaya Lal Gauba) to Islam (Khalid Latif Gauba). See Gauba (1975).

forces" of trying to convert it into an Assamese–Bengali problem, whereas "The life and death question of Assam today is who would in the near future be the majority community—Muslims or Hindus. [All Hindus] must unite to save Assam from becoming a Muslim majority state [p. 11]." "Will not then," a retired I.C.S. Officer warned, "the cry to join Bangladesh be revived by Muslims in Assam [Moitra, 1980:9]?" He blamed the central government's indifference to this danger on its reliance on Muslim "vote banks" in Assam as elsewhere (see also, Kamath, 1980).

Muslim apologists sought, on the other hand, to demonstrate (Bhuyan, 1979; Madani, 1980) that Muslim Bengali immigrants had adopted Assamese as their mother tongue over the years, obtained Indian citizenship and were now being illegally evicted by police of an unsympathetic Janata Party state government. Actually, the issue has crosscut religious cleavages somewhat as evidenced by the presence of Muslim names on the Assamese movement's committee and by the victimization of some Hindu Bengalis by Assamese terrorists.

A curious inversion of the Assamese situation is provided by Kashmir, where in 1982 Shaikh Abdullah introduced a bill into the Jammu and Kashmir legislature to permit Kashmiri Muslims who had emigrated to Pakistan in 1947 to resettle in the state in order to *preserve* the Muslim majority in India's only predominantly Muslim unit (Reddy, 1982).

CENSUS MANIPULATION

Students of minority phenomena have been prone to take for granted the objectivity, if not always the accuracy, of official census figures. But where the returns may have a crucial effect on the distribution of offices or other political or economic benefits between two or more ethnic groups, the temptation to influence or even falsify statistics may become irresistible to the point of rendering the census operation infeasible. The classic case, of course, is Lebanon, where the Christians and Muslims have been so close in numbers and the National Compact has institutionalized the proportional allocation of offices between them that no census has been held since 1932.[25]

More recently, James F. Guyot (1975) has drawn our attention to the fact that "Who counts depends on how you count [p. 1]," even in the United States as affirmative action goals for minority group employment have become a part of government policy.

Meanwhile, Paul Brass (1974) has demonstrated that the much vaunted British censuses of India, as well as those conducted since by the Republic, suffer from severe limitations as objective measures of the dis-

---

[25] The same is now said to be true of Nigeria.

tribution of languages like Hindi and Urdu, both because of philological difficulties in defining and naming the classifications of language and dialect, and because, however impartial the census officers, the census "becomes an extremely useful political document, which reveals the relative success of competing cultural-political organizations in their decennial census drives [p. 75]." For instance, Visaria (1971) reports deliberate misreporting of religion in the 1941 census for undivided Bengal and Punjab because of conscious efforts by both Hindus and Muslims to inflate their counts for political reasons.

Since Independence, the Urdu movement, largely Muslim, has charged that census figures do not accurately reflect the true numbers of Urdu speakers in Uttar Pradesh and Bihar because of falsification by Hindi-speaking Hindu enumerators. Brass (1974) reaches the sweeping verdict that "No census of Hindi and Urdu speakers in either state has ever in any way accurately reflected (their) number and relative proportions [p. 190]." Elites, he explains, instill in the unmobilized rural population knowledge of the "correct" name of their mother tongue. Similarly, Muslim organizations have attacked the census of religions as "fake" (Khan, 1973).

On the other side, Hindu militants like Hendre (1971) demand that Jains, Sikhs, and Buddhists be listed in the census as Hindu in order to reinforce the majority's advantage. He charges that "The census of India is a ten year periodical race between Hindus and others when they turn back just to check who is in the majority [p. 114]." Mathur (1972) even lists "proximity of the census" as a cause of religious disturbances in India, and Khalid Bin Sayeed traces the Hindu *Shuddhi* movements of the 1920s described earlier to publication of the census returns showing Hindus are declining relative to Muslims. In the long run however, census manipulation is only a marginally useful method of concealing or revealing population trends that would probably eventually become publicly evident even without a published census. If two communities already eye each other with suspicion, the census returns then may be used or distorted to serve their leaders' preexisting purposes.

SUMMARY AND CONCLUSIONS

Given the large, overall disproportion between the Hindu majority and the Muslim minority in India, when and why does the "numbers game" flare up recurrently, and who agitates the issue? Some tentative conclusions are as follows:

1. Modernization including merit recruitment has brought previ-

ously functionally specialized, noncompeting communities into collision.

2. The British decision to create separate electorates with representation roughly proportional to group percentages made numbers politically relevant.

3. The Partition of British India largely on the basis of which community had a majority in each province and district imbedded fears and hopes of more partitions in marginal areas.

4. The decennial censuses allow communal leaders to compare the growth or decline of their communities relative to their rival's, which gives a certan periodicity to agitations over numbers.

5. The mass conversion of Untouchables to Buddhism in the 1950s, like Christian missionary successes with tribals earlier, may have rearoused Hindu fears and Muslim hopes that other large sections of the majority community could be detached by conversion.

6. Increasing elite attention to the population explosion and family planning programs in the 1960s made laymen aware of the demographic concept of differential group fertility.

7. The general politicization by socialism and the welfare state of economic decisions has raised the saliency of ethnicity, as cogently argued by Glazer and Moynihan (1975).

8. The numbers game seems to be another application of the thesis of Brass (1974):

Political elites choose the cultural symbols upon which they wish to base their claims for group rights . . . and then work to make other cleavages congruent with the primary cleavage. . . . Political conflict may reduce cumulated cleavages just as the reverse process may occur. . . . Political organizations and party and government policies are more often than not decisive in both the formation of group consciousness and in the character of inter-group relations [pp. 22, 28, 36, 423].

REFERENCES

Agarwala, S. N.
    1974   Will Muslims outnumber Hindus? *Illustrated Weekly of India* **XCX**(1 January 13):16–19.
    1976   Make sterilisation compulsory—now. *Illustrated Weekly of India* **XCVIII**(8 February 22):11.
Aggarwal, P. C.
    1971   *Caste, Religion and Power, an Indian Case Study.* New Delhi: Shri Ram Centre for Industrial Relations.

Ahmed, I. (Ed.)
   1973a   *Caste among the Muslims.* Delhi: Manohar Book Service.
   1973b   Endogamy and status mobility among the Siddique Sheikhs of Allahabad, Uttar
           Pradesh, in *Caste among the Muslims* (I. Ahmed, Ed.), pp. 157–194.
Amir-Ali, H.
   1970   *The Meos of Mewat.* New Delhi: Oxford and IBH.
Apte, D.
   1966   The story of Muslim penetration of Assam as told by census officers. *Organiser*
           October 30:15.
Arnold, T. W.
   1935   *The Preaching of Islam: A History of the Propagation of the Muslim Faith.* London:
           Luzac. (Originally published, 1896.)
Barrier, N. G.
   1968   The Punjab government and communal politics. *Journal of Asian Studies* **XXVII**(3
           May):523–539.
Bhatia, V. P .
   1971   Spectrum. *Organiser* **June 19**:3.
Bhuyan, M. N. H. M.
   1979   Foreigners in Assam: myth and reality. *Secular Democracy* **December**:27–33.
Brass, P. R.
   1974   *Language, Religion and Politics in North India.* London: Cambridge University
           Press.
Chand, G.
   1972   *Population in Perspective, A Study of the Population Crisis in India in the Context
           of New Social Horizons.* New Delhi: Orient Longmans.
Cobban, A.
   1944   *National Self-Determination.* Chicago: University of Chicago Press.
Dale, S. F.
   1980   Islamic society on the South Asian frontier. Oxford: Clarendon Press.
Davies, C.
   1976   The relative fertility of Hindus and Muslims. *Quest,* **99**(January–February):
           19–32.
Davis, K.
   1951   *The Population of India and Pakistan.* Princeton: Princeton University Press.
A Defense of the Urdu Language
   1900   *A Defense of the Urdu Language and Character.* Allahabad: Liddell's.
Despande, G. S.
   1966   When we will need to export our soldiers. *Organiser* **November 27**:12.
Devasenapathi, V. A.
   1966   Religious conversion: a Hindu view. *Religion and Society* **XIII**(4 December):
           43–46.
Eaton, R. M.
   1978   *The Sufis of Bijapur.* Princeton, N.J.: Princeton Univ. Press.
Elliott, C.
   1974   Decline of a patrimonial regime. *Journal of Asian Studies* **November**:27–47.
Faruqi, Z.
   1963   *The Deoband School and the Demand for Pakistan.* Bombay: Asia Publishing
           House.
Franda, M. F.
   1972a   *Militant Hindu Opposition to Family Planning in India. American Universities
           Field Staff Reports, South Asia Series* **XVI** vol. 11 no. 2.

1972b   *Population Politics in South Asia,* Part II: *Refugees and Migration Patterns in
         Northeastern India and Bangladesh. American Universities Field Staff Reports,
         South Asia Series* XVI, vol. 3 no. 6.

Frykenberg, R. E.
1975   The impact of conversion and social reform upon society in South India during
         the late Company period. Unpublished ms. available from University of Wis-
         consin.

Gauba, K. L.
1973   Exchange of population, in *Passive Voices,* pp. 43–50. New Delhi: Sterling Pub-
         lishers.
1975   *Friends and Foes.* New Delhi: India Book Company.

Glazer, N., and Moynihan, D. P.
1975   *Ethnicity, Theory and Experience.* Cambridge, Mass.: Harvard University Press.

Gopal, R.
1959   *Indian Muslims, a Political History 1858–1947.* Bombay: Asia Publishing House.

Gordon, M. M.
1975   Toward a general theory of racial and ethnic group relations, in *Ethnicity, Theory
         and Experience* in (N. Glazer and D. P. Moynihan, Ed.), pp. 84–110. Cambridge:
         Harvard University Press.

Goswami, R. M.
1980   Assam editor's request to Calcutta press. *Organiser* **May 18**:11.

Gupta, N. R. S.
1968   How East Bengal became a Muslim majority area. *Organiser* **April 21**:5, 12.

Guyot, J. F.
1975   The Puerto Rican population of New York City: Who counts depends on how
         you count. *New York City Perspective* **2**(2)1–8.

Haq, M. A.
1972   *The Faith Movement of Maulana Muhammad Ilyas.* London: George Allen and
         Unwin.

Hallow, R. Z.
1969   The blacks cry genocide. *The Nation* **CCVIII**(April 28):535–536.

Hardy, P.
1972   *Muslims of British India.* London: Cambridge University Press.
1977   Modern European and Muslim explanations of conversion to Islam in South
         Asia: a preliminary survey of the literature. *Journal of the Royal Asiatic Society*
         2:177–206.

Hendre, S. L.
1971   *Hindus and Family Planning: A Socio-Political Demography.* Bombay: Supraja
         Prakashan.

Hindustan Times
1978   *Hindustan Times* **December 22**:3.

Hoque, Z.
1970   Religion of Islam and family planning. *The Islamic Review and Arab Affairs*
         LVIII(1 January):6–10.

Huntington, S. P.
1968   *Political Order in Changing Societies.* New Haven: Yale University Press.

Hussain, K.
1969   Pros and cons of family planning. *Radiance* **March 23**:13.

Jain, P. C.
1970   Are Indian Muslims really a minority? *Organiser* **June 27**:12.

Jhangiani, M. A.
    1967   *Jana Sangh and Swatantra*. Bombay: Manaktalas.
Jeelany, S.
    1969   The immorality of religious conversion. *Organiser* **September 27**:6.
Jones, K. W.
    1968   Communalism in the Punjab: the Arya Samaj contribution. *Journal of Asian Studies* **XXVIII**(1 November):39–54.
    1976   *Arya Dharm*. Berkeley: University of California Press.
Kamath, M. V.
    1980   Neglected Assam. *Illustrated Weekly of India* **January 20–26**:2–9.
Kautsky, J. H.
    1962   *Political Change in Underdeveloped Countries*. New York: John Wiley & Sons.
Khan, M. A.
    1973   Muslims and the census of India. *Mainstream* **XI**(50 August 11):27–28.
Khan, M. E.
    1975   Is Islam against family planning? *Islam and the Modern Age* **VI**(2 May):61–72.
Khan, R. R.
    1974   Growth of Muslim population in India. *Interdiscipline*:56.
Lal, K. S.
    1973   *The Growth of Muslim Population in Medieval India*. Delhi: Research Publications in Social Sciences.
Levtzion, L. (Ed.)
    1978   *Conversion to Islam*. New York: Holmes and Meier.
Madani, M. S. A.
    1980   Assam and so-called foreign nations. *Secular Democracy* **May**:20–24.
Malik, H.
    1969   The Muslims of India and Pakistan. *Current History* **LVI**(March):154–155.
Malhotra, A.
    1975   Hinduism's second shot at becoming a missionary religion. Paper presented at the New York State Conference on Asian Studies, Hamilton, N.Y.
Mason, P.
    1971   *Patterns of Dominance*. London: Oxford University Press.
Mathur, Y. B.
    1972   *Muslims and Changing India*. New Delhi: Trimurti Publications.
Maudoodi, S. A.
    1959   *Process of Islamic Revolution*. Rampur: Markasi Maktaba Jama'at-i-Islami Hind.
Mohsin, F. H.
    1976   *National Herald* **April 28**:4.
Moitra, S. M.
    1980   Assam: there is no business like vote business. *Organiser* **June 1**:8–9.
Mufakkir (pseud.)
    1971   Plan the economy and not the family. *Radiance* **December 5**:4.
al Mujahid, S.
    1970   Eviction of Muslims, in *Indian Secularism*, pp. 130–148. Karachi: University of Karachi.
Mukherjee, J. N.
    1967   Muslim dominance in Bengal. *Organiser* **October 29**:21–22.
Nizami, K. A.
    1961   *Some Aspects of Religion and Politics in India during the Thirteenth Century*. Bombay: Asia Publishing House.

Organiser
    1969   *Organiser* **March 13**:8.
Organiser
    1969   *Organiser* **May 17**:15.
Organiser
    1972   *Organiser* **September 2**:3.
Owaisy, M. A., and Kapur, C.
    1970   Islam and family planning. *Family Planning News* **XI**(August–September):14–16.
Pethe, V. P.
    1973   Hindus, Muslims and the demographic balance in India. *Economic and Political Weekly* **January 13**:75–78.
Radiance
    1971   Shyam Sunder, not Shujast Ali. *Radiance* **August 29**:1.
Radiance
    1972   Meaning of census figures. *Radiance* **July 2**:1.
Radiance
    1972   Announcement. *Radiance* **July 30**:15.
Radiance
    1972   Increase in Muslim population. *Radiance* **October 8**:2.
Raza, M.
    1976   Changing Purdah system in Muslim society. *Islam and the Modern Age*. **VII** (1 February):57–78.
Reddy, G. K.
    1982   Centre takes serious view of J & K bill. *Hindu Weekly* **June 12**:1.
Richards, J. F.
    1974   The Islamic frontier in the East: expansion into South Asia. *South Asia* **4**:91–109.
Sayeed, K. B.
    1860   *Pakistan, the Formative Phase*, Karachi: Pakistan Publishing House.
Shakir, M.
    1970   *Islamic Neo-Revivalist Renaissance: The Mind of Maulana Maudoodi.* New Delhi: Sampradayikta Virodhi Committee.
Sharma, S. L.
    1966   "Approach to the study of 'socio-cultural outcome of conversion.'" *Indian Journal of Social Research* **VII**(December):194–197.
    1968   Comparative styles of conversion in major religions in India. *Journal of Social Research* (Bihar) **XI**(2 September):141:148.
Sharma, S. L. and Srivastava, R. M.
    1967   Institutional resistance to induced Islamization in a convert community. *Sociological Bulletin* **XVI** (1 March):69–80.
Schermerhorn, R. A.
    1970   *Comparative Ethnic Relations.* New York: Random House.
Smith, D. E.
    1963   *India as a Secular State.* Princeton: Princeton University Press.
D'Souza, V. S.
    1973   Status groups among the Moplahs on the southwest coast of India. in *Caste among the Muslims* (I. Ahmed, Ed.), pp. 45–60. Delhi: Manohar Book Service.
Titus, M.
    1959   *Islam in India and Pakistan* (revised ed.). Calcutta: YMCA Publishing House.

Thursby, G. R.
   1975   *Hindu–Muslim Relations in British India*. Leiden: E. J. Brill.
Vasfi, S. A. S.
   1972   A much-maligned and most misunderstood body. *Radiance* **April 2**:4,15.
Visaria, L.
   1974   Religious differentials in fertility, in *Population in India's Development, 1947–
           2000* (A. Bose, P. B. Desai, A. Mitra, and J. N. Sharma, Eds.), pp. 361–373. Delhi:
           Vikas Publishing House.
Weiner, M.
   1973   Socio-political consequences of interstate migration in India, in *Population Pol-
           itics and the Future of Southern Asia* (H. Wriggins and J. F. Guyot, Eds.), pp. 190–
           228. New York: Columbia University Press.
Wriggins, H., and Guyot, J. F.
   1973   *Population Politics and the Future of Southern Asia*. New York: Columbia Uni-
           versity Press.
Wright, T. P., Jr.
   1966   The Muslim league in South India since independence: a study in minority
           group political strategies. *American Political Science Review* **LX**(September):579–
           599.
   1970a   The Muslim personal law issue in India: an outsider's view. *The Indian Journal
           of Politics* **IV**:69–77.
   1970b   Muslims as candidates and voters in the 1967 general election, in *Fourth Gen-
           eral Election in India* (S. P. Varma and I. Narain, Eds.), pp. 207–224. Bombay:
           Orient Longmans.
   1972   Identity problems of former elite minorities. *Secular Democracy* **V**(August 8):43–
           51.
   1977   Muslims and the 1977 Indian elections: a watershed? *Asian Survey* **XVII**(12
           December):1207–1220.
   1978   Indian Muslims, the Bangladesh secession and the Indo-Pakistan war of 1971,
           in *Main Currents in Indian Sociology*, III (Giri Raj Gupta, Ed.), pp. 128–148.
           Durham, N.C.: Carolina Academic Press.
   1983   The movement to convert Harijans to Islam in South India. *Muslim World*
           (forthcoming).
Zakaria, R.
   1970   *Rise of Muslims in Indian Politics*. Bombay: Somaiya.

Index